Becoming Partners with Children
with Children
From Play to Conversation

James D. MacDonald

Nisonger Center
Department of Speech and Hearing Science
The Ohio State University

Special Press Inc.

The development of this work was supported in part by the Bureau of Research in Education of the Handicapped, Office of Special Education and Rehabilitation Services, United States Department of Education, grant # G008430049-88; and the Bureau of Maternal and Child Health and Resources Development, Health Resources and Services Administration, United States Department of Health and Human Services, grant # MCJ00922-22-0.

Published by Special Press, Inc.
11230 West Avenue
Suite 3205
San Antonio, Texas 78213

For information about our audio products, write us at:
Newbridge Book Clubs, 3000 Cindel Drive, Delran, NJ 08370

International Standard Book Number 1-55990-010-5
Printed in the United States of America

2   3   4   5   6   7   8   9   10   96 95 94 93 92 91 90

Contents

PART II DEVELOPMENTAL GUIDES

I dedicate this book to all the parents and children who have become closer partners in play and communication, and to a few in my own life.

To Carolyn MacDonald, who lived the principles in this book on her own, and to
Larry, Kyle, and Jackson
who have made it easy for me to be invested in children

To Mac MacDonald, who taught me the value of unnoticed people

To Margaret MacDonald, my first conversation partner, and still going

To "Monie" Lorenz, our adopted grandmother, who showed the profound results child care can have

and

To Helen Murphy Pluta, one of those women who has kept strong conversational relations with her children under great stress and with remarkable success.

Why I Wrote this Book

To make a long story short, I had to. My 18 years of getting children and adults together had become so rewarding to me and my students that I had to see if the ideas could stimulate others to become partners with children. Most of the adults we have known have been invested in children but seemed not to have a map to guide them. This book is intended to be a map that children and adults can follow from the earliest play routines to sophisticated conversations.

I also wrote the book because I was told to by the parents I served, by the students who wanted tools to carry out the ideas elsewhere, and by the clinicians and teachers in many workshops who said, "I like it; so where is it?"

But certainly the most powerful reason was the hundreds of children I have known who were ready for communicative relationships much more than was expected. This book, then, is written for large populations of children with some of the following problems. Some rarely play with others or have much of a sense of give-and-take with people and thus they live virtually isolated lives. Then there are the children who communicate much less than they know and are treated by society as if they were less competent than they are. Many of the children I've known do not seem to stay in interactions in ways that let them learn to become social and communicative.

The book is in great part a report of my clinical and research experiences directed to one overriding question: How can adults interact and communicate with pre-conversational children so that those children spontaneously learn to become social and communicative with those adults? While this may seem a presumptious task, it has been an attempt to carefully integrate early developmental research and theory with our own years of studies of children and their parents and teachers. In this book, I have tried to bring alive the many barriers and successes I have faced in our attempts to help adults and children become learning partners.

I also wrote this book to communicate with several groups of adults who have the responsibility to integrate children into society. It has been my experience that no matter how well-trained adults are professionally, their effectiveness with children may well depend on the way they communicate and develop sensitive, reciprocal relationships with them.

Recent laws mandating education for children with delays from birth to age 5 have been an attempt to prevent more lasting delays and provide training in cognitive and social skills that, to date, has been generally unavailable. As expected, services speaking to new laws take a while to emerge. Consequently, few teachers, speech therapists, and other child care workers have been trained in the fundamental skills children need in the early years. The work in this book provides a developmental guide to accompany these children from the most primitive play to conversations for friendship and learning. For professionals, it is designed for three purposes: first, as a text during their training to be child specialists; second, as a clinical guide for their interactions with children; and third, as a model for working with parents.

In addition, my work with parents of children with many delays has convinced me that parents are a greatly underestimated source for assisting their children's development. This book, then, is a direct attempt to put into parents' hands a way to learn about their children and to guide them to become more social and communicative. The book represents the experiences of a great number of parents as they learned to become playful, communicative, and conversational with their children. The book also provides a map for parents of children with apparent normal development because the basic notions come from studies on normal child development.

A major motivation for this work has been to encourage educators responsible for training clinicians, teachers, and child care workers to systematically prepare students to competently assist children in early social and communicative development. The strategies discussed here, taken together, are proposed as a style of interaction that enables children to learn more readily from professionals.

As I said when I began, I wrote this book because I had to. It became a report of a long series of conversations I have had with parents, students, and peers.

Acknowledgments

I am indicated on the title page as the sole author of this book, and it is true that I wrote down the words and did most of the thinking that produced them. Accordingly, all of the oversights, blunders, and downright mistakes are mine; if what you read irritates you, yell at me. At the same time, the book is a product of a great many partnerships with people ranging from professors to infants. In writing this, I took the role of participant observer. As a kind of reporter in the trenches, I have tried to describe what I saw as children and adults struggled to become more playful, interactive, and conversational. As I reported, I also participated; this book reflects both objective and subjective analyses of my own experiences with hundreds of children and their significant adults.

Three organizations have provided the atmosphere for the kind of work reported in this book. At the Ohio State University, both the Nisonger Center and the Department of Speech and Hearing Science have provided the students, clients, and environment where innovative programs could struggle and proceed. The Office of Special Education in the federal Department of Education has moved steadily to support early intervention approaches. Grants from the department have provided support for a number of the research and development activities discussed in this book. A special word is due to the Nisonger Center. As an interdisciplinary training center for developmentally delayed children, its mission has been to simultaneously provide student training and programs not available in the university but needed in the community. I hope this book is some evidence that the center is meeting its mission. I would like to thank a number of administrators who have made sure that such opportunities continue: Vern Reynolds, Bill Gibson, Ben Benson, Mike Guralnick, and Steve Schroeder.

The work and thought leading to this book have spread over many years with clear influence from people ranging from infants to professors. As a client in speech therapy, I became intimately familiar with the variety of approaches to help children communicate. In my first professional positions in two state hospitals (Philadelphia and Fairboult), the patients taught me the devastating effects of having few or disturbed social skills. Then, at the University of Minnesota, I studied communication from both behavioral and cognitive perspectives. I am still influenced by one professor in particular, Dick Martin. Dick taught me to make sure others can see what I say. I hope this book is as clear as Dick would have it.

One powerful influence in this work has been the constant flow of students training to be clinicians and educators; their encouragements and frustrations went far to shape the model presented here. If students couldn't do it or care about it, it went back for more work. Certainly the student most influential to this work was Yvonne Gillette, who evolved from student and clinician to an instrumental role in developing the model. Her dedication and perseverance have strengthened the work substantially. You can find her work in the other volumes in this series.

Surviving in the field with new approaches is much more difficult than going along with status quo. Many students have forged ahead on their own with the approach in this book. Tom Almerico has made the model almost an institution in Utah; his successes and prodding have given me faith at many points. While I encourage students to start easy, Joanne Gerenser ignored me and developed a system for conversations with adolescent autistic children in New York. Linda Lombardino in Florida makes the ideas live in her graduate students. Jeanne George juggles the model across several classrooms. To these troopers and many more, thank you! You have kept my spirit in the wondering times.

Two more students who have had special influence were Deanna Horstmeier and Jenny Young. In the beginning, there was Deanna Horstmeier, first a client mother and then a partner. Deanna is a true developmental model; even her careers have followed her son Scott's needs from play to community life. And, during the last 2 years, the writing years, Jenny Young has been just the sidekick I needed— bright and invested—with unfailing enthusiasm, a real marathon lady. With her enthusiasm and creativity, Jenny made reaching the finishing line much easier.

None of this would have happened if a great number of parents had not been willing to expose themselves and change with their children. This challenge is not to be taken lightly. Consequently, I want to acknowledge representatives of the many parents. Elaine and Jan, mothers of severely at-risk infants, fought through their daughters' illnesses to build a strong communicative relationship. Maureen, mother of autistic-like twins, found her children's world and has never left them. Ginnie organized a family of six to make sure her son with Down syndrome became a conversationalist. Barry, the professor who relinquished his academics for his son, became a fine-tuned partner. Ann learned to "read" her withdrawn, highly distractible son, Nick; by getting into his world, she brought him into hers. Carol, by slowing down and doing less, allowed Jonathon, with cerebral palsy, to become her communication partner. It is these and many other parents who, through their stamina and openness, are the original writers of this book. Thank you for the investment and the surprises!

Writing this book also required some strong personal supports. Through every step of preparing this book, there have been a few persons who have provided me invaluable personal support. Norman Shub, a powerful teacher, has crystalized for me a primary theme of this work, awareness and responsibility in relationships. And, Norman, even 2-year-olds can be responsible. Publishing sounded bureaucratic to me until I was continuously encouraged by the personal and conceptual support from my publisher, Tom Hutchinson. He always made me feel the work spoke to real needs. Many thanks, too, to his partner, Francie Margolin, who kept it all together. Finally, I realized that if an attorney could get excited about a book about children, we had something. Glenn Kacic heard more about the book than he wanted but responded with an interest and expectation that kept me going.

Part

1

BACKGROUND OF THE ECO MODEL

1 | *Introduction*

SOCIAL
social
PLAY
play
TURN
tur
TAKING
taking
COMM
com
UNICATION
munication
LAN
la
GUAGE
guage
CONVE
conve
RSATION
rsation

Many children appear to become social and communicative with little effort on their part or on the part of their caregivers. The process of becoming communication partners with others begins as the child and parent give and take in playful interactions. Within these natural interactions, they begin, first with movements and sounds and then with words, to communicate together. In these spontaneous exchanges, the child and adult are building social and cognitive skills without teaching in any formal sense. Although this natural process appears effortless and simple, it actually involves a rich network of finely tuned and progressively related interactions.

The **ECO** model for intervention proposes a system for guiding the development of interactions between children and their caregivers. For, despite our expectations that children will become social and communicative "on their own," not all children do. Many children simply do not learn adequately in their natural interactions. A major assumption of the **ECO** model is that children will learn in their natural contacts to the extent that they have balanced, matched relationships with others who are important to them. Therefore, the **ECO** program and its corresponding materials (described below) are designed for children with some of the needs described in table 1.1.

The primary purpose of *Becoming Partners with Children* is to bring children and adults into relationships in which the child can spontaneously learn to be an increasingly social and communicative person. First of all, it is designed to be a guide to the development of a child's interaction—a guide from initial social play to mature conversational relationships. With this book, I hope that both professionals and parents will learn many of the skills children need in order to become as socially competent as they can. Equally important, I hope you will learn a system of ways you can interact and communicate with children so that they learn from you in daily interactions. Whether they are professionals or members of a child's family, adults need to understand better the genuine power and influence they can have with their children. I have written this book with the sincere intention of empowering adults with specific skills to help the development of children with whom they now feel little influence.

As the title suggests, *Becoming Partners with Children* views interactions between an adult and a child as the indispensible process by which a child becomes social and communicative. It follows from this view that a child will become an habitual, social learner when clinicians, parents, teachers, and others responsible for his nurturance change reciprocally with him. After years of work with parents, teachers, and students, I am encouraged that changing interactive styles with children is not merely a feasible goal but one that unites the adults and children in more effective learning relationships.

Table 1.1
*Who Is
The ECO
Partnership
Model For?*

CHILDREN WHO NEED TO:

PLAY

- Play meaningfully with things.
- Stay in play with others.
- Play genuinely with people, not just in parallel ways.
- Imitate others or follow others' models.
- Attend to others.
- Make personal attachments.
- Learn to prefer being with others to being alone.
- Play in less self-centered ways.

INTERACT

- Give and take with others.
- Respond to others' contacts.
- Initiate contacts.
- Keep others actively with them.
- Take turns with others.
- Play less passive roles.
- Take more social initiative.
- Cooperate in rather than dominate interactions.
- Respond sensitively to others' concerns.
- Stay on activity topics for extended exchanges.

COMMUNICATE NONVERBALLY

- Regularly exchange meanings with others.
- Initiate communication.
- Respond to others' communications.
- Communicate with increasingly creative movements.
- Communicate with increasingly natural sounds.
- Communicate to get their needs met.
- Communicate more to others than to themselves.
- Communicate for social, friendly reasons.
- Try to communicate as others do.
- Communicate in creative, pretend ways.

LEARN LANGUAGE

- Talk as a natural part of their interactions.
- Use increasingly new language.
- Move from body language and sounds to words.
- Talk about their interests.
- Talk more with others than to themselves.
- Use language assertively, not passively.
- Pace their language, waiting and not interrupting.
- Talk about others' concerns.
- Stay on a verbal topic.
- Use more child-world language than academic language.
- Actively communicate when they talk.
- Use more varied language rather than continually repeating a limited set of expressions.
- Talk from another's perspective.

BEGIN TO CONVERSE
- Have conversations as a major activity with people.
- Have age-appropriate conversations.
- Stay in conversations beyond brief contacts.
- Invite and pursue conversations rather than avoid them.
- Communicate less for instrumental reasons than social ones.
- Ignore or fail to pursue social conversations.
- Use language less for talk to themselves and more for socialization.
- Take turns and wait.
- Talk more on topics and less in irrelevant ways.
- Talk in more socially engaging, less socially aversive ways.
- Use language that is more emotionally appropriate.
- Reduce their control and disruptions in conversations.
- Share the lead in conversations.
- Develop a topic rather than perseverate on it.
- Show more interest in conversation as a pastime.

Another intent of the book, then, is to provide concerned adults with information for monitoring their own interactive style in relation to their child's emerging social skills. I would like you to consider *Becoming Partners* an ongoing map for adults and children as they move from spontaneous play through the competencies entailed in becoming social andcommunicative.

Still another purpose of this book is to provide educators with a resource for developing Individualized Education Plans that address the first few years of development. By incorporating specific goals and objectives for building interaction competencies, these plans may help educators enlarge their curricula to include communication as well as language. These social and communicative competencies will help preconversational children more readily acquire the social skills required for nearly all learning and generalization in daily life. Although the **ECO** program does target discrete skills, its authors are more concerned with helping children and adults become natural social learners, that is, generalize specific competencies in social learning to anything they might need to learn. At times, *Becoming Partners* may challenge you by questioning the traditional view that children's cognitive skills are the province only of teachers, and communicative problems the province of therapists, and social development the province of parents. The **ECO** approach calls a variety of professionals together with the parents to coordinate a mutually supportive action plan for the child to become social and communicative. It assumes that, regardless of the kind of delays or disorders a child shows, the social nature of his home, school, therapy, and other critical environments greatly influences the kind of learner and social partner he will become.

PREVIEW OF THE ECO APPROACH

The five **ECO** competencies stand for several developmental stages in which the child and adult develop together from primitive play to conversational habits.

Play

The first set of competencies focuses on helping children and adults become the kind of social play partners they need to be if the child is to learn spontaneously with others. By learning to be more playful, adults make themselves more accessible for learning. Through play, they build such a finely tuned relationship with their child that both of them feel successful and motivated to interact more often.

We developed this set of competencies in response to the many children we found playing alone or in parallel with their adults. These children, even those who were verbal, seemed not to be motivated to socialize with others. When we helped the adults become more childlike and playful, we found the children were more motivated to learn and communicate with the adults.

Turntaking

The second set of competencies builds interactive habits between children and adults across a range of contacts that includes caretaking, play, learning, and leisure. Because any interaction is an opportunity for both communicative and cognitive learning, an intensive habit of give and take with others is optimal for learning. Through turntaking, the child and adult learn the kind of balanced interaction that allows each person to participate fully in the exchanges. This educates the adult to keep the child in more frequent and increasingly longer interactions of the kind that further communicative and cognitive learning.

The set of turntaking competencies is for those children, regardless of communicative level or cognitive ability, who do not respond when addressed, who rarely interact with others, who stay only briefly in interactions, or who interact only to satisfy needs and not to build relationships.

Nonverbal Communication

The nonverbal communication competencies recognize that children need to learn to *communicate* with any physical or auditory means available before they can learn language. Intentional communication must become habitual before language can. Although attention to preverbal communication is often sacrificed for efforts to teach language to children with delays, it can prepare the child to learn language by first making him a habitual communicator. These competencies enable adults to become partners who match their communication to the child's level to guide him to more mature communications.

These competencies speak to the many children who communicate much less than they know or seem able to communicate with words alone. They also speak to the many frustrated adults whose adult language forms consistently fail to engage the child in communication.

Language

The *language competencies* view language as evolving from the play interactions and nonverbal communications developed by the first three sets of competencies. Learning language then focuses on the adults using language to translate the child's earlier communications and experiences into words that are immediately useful and highly meaningful because they relate directly to the interaction in progress.

The **ECO** language competencies are more interactive than academic in that they focus on helping the child to talk about his current knowledge. These competencies are for children with delays, who may have language for school tasks (for example, numbers, colors), but who still often communicate much less than they know. Several competencies also help the child develop and stay on topics long enough to learn new language and new skills.

Conversation

The ultimate goal of the **ECO** program is that the child have increasingly broader conversations for educational, social, and vocational relationships. The competencies for building conversations span a range of pragmatic roles. That is, the children and adults learn to communicate as much for the social reasons that bind people together as for the instrumental reasons of directing and controlling each other.

These competencies are meant for the many children who rarely have conversations even though they have considerable language. The child who initiates verbally but then leaves an interaction, as well as the child who plays a passive role in conversations, is unlikely to learn as much from others as he could otherwise, to be well-accepted in society, or even to be able to capitalize on what he knows.

THE ECO MODEL

The **ECO** intervention model has evolved out of several activities and purposes related to understanding and serving children as they become social and communicative. This approach to early child development began as we faced more than 100 children a year who had a wide variety of developmental delays. Along with our clinical responsibilities for these children, we directed an academic program, training clinicians, teachers, and other child development specialists. Beyond preparing professionals to work with children, we conducted regular parent training with their children. After several years of clinical work and teaching, we received a series of federally funded research grants that enabled us to systematically build the intervention model and experimentally develop an assessment (*ECOScales*) and treatment curriculum.

Developing the model, then, involved integrating years of clinical, teaching, research, and development work that addressed a single goal: to define an interactional model for building social and communicative relationships between children and their significant others. What follows are brief messages to parents and other caregivers, clinicians, classroom teachers, and trainers of professionals, to whom we now offer **ECO** as a way to help all their children grow and learn.

TO PARENTS AND OTHER CAREGIVERS:

As I look back to watching my own children—Larry, Kyle, and Jackson—develop, it seemed that learning to interact and communicate happened effortlessly, the way a tree grows without apparent help from anyone. Like so many parents, I never thought it was anything we did much about. Now, years later, I realize how much their relationship with us, especially with their mother, influenced their social and communicative development. This realization does not disregard the genetic influences that may have been at work, but it is the environmental ones that were more directly under our control.

Now, after working closely with children with various delays, I realize how absolutely critical it is that parents and caregivers examine how they interact with their children and how those ways of interacting help their children to become active learners and social partners. A great part of my motivation for developing this model has been the hundreds of parents and professionals who are concerned about how well their children will fit into society and benefit from social relationships.

The majority of parents who have come to us over the years have hoped we could take the child and to some degree either "fix" him or her or at least do the bulk of the work ourselves. To the surprise and initial discomfort of many parents, we immediately informed them that our role would be to teach them about their child's development and, most importantly, how they could help their child interact and communicate within their natural interactions. Many were surprised that we had no teaching drills, but only carefully matched, interactive partnerships as our teaching resources. In a nutshell, our philosophy with these parents has been this: "We will help *you*; then *you* will help your child." We hope you will read this book in that spirit.

What *Becoming Partners with Children* does offer is a map to guide you to know what children should do to become social and communicative and to see how you can shape your interactive style to help your children learn. Understandably, most parents are concerned that their children acquire the skills needed to progress in school. Unfortunately, as David Elkind (1987) has argued, we too often teach children academic skills before they have the social and communicative skills to use that information. Unless a child is social and communicative, he is likely to learn little in school and even more likely to be unable to show what he has learned. A primary purpose of both preschool and kindergarten is to socialize children into the new milieu of working in groups and doing tasks with relative strangers. Our approach strongly encourages parents to make sure their children are socializing and communicating before they are put into these situations. In preschool and in school, an adult's need to direct a group might encourage delayed children to be so passive that their natural learning is limited. In your hands, your movements, and your words, you hold the power to influence your children to be social and communicative.

After 18 years of coming to this philosophy, I now feel a greater commitment to it with every new family I meet. For example, my most recent clients have been Francie, age 11, diagnosed with learning disabilities and using immature conversation skills; Nick, age 4, with inconsistent social communication and frequent autistic-like behaviors; and Colin, 28 months, an apparently happy, playful child who communicates effectively with body language but shows little verbal language. In each of these recent cases, I could not support a form of treatment that isolated the child from the relationships inevitably responsible for his or her development.

One of our most basic assumptions is that children do not learn either to interact or to talk from traditional, directive methods of the kind used to teach topics like math and history. Instead, they learn to interact by habitually relating to people who are finely tuned to their abilities and interests. A key to social learning is that a child will learn to be sociable more readily if interactions are free of stress and involve warm, emotional attachments.

As we have developed this model, it has been the parents themselves who have sustained me and driven me on. Beyond our own clinical findings and the support of similar findings by other researchers, the parents have expressed in many ways how they have learned to feel competent in helping their child become social and communicative. And perhaps just as important, they have discovered how they enjoy their child more, how they feel that the child gives them more, and how they have found it easier and more rewarding to raise their child as a partner than as a caretaker.

I recall a long list of parents whose reactions to the program encouraged me. These people have also shown me the remarkable resilience and commitment parents can have in the face of highly frustrating, unrewarding relationships with children. Jim is a father who worked extremely hard with Jeremiah, an autistic child; he faced what he felt were many failures. Then Jim learned to accommodate his world and his boy's. He found that success is not always getting what you want.

Diane was a business woman in her early forties; she never expected to have children and then she had Mitchell, who came to us as a hyperactive and socially inconsistent 4-year-old, and his brother Daniel, who is deaf and who was 2 when we first saw him. Diane immersed herself in the ideas of the program. She was determined to have children that she and world wanted to be with.

Bernice was determined that Damon, age 8 and considered emotionally disturbed, should be her friend and that others see what he was able to do. Watching their friendship develop—from a stressful, directive tug-of-war into increasingly meaningful conversations—gave me still more conviction that parents are often the best learning partners.

Not only did Elaine have real difficulties accepting Emilie's Down syndrome, but she lived with stress produced by the extremely high-risk medical problems that threatened Emilie for most of her first 3 years. Trying to get a critically ill child to stay in the interactive world was one of the most difficult tasks I have seen a family endure.

And there was Barry, the college professor who studied Jeff's problems and was very much an expert in his own world. To go from expert to student, responding to our encouragement to change, took not only great flexibility and a concerted focus on his child but the courage and willingness to admit he wasn't the expert on everything.

While each of these parents seems to have a little of the hero in him or her, I have been equally inspired by those parents who would have accepted their children with delays more or less as they had been defined by professionals. Instead, these parents learned to expect more from their children on a daily basis, just as they did with their other children who had no identified problems.

So, what does this book have to offer parents of children with social and communicative delays? First, it is a developmental guide to following your child as he develops the playful and interactive skills he needs for later learning. It also shows you how children first communicate without words and then develop language. It helps you see how children learn to have conversations in which they learn more language and through which they build social relationships. And finally, it will turn out to be a book not just about your child's needs and what he or she can do, but about you and what you can do to move your child into playfulness, communication, and conversation with you and other people who are important in his or her life. It also describes changes made by 25 families who used the principles and activities described in the book.

TO SPEECH-LANGUAGE CLINICIANS:

In 1971, when I became responsible for the language programs at the Nisonger Center at the Ohio State University, I supervised assessments, treatment clinics, and classrooms for a wide range of children with delays. I realized I had a lot to learn. Like many of you perhaps, my training had concentrated on communication development and intervention for clients already having a conversation habit. Theoretically, these clients have the social skills they need if they are to use and generalize into their conversational worlds the new skills we teach them.

I soon faced more than 100 children with a wide range of delays, few of whom had generalized conversation habits. Some of the children were mainly noninteractive, with little awareness of what to do with people. Others would play occasionally with people but rarely communicated. There were also children with functional skills in nonverbal communication (often idiosyncratic to familiar people) but with little use of language. Other children clearly had language but little pragmatic range, using language mostly to get needs met or to respond passively. There were even children who had considerable language but rarely engaged in conversations or shared topics with partners.

As I came to know this population of preconversational children and saw the genuine commitment of their parents and teachers, I realized something: I was not trained to address these problems or to involve parents and teachers. Indeed, if I did what I was trained to do, I simply would not speak to the problems that kept these children from entering society and communicating. The **ECO** program, and especially this developmental guide, is the result of 17 years of relationships with children, parents, and professionals during which we have trained each other to help children develop from initial play competencies to competencies with conversations for friendship and learning.

One early realization I had as Yvonne Gillette and I developed a clinical model for these children was that the traditional, one-to-one therapy model—with the clinician and child working in isolation from his natural learning relationships—would not work. *I am not saying that a one-to-one therapy model is never appropriate.* I am saying that we have found, theoretically and practically, that preconversational children learn to communicate *within their natural interactions.* Therefore, to help these children change, we professionals must help both them and the adults who play a significant part in their lives to do so within the ecology of those natural interactions.

In our experience, this move from isolated, one-to-one therapy to a consultant/training role seems too radical a change for many professionals. We are often told that this new role runs counter to much of the structured, directive approaches that are the hallmarks of sound clinical practice. This sentiment is understandable because most of us (perhaps you as well) were trained to improve the structural features of communication for people with intact conversation systems. But for a wide range of people who are not yet conversational, the goals cannot be the same. Instead, the first goal must be to develop *social relationships* in which communication can be learned spontaneously, where the fundamental process of learning to be communicative begins. Consequently, *Becoming Partners with Children* proposes a clinical model whereby you engage children and their significant adults in building partnerships that allow communication to develop and flourish.

Becoming Partners with Children is designed to assist speech and language clinicians and others responsible for communication development:

1. To learn more about the critical processes through which a child develops from first interactions to habitual conversations
2. To explore a new intervention model for communication-delayed children and other individuals who are preconversational
3. To learn to identify and integrate three critical components of a clinical plan
   a. Child goals for developing play, interaction, preverbal communication, language, and conversation
   b. Adult strategies and interactive styles that stimulate and reinforce these child competencies
   c. Problems that interfere with these child goals and adult strategies
4. To learn to educate parents, teachers, and others influential in the child's world
5. To provide parents, teachers, and others with tools for training themselves in their natural settings
6. To develop a consultant model, one in which you work with parents and teachers in building interaction and communication habits with the child

As you may suspect, adopting a new clinical model can be frustrating and uncomfortable, especially if it counters some traditional habits. But I have found great encouragement in the feedback from many speech clinicians who report success in applying the **ECO** model. I will acknowledge only a few here, but I want to express my genuine appreciation to many others who have supported the work with feedback of successes.

I have been pleased to see the model used in infant programs that may produce our most lasting effects. Jenny Young in Mansfield, Ohio, Linda Smith in Red Deer, Alberta, and Minda Bickley in Lancaster, Ohio, have used **ECO** in educating parents and professionals to adopt interactive styles that build stable social habits in the first year of life. Tom Almerico, in Salt Lake City, has built a broad consulting system by independently adapting evolving phases of **ECO** over the last 10 years. Tom creatively integrated **ECO** into a school system, not only training parents and teachers but assisting in redesigning curricula and helping trainees train others. He has done things I had not imagined, such as adapting **ECO** to interacting with severely multiply handicapped, as have Linda Lombardino and Dan McClowry in Florida.

In Eau Claire, Wisconsin, and Winona, Minnesota, Joyce Olson and Janet McCauley have been very ambitious; after clinically adapting **ECO** for a few years, they have developed the video-mediated inservice program for training teachers and caregivers in early social and communication development. Much of the program is a direct translation of *Becoming Partners*. (This video training program is also available from Special Press.) In New Jersey, Joanne Gerenser has adapted the model to a conversation-based approach with autistic adolescents that involves daily life classrooms and parent education.

It is particularly exciting to see language clinicians and teachers combine their talents to design classrooms that focus on interaction development. Increasing numbers of preschools for children with language delays— "communication classrooms" as they are often called—are viewing interaction and communication as the fundamental processes for learning. In Iowa, Steve Oberman has been adapting **ECO** to his field work for several years. In Columbus, Ohio, Marty Starky and others have communication-based classrooms using **ECO** principles; and at the Nisonger Center, Jeanne George directly applies the **ECO** program to preschool classrooms.

Perhaps my most consistent role has been to train students and professionals concerned with communication disorders. Many have told me of how exciting and frustrating it has been to attempt to build interactions between children and adults who did not know the importance of strong communicative relations with children. It is my hope that you will join them to enrich your lives and the lives of children and adults who can have stronger natural relationships.

TO TEACHERS:

In countless classrooms over the past 18 years I have witnessed the dedication with which many preschool and infant teachers work to help children develop. Traditionally, teachers are trained to work on preacademic or academic skills with children who can socialize and communicate. Learning these skills requires a child to be social and communicative enough first to learn them and second to generalize them. However, for children who are not socially and communicatively ready to learn many typical school tasks, the lack of interaction skills is a continually widening gap between the child and access to learning in natural, daily exchanges with others.

The **ECO** partnership model bridges this gap for children whose social and communicative skills are not adequate to allow them to learn on their own. In my experiences with children in classrooms, it has been the interactive and communicative children who seemed to benefit the most and the children who socialize and communicate little who have the greatest difficulty. Thus the **ECO** approach often provides teachers with two things: a curricular guide for children's development and an interactive guide for fine-tuning their own social and communicative style with the children.

ECO includes a system for helping children develop the early play and interaction competencies they need even before they become communicative. The **ECO** competencies provide a behavioral map of the early social and communicative skills that have been left out of early education curricula and left to the teacher to address strictly on her own. (Only recently have preconversational children even been expected to be educated.)

Before preconversational children are ready for traditional educational goals, they need teachers who help them become social learners. They need teachers who view interaction skills as elements in the curriculum that are fundamental to other learning. Thus, **ECO** addresses this question: How can teachers and other adults interact and communicate with children so that those children stay interacting and learn from them? The **ECO** response is a series of strategies or interactive styles that appear to facilitate a natural learning relationship with the children.

In short, the **ECO** program offers teachers a model of what to teach and ways to teach children who are not yet socializing and communicating adequately to learn and generalize what they learn. We find that when teachers build more sensitive relationships with children, the children are not only much more attentive but more naturally motivated to learn. These changes alone are rewards for a teacher, and they are generally followed by parallel changes in the children's enthusiasm and successes.

We hope that **ECO** helps you discover ways to make your classrooms increasingly interactive and communicative. We genuinely believe that the more interactive a classroom becomes, the more the children practice and respond to instructive feedback. Teachers cannot be responsible for directly teaching every concept or relationship a child is expected to learn in school. The child must also learn to learn on his own. To this end, teachers can build relationships with children and an interactive environment within which those relationships will stimulate and nurture incidental as well as directed learning.

Finally, the **ECO** program offers teachers ways to work together with parents and clinicians or other professionals. Its ecological focus assumes that the burden for social and communicative development cannot fall on any one person's shoulders. What we now know about communication development argues strongly that no one person can lead children to learn to communicate in all their interactions. We hope that this book will show you directions for helping your children become more social and communicative, with you, with other adults, and with their peers, and that teaching these children will become more rewarding for you.

TO PRESERVICE AND INSERVICE TRAINERS OF CLINICIANS, TEACHERS, AND CHILD DEVELOPMENT SPECIALISTS:

In recent years, approaches to early education have changed in major ways. Awareness that early intervention is critical for many children to become ready for school and society is growing. Federal laws mandating education for young children with delays have made policy of widespread findings that the first few years are indispensible in preparing children to become successful learners and accepted social part-ners (Brazelton, Koslowski, & Main, 1974, Elkind, 1987; Piaget, 1952). Another change in early education is a reassessment of the role of parents, other natural care-givers, and teachers in guiding children to become social and communicative (Bruner, 1983; Stern, 1985). An overwhelming body of theory and research now makes a power-ful argument for early attention to children's preconversational development. No longer is it realistic to expect children to interact and communicate on their own, especially when there are physical, intellectual, or emotional risk factors that could interfere.

Because of the recency of much of this research, preservice programs are only now beginning to train students to foster these competencies that children need for social and communicative development. Until recently, we have trained students largely to work with children whose speech or language problems merited attention but whose social and communicative relationships were reasonably well-established and stable. Thus, the **ECO** model provides faculty with a developmental guide for helping as-piring professionals understand the critical processes involved in helping children (and guiding other adults to help children) become communicative enough to learn in school and to generalize their learning to social and vocational relationships.

Becoming Partners with Children is designed to be able to serve as a text for students preparing for clinical, teaching, or other supportive roles with preconversational chil-dren. We use this text in our own courses in early communicative and language de-velopment. The other three manuals (see the description below) are companion tools for teaching early assessment and intervention approaches, and we use them in our courses on early intervention and clinical practice. Although we believe these books to be among the most comprehensive available for training preservice and inservice professionals in social and communicative development, we have tried to maintain an easy, conversational style. We realize that many of the notions in these works may seem novel to clinicians or teachers currently working with children. We hope that the conversational approach encourages readers to see this approach to development not as directive or didactic, but rather as reciprocal exchanges between the learners who learn not only because it is their work but also because of the social interchange that can accompany any exchange of ideas.

THE ECO COMPONENTS

The **ECO** program has been used with infants and children of preschool and school age and even with adults who had severely limited interaction and conversation skills. Although the **ECO** principles and goals cross both disciplines and categorical def-initions of developmental and communicative delay, it is helpful to think of the pro-gram as focused on individuals, and those with whom they live, who have these characteristics:

1. They are often noninteractive.
2. They are interactive but not communicative.
3. They are communicative but not linguistic.
4. They are linguistic but not conversational.
5. They have limited conversation skills in daily contacts with others.

One or more of these problems are generally observed among infants at risk and older children with conditions labelled emotional disturbance, behavior disorders, learning disorders, Down syndrome and other developmental disabilities, hearing impairment, cerebral palsy and other motor delays, and autism and other social isolation problems.

The different **ECO** components were developed to speak to the many different individuals who have the power to help people with communication delays become more interactive and communicative. The following paragraphs describe each of these components briefly.

This book, *Becoming Partners with Children: From Play to Conversation,* is a developmental guide for parents and professionals. It provides the most complete description of the **ECO** research base and **ECO** principles, goals, and strategies. Although it is organized so that it can serve as a text in training professionals, *Becoming Partners* is also meant to be a kind of reference that parents and professionals can pick up and read as they need information, guidance, assistance, or support.

Ecological Programs for Communication Partnerships: Models and Cases is a practical guide for professionals who are planning and implementing communication programs for children and adults. As its title suggests, this book helps professionals adapt **ECO** principles and strategies to the particular service models within which they are currently working or may be considering as alternatives to their current model. The cases in the book come from our experience with actual children and adults, although their names have been changed to preserve their privacy. These cases add flesh and blood to the outline recommended for systematically assessing, planning, and delivering treatment.

The *ECOScales* are a tool both for observing and building social and communicative competencies. They are accompanied by a manual that describes how to observe and rate interactions and how to develop profiles of the competencies and the partners in the interaction. The manual also provides information about the validity and reliability of these scales.

The *Practice Plan and Record* is a hands-on way to keep track of the current plan and how the partnership is changing as the plan is put into action on a daily basis. This simple record provides a summary of interactive goals, key strategies, problems to avoid, and daily activities to use as opportunities for interaction, plus a calendar and diary for noting what happened and when.

The *ECO Resources* are tools for professionals to introduce the **ECO** program to parents and other adults by selecting only the most immediately relevant topics or problem-solving strategies that each particular situation warrants. The **ECO** Tutors are actually topical guides that explain the **ECO** competencies, and they parallel the *ECOScale* items (including separate guides for preverbal and verbal children). The Conversation Routines are concrete ways for parents or other adults to get started, not by making radical changes in their daily routines but by turning regular daily activities with a child into opportunities for communication. The Sample IEPs and Problem Solvers provide a small library of concrete examples for parents and professionals when the time comes to sit down together and develop in paper and ink a plan for the intervention.

Communicating Partners Videotapes include examples of children and adults (both parents and professionals) before and after **ECO** principles and goals were used to help the child and adult become communicating partners. At present, there are a total of four videotapes, with others planned (some prepared by the **ECO** authors and others by professionals who have used the **ECO** approach with children and parents).

2 | *Principles of Communication Development*

RSATION
rsation

CONVE
conve

GUAGE
guage

LAN

UNICATION
unication

COMM

TAKING
taking

TURN

PLAY
play

SOCIAL
social

It is apparent to anyone intimately familiar with people who have developmental delays that most have extremely limited social and communicative skills. Whether their failures lie in the areas of playing with others, interacting spontaneously, communicating what they know, using their language in conversations, or building sustained relationships, the heart of the problem seems to be that they have not established social partnerships with adults or peers. The critical problem is not what is often labeled a "speech" or "communication" problem. Instead, it appears to be a fundamental failure to develop relationships that generate spontaneous learning.

The **ECO** model for social and communicative development asserts that, if social relationships are indeed vital for a child to learn to communicate spontaneously and to generalize formal learning to natural interactions, we must consider broad changes in how we serve communicatively delayed children. These changes need to be considered in terms of several questions about our role in helping preconversational individuals to develop: What is the appropriate curriculum or content of our efforts? Who is best fit to aid their development? What training for professionals is needed? And what adult interaction styles best serve the social and communicative development of these individuals?

Many clinical and educational programs for children with delays seem to assume that the child has the social and communicative competencies to use and generalize the academic content that is taught. However, when we look at our management of "normal" children's education, we see that preschools and kindergartens see the function of socializing the children as a prerequisite to teaching academic skills. Elkind (1987) has recently argued that even now "normal" children suffer from the problem of "miseducation," his term for imposing academic and competitive goals on young children before they have a stable base of social relationships. What results is a series of "circus tricks" that are not integrated into the fabric of the child's social learning.

As professionals and parents scrutinize their goals and strategies for children with delays, they must ask this pivotal question: *To what extent do our plans for a child give him tools to become as socially independent a learner as possible?* Given the general goal of providing the least restrictive environment, we should not ignore the possibility that school and home curricula can actually be sources of restriction. When clinical and educational demands for preconversational children focus on academic goals at the expense of social and communicative skills, we must ask who is being served. What use will the goals serve if the child's social relationships are limited to satisfying immediate needs and responding to an agenda determined by others?

Since the early 1970s, research across several disciplines on initial social learning has arrived at surprisingly consistent findings regarding the key processes necessary for developing social relationships (Bates, 1976; Bruner, 1977a, 1983; Bell, 1977; Bullowa, 1979; Crnic et al., 1984, 1986; Field, 1980; Goldberg, 1977; Kaye, 1980; Lewis & Rosenblum, 1977a, 1977b; Mahoney et al., 1981, 1988; Marfo, 1988; Stern, 1977, 1985; Trevarthen, 1977, 1979). These findings are beginning to be applied to clinical approaches to developmentally delayed children (Bromwich, 1981, 1987; Dunst, 1985; Girolometto, 1988; Greenspan, 1985; MacDonald & Gillette, 1984, 1988; McConkey, 1988; Mahoney, 1988).

This research has concluded that there is a central core of child and adult competencies that occur in stable social attachments. A particularly interesting finding is that the child is an active participant in his own development (Bell, 1971: Deci, 1975; Lewis & Rosenblum, 1977); to the extent that his significant adults interact in the following ways; by allowing a balanced, reciprocal partnership (Goldberg, 1977); by being behaviorally and cognitively matched (MacDonald & Gillette, 1988; Mahoney, 1981) as well as sensitively responsive (Mahoney, 1988; Snow, 1972); by being child-directed (Bruner, 1977a, 1983); and by being emotionally attached (Greenspan, 1985; Stern, 1985). Thus, it appears that the kind of adult, interactive style that supports a child's communication development has certain characteristics that are needed from early interactive stages through verbal conversation.

This latter finding, namely that certain adult styles are more productive than others, is so pervasive that it strongly suggests that adults such as parents and teachers need to be educated as much as the children themselves. Because the goal of the **ECO** model is a social and communicative partnership, our clients and students include both the child and his significant adults. Consequently, they role of the professional is more than that of a teacher or therapist with the child alone.

The remainder of this chapter both describes the **ECO** model for developing social and communicative partnerships and proposes directions for future education, research, and community action. First, a series of principles is presented; these principles are critical in generating a stable social and communicative partnership. These principles pervade the majority of **ECO** learning relationships regardless of the content of the curriculum.

PRINCIPLES OF THE ECO MODEL

The following principles for developing a social and communicative partnership have evolved out of a growing field of research into early adult-child interactions. As such, they are recommended to educators and families as instructive guides to help the child learn to become social and communicative with them. While these principles are in many ways counter to traditional didactic approaches to teaching, keep in mind that the children in question are preconversational, that is, not yet readily learning and generalizing in social relationships. These principles address the question of how adults can interact and communicate with children so that the children learn to be social and communicative with them.

The Partnership Principle

Are you sharing your child's learning in a balanced, give-and-take relationship?

Perhaps the most obvious fact about social and communicative development is that the child cannot do it alone. Not only does he need other people, he appears to need certain kinds of relationships. It is predicted that, for such development, a child needs balanced reciprocal partnerships (Bruner, 1983; Bronfenbrenner, 1979; Kaye, 1979). A basic notion here is that a child will learn from adults to the degree that the adult is an active partner who acts like the child, follows his motivations, and has a meaningful relationship in which give-and-take is the rule of interacting more than are onesided controls.

In his ecological theory of human development, Bronfenbrenner (1979) proposes a child and his significant adults develop together in joint activity pairs where both child and adult perceive themselves as doing something together. In such joint activity, he proposes, a partnership forms as long as three things happen: reciprocity, balance of power, and an affective attachment.

Reciprocity occurs when each person influences the other, unlike the one-sided relation often observed in didactic settings where an adult controls the direction and content of the interaction. Being reciprocal, each partner has to coordinate his activities with the other. Reciprocity leads to mutual feedback, which gives rise to a momentum of its own that motivates the participants not only to persevere but to engage in progressively more complex interactions. Without such reciprocal interactions, a child may be unlikely to learn much spontaneously from others. One strategy that has helped us build reciprocity is turntaking, in which the child and adult build a habit of mutual give-and-take (MacDonald & Gillette, 1988).

Turntaking then leads to a balance of power between adult and child in which each person has substantial influence on the other. Thus, the child is actively encouraged not to take the passive, responsive role often characteristic of children with developmental delays. A balance of power in interactions allows the child both the active participation he needs and regular access to the adult's feedback. Children appear to be more motivated to learn when they have some clear control over their environment and can have concrete effects on their significant people. Research with handicapped and nonhandicapped children and their parents has reported less reciprocal turntaking in the handicapped pairs (Buckhalt et al., 1978; Cunningham et al., 1981; Jones, 1980; Mahoney et al., 1985). While some studies have reported that adults dominate the turns with their children (Girolometto, 1988; Young, 1988), others such as Kogan and his colleagues (1969) report that adults and children operate in a "simultaneously neutral" position in regard to each other.

Finally, the most favorable condition for learning and development appears to be one in which the balance of power between adult and child gradually shifts in favor of the developing person, that is, when the child is given increasing opportunity to exercise control of the interaction (Bronfenbrenner, 1978, 1979; Goldberg, 1977; Hunt, 1961; Mahoney, 1988; Vygotsky, 1962).

One feature of partnerships often not specifically targeted in clinical or education programs is an active emotional attachment between adult and child. In a partnership model, it is essential that the child and adult reinforce each other by means of their social contact alone. Unless the adult's contact itself motivates the child to interact, the child will not likely develop a strong habit of initiating and maintaining interactions with people. Once people become generalized reinforcers, the child is more likely to choose a social world over a solitary world. Children appear to choose the world that allows them the most freedom, support, and access. In balanced, reciprocal relationships—the goal of this approach—each person has opportunities to experience success and feelings of competency that come from influencing the other. Another principle that is indispensible in building partnerships is using language and actions that are matched to the child's competencies, motivations, and communications.

Matching

Are you interacting and communicating in ways that your child can do and that allow him success?

Matching refers to the more developed person in a pair performing in ways the less developed person can perform, and in ways that relate meaningfully to that person's immediate experience. Specifically, progressive matching is the habit of interacting sensitively with a child in ways that both ensure him success and show him a next developmental step. There is evidence that adults frequently act and communicate far beyond the developmentally delayed child's physical and cognitive capacities, imposing on the child notions that do not match his experiences or motivations (Lieven, 1984; MacDonald & Gillette, 1988; Mahoney, 1988). Further evidence of mismatching to developmentally delayed children (Cross, 1978; Ellis & Wells, 1980; Girolometto, 1988) is that parents' communications to delayed children are less meaningfully related to the children's speech or actions that are those of parents of nondelayed children. Thus, whether adults provide models beyond the child's reach or communicate outside the child's experience, matching is a global strategy for helping a child learn naturally in an interaction.

Until recently, the notion of match was restricted to whether traditional learning tasks were sufficiently close to the child's ability level for him to master them. Thus, Hunt (1965) and other educators have specified that curricular objectives (such as in sensory-motor skills, math, and so forth) be finely tuned to assure the child's cooperation, motivation, and success. However, as we analyzed parent-child interactions during the development of the **ECO** model, matching consistently appeared as a critical feature differentiating those interactions that continued from those that did not. We discovered that the critical task was to match the adult's behavior to the child rather than to match the objects or curricular tasks to the child.

We decided that, if the child's goal was to socialize and communicate, we could no longer use a curriculum consisting of academic tasks alone. In fact, we concluded that, for our purposes, the curriculum for the child lies in the social partner herself, in her actions, communications, and interactive styles. That is, if we are to help a child become social and communicative, parents and professionals must allow themselves to be so finely tuned to the child's cognitive, communicative, and motivational states that the child can learn to model them spontaneously and build productive relations with them. This finding—that the adult's actions, communications, and interaction style are the precise curriculum or what the child needs to learn first—greatly influenced the development of the **ECO** model. It compelled us to move away from a teaching focus on sensory-motor and other academic tasks and toward a focus on directing the child to master the spontaneous behavior of adults and peers in order to become social and communicative.

After studying 60 developmentally delayed children and their mothers, Mahoney (1988) concluded that matching does indeed relate to greater interaction and learning. He concluded that the child's ability to participate in social interaction depends on several matching factors that can serve as guidelines for parents and professionals. First, the style of interaction adopted by the adult must be compatible with the child's interaction style. Second, the focus or topic of interaction must be congruent with the child's current interests. Third, the complexity of the adult's behavior must not exceed the child's capacity to process information. Fourth, the difficulty of the activity that occurs during the interaction should not exceed the child's current level of competence.

Sensitive Responsiveness

Are you responding to those subtle behaviors that are your child's developmental steps?

In developing a learning partnership that is mutually reinforcing to adult and child, the adult must respond to the child's subtle developmental steps so sensitively that the child pursues them himself. While matching takes the adult into the child's world, it is not enough. Contingent responding across levels is also necessary, for example, responding to the child's primitive interactions (Goldberg, 1977), his emerging nonverbal communication (Bates, 1976; Sugarman, 1984), his conceptions and experiences (Snow, 1984) and his language and topic (Cross, 1984).

In the **ECO** model, we first ensure a positive emotional attachment and then foster a contingent responsiveness through modeling. This responsive modeling in turn leads the adults to an awareness of the critical child behaviors they may never have noticed before. Through emotional attachment the adult becomes a functional reinforcer so that her responding will support and maintain the child's interaction.

Although any concerned adult may genuinely believe she is sensitive and responsive to children, we have found that even the most concerned and devoted adult cannot respond appropriately without some awareness of the developmental steps the child must travel through to reach the adult's goals. Thus, parents and professionals alike, most of whom have very little training in early social and communicative developmental, need to learn what to observe as well as how to respond. The **ECO** model described in this book gives adults a developmental curriculum to sensitize them to both their child's development and their functional role in that development.

The value of sensitive adult-responding is now becoming central to a wide variety of scholarly approaches to early education and child development. One unifying feature of many recent approaches to social and communicative development is that learning proceeds best when it is focused on the child's current knowledge and experiences (Bruner, 1983; Field, 1980; Stern, 1985) rather than on adults' agenda or choices of goals. This growing respect for the child as competent in generating his own direction for learning leads us directly to encourage adults to take the role of a sensitive responder who is finely tuned to the child's current capacities and motivations to perform (Newson, 1979b; Stern, 1977; Trevarthan, 1979).

In developing the **ECO** model we have accumulated extensive evidence on videotape that many parents respond much less to their children's preverbal behavior than to their vocal or verbal behavior, even when socially directed. A series of research studies support these findings (Eheart, 1982; Jones, 1980; Peterson & Sherrod, 1982). These studies and ours show that mothers of delayed children appear less responsive to noncommunicative behaviors of their children, thereby providing less meaningful support to child-oriented activities that are the critical precursors to communication. This finding is cause for concern when we consider the developmental evidence that communication emerges from nonverbal behavior (Bates, 1976; Bruner, 1983). The problem may well be that adults who fail to respond to preverbal play behavior actually discourage their children from practice-ing and making interactive the very behaviors that should be supported as the functional steps to becoming social and communicative.

In his research with mothers and handicapped children, Mahoney (1988) found strong facilitative effects on the child's learning when mothers actively acknowledged their children's actions and emerging communications. His following conclusions crystalize our experience as well. When parents are generally responsive to their behavior, children may develop their sense of control by recognizing that they can lead their parents during interactions. They may become more attuned to their own intrinsic cues as their parents respond to activities that interest them. The general acceptance that parents manifest by responding positively to their children's activity may enhance children's feelings of competence of self-worth (Mahoney, 1988, p. 210).

Child-Based Nondirectiveness
Are you allowing your child sufficient control over his learning? And are you permitting him to express himself?

We have consistently found that an adult who directs and controls a child, especially a child with delays, usually does so out of habit, a habit that is deeply ingrained and resistant to change. Adults who make statements like "All he needs is discipline" or "As long as I just get him ready for school" fail to realize that their child's most important learning lies within themselves, in affectionate, reciprocal partnerships, not in teaching drills.

The principle of non-directiveness does not mean that all directions and controls are to be eliminated. Occasional regulation and instruction are necessary, but social and communicative development is much less a matter of external regulation than of self-motivated interactions. The issue here is that direction and control should not be the primary reasons that adults interact with children. The sight of a 5-year-old girl with minimal self-esteem learning to withdraw socially is only worsened by the sight of an adult directing and evaluating her behavior into goals only the adult chooses.

The notion of *learned helplessness* relates well here. Children with delays are, often and in many ways, slow, imprecise, and unlikely to initiate their own activities. On the other hand, parents are often anxious for the child to perform. When the child does not respond at once, parents begin questions and commands that require the child to leave his frame of reference in order to get into his parents' thoughts and motivation. More often than not the child fails, and this failure provides feelings of failure in the adult as well. Thus, these tools that parents believe to be necessary for teaching, such as questions, commands, and directions, often become tools that simply terminate the interaction and present another opportunity for the child to learn.

A nondirective style of interaction with children who are learning to communicate allows them a kind of *guided freedom*. This freedom lets the child pursue his own inner motivation and physiological cues, which are his optimal stimuli for learning. With guided freedom the child is bound to have some successes, and therefore an increased self-esteem that may increase his willingness to interact. Without such freedom the child regularly fails to satisfy the adults' mismatched models, thereby limits his social contacts, and reduces his opportunities to learn. When adults interact in a style that does not constrict the child's options, then he is motivated to learn by his own personal images and responses, not simply by what others have chosen for him.

If left to interact only with a controlling adult, the child with delays often assumes a passive, dependent style, responding when directed but rarely asserting his own motivations or competencies. Directive styles also interfere with the child's own natural learning from his current activity. A child who is constantly directed or ignored may come to believe that he is incompetent and that the right things to learn come not from his own experiences but only from others.

As Stern (1977) portrayed in his exquisite view into parent-infant interactions, a major task of the young child is to learn ways to successfully regulate his external world and, as a by-product, his inner state through the use of emotional communication. The danger of directive or otherwise controlling behavior is that it interferes with the child's ongoing learning and motivation. When regularly directed by another's interests, a child is missing the opportunity to regulate his world. When he does begin to communicate, the effect may be that he does not know how to express his experiences.

Mahoney's (1988) investigation of 60 developmentally delayed 1- to 3-year-olds showed three interaction styles to prevail in the mothers: communicatively responsive, didactic or instructional, and communicatively ineffective. The didactic or instructional group tended to use language to direct their children's activity and to provide new information. They tended not to be responsive to their child's activities, but rather to focus primarily on topics that interested them. On the other hand, mothers with a communicatively responsive style were readily attentive to the child's communicative attempts. They tried to make sense of their children's communication, and they engaged in conversations in which they treated their child's communicative attempts as though they were meaningful or significant.

When Mahoney studied the children associated with the different maternal styles, the communicative styles were related to the rate of the children's language development. Generally, the children who achieved the highest level of communicative functioning had mothers who were responsive to their communication, while children at the intermediate and lower levels had mothers who were didactic or ineffective communicators. In separate studies, Mahoney also found that a didactic or controlling style of interaction was related to lower levels of functioning.

If we view the child as an active rather than passive participant in learning, we may be more encouraged to maintain a responsive, nondirective role with children. Within true partnerships—ones that are reciprocal, matched, and responsive—the flow should become so regular that the child incorporates his internal motivations and competencies as well as the external support of the adults.

Emotional Attachment

Is your social attitude effective in helping your child to be social?

A renewed interest in the emotional attachment between mothers and their young children occurred in the 1970s (Greenspan, 1985; Kaye, 1980; Lewis & Rosenblum, 1977; Stern, 1987). Research into parent-child interaction (Bruner, 1977; Newson, 1979b; Schaeffer, 1977; Trevarthen, 1979) began discussing the notion of "inter-subjectivity," the idea that infants and mothers achieve a degree of emotional and intellectual understanding of each other when their interactions are reciprocal and emotionally sensitive. From very early on, the active social presence of the mother and other caregivers is well established for most infants studied (Goldberg, 1977; Newson, 1979a). That is, people are, almost from the beginning, functional reinforcers for the child; he will show affect both upon the appearance and disappearance of the adult and he will exert no small amount of effort to maintain the adult's interaction. The mere presence of a significant other motivates the child to interact and increases those child behaviors it follows.

With children displaying developmental delays, the degree of emotional attachment may be lessened or disturbed (Greenspan, 1985). While there is tentative, emerging evidence that the interactions between children with delays and their parents may undergo disturbances, the issue is long from being resolved. The clinical reports that many mothers of handicapped children undergo a series of mourning periods (Blacher, 1984; Goldberg, 1977; Solnit & Stark, 1961) raise the question whether, for certain parents, the stress and shock of an unexpectedly "different" child may interfere with building the natural learning partnership the child needs in order to flourish.

In our experience with parents of handicapped children, we have found some evidence that parents prefer to have a more instrumental, businesslike relationship with their child than an animated, playful one. Although these obervations were made in the clinic and may not reflect home performance, we found that this style interfered with the child's easy access into a relationship with the parents. In the **ECO** program, we begin with intimate, failure-free play, with the only goal that parent and child stay with each other and adjust until they are enjoying the interaction. The principles of matching, responding, and allowing the child control serve to give both child and adult successes.

One view is that emotional attachment between the adult and child depends on the degree of success they experience with each other. In the **ECO** model, we do work through feelings with parents, but we immediately show the parent how to have some interaction success with their child. This usually means that we have to educate them to see how the child's little steps, which would otherwise go unnoticed by them, are truly critical. In developing the model, we learned that the emotional state of the mother and her respect for the child often shifted positively once they began interacting with success. And although states of grief remain, parents often report fewer feelings of frustration and depression as they become successful in effecting positive changes in their children.

This view of success-generated emotional attachment has support in Goldberg's (1977) concept of "mutual efficacy" in mother-child interactions. This notion proposes that both mother and child need to be effective in the interaction in order for such interactions to become habitual and for emotional attachment to develop.

For the parent this need is fulfulled by eliciting new and interesting behavior from the child. For the child, successes come from the mother's show of affection, her matched and responsive behaviors, and the child's control over the mother's behavior. In other words, when the mother and child succeed in maintaining each other's interaction, they are then emotionally prepared to build a partnership in which spontaneous learning can occur. Throughout the **ECO** model, we are concerned with strengthening the adult's competencies as well as the child's. Perhaps a rule to consider is that *"in order to have a socially competent child, he must be in partnership with adults who are child-directed and socially competent."*

As Goldberg (1977) predicted in her theory of social competence, emotional attachment that leads to growth will result from a habit of interaction in which both the child and adult experience regular success with each other. The **ECO** model is, in part, an attempt to guide adults to see both their child's next appropriate successes and the effects of their own natural strategies designed for success.

Thus, when the child and adult feel emotional efficacy, they are combining their experiences of success with the actual intellectual and social achievement. Thus, the more that adults can be helped to have successes with their children, the greater the likelihood of increased emotional attachment. And, the more emotional attachment, the more likely will interactions become habitual. Thus, at every stage of a child's development, emotional attachment with an interactive partner is likely to result in greater interactive practice, deeper learning, and greater motivation for the child to engage in other social contacts as a way of life.

BE A BALANCED PARTNER

General Principle

Children learn to be social and communicative within partnerships that are balanced and reciprocal and that penetrate both casual and structural interactions.

Development Principles

1. "Give as well as take." To become social and communicative, a child needs to give to others as well as take; the frequently observed passive role of some children and aggressive role of others suggests that they do not have this critical give-and-take habit.

2. "Learning is inevitable." A child is learning either how to or how not to communicate in every interaction he has, regardless of whether the adult intends to teach something.

3. "Motivation to learn." A child becomes more motivated to learn when he has feelings of competence; balanced interactions allow a child the time to succeed.

4. "Frequency counts." Frequent interactions just for the sake of the social contact are indispensible for a child's social and communicative development.

5. "Children stay when they have control." Children appear to stay for more interactive learning when they are frequently controlling their effects on others.

6. "Reciprocal, not one-sided." A child's interactions must not generally be one-sided, with child or adult dominating the turns; rather, they should be reciprocal. That is, each person should respond meaningfully to the other and share the lead with the other.

7. "Give the child some power." A child learns as his significant people shift the balance of power in his favor when he can do more.

8. "Communication comes with control." Children appear to be more motivated to communicate if they frequently have control over interaction.

9. "Enjoyment accelerates learning." Appropriate social play can be gauged by the child's enjoyment level; assume that the more a child enjoys being with others, the more he is learning from them.

10. "Being accepted in society." Society accepts people to the degree that they interact by giving as well as taking. Learning to interact in balanced ways is as or more critical to a child's development than learning facts and skills.

11. "Stay for one more turn." A useful general rule for helping children be more interactive and communicative is to keep the child with you for one more turn than usual.

BE A MATCHED PARTNER

General Principle

A child will learn from others to the degree that the others act and communicate in ways the child is able to do. Their behavior must match the child's competencies, interests, and style.

Development Principles

1. "Learning involves changing to be closer." A child's development is a process of accommodation in which the child gradually changes his ways of in-

teracting, communicating, and thinking to be more like those of the people close to him.

2. "Matched actions are more easily learned." The actions of adults are more likely to become part of the child's interactions to the degree they are ones the child can readily perform.

3. "Matching motivates." The child appears motivated to attend to and assume adults' ideas and interests to the degree that they match the difficulty level, interest, and style of the child's. Thus, the child is unlikely to be motivated to interact in events that are difficult, unrelated to his interests, and incompatible with his style.

4. "Do what the child can do." A child more more likely to learn to communicate from people who match him by communicating in physical and linguistic forms the child can follow.

5. "Match the child's ideas." A child will be more motivated to communicate with adults when they frequently interact and communicate about his ideas.

6. "Make the stimulation fit." Each child has his own optimal capacity to respond to stimulation; if stimulation is too little or too much, a child will be less likely to interact and to learn.

7. "Read the child for what to match." In order to match, adults need to read the child's behavior; "reading the child" means observing the little things he does and interpreting them, then matching back to the child so he can continue the interaction.

8. "The curriculum for communication is people." For learning to communicate, the curriculum or body of tasks to be learned lies in daily contacts with people. The forms, contents, and intentions of people in a child's world compose the active curriculum for learning to communicate.

9. "Match before and after." In specific interactions, matching assists learning in at least two general ways. First, matching before a child acts or communicates increases the probability that the child will interact and act more like the adult. Second, matching after the child acts or communicates will encourage him to stay interacting and learn from the adult.

10. "Mismatch for failures." The more mismatched adults are with children (that is, the more they do things the child cannot do), the more failures the child will experience and the less likely he is to stay and learn from those adults.

11. "Learn the child's competencies." By being sensitive to a child's abilities, adults can fine-tune themselves to the child, thus offering him models he can do.

12. "Imitation is not enough." While imitating a child is one useful way of matching, matching is much more than doing exactly what a child does. Matching can also involve new actions and communication at the child's level.

13. "Show the next step." Progressive matching is also necessary. By progressively matching, adults still do what the child can do but also show him a next step, a new or higher-level action or communication.

14. "Staircase partner." Adults should consider themselves on a developmental staircase with the child; each step is the child's action and communication level. The adults' job is to be both on the child's step and on the next step, showing him what else to do.

15. "Competent adults." A child's successful development also requires that his significant adult feel competent. Matching helps adults be competent by helping them keep the child interacting and succeeding.

BE RESPONSIVE TO THE CHILD'S EMERGING INTERACTIONS

General Principle

A child's social and communicative development depends on his significant others responding sensitively to subtle, emerging behaviors that are developmental steps to interaction and communicating.

Development Principles

1. "Natural Reinforcer." When there is a positive emotional attachment between adult and child, any adult response can serve as a natural reinforcer for what the child does; the child will then perform for the attention and communication itself.

2. "Influence." Adults can be more powerful developmental influences on children by sensitively responding to them.

3. "Self-esteem." Responding to a child in a matched way fosters self-esteem and motivates the child to stay learning with others.

4. "Read the child." In order to respond sensitively to the child, the adult must learn to READ the child; that is, to observe and respond to any behaviors that could be functional building blocks to social or communicative behaviors.

5. "Every invitation counts, at first." Adults should be sensitive and responsive to whatever behaviors the child initiates; this will encourage him to initiate social contacts.

6. "As if." A child's actions and sounds can become communicative messages if adults regularly respond to them as if they were communications.

7. "Respond with appreciation." Even when a child's behavior is much less mature than that of his peers, adults should appreciate the child's effort and understand that it can be a valuable step to more mature interactions.

8. "Fertilize the flowers." Children will do more of those behaviors adults respond to than the ones they ignore. Consequently, a rule to guide adults is to "fertilize the flowers not the weeds"; that is, attend to the behaviors that can build into communications and will strengthen them. Conversely, attending to inappropriate or maladaptive behaviors will also support their development. Thus, adults will be more productive when they learn to distinguish between the child's developmentally positive and negative behaviors and respond accordingly.

9. "Do not take the child for granted." Children will do less of many necessary emerging social behaviors if adults fail to sensitively respond to them. Taking a child's emerging behaviors for granted and not supporting them may discourage his development and widen the interactive gap between the adult and child.

BE NONDIRECTIVE

General Principle

Children learn most efficiently and stay interacting more when they have freedom to initiate and respond from their own experiences and motivations rather than when they are in a passive role of responding to others' directives and agenda.

1. "Avoid making passive." A directive and controlling teaching style, dominated with questions and commands, is likely to result in a passive, unresponsive child who does not pursue interactions spontaneously.

2. "Feelings of competence." A nondirective style of interacting that allows the child to express his own communications appears to support the child's feelings of competence.

3. "The power of commenting." A nondirective style, involving commenting and expectant waiting, is a powerful general strategy for motivating a child to communicate; comments announce the adults' ideas and allow the child to choose his own.

4. "Image builder." A nondirective style allows the child to communicate and create his own images rather than to defer to another's agenda.

5. "Never say never." Being nondirective does not mean never questioning or regulating a child; such directions are often useful and instructive, but as a general interactive strategy they do not appear to foster the habit of reciprocal interaction necessary for communication development.

6. "Nondemanding give and take." Social relationships are the place and the process for learning to communicate; in order to flourish, social relationships require a nondemanding give-and-take style in which the child can express himself, make mistakes, and have successes. Persistent questions and commands do not allow a child to develop the social relationships he needs.

7. "Don't be a lone ranger." A directive and controlling adult interactive style with a child may result in the child choosing to operate alone, thus missing many opportunities for social and communicative learning.

BE EMOTIONALLY ATTACHED

To become a habitual social communicator, a child must be attracted to people as a powerful source of reinforcement and modeling.

1. "Enjoyment for the child." To learn to communicate, a child must actively enjoy being with people.

2. "Adults need enjoyment too." To consistently help a child communicate, adults must genuinely enjoy the child, at least a good deal of the time.

3. "Interaction—a top priority." Interacting with people should be more interesting than being alone, at least some of the time.

4. "Attachment comes from competence." To be emotionally attached, both adult and child must feel competent with each other. They must experience success with each other. Emotional attachment between adult and child is likely to increase as the adult does the following: becomes a partner by allowing the child his turns; matches the child by doing things he can do and is interested in; sensitively responds to child by attending to and supporting emerging skills; becomes more nondirective by sharing the lead with the child and allowing him to communicate from his own perspective.

5. "Emotion motivates communications." The more active an emotional relationship a child has with a person, the more easily will interactions flow.

6. "Emotion can also discourage communication." Subtle expressions of judgment or disregard, especially to a child with a history of interactive failures, can diminish a child's interest in communicating.

7. "Reduce communicative risks." For many children, each communication may be a risk. A child may be taking the chance that he can't be understood or accepted. While judgmental responses may teach a child a single "correct" fact, they might reduce the chance the child will stay or return for more learning.

3 | *Competencies of the ECO Model*

SOCIAL PLAY
social play

TURN TAKING
turn taking

COMMUNICATION
communication

LANGUAGE
language

CONVERSATION
conversation

Educators, clinicians, and parents are regularly faced with the question of what are the next appropriate goals for a child with developmental delays or communication disorders. The traditional answer—"I want him to learn" or "I want him to talk"— is much more involved than it appears to many people. In the **ECO** model, social and communicative competencies are seen as much more than talking. They involve a sustained habit of social play and reciprocal turntaking interactions (Bruner, 1983; Lewis and Rosenblum, 1977b), and they develop first into preverbal and nonverbal communication skills and only later into language and conversation. These five competencies are seen as necessary for the adult and child to move from a noninteractive to a conversational relationship, that is, from a non-learning one ot one that fosters cognitive and social learning. There competencies are recommended as guides to future curricula for parents and professionals alike. This book contains a separate chapter on each of these competencies.

Traditionally, language is the only one of these five competencies that has been widely encouraged in professional training programs, and only recently have teachers and clinicians become familiar with the other four as regular tools for their work. Approaches to developing communication have traditionally focused on speech and related structural aspects of children who already demonstrated conversational skills. However, children with developmental delays are well known for having limited social skills for building reciprocal relationships, let alone the conversational skills needed to generalize from "speech" training. The primary goal of the **ECO** model is to unite adults and children in the kind of interactive relations where children can become communicative. in progressively more advanced ways.

The clinical research model presented in this book, the **ECO** model, views communication development as a function of five interactive competencies. The competencies unite a child and his significant others in balanced interactions from their initial contacts to habitual conversations. The five competencies of the model provide a map for adult and child to follow as they develop together.

Why Five Competencies?

As a child develops a habitual conversation system, he and his significant others acquire several competencies. Five of these competencies are the focus of the **ECO** model: Social Play, Reciprocal Interactions, Preverbal Communication, Language, and the Pragmatics of Conversation. The names given here to the five competencies are often used interchangeably in everyday language. Although each term has its own common sense meaning, each is used theoretically, clinically, and educationally to refer to a specific aspect of interaction. The definitions given in this chapter reflect the ways these terms are used in the **ECO** model. Each of these competencies includes distinct child skills, specific adult strategies, and problems that can interfere with the interaction. The **ECO** model is a system for observing, assessing, and teaching these five competencies within the context of building relationships. This natural interactive context is viewed as both the focus and process for communication development. Consequently, each competency in the **ECO** approach focuses as much on the adult's role in the child's development as on the child's skills themselves. For communication, a competency is always seen as a function of two persons interacting.

We selected the five competencies on the basis of the last 25 years of theory and research in child development as well as on our own work in researching and developing adult-child communication programs. We have developed the **ECO** model with a wide variety of individuals who have yet to develop generalized conversations. The literature has carefully shown that these five competencies are not just intimately related but functionally dependent on each other. Until a few years ago, the study of speech and language development was largely restricted to the oral communication abilities of people with the generalized conversation skills needed to actively develop more and more complex communication. The focus of the **ECO** model is the development of those very social-conversational relationships that underlie oral communication development.

The structuring of **ECO** into these five competencies grew not just from the theoretical and research base that has developed in the last few years, but also from the needs of hundreds of children with communication disorders. In assessing clients in evaluations, classrooms, parent-based programs and institutions since 1965, we have found that the most critical problems with the client's communication development were often not the typical "speech" problems for which speech and language therapists are usually trained, or even the "language" problems that classrooms traditionally address. Our work has involved children and adults with five markedly different levels of development: noninteractive, interactive but minimally communicative, communicative but not linguistic, linguistic but not conversational, and conversational with limited pragmatic range. These five competencies evolved directly from these problems, as seen in hundreds of clients in a variety of environments.

A final reason for attending to all five areas is what might be called the "squeaky wheel" approach to assessment and treatment. For example, when faced with a 4-year-old whose articulation is similar to that of an 18-month-old, it is tempting to identify the major problem as misarticulation. However, children with "squeaky wheels" such as this often face more basic barriers to development in the form of limited interaction skills, social isolation, limited play relations, and environments in which significant adults provide few matched models or child-world language. Our own clinical work, and much of the literature, supports the conclusion that traditional speech disorders are actually a function of a variety of interaction processes often ignored if only the isolated speech problem is treated.

These interactive processes are the basis for our use of the term ecological, by which we mean that communication develops not within the child alone but as a function of the kinds of social relationships the child has. Thus, an ecological approach to studying and treating communication delays attempts to assess and program for the child's primary relationships, that is, the child and his caregivers.

Of course, these competencies are closely interrelated. Rather than think of them as hard and fast limits on interaction, use them to help differentiate behavioral features, problems, and processes that span the continuum from primitive interactions to rich generalized conversations.

Notice too that the definitions include not only the child's but the adult's participation in the relationship. Thus, throughout this book the focus is on developing parallel competencies in both child and adult. Communication is like a marriage: its natural development, problems, and clinical development necessarily involve two persons.

SOCIAL PLAY

Social play is the competency shown when a child and adult regularly engage in genuinely joint activities, activities where each person is attending to and participating in the same things. The stronger the social play the more the two perform as a unit, and the power gradually shifts from the dominant person to the developing person. Social play has no predetermined rules or content. Anything can be play, and it may be planned or spontaneous. As the two partners grow in this competency, their playful style becomes evident in more and more of the child's interactions.

As the child develops in social play, his actions become more functional, intentional, and symbolic, and they will begin to take on more of the properties of those of the partner. Through social play the child will be able both to develop his own meanings and to learn new functions and meanings from his partner's intimate participation in his activities. People will begin to take ona more positively reinforcing value, this will become more natural in signaling for interactions.

As the adult develops in social play with the child, she will become more truly accessible in several ways. Through matching, she will become more like the child, doing things he can do, providing him successes, and showing the next developmental steps with little stress. Through sensitive responding, she will support the child's natural steps in development, keeping him motivated to interact and learn. The adult will become more facilitative and less directive. The goal of social play is more to express naturally one's current motivations and abilities than to get a specific job done.

In social play, both the adult and child engage in a habit of stress-free, joint-activity routines. These routines allow the child to become emotionally attached to the adult in a context that gives the child increasingly greater control and success (Bronfenbrenner, 1979; Lewis & Rosenblum, 1977; Stern, 1977). In our experience, children and adults do not often show the active joint togetherness that underlies the social support system a child needs (Bruner, 1983; MacDonald & Gillette, 1988) for communication learning. Our experience also indicates that adults frequently fail to see how critical adult-child play is to a child's cognitive and social learning. Play is more typically seen as the child's business and not worthy of serious adult attention or participation. Thus, the children and adults we have studied regularly operate in distinct worlds—the child in an action world and the adult in a linguistic, task-oriented world. This gap can be extremely limiting to the development of a child with delays. However, if educators and parents interact with children from an intimate, playful attitude, they become more effective natural teachers. Social play is thus seen as the beginning competency, even for children who have some communication and language but few playful relationships.

The first goal is that the adult and child become play partners. To accomplish this, they play actively together with a shared focus, balance the amount of each person's activity, and act and communicate the way the other does as they share directions and decisions in play. The child's primary goal is to stay actively in play with others. To do this, he initiates as well as responds to others, and he engages directly in the activity of the other. As the child grows in this competency, he actively keeps the interactions going and uses a greater range of functional and meaningful actions that gradually reflect what the adult does. Children then play more and more with others and less alone.

The goals for the adult in social play are equal in importance to the child's goals. To support the child's own motivation, they keep childlike play going by matching the child's actions, responding sensitively to the child, and making themselves more interesting than the child's distractions. They match their own communications to the child's level, communicating about immediate experiences, and then reduce their control to allow the child more successes. This playful attitude is more than a way to play games; it is a habit that helps the child become social.

TURNTAKING IN RECIPROCAL INTERACTIONS

The essential characteristic of the turntaking competency is the attitude of give-and-take. A passive child and directive adult show limited give-and-take. For communication to develop, the child and adult must establish a flow, back and forth, in which each person both initiates and responds meaningfully to the other person's turns. Beyond this pattern of give-and-take, the critical feature of a mature turntaking competency is that each person will actively keep interactions going.

The turntaking child learns that he can interact with any behavior capable of engaging the adult's attention. Depending on how responsive to him his adults are, the child begins to explore people as he does toys and learns to accommodate to them, thus refining his play behavior into social behavior. He moves gradually from being primarily a taker to being a giver. At first he will give more attention than action, but gradually he will direct more of his actions to others, and eventually he will extend his turntaking to communicating. As the competency grows, the child will become more adept at shifting back and forth between the roles of follower and leader, and he will see his role as giving and taking with others.

The turntaking adult learns to adjust her expected role of giver to one that helps the child give and exchange. She learns that giving without allowing the child to actively participate severely limits his social development. She learns that a major responsibility of a caregiver is to show a child how to give to others interactively as well as to get from them. She learns that timing is critical with a child, and so she waits and shows the child she expects him to interact. The critical aspect to becoming interactive is to keep the child interacting with the notion that every social turn is another opportunity to learn.

The critical skill of reciprocity, or mutual give-and-take, appears barely evident between many children with delays and their significant adults (Field, 1980; Girolometto, 1988; Jones, 1980). If a child assumes a primarily passive or responsive role in interactions, it is unlikely to give his partners enough feedback to warrant them staying in interactions. This lack of interaction only further deprives the child of the spontaneous opportunities for learning that are necessary to become a communicating partner. Consequently, the goal of turntaking is to establish a give-and-take habit from the most primitive movements to the most complex concepts in a conversation. The child and adult learn that the child has as much responsibility to give to others as to take from them and to give in ways that are meaningful to the other. This notion, that a child with delays has the duty to give as well as get, has been a powerful one in our work.

At first, turntaking is based on the child's own available set of behaviors but is soon extended through imitation and modeling to a more socially responsive range of behaviors that begin to approximate those of his adults. Turntaking, then, begins to pervade people play as well as object play and spontaneous contacts in daily routines. A related goal for the child is to extend into social use, skills he already uses when alone. How often we have heard, "Oh, he does that," only to find that the child did it only when directed but not as a part of his social life. Turntaking is a tool for making the skills a child *has* into skills he *uses* socially.

Two adult strategies that have proven powerful in engaging children in extended interaction are matching—acting and communicating like the child—and expectant waiting—expressing visible anticipation as one waits for the child to respond. These habits, matching and waiting, often require adults to alter their well established patters. Without such changes, however, the child is frequently at a loss for what to do and when to do it, so that he may become discouraged from trying to compete with the rapid flow of adult behaviors.

But knowledge of matching and waiting is not enough. We have found that parents and professionals must develop a lasting commitment to the child's need for regular interaction. Unless they genuinely recognize how important habitual interaction is for a child with delays, adults can easily be distracted from this essential job of monitoring the child.

PREVERBAL AND NONVERBAL COMMUNICATION

Two maxims are critical to the competency of preverbal and nonverbal communication: first, any behavior can communicate; and second, children communicate long before they speak and their nonverbal messages are vital to learning language. Preverbal communication involves sending, receiving, and exchanging messages with any behaviors other than words or signs. Even a child's actions and sounds not originally intended as communication can become communicative if the adult responds sensitively to them. Preverbal/nonverbal communication is not a stage separate from the first two competencies, play and turntaking, but social play and turntaking are fundamental to build a communication habit.

A child's general activity level and specific actions relate directly to his potential for communication. Beyond satisfying his own physical needs, the child must extend his actions and sounds into social encounters through repeated, playful relations. He must first interact on any frequent basis before he can be expected to extend those interactions into communication. The child must have stable skills of imitating, responding, and maintaining communication with the adult.

The importance of the adult's competencies here cannot be overstated. The adult's communications must be accessible to the child if the child is to imitate them. Consequently, the adult must be able to fine-tune her actions and match the child's actions with competent adult forms the child both comprehends and can use as models for what to do. She must sensitively respond to her child's intentions and emerging behaviors, enticing the child to become a communicator. As the adult becomes sensitive to this role in shaping the child's actions and sounds into communications, she begins to build a bridge that will allow these communications to become words.

The natural unfolding of communication, from playful and functional actions to gestures and sounds to verbal language, has been carefully mapped (Bates, 1976; Bullowa, 1979; Siegel-Causey, Ernst & Guess, 1987; Trevarthen, 1977). However important these preverbal attempts are for social and linguistic development, clinical and educational approaches to handicapped children rarely concern themselves specifically with the preverbal conversations that are necessary building blocks to speech (Snow, 1984). In fact, we have found that parents and professionals are often unaware of how important preverbal communication is in actively preparing both the child and adult for the child's language and conversation.

Like others who have studied this area, we have found that adults often fail to match the actions or sounds of a preverbally communicating child. Instead, they use predominantly verbal language that is beyond the child's level of successful performance (Girolometto, 1988; Holtom, 1987; MacDonald & Gillette, 1988).

In fact, nonverbal communication can provide rich practice in developing the semantic intent and pragmatics that prepare the child for the form, content, and use of language (Bloom & Lahey, 1978). Repeated practice in these aspects of language establishes the habit of communication that then supports the emergence of language in natural interactions.

This third competency grows out of the play and turntaking competencies as the adult comes to treat the child's actions as communications and as the child attempts to model the matched communications of the adult.

A major goal of this competency is that the child increase the rate of his communications, whatever their form or intelligibility, to provide a foundation for the emergence of language. Related goals include the habit of initiating as well as responding, maintaining communicative turntaking, and maintaining a balance between the social and instrumental purposes for the communications.

The adult's role here continues to be a playful, interactive one, now with a specific focus on progressively matching the child's actions into communications and on translating his sounds and gestures into words. This matching process is not unlike the process of learning a second language, because the adult treats the child's preverbal behavior as the child's first language and assumes the role of translator as she translates it into her own language. Not only does this translation take place at the moment the child is most likely to want to learn it (Mahoney, 1988), it is also directly responsive to the child.

LANGUAGE

A traditional definition of language often reads like this: A rule-governed system for expressing information in symbols. When extended to an interaction model such as the **ECO** model, this traditional definition might read: *Interactional language is a system in which the child develops symbols for communicating from* *his own knowledge, meanings, communicative intentions, and motivations, aided by others whose language is matched to the child's capabilities, interests, and communications.* Interactional language includes the communication partner in its definition.

For the child, the task of learning language involves, first, translating into audible or visual symbols knowledge he already has. The term knowledge-communication gap refers to the widespread finding that many "talking" children communicate much less than they know. The implication here relates to the issue of what language children should learn. The position taken in the **ECO** approach is that a child's language curriculum or program may be most efficient and useful when it focuses on language representing three areas: what the child knows and does (cognition); what he communicates about and has probable cause to communicate about (communication); and what is currently reinforcing to the child (motivation).

Consequently, the adult's success as a natural language teacher is likely to depend on how sensitive she is to the child's knowledge, communicative intents, and interests. Adults often find that a child participates only a little with them when they use or impose language that comes from adult interests or requires school learning. However, the adult finds a more linguistically involved child when she becomes a "living dictionary," one who codes her child's actions, communications, and interests as she engages the child in regular verbal interactions on extended topics.

When language is also seen as developing within matched, responsive partnerships (Brown, 1973; Cross, 1984; Snow, 1984; Wells, 1986), the task of teaching language must specify the adult's language content and style to the child as well as language goals desired of the child. That is, it is proposed that a curriculum for language development must include goals for both the child and adult. The context for language learning remains the same responsive, nondirective, joint activity routines (Bruner, 1977a; Stern, 1985) that have kept the two together while learning to interact and communicate. What is new is the content to be learned.

Our experience with children with delays has revealed two widespread problems: the "knowledge-language gap" and the "academic language" problem. The first problem is that children often know much more than they attempt to communicate. They often appear unaware that one valuable thing to do with their knowledge is to express it in language. Language for them appears to be something more to store than to use. The second problem is seen in the child who has language for many school-motivated notions, such as body parts, colors, and numbers, but little language to express his current experiences, nonverbal communications, and motivations. Too many children have difficulty linking their experiences and communications with their language skills, apparently viewing language as a tool to communicate only to others' expectations, not as a tool for personal expression.

A child-based language curriculum, then, involves the vocabulary that represents those meanings that developing children consistently show in their first language (Bloom, 1973; Brown, 1973; MacDonald, 1978). In place of traditional academic language, communicatively appropriate early language reflects child meanings. These include agents, actions, objects, locations, and feelings that can be combined efficiently into a wide range of early sentences in conversations for solving problems and building friendships. At first this content capitalizes on the child's natural reasons to use language in communicating with others and in his own private coding of his experiences.

Before the child is habitually conversational, the parent, teacher, or other adult can act as a kind of interactive dictionary, coding the child's own experiences and motivations. By using language that is immediately responsive and meaningful to the child, adults reduce the cognitive demands on the child and allow him to focus more on the adult's language than the adult's topic (Lieven, 1984; Snow et al., 1984). Considerable research shows that children engage more linguistically with adults when the adult's language is immediately and meaningfully related to the child's moment and knowledge than when it is not.

CONVERSATION

The competency of conversation involves the variety of social roles and reasons for building conversations. The study of language use (pragmatics) goes beyond the issue of what language is needed to the question of why the language is used. The prevalence of children who are only passive and responsive communicators should cause us to ask as much about the reasons and uses of language as about the form or content of the language used. Children with a broad vocabulary but few skills in conversation may miss many lifelong benefits of their language in personal relationships and in the larger world. This competency is defined in part by three broad reasons why children and adults communicate: to get or to manipulate (instrumental); to establish a social connection and to enjoy the contact (social); to accompany actions or for one's own stimulation rather than to communicate (self-directed); (Halliday, 1975; Searle, 1969; Piaget, 1952).

For the child, instrumental and self-directed communication appears obvious and natural. So does social communication, at least in infancy. The lack of social communication is usually one of the greatest barriers to learning and socializing faced by children with delays. It is common to see children talk readily when they are questioned and directed but show little or no language in the kinds of social conversations that make up most of life. Within the primary goal of communicating socially, the more immediate goal of staying in conversations may determine the degree to which the child continues to learn on his own and becomes socially acceptable.

For the adult, assisting the child in becoming habitually conversational requires a careful evaluation of her role in communicating with the child and its effects on his communication with others in his world. When adults direct and control a child's communication, they appear to limit severely the children's language and social participation, with the frequent result that the child experiences few successes and withdraws from social contacts. On the other hand, a child-based social style of conversation appears to yield more from the child, with the result that he more readily becomes conversational.

The passive, responsive roles taken by many children, showing little active participation in conversations, offer a dim forecast for their future in friendships or productive partnerships of any sort. Similarly, children who have only brief, undeveloped, verbal contacts with others not only miss much social learning but also make themselves unaccessible to others ready to teach them. Though far from passive, an aggressive, dominant child also discourages a partner from participating and thereby reduces the opportunities for successful conversations. Thus, whether the child takes a passive, overactive, or controlling role in conversations, the problem centers on pragmatics, or the use of language: the child has not learned the rules of conversation and does not use language to build or sustain relationships. Many parents and professionals seem to view conversation as an adult enterprise. In the **ECO** model, conversation is seen as the primary means by which people learn from one another, especially language. Thus, we strongly encourage regular conversations as a fundamental goal for classrooms and homes, regardless of the content to be learned.

Many adults also see a need to direct and control handicapped children, not to engage in conversations with them. This attitude may derive from the child's apparent helplessness, and it is consistent with professional training that stresses academic content more appropriate for children who are already conversational. Unfortunately, too many adult questions and commands prevent handicapped children from taking an initiative role in conversations, set them up to fail in many of their responses, and discourage them from the conversation process itself (Girolometto, 1988; Mahoney, 1988; Mahoney et al., 1985).

Thus, if children are to master conversation skills, their home and classroom environment should reflect a commitment to conversation as an indispensible process. No longer will adults be satisfied with an obedient, responsive child who rarely asserts himself. Instead, they will help the child communicate for a variety of reasons: to comment, to reply, to inquire, to maintain attention. Their style of relationships will become more social than instrumental, initiated for the value of interaction itself.

As adults extend their conversational habit into intentional as well as spontaneous contacts with the child, they will maintain the child's interaction and show the child how to develop social partnerships with others, partnerships rich in new language and new skills for the child to learn.

COMPETENCIES FOR SOCIAL AND COMMUNICATIVE DEVELOPMENT

What do children need to learn to become social and communicative? What goals should early education and clinical approaches address in order to foster social and communicative development? What do parents need to know about how children learn to communicate? What can they, as parents, do to help them communicate? Why are these particular competencies necessary?

NOTE: *Competency* here means a generalized habit of behavior that is needed across the child's range of social relationships; as such, a competency involves a system of related skills, attitudes, and patterns.

BECOMING PLAY PARTNERS

General Competency

Social play is the competency in which a child develops increasingly close and more habitual joint activity relations with people. It is with these skills that he begins to engage others in extended playful interactions as his natural way of being with people. As he develops social partnerships, the child gradually becomes more like his partners, following their social rules and learning their skills to the degree they are behaviorally and motivationally matched. Social play is to be distinguished from traditional work or teaching in that learning to be social generally involves no externally imposed goals; while social play results in considerable learning, it occurs in a context of balanced, undemanding social exchange.

What can a child do to become social?

1. Respond to others with interest.
2. Frequently prefer social contact to being alone.
3. Stay with others for increasingly longer periods.
4. Initiate and respond to others.
5. Actively participate in the same activity with people.
6. Successfully have effects on others.
7. Imitate others' actions and communications.
8. Allow others to engage in his play.
9. Frequently lead others in his choice of play.
10. Actively include others in his play.
11. Continue his personal explorations with others.
12. Frequently follow others' leads in play.
13. Play functionally and meaningfully with others.
14. Play imaginatively with others.
15. Successfully control others in play.
16. Successfully assert himself when dominated.
17. Spontaneously interact with others outside play.

1. Present a playful, childlike atmosphere, getting directly into the child's play and spontaneous behavior.
2. Allow the child some control over the adult and the activity.
3. Insure the child has some success.
4. Encourage the child to stay in the activity for increasingly longer amounts of time and allow him the freedom to explore and create.
5. Be a matched, childlike partner. Matching means acting and communicating in ways the child can match.
6. Act like the child; this helps him act like the other person.
7. Match the child's *interests;* do things related to his concerns.
8. Match the child's *actions;* be a physical model of behaviors he can perform.
9. Match the child's *communications;* use sounds, actions, and words like his.
10. Match *progressively;* show your child a next developmental act or communication.

BECOMING TURNTAKING PARTNERS

General Competency

Turntaking refers to the generalized habit of frequent reciprocal interactions in which the child interacts in a give-and-take style and regularly shares activities and communications with others. Such interactions are necessary for learning to be social and communicative.

Why is turntaking important for social and communicative development?

A turntaking habit is necessary for a child to learn to give socially as well as get; without this habit, others are unlikely to build relationships with the child.

To have lasting effects, turntaking must be reciprocal; that is, each person is responding meaningfully to the other and neither is always taking the lead.

For optimal learning, adult and child should shift the lead back and forth so that each can fulfill his own motivations.

Turntaking means a general give-and-take style with true exchanges; it does not mean rigid question-answer routines or rote back-and-forth routines with little changes. Also, turntaking does not mean "all the time"; both child and adult need their own freedom to operate on their own.

Without frequent turntaking, a child is unlikely to get sufficient practice to learn to communicate like others and to get the immediate feedback that is critical to his learning.

Turntaking provides the child with the skill of staying in interactions that provide frequent practice and immediate feedback on emerging cognitive and communicative skills.

What can a child do to learn to take turns?

1. Frequently initiate contact with others.
2. Frequently respond to others' contacts.
3. Interact in an increasing number of activities.
4. Take a turn and then wait for the other to take a turn.
5. Take turns imitatively.

6. Take creative turns, not only imitative ones.
7. Take turns spontaneously, without being prompted.
8. Take turns with meaningful actions.
9. Take turns with gestures and sounds.
10. Take turns with words and sentences.
11. Direct actions and communications to others, not to himself.
12. Show interest and expect others to respond.
13. Actively keep interactions going.
14. Act reciprocal; respond to others meaningfully.
15. Show interest in the partner's point of view.
16. Generally do only about as much as the other.
17. Show ability to get his own turn if dominated.
18. Interact in activity of partner's choice.

How can adults and peers help the child take turns?

1. Be committed to the importance of the child's interacting.
2. Match the child's actions and communications.
3. Respond immediately to little behaviors.
4. Generally, expect the child to interact.
5. Accept any safe interactions at first.
6. Take one turn then wait silently.
7. After waiting, signal the child to take a turn.
8. Physically prompt a turn, if necessary.
9. Keep the child for one more turn than usual.
10. Maintain an easy back-and-forth flow.
11. Occasionally get from the child, as much as give to the child.
12. Enjoy interacting with the child.
13. Be more interesting than the child's distractions.

BECOMING COMMUNICATING PARTNERS

General Competency

Children first exchange messages (communicate nonverbally) with any physical or audible means they have. A child needs to frequently communicate with any means in habitual interactions before he will talk or build natural learning relationships. The more this competency develops, the more the child learns he can affect other and the more motivated he becomes to communicate.

Why is nonverbal communication important? A child will become an habitual communicator to the degree he freely contacts others with all forms of sound and movement at his disposal. A child will learn to communicate more readily with people who sensitively respond to his subtle behaviors.

A child will communicate more readily with people who communicate in ways he can match. A child will communicate more readily when adults communicate about the child's interests and immediate experiences. A child will learn to communicate best in relatively nondirective interactions where he has some freedom rather than in adult-directed teaching contacts where the child is passive. A child's nonverbal communications will become verbal language to the degree that others treat them as communications and translate them into words. A child will become communicative to the degree that his emerging behaviors have clear effects on others. A child's communication will become more like that of others when those others regularly match and wait for more. A child will learn to communicate to the degree that he communicates for a variety of reasons beyond having his needs met.

What can a child do to develop the habit of nonverbal communications?

1. Communicate on sight of a person.
2. Initiate as well as respond.
3. Take turns with communications.
4. Wait for others to communicate.
5. Keep communicative interactions going.
6. Freely and frequently communicate with movements.
7. Freely and frequently communicate with sounds.
8. Freely and frequently communicate with words.
9. Respond in ways other than communicating.
10. Communicate to play by himself.
11. Communicate to get needs met.
12. Communicate just for friendly contacts.
13. Communicate about his own interests.
14. Communicate about others' interests.
15. Communicate messages clearly without words.
16. Communicate assertively.
17. Try to make himself understood.
18. Change his communication to be more like others.

What can adults and peers do to help a child become nonverbally communicative?

1. Communicate on sight of the child.
2. Clearly communicate for a response, not at the child.
3. Communicate frequently with the child.
4. Take turns communicating with the child.
5. Communicate once and then wait for the child.
6. Wait silently with anticipation for the child to communicate.
7. Match the child's communication with a communication he can use.
8. Match child's sounds with clearer sounds or easy words.

BECOMING LANGUAGE PARTNERS

General Competency

A child's language evolves from both his knowledge and his communication skills. Consequently a child will first talk about his experiences and interests as well as those notions that are communicatively useful to him, both socially and instrumentally. A child is likely to learn language to the degree that he has partners who communicate within shared activities.

How do language skills help a child's social and communicative development?

A child will learn language to the degree he interacts with a shared focus with others.

Language learning is more likely to the degree a child stays in balanced, turntaking interactions that allow him modeling, feedback, and practice.

Language learning and language teaching are often distinct processes; language learning is less likely to occur in conventional directive teaching settings that make the child passive and are related to his motivations.

Children appear to learn language to the degree that the language has regular communicative use for them.

Most children begin to talk about a few similar meanings: agents, actions, objects, locations, and feelings. These meanings are a more effective base for first language than many academic goals (like colors, shapes, and numbers) that have less power to motivate and communicate.

What can a child do to continually learn language?

1. Stay for more frequent interesting language.
2. Use language to play by himself.
3. Use language to show what he knows.
4. Use language to communicate with others.
5. Use language both to initiate and respond to others.
6. Use language with confidence.
7. Talk about himself and his actions.
8. Talk about others and their actions.
9. Talk about feelings.
10. Steadily add new words to his vocabulary.
11. Imitating and otherwise modeling what others say.
12. Use language more than to get needs met.
13. Combine his old words into sentences.
14. Stay on topics of his own choice.
15. Stay on topics of others' choice.

How can adults and peers help a child learn language?

1. Believe that you are the child's best language teacher.
2. Realize that playful interactions are the best way to learn language.
3. Use language with the child that is frequently useful to him in communication.
4. Realize you are a natural teaching dictionary for your child.
5. Match the child's nonverbal communication with a useful word.
6. Match your language to the child's interests.
7. Match your amount of language to what your child can do.
8. Keep him for one more turn with language.
9. Use words that match his interests.
10. Accept any words at first without judgment.

11. Comment without pressure; this often keeps the child talking better than questions and commands.
12. Keep the child on topics one or two turns more than usual.
13. Keep child talking on a topic of his choice.
14. Use talk that stimulates images instead of rote responses.
15. Be more interesting in your talk than the child's distractions.

BECOMING CONVERSATION PARTNERS

*General
Competency*

Children will learn to become social and communicative to the degree that they learn to engage in extended verbal exchanges with a variety of pragmatic intentions and to shift flexibly between their own and others' topics.

Conversation skills begin in infancy, when the child and adult exchange their first imitations, requests, protests, and the like.

Children appear to learn more readily in conversations that are social and non-directive than in directive and controlling ones.

Changing from a questioning adult to a commenting one often leads to more conversational children.

Directive, controlling conversations with questions and commands are deeply ingrained in many adults.

Conversations are often best begun with the adult and child actually doing something together.

Children learn to be conversational to the degree that they have control over what and how to communicate.

Until habits develop, it is more important for a child to stay in conversations saying anything than saying "the right things, the right ways."

Conversations are a highly efficient and effective way for a child to develop many cognitive and social skills.

The stronger a child's communication skills, the more natural learning is likely.

Conversations can be effective generalization tools.

*What can a child do
to build the
conversation habit?*

1. Communicate for a response, not at others.
2. Acknowledge that language has many uses (pragmatics).
3. Communicate for critical social reasons, such as commenting, replying, nurturing, sharing, information, giving affection, and getting attention.
4. Limit instrumental communications, such as meeting needs and manipulating others, to occasional use.
5. Weave conversations in and out of his play.
6. Carry out imaginary conversations.
7. Communicate in ways that get responses.
8. Keep conversations going without prompting.

9. Initiate a conversation on his topic.
10. Respond meaningfully to what others say.
11. Play an active rather than passive role in conversations.
12. Stay in conversations on others' choice of topics.
13. Shift back and forth from one's own topic to the other's.
14. Communicate turns with partners rather than dominating them.
15. Balance turns with partners rather than dominate them.
16. Take the other's point of view in conversations.
17. Develop a topic beyond an initial notion.
18. Show assertive interest in having conversations.

What can adults and peers do to help a child become a conversation partner?

1. Believe that conversations are necessary for learning and friendships.
2. Believe that every conversation teaches some language.
3. Believe that children with delays communicate much less than they know.
4. Believe that conversations are the best way for a child to show what he knows.
5. Believe that a playful attitude in conversations results in more learning than a work attitude.
6. Believe that frequent conversations are the most powerful language teachers.
7. Comment on your experience with the child rather than questioning and commanding.
8. Respond to the child's comments with nonjudgmental replies.
9. Respond to the child in ways that keep him communicating.
10. Make extended chains of your turns.
11. Build on the child's turns with new, related ideas.
12. Limit questions and commands to genuine ones that serve a real need.
13. Communicate with clear expectancy for a response.
14. Allow and support a turntaking flow.
15. Communicate in ways that match the child's ability and interests.
16. Allow the child to contribute to a conversation with gestures, sounds, or any other means.
17. Consciously keep the child for one more turn than usual.
18. Respond to the child's ideas with new but related ideas.

Part

II

DEVELOPMENTAL GUIDES

4 | *Becoming Play Partners*

SOCIAL PLAY

TURN TAKING

COMMUNICATION

LANGUAGE

CONVERSATION

Children and adults must learn to stay and to play with each other before the child can learn to be social and communicative in natural interactions. Parents and other adults often do not believe that play is critically important to every child's development (Bronfenbrenner, 1979). When adults do see play as important, they frequently assume that playing alone is enough for a child. Playing alone does help a child to think in many ways, but playing with people helps a child think and communicate. This program aims to help adults become the kind of play partners who can spontaneously show a child how to develop as a social communicator.

In this program we define play as any interactive activity that is motivated by the shared interests of the child and adult and that involves no pressure to get a job done or perform in specified ways. Play can be planned or structured, as with a game or playing house, or it can involve casual brief contacts with no purpose other than enjoying each other. Critical to such play are joint activity routines (Bruner, 1983), in which the child and adult engage in play that directly involves both of them in the same physical or communicative activity. Such routines allow predictable (hence, routine) give-and-take exchanges that create a cognitively and socially safe situation in which the child can try out new skills successfully.

Routines allow a child to participate in a repetitive event he or she can master. Then, within a successful exchange, the child and adult can experiment with new skills. Routines also allow the practice and matched feedback the child needs to learn the intricacies of newly emerging skills. The playfulness of the routines ensures that the child maintains the enjoyment and success necessary to develop habitual social attachments. Common routines include "pat-a-cake," winking, stacking games, and any other events that are predictable and to which we can add something new like sounds and words. Here we do not mean sit-down play that takes the adult away from other things that must be done; interactive play is best when it is salt-and-peppered throughout the natural time adults spend with their children.

Many researchers and clinicians have concluded from intimate involvement with children developing language that play with people is a necessary habit for developing communication, language, and conversation (Brazelton, 1973; MacDonald & Gillette, 1987; Snow, 1972; Tronick, 1982). The work begun in this play program never ends. The skills learned here will need to be strengthened and maintained throughout the later stages of social and communicative development, indeed into the increasingly complex conversations of adulthood. Without learning to stay and play with others, children are unlikely to learn how to move to the next stages of communication, language, and conversation.

The **ECO** program takes its name from the term ecology, which refers to the balanced interaction of developing individual elements in a complex structure of living things (Bronfenbrenner, 1979). An ecological approach to communication is based on problems identified in the child's own interactions with the world around him or her, and it focuses on three related sets of goals: those for the child, those for the adult, and those for the enrichment of the interaction. This approach is based in part on the assumption that a child's communication does not develop alone; rather, the child and adult are a developing pair who grow and change together in part as a function of how they interact with each other. The goals for the child will help him become more social and communicative. The goals for the adult translate into strategies that help to overcome the problems and allow the child to fulfill his goals. The interactive goals deal with adult and child not merely as individuals interacting but as a dynamic unit to be assessed and served as a unit.

The **ECO** program views its primary mission, then, as helping two clients, child and adult, change together to build greater interaction in a growing communicative partnership.

The remainder of this chapter explains and discusses the goals and strategies involved in becoming play partners. These goals and strategies are the first stage in developing communicative habits. If a child is not habitually interacting and communicating with you and others, this first program is for you. Even if he does communicate, even talk, occasionally, this program is for you. It will help you begin to form the kind of relationship you need for later communication, language, and conversation. Regardless of the level of the child in your care, we hope you read this chapter to get a personal feel for the interactive world you and your child share. And we believe that you will come back often to this chapter, to discover ways you can help your child learn more from you.

Interactive Goal

1. BECOME PLAY PARTNERS

What Can You and Your Child Do Together?

If a professional is available, his or her role in the **ECO** program will be to help two people come together in an active partnership that helps the child not only to communicate with the adult but also to build similar partnerships with others. Brief clinical contacts between professionals and a person with delays cannot alone be expected to build new habits that will endure for life. It is only within the ecology of daily interaction between two people that communication will emerge. If professionals are not available, parents and other caregivers can still learn much from this program about how to become closer to their children.

Your child learns as both of you change together.

This program is different from traditional approaches to teaching language to children with delays. To begin with, in an ecological approach the child is no longer considered the only person to be served. What is more, the primary goal is not to teach a particular core of concepts, words, gestures, or sentence structures. Rather, the primary goal is to develop a play partnership between adult and child, because child-oriented play offers the richest, most natural, and most frequent opportunities to learn. Traditional teaching or therapeutic tasks alone are not adequate for building the social relationships needed for communication.

Play is the important work of your child.

Do not conclude, however, that the emphasis on play is intended to make light of a serious need. Play is not taken lightly here. Like many adults, you may view play was what you do after work is done. For the developing child, many scholars in child development (see Bruner, 1975; Newson, 1979b; Piaget, 1952; Stern, 1985) agree that play is the child's most important work, allowing him or her to create and re-create new problem-solving skills. Thus, if you and others join in your child's play, you will be precisely where he learns best. The goal, however, is not for adults to play on the floor all day long, nor is it to abandon the curriculum of other skills the child needs to learn to mature. Rather, the goal is to make contact, to learn to play in the child's world. And having made contact, you will soon learn how to make play out of even the child's simplest contacts with you. The goal, then, is a playful attitude, and that will get a great deal of learning done.

One of a great many advantages to playing together is that it requires very few developmental skills of your child or specific training from you. There is extensive evidence available showing that, soon after birth, infants regularly play elaborate give-and-take games with their mothers. During these games the mothers sensitively fine-tune themselves to the child (Brazelton, 1973; Field, 1980; Kaye, 1976; Stern, 1974), and the child actively reciprocates, showing he is changing as his mother changes. In fact, recent researchers now credit the infant with a considerable amount of control of the mother, indicating an active as well as responsive learner (Bell, 1979).

Children who have few play relations with adults appear to be missing some of the most critical natural tools to learn what others do and how they can become like them. The literature on delayed and disturbed children reports striking lacks of such reciprocal social skills. Problems of this sort are often the hallmarks of people labelled autistic-like (Fey, 1986; Prizant, 1983), emotionally disturbed (Greenspan, 1985), behavior disordered (Forehand & McMahon, 1981), hearing disordered (Kretchsmer & Kretschmer, 1978), Down Syndrome (Mahoney & Robenalt, 1986; McConkey, 1988), and blind (Frailberg, 1977).

Widespread reports indicate that attention problems may also be related to children's habits of social interaction (Peck, in press). For example, while children with Down syndrome have a reputation of being social, our experience is that many of them have limited social "staying power," which in turn reduces their opportunities to communicate and build relationships (Young, 1988). The degree to which adults can motivate children to stay attending to and interacting with them may reasonably relate to a great number of learning successes or failures (Mahoney, Finger, & Powell, 1985).

The social isolation of people with other kinds of developmental delays has been widely documented (Field, 1980; Schiefelbusch & Bricker, 1981). While they often have academic and vocational successes, these successes may sit as only unused knowledge if they do not have the social skills to generalize them into relationships. Wells (1981), McConkey (1988), and others have viewed communication problems as primarily a problem in social interaction skills rather than in cognitive skills only. That is, the problem is often not that children lack the knowledge but that they lack the social skills to use that knowledge to relate in the world. An example is the boy who shows he knows many meanings and functions of things in his play but rarely uses that knowledge when others give him similar tasks to do. A common case in point is the testing situation where parents claim that their child, when left alone, "can" do many of the things he has just failed on a test in a social context.

We agree with those professionals who find that playful interactions within the child's world are the indispensible learning format that is necessary before language and communication can emerge. Becoming play partners, then, might be viewed as a major step in the prevention of severe social and communicative delays. We are often surprised at what we see a child do when we allow ourselves to genuinely play with him. It is, in great part, these experiences that motivate us to continue our own work.

This program is an attempt to place in your hands, as a parent, professional, or other primary caregiver, the skills for building communication within interactions that can become a part of daily routines. Consider now five important guidelines that can help prepare you for eventual language and communication learning with your child.

Subgoal
Play with, not only at or beside.

a. Be actively together.

The kind of play relationship your child needs is one in which each of you is clearly playing with the other, not only at or beside the other. Thus, the two of you must attend to each other and respond sensitively to each other's actions. Do not be satisfied merely to be playing in parallel, with each "doing his own thing." The key is that you should both be doing the same thing in a joint activity. The more you do the same thing, the more you will share the same world of ideas, and this sharing of a common world is essential for a communicative relationship. This common universe of experience will allow each of you to learn the other's ideas and motivations. Furthermore, as an adult, you will be better situated to build on what the child knows if you have a personal and physical knowledge of the child's experiences. For example, as you build a bridge of blocks, you could "play at the child" by stacking the blocks and telling him what you are doing. Or you could "play beside" him by working one side while he made the other. In contrast, to be actively together, you could place a block, wait for him to place one, and each continue responding sensitively to what the other one did. Note that we again do not mean specific games as play; you can be most effectively playful by incorporating play as a part of all kinds of contact.

Subgoal

b. Play with the same focus as the other.

Your child will learn more if you are actually involved in the same activity. If your child is pushing cars, putting away toys, or having a snack, you do it too. Get into little back-and-forth routines, where each of you is trying to act like the other, with you gradually showing him a new thing to do. The more you focus on what the child is doing, the more easily will you be able to do things he is able and motivated to do. We find that children enjoy this togetherness and attend to us more if we are an intimate part of their activities. Sharing your child's focus will also give you a clearer feel of what he knows, what he wants, and what he can do.

You do not always need toys for this play; be sure some of your time together is just with you or another person. Your child needs to learn that people are rewarding just by themselves. Then he will stay and learn from them.

You may ask, "But what do I do with him? I don't know how to play any more." The answer, in the beginning, is anything safe. We often begin by imitating what a child is doing. This often catches his or her interest. Then we proceed by being more interesting than the things distracting the child. And we let the child know that anything safe goes as long as he or she stays with us briefly on the same activity.

Remember that your first job is to convince your child that staying with people will be rewarding and that he will have many choices of his own to follow in the play. Do not expect the toys to keep him with you. If toys are keeping your child with you now, then he is probably not attending enough to what you are doing to be learning from you.

Subgoal

c. Do about as much as each other.

Once the child and adult are together, the child needs the opportunity to do what he can do. Increasing evidence suggests that a child may learn best when he has some control over his activities. Even a little choice allows the child to explore and create in a spontaneous match between his perceptual-cognitive skills, motivation, and the opportunities of the moment (Deci, 1975; Goldberg, 1977). Clearly, many children with delays are often slow to respond and perhaps even slower to figure out exactly how to initiate social contacts. They need time. We must give them that time and keep attending to them as they proceed. We have observed a strong tendency in adults to dominate much of the activity in play. These adults do so much that the children can't show what they know. Instead, the children often become passive and thus appear not to try. They seem to refuse to compete with the faster and much more competent adult, and the consequence is not just that they learn less but that they fail even to know how to be with people. And people must be their primary resource for learning.

Give your child time.

To learn, the child must actively participate, not just watch or have things done for him. When the adult and the child each initiate about as much as the other does (that is, balance interactions), the child is able to try out his skills and receive supportive feedback from the adult. While the more general rule is that adults are the ones who dominate, it is not unheard of for a child to dominate the interaction and prevent or ignore the adult's participation. In this case, children need help learning that, to be socially acceptable, interactions require doing with, not doing alone, and giving as well as getting.

Subgoal

d. Play and communicate like the other.

Matching, a term used throughout this book, is a skill that applies to every stage of development. Matching refers to the adult doing something the child is likely to be able to do. Children appear to learn more readily when adults match their behaviors. That may sound self-evident, but if you observe adults and children together, you are likely to see the opposite happening. Adults often do something children could not even attempt, and yet the adults act as if they want or expect the child to do it.

Get in the habit of matching.

Widespread research on the motivation of young children suggests strongly that children perform best on tasks that are at their performance level or just slightly above it (Deci, 1975; Hunt, 1961; Mahoney, 1988; Vygotsky, 1962). Although the tasks were mostly school-like rather than conversational, these researchers did conclude that matching helps the child learn in several ways. Most important, when an adult matches a child, the child's chance of success increases, which in turn motivates the child to do more, thus increasing learning opportunities. Another result is that the child is less inclined to avoid learning situations. Matching shows respect for the child and an acceptance of his current level of performance. We find that in response to our matching, children are more likely to then enter our world.

Thus, when matching is applied to the task of communicating, the child is no longer trying to master a task with objects but a task who is a person. In other words, every adult can become a kind of finely tuned task that motivates the child to have easy successes, successes that will keep the child in the interaction for still more learning. As adults become more and more like the child, doing what the child can do and showing a next step, a partnership emerges in which the child and adult come to act in tandem rather than alone together. While the word matching may be new to you, the idea is probably not. We suspect that you yourself stay and attend more with persons who match you by doing things you can do and that interest you.

Subgoal

e. Share directions and decisions in play.

In a play partnership, the major goal is to keep both people in the partnership, each enjoying the other. When beginning a play habit, there are no right and wrong ways of acting, no jobs to get done, and no agenda other than to enjoy each other. Mahoney and his colleagues (1985), in a series of longitudinal studies of children with delays, have demonstrated that mothers who are more playful than task-oriented have children who are socially and cognitively more advanced than do mothers who were mainly directive, controlling, and judgmental. Likewise, a play partnership requires that children are not controlling the adult, but rather are cooperative, playing for the fun of it and not only to attain some goal.

As adults, our own most rewarding conversations often have no goal to accomplish or job to get done. Instead, the shared contact is its own reward. This is the kind of play partnership we want for you and your child. Consequently, it is essential that play not become drudgery for either you or your child. The habits your child learns in play with you may determine the kinds of conversations and relationships he may have later.

It's Your Turn

COMMENT: If Larry and I became the kind of partners you suggest, I would have to stop doing a lot of things I think I should do for my child. I was even taught to do many of them.

REPLY: Exactly. And that is why this approach, while it sounds simple, actually challenges many of our views of how children learn. The first step in tackling this dilemma is to watch Larry and ask yourself a few questions. Do you believe he learns from you in daily casual interactions? Do you feel he can learn if you don't give him the time to practice? Do you think he can do the complicated things you do? Does he do better when you do things he can do? If he does learn from you, do you think he's likely to stay to learn more if you run the show and direct what he does? Or will he do more if you make friendly, low-stress play out of your time together?

We find that children learn more from professionals and parents when those adults think less about what they should do and concentrate more on responding sensitively in ways that keep the child with them and allow the child to become more like them.

COMMENT: I enjoy playing with my son Teddy, but I get stuck doing the same things over and over. Teddy doesn't get bored but I do. What should I do?

REPLY:

Every moment together can be playful. Let any situation lead you into play. Be sure you stay together actively in three kinds of activities. First, stay in "people play" so Teddy learns to stay just for the value of being with people; he will need that for communication. Second, keep your son in frequent contacts playing with things he enjoys. Third, make easy balanced play a part of the daily routines you do.

Table 4.1 lists some of the activities we find successful in keeping children in playful interactions.

Table 4.1
Activities:
Generalization

Object	Routine	People
Blocks	Getting dressed	Playing with feet
Dolls	Setting the table	"Rocking" game
Trucks	Doing dishes—soap play	Play "airplane"
Shoes	Riding in the car	Swinging around
Books	Cooking/preparing food	Hiding
Empty can	Getting ready for bed	Patty-cake
Ball	Bathing	Tickling
Airplane/airport	Tying shoes	Making faces
Toy house/people	Yard work; bagging grass	Peek-a-boo
Paints	Looking in the mirror	Making noises

Self-Assessment:
How Are You
Doing?

Describe your play partnership with your child. Use a 1 to 9 scale where 1 = never or very poorly; 5 = occasionally or fairly well; 9 = always or extremely well.

_____ 1. Be together. We genuinely attend to and share with each other.
_____ 2. Be balanced. Frequently, each of us does about as much as the other.
_____ 3. Be matched. Each of us does what the other can do or is able to try to do.
_____ 4. Be motivated. Each of us does much of what the other wants.
_____ 5. Be friendly and nondirective. Our contacts are more for enjoyment than to get something specific done.

Note: You can also ask professionals or friends to assess you and your child on this scale. Their views may help identify how you can build a stronger base for your child's communication development.

Interactive Problem

2. LACK OF PLAYFULNESS

Think carefully about how important you think play is and how playful your child perceives you to be. Several problems can interfere with playfulness: the way you think, the way you act, and the way your child acts and sees you. If you think that play is only a vacation from "real learning," as golf may be for you, you are not likely to be very playful with your child. Many people believe that play

Play is not only child's work.

is important for a child to learn to explore, manipulate, and master his environment, but may also believe that most play can be done alone or only with other children. Rarely do we meet adults who believe that playing with adults is necessary for a child learning to communicate.

True, observing normally developing children can make it seem that they learn most through playing on their own. But these children usually have learned much earlier in their development the social skills needed to share their knowledge in relationships with people (Lewis & Rosenblum, 1977). In fact, by the end of their first year, most normally developing children have mastered the skill of people play that is the critical base for communication (Bullowa, 1979); it is only by being a competent social partner that children can move to learn to be communicators.

Your playfulness is more valuable than you may believe.

Another barrier to playful habits is the lack of confidence of many parents and professionals that their own casual time contributes to their child's learning. Adults sometimes assume that only specialists can make a real difference. They fail to see the many skills they already have and have used to help their child come as far as he or she already has. Still another problem is the view that play needs to steal time from the duties of the day. This view does not acknowledge that most daily activities can include playful interactions at no extra expense in time or energy.

If their child is delayed, parents may have felt pushed away and unsuccessful for so long that they now believe the child does not want them or cannot learn from them. This view is potentially very harmful to both the child and adult. Playfulness can help spark or renew those enjoyable interactions that characterize contacts between most infants and their parents.

Don't allow your child to not play with you.

Before many adults can get to the point of easily accepting play as valuable, they need to overcome another problem: expecting too much. In our product-oriented world, it is not surprising that parents and professionals do not find the child's small steps as rewarding as the pace an adult would prefer (Elkind, 1987). Thus, it is easy to forget to reward the child for things that you do not find rewarding in themselves. Unfortunately, without rewards for even the smallest steps, the interaction may stall and the child may learn nothing new or learn only to stay away.

A similar obstacle to playfulness is the adult's insistence on goal-oriented rather than child-centered play. Play that produces stress or results in more failures than successes is more punishment than play. The notion that there can be only a right and a wrong way to do things often deters the child who is not yet ready for the whole thing. For instance, the father who drives his son to build a complete bridge

"Right" may often be wrong.

when the child is ready only to stack blocks is too common an example of stress the child may seek to avoid, thereby avoiding the chance to learn from people. If your child were learning to climb steps, you would certainly not place him on the bottom step, run to the top, and say, "Come on up and get me." You already know how to expect and help your child do some things one step at a time. Ask yourself if you are preparing your child for success or failure when you play with him.

Parents and professionals regularly want their children to play with things in the "right" way. They often believe that "educational" toys are best for children and that there is a preferred way to play with them. Little do they realize that people may be a child's best toys. Because a child will be communicating more with people than with toys, recognize that you can be a plaything if you are animated and inviting. If you can become a playful toy that keeps your child interacting, you will be teaching your child something he absolutely needs: a positive value for people. Believing that you are your child's most valuable educational toy can help you get much closer to the child and make learning effortless for you and your child.

For social and communicative learning, you are your child's most important toy.

Watch for these
signals of a problem
in playfulness.

The event we will describe next can alert you to possible problems in your child's playfulness with others. These problems usually seem to be a result of adults and children doing what they believe they should be doing. It is reasonable that neither the child nor the adult appreciates the value of playing with the other. Few adults are taught that child play is critical to a child's social and communicative development; few children will stay in social play if it is not as rewarding as playing alone. Clearly no one is at fault here.

In our work with children of many ages with many diagnoses, we find that these problems interfere with interactions that are valuable for learning. Often as we discuss these problems, parents, professionals, and students get defensive and give reasons for why they do what they do. Many feel guilty. Neither of these reactions is necessary. Before we spent years studying children and adults, our interactions with children showed all of the problems discussed below. In fact, they still do, at times. We are not striving for perfection from either you or your child. Consider these problems as events to think about and avoid when you and your child are together.

Subproblem

a. little enjoyment of or interest in each other.

Just as with adults, when we do not show enjoyment or interest in what a child does, we may be actively discouraging the child from continuing that activity or, worse, from valuing it himself. Many children with delays are vulnerable to adult judgments and lack of support for their play activities. This problem can hinder many kinds of learning if the child loses confidence in the value of his play. Further, few children will involve their adults in play if they realize those adults do not enjoy it; consequently, many indispensible learning interactions will be lost.

This problem also works in reverse. How do you feel when your child shows no pleasure or interest in what you do? When this happens to us and to adults we know, we seek other things to do and the child again misses many opportunities to learn.

Subproblem

b. Minimal sensitivity to each other's emotions and motivations.

It is easy to ignore a child's feelings unless he or she is in special need. It is equally understandable to be too busy to attend to many of your child's motivations. However, it is precisely those subtle emotions and interests that are the best links between us and the child. Unless we sensitively attend to a child's feelings, he may keep them to himself and become less social; we will be less able to keep him learning with us. For example, by simply responding to your child's excitement when the doorbell rings, you support his new behaviors and have the chance to show him how to interact further.

Similarly, it is reasonable to expect your child to have a problem learning to communicate if he is not actively sensitive to your emotions and motivations, because he will not be likely to understand you and give you what you need interpersonally. It is by becoming aware of the interests of others that your child will learn to take their perspective; without that skill, he will be accepted as a communicating partner less easily.

Subproblem

c. Minimal affect or expressiveness.

Consider a child's world to be a circus, full of entertainment ready for the taking. In a circus, many of the most effective performers show the most affect or emotion and express themselves in many ways to fit the audience. With children with delays and adults, neither may show much affect or attempt to keep the audience (each other) interacting and interested. The problem here is that children, especially ones with delays, need to see other people as more stimulating that the object world. The child will learn to be social and communicative with people only by interacting with them with increasingly more interest and frequency.

Subproblem

d. Stressful or task-oriented activities.

Children operate with many of the same rules adults do. Like us, they avoid stress and failure. Activities that focus more on the adults' goals and difficult tasks are likely to result in two potentially serious problems. First, they may reduce the child's freedom to explore and communicate his own intentions. Second, they may lead him to see adults, in general, as something to avoid rather than join.

Subproblem

e. Focus on right or wrong.

Children develop best along their own small, evolving steps. When we face them with our views of right and wrong, such as when we urge a child who is just beginning to talk to use adult articulation or when we encourage a toddler to play with a toy in a prescribed way that is too complex, we face the danger of creating failures for them and discourage them from interacting with people.

Subproblem

f. Minimal spontaneity.

Do you ever feel you learn best when something happens unexpectedly and all the conditions—in you and in the situation—are just right? Too often adults act as though children learn only when adults teach. If adults and children do not unite spontaneously, they might miss the best motivational times for learning. If a child is discouraged from acting upon his own immediate interests as he senses them and if his contacts with adults are too structured, he will lose interest and learn less. Adults have often told us that they believe they must continually be teaching or directing children with delays. They fail to see how much learning happens on the run, when both the adult and the child spontaneously hit upon a common awareness ("Look at that silly man!") or activity ("Oops, let's clean it up!").

Subproblem

g. Limited use of active playful movements.

The ways you move can be signals for your child either to be childlike or not. Time and again we see adults and children play a game as if they were in a trance, moving very little. Playful movements can be a rich source of new meanings and communications; the less playfully active you are, the less communicative your child may be as he plays with you.

It's Your Turn

COMMENT:

Playing with children sounds good, but I simply do not enjoy it. I have a 3-year-old boy with autistic tendencies and an infant girl. How can I learn to enjoy play?

REPLY:

You need two things to get started: first, a firm belief that play with people is almost as necessary as food for your children; second, a feeling of freedom to do anything with no pressure to get a job done. You may not enjoy play because you may not feel successful. At first, just keeping your child with you is an important success; let yourself feel it is an accomplishment when your child stays longer. Then practice being childlike with nothing to get done. We find that a child will stay and do more when you act like him and make no demands other than for him to stay doing something with you. Keep track of two things—how long he stays and new things he does. Make those your rewards.

COMMENT: I have been a principal of a special education school for 22 years. I firmly believe that my children need structure and direction, not to go and play freely.

REPLY: You are not alone in your conviction. As you will see in this book, we propose considerable structure to adult-child relationships. But unless a child voluntarily interacts with people playfully, he is unlikely to become social and communicative. And no matter what he learns in structured teaching, he may never use it and benefit by it if he does not have strong social habits. Once a child has relationships, he then can continue to practice and learn what he is taught. We are concerned that the child not limit his learning to structured teaching situations and miss the natural learning available only in social contacts.

COMMENT: I don't understand when you say that focusing on right and wrong is a problem. I studied for years to teach children to do things right. Am I wrong?

REPLY: No. Of course, we want your child to do things right, but it must be right for his own development, not for your expectations. For example, the right way to build a tower of blocks or greet someone in the morning will differ for two children. A complete tower may be right for Manuel while stacking only two blocks might be right for Julia. Similarly, a full "Good morning, Gloria" may be the right next step for Manuel while Julia might be developmentally correct with a glance and a wave. If we pressure a child to do things our "right" way, we may give the child failures and drive him away from the interactions he so needs. Remember that the child must stay interacting to learn from you. Consequently, the one right thing you should always work for is the child staying with you, and then gradually go after the other right things.

Self-Assessment: How Are You Doing?

Describe how you feel about your play problems with your child. Use a 1 to 9 scale where 1 = disagree strongly; 5 = neither agree or disagree; 9 = agree strongly.

____ 1. Play is for fun, not for learning.
____ 2. I don't have what it takes to teach my child.
____ 3. I am not interested in playing with my child.
____ 4. My child is not interested in playing with me.
____ 5. Playing with my child is stressful.
____ 6. I don't feel successful when playing with my child.
____ 7. I don't expect my child to do much.
____ 8. I feel a pressure to get a job done when playing with my child.
____ 9. I expect more than my child usually gives me.
____ 10. I feel I need toys or things to play with my child.

Adult Problem

3. DIRECTIVE, CONTROLLING STYLE

Children appear to learn best as they explore freely with guidance from others when needed, but the notion of guided freedom requires a careful balance between leading your child and following his lead. If adults are regularly directing and controlling a child, several things are likely to happen. The child will be less motivated to learn than when he has some control and choices. He will fail more often if the directions do not match his immediate interests and needs; thus he may avoid just those social interactions he needs to become social and communicative. He will see social contacts as more work than play. He may come to think that what others want him to do is more important than what he wants. In all, when adults direct and control children, those children appear to learn less and become more passive, thus less actively participating in learning opportunities (Elkind, 1987; Mahoney, 1988).

Of course, we must occasionally direct and control children. The issue here is the general style to take with a child. We know children who interact and communicate freely in some environments and not in others. The difference in those environments often lies in the degree to which direction and control is the name of the game. Highly interactive children often become passive in settings like those classrooms, where their spontaneity is seldom supported and where directions are the primary adult style.

Subproblem

a. Takes majority of turns.

Frequently we see adults act as though they believe that the more they do or say to the child the better the child will be. And so we see a father building a full bridge of blocks with a child who is ready only for a few at a time, or a grandmother who wants to show the child who is just beginning to speak how to talk. So she says "Look at all those things in that toy house; there's a stove, and refrigerator, and a table, and up there there's a bed and a potty chair. . . ."

Domination discourages children.

In these cases the child has no time to participate and is given models that he cannot be expected to attempt. Children treated like this often take a passive role as if they expected they were supposed to sit and listen and watch, not to interact. When we discuss this "turn dominance" with adults, they often say they want to give the child as much as they can and they expect the child will figure out what to do next "somehow." Without time and models the child can at least approximate, it will be excessively difficult for a child to learn to socialize and communicate. And when we consider that parents of infants usually give them time and matched models, we realize that adults can match and wait if they believe, as they apparently do with infants, that the child needs it.

Subproblem

b. Little waiting.

Children who have been slow to develop social and communication skills are often also slow to initiate and respond. Unless adults wait sensitively, the child with delays will not have time to process the situation, decide what to do, and act. Moving and communicating is physically difficult for many children. When adults do not wait for a child, not only do they prevent him from the practice he needs, they may actually be teaching him to not try, to avoid the work of learning and let others act and communicate for him.

No time to act.

Not only do adults frequently not wait often or long enough for a child to participate, they also often do not let the child know they expect him to do something. Simple facial or gestural signals let the easily distracted child know he is supposed to do something with another. Parents and teachers who report that they feel that all they do is give to the child often do not allow the child to give something back by waiting or informing him of his responsibility to give back through signalling.

c. Controlling atmosphere.

Even when an adult is responsive and childlike, there can be a controlling atmosphere. If the child has little opportunity to act or communicate on his own without someone monitoring what he does in some way, he may be much less motivated to be with others than to be alone. Children can read the social rules of an environment. If a child sees other children regularly directed, he may redirect his social behavior as if he were learning the rules of the room. A controlling atmosphere is one in which the adults are the ones who choose and direct the activities and where children are not seen as the best sources of their own learning activities.

d. Ignores child behavior.

Children need sensitive attention to build their behavior into social and communicative skills. Adults can effectively control or limit child development by ignoring those emerging social, motor, and communicative behaviors that are the building blocks for language and conversation. Ignoring a child's early sounds, movements, and words may be, in effect, teaching the child not to practice them, or at least not to use them with people. Unless adults attend to a child's behaviors as if they were important and communicative, the child may not learn to use them to build relationships.

e. Disregards child's motivation.

Similar to ignoring a child, when adults disregard the child's interests, children often lose interest in social contact. Parents and teachers often tell us that they did not realize that a child may know what he can best learn. He knows himself, his abilities, his readiness, and his motivation—often better than anyone else does. When we follow a child's motivation occasionally, he usually participates more actively, as well as allow us to lead him into our interests. The value of the child's motivation as the most useful leader to his learning is a value that has benefited us greatly in our work with children.

f. Lack of sensitive responding.

Sensitive responding means reacting immediately to the child's current state, that is, a child needs others to attend to him in ways that tell him they understand and appreciate what he can do and his concerns. Often we see adults respond to the superficial aspects of the child's behavior (the way a word is said or a task is done) and ignore the intentions and genuine attempts the child is showing. The more a child realizes that his feelings and efforts are being supported, the more likely he will become social and learn from people.

g. Control of topic choice and direction.

Many adults we know report they believe that they know better than the child does, what the child needs to learn in order to be communicative. Of course, they are older and much more experienced. Consequently, they often initiate the topic of play and conversation or control its direction soon after the child chooses a topic. Unfortunately, we then regularly see the child lose interest and leave the interaction. Parents and teachers we know have later learned two critical truths about learning to communicate. First, a child is more likely to stay with you if you allow him to control the choice of topic or activity at least some of the time. And, second, regardless of the topic or activity a child chooses, there are ample opportunities to show a child how to be social and communicative about it. Remember, at this stage the goal is to keep the child interacting. Without this habit of interacting, any chance for developing genuinely social use of communication is very small. As your child develops through later stages, when you and your child seem stagnated, going nowhere in an interaction, it can be useful to stop and let him have control over the topic or activity. Allowing a child to take the lead often maintains his interest and the participation he needs for learning.

Subproblem

h. Overuse of questions and commands.

There is increasing evidence that questions and commands, in excess, result in passive, noninteractive contacts in which the child shows much less than he knows. A high proportion of parents and professionals with whom we have worked state clearly that they believe questions and commands are the most effective way to get a child's response. What they come to realize is that questions and commands, while occasionally getting a response, do not achieve a number of goals that adult communication must meet to help a child to communicate. First, they often end the contact, allowing no more learning. Second, they generally direct the child to act from the adult's framework, thus not allowing the child to pursue his own ideas and directions. Third, the child's need to become an active, assertive partner may be discouraged and he may become passive and unassertive, a role that will serve him very poorly in his task of learning to communicate spontaneously. Passive children, by definition, do little that is social. Consequently, a passive child is unlikely to have the number of self-motivated social contacts that are needed for successful communication development.

Subproblem

i. Behavior more like that of a teacher than a partner.

Often adults report that they need to act like a traditional teacher, controlling and directing, in order for their child to learn. Once they discover, through experience, that children are more social and communicative in balanced partnerships than in dominant teacher-student roles, they learn to share the learning task with the child, occasionally following his lead, responding sensitively to him, but also assertively keeping him interacting for increasingly longer times. The traditional directive teacher style is certainly appropriate at times. However, if the child is not also learning to be social in his learning, much that is "taught" may be stored in memory and used little in social life.

It's Your Turn

COMMENT:

You seem to be telling me not to be a teacher. But I am a teacher; I'm hired to teach children with delays.

REPLY:

We realize how strange this approach may seem. Teaching often refers to an adult's directing and controlling a child so that he learns specific facts and skills. Unfortunately, we know many children who have been carefully taught many concepts but who have not learned to socially learn spontaneously. Until a child learns to be a social partner who stays learning with others naturally, all the school-like learning may do little for him.

We do not intend to discourage you from teaching. The point is that teaching children who are not yet conversational requires different goals and strategies from teaching a child who is already socializing what he knows. Be sure when you teach something that the learning does not just sit there unused unless you ask questions and give commands. Your children will have a great many more opportunities to learn from natural social contacts than from the few chances you have to directly teach them. Don't waste your valuable teaching time; be sure your children are socialized to learn on their own.

COMMENT: I have four children, 12, 9, 5, and 3. It wasn't until I was frustrated teaching my 5-year-old with cerebral palsy that I realized he chose to be with me more when I took the pressures off and really played together with him. Now, both the 3- and the 5-year old want to be with people more. I wish I had learned to be more interactive and less directive with the older ones; they avoid me and other adults like a dreaded job.

REPLY: It's good to hear your story. But don't give up on your older children. Call a truce on questions and commands that put them on the spot; then wait, wait, and then wait a little more!

COMMENT: I've been a teacher for 22 years and I know that children must be regulated to know their limits and how to do things right.

REPLY: We know many children whose parents and teachers have insured that the children are well regulated. Often they look like they are waiting to be told what to do, with little enthusiasm for learning on their own with people. The problem is that only a small part of a child's learning needs to be regulated by others. A child who is well regulated often is one who rarely learns spontaneously or develops relationships to share his knowledge and learn more. Be careful that your well-regulated children do not become so dependent on others for learning that they miss countless opportunities to learn from their own motivation.

COMMENT: I used to feel I needed to control the preschoolers in my daycare with questions and directions. They were obedient but took little initiative and seemed quite unfriendly. Once I began to wait, respond to their interests, and make sure they had successes with me at their level, they became alive and began to learn much more. They also finally showed me they were learning those things I taught in lessons.

REPLY: To become social and communicative, children must learn that they can be successful and have some control over their people. Nothing seems to result more in a child wanting to come back for more than having successes with others.

COMMENT: After years of barraging children with questions and commands, I realized that I was the one who was learning the most—learning what the child knew and could do. The child was learning to be passive and to try to second guess what I wanted rather than to respect his own learning sources. Now that I do and say things with him and not at him, I see him learning more from me.

REPLY: A very important insight. We find that children cooperate and learn much more from our modeling that lets them respond freely and take the lead than from our controlling and testing.

Self-Assessment
How Are You
Doing?

Describe how you feel about your relationship with your child. Use a 1 to 9 scale where 1 = disagree strongly; 5 = neither agree or disagree; 9 = agree strongly.

_____ 1. I generally control my child when we are together.
_____ 2. I rarely wait for my child to initiate or respond.
_____ 3. I generally determine what my child should be doing.
_____ 4. I correct my child when he makes mistakes.
_____ 5. My children need me to teach them more than to play with them.
_____ 6. Time with my child is more work than play for both of us.

Child Goal

4. STAY WITH OTHERS IN PLAY

What must your child first do to become a play partner? Anything is acceptable—anything safe and socially acceptable, that is. To start interacting, a child must be free to do whatever he can do. Beyond the restrictions of safety and social acceptability, the goal is simply that the child stay with people, actively doing something back and forth with them.

"Anything" is where to start.

At first, the actions need not be useful or even meaningful. A play partnership begins with any friendly exchange of actions or words. Any little behaviors are important—you can build almost anything into communication (Bates, 1976; Sugarman-Bell, 1978; Watzlawick, Beavin, & Jackson, 1967). When you begin with the "anything" principle, you guarantee successes for the child because you regularly accept what he does and encourage him to continue. Once he learns he can get you back with simple movements, you can show him how to change gradually to do new things, such as make sounds or meaningful movements.

Success will keep your child with you.

Many adults work hard to get a child to do a specific job—clapping or pointing to the doggie. Then, when the child does not do it just right and the adult corrects him for it, the child leaves the interaction. "Why won't he stay with me?" the adult wonders. Perhaps because there was not enough incentive for him to stay. Failure is small incentive for anyone. But your accepting him and continuing to play with him as simply as he now is able to can be a success that keeps him for more. Children are likely to stay spontaneously on adults' terms only after the adults show they will stay on the child's terms. Learning specific new things must wait until the child is staying in interactions; otherwise, new demands may drive the child away, and all chance for learning is lost.

Stay to:
initiate
respond
maintain.

In this first **ECO** program, the child will learn to stay in three primary ways: to initiate, to respond, and to maintain the other's participation. Often, children stay with others only by responding. For example, 11-year-old Alison, diagnosed with learning disabilities, responded whenever anyone spoke to her, but her father reported that he often waited 20 minutes in a car ride for her to contact him on her own. On the other hand, Ben, a 6-year-old with Down syndrome, would initiate and respond but never did anything to keep the interaction going. It appeared that Ben thought of interacting with people as a one-shot act of "give and take and go." Staying with people was not on his play agenda, and he found more freedom to explore when he was on his own than when people put demands on him and set him up for failure. It is healthy and encouraging when a child seeks out successes. If adults want the child to stay in interactions, they must be sure he succeeds with them.

As you engage in joint activity routines with your child, you will move closer to using functional and meaningful actions that are appropriate to the events. However, while functional behavior is desirable, it is secondary to the need of the child to avoid regular failure in first learning to be social.

Another goal for the child is to learn to actively keep others interacting with him. Moving toward this goal is a sign that the child is becoming motivated to stay with people and get something from them. Such progress may also let others know he actually wants the interaction; thus, they feel more competent in keeping him as they stay and build a partnership with him.

A final goal for the child in playing together this way is simply to increase his or her range of actions, no matter what the actions are. Children with delays too often do the same things over and over. But new and different actions lead to more new and different thoughts to communicate. This is why it is so important that the child explore as many new actions as possible, actions that you then can show him how to make more meaningful. Eventually, the goal is for your child to begin acting more and more like you. For now, though, the goal is just for your child to do many things with you.

Accomplishing these major goals will be easier if you take small, concrete steps at the start. Let's look at a few that have been effective for us.

Subgoal

a. Play in the same activity as the adult.
Your child will learn from you to the extent that the two of you share the same experiences. Playing in the same activities you engage in does not mean acting like an adult. It means that once you get into his world, he will stay with you and begin trying to do the things you do. Staying in the same activity is like staying together on a conversation topic; unless your child stays on the same ideas and activities, he is unlikely to continue learning from you. For example, rather than playing on the kitchen floor with her truck, Peggy could climb up and join her sister Megan in washing dishes.

Subgoal

b. Use actions to initiate as well as to respond to others.
Often we are so pleased when a child with delays responds to us at all that we forget he must also learn to initiate. What kind of social and learning relationships will he have if he never starts a contact or shows what he's thinking? Be sure your child is not staying with you only responsively. The world will not always come to him; he cannot expect others to do all the work. Unless he asserts himself no one will know his world, which is the best place from which we can begin to teach him. Jacob's mother was tired of always going to him. One day she started playing with his toys and waited for him. Soon he came and showed her how to play with them his way.

Subgoal

c. Actively keep play interactions going.
We all want to be with people who want to be with us. Your child must learn he has the right and responsibility to keep others with him. Does your child actually do something to keep you with him? Will he pull you to stay or otherwise keep you interacting with him? Unless he learns to keep people with him, he will become almost solely dependent on others for his opportunities to learn. Leslie's grandfather enjoyed playing cards with her but he noticed that she always waited for him to tell her it was her turn. One weekend he started taking his turn and

then putting his hand down. Leslie soon got the idea and started keeping the exchange going on her own.

Subgoal

d. Use functional and meaningful actions with others.

When your child plays, he can begin with anything he can do, whether it has meaning to you or not. His first job is just to keep playing with others. Gradually your child will learn to play with things appropriately and in ways that are meaningful to the world at large. The more you play in ways your child does, the better position you are in to show him how to use things meaningfully. For example, as your child bangs his cars and cups, you can bang his cars and cups. Then, as he responds, you can show him how a car runs and how a cup can feed him.

Subgoal

e. Play with others rather than alone.

Be careful that your child is genuinely with you and not just beside you. He should be initiating and responding to you and making you feel that he is having effects on you as well as you on him. Remember, we have almost never seen a child who did not want to be and play with others. If a child seems not to want to play, we look first to change what we are doing before we say he "can't" or "won't." Perhaps our idea of play is not his. But generally, he will have one. Like all of us, a delayed child can comprehend that people don't want to be with him. It is absolutely essential that delayed children do not come to believe this about themselves.

It's Your Turn

COMMENT: My son Kyle and I play in the same activities all the time. He plays with his toys and I talk to him about what he's doing. My mother thinks I'm a good playmate. Is that what you mean by being a play partner?

REPLY: No, we mean actually performing similar actions on the same things. That way you get into his world and learn to act like him, so he can learn from you. For example, you can play together by putting people in a play house or by petting your cat, or by drawing a picture together. Perhaps your mother is responding to your warmth and friendliness; that's good, but you need to transfer those qualities to together play.

COMMENT: I am a speech therapist and it is very hard for me not to get my clients to do things the right way. If I clap and they wave, it seems wrong for me not to correct them. Convince me that what's wrong for me is right for them.

REPLY: You've hit on an extremely important point for parents and professionals alike. It is very easy to think that what is right for us is right for our children too. Think of a child's development as an endless staircase, one that the child must approach step by step. Then it may be easier to see that it is not a simple matter of doing what we do, but rather a matter of coming toward what we do one step at a time. If your client were on a bottom step of a real staircase, you would not stand at the top and expect him to take all the stairs at once. You would go to the step he was on and lead him up, one step at a time. Show him he can take the first step by acknowledging things he can already do.

Remember two points we talked about here. First, a child must do things in the small developmental steps he can handle. Any bigger leaps may discourage him. Second, he must stay with you if he is to learn from you. In your clapping example, at least the child moved when you did. If you waved back, then clapped without judging his waving, he might have stayed to clap with you. If we look at a child's next steps, they are the right way for him even though they would be wrong for you as an adult. But it is not wrong for you if you are doing it with him.

COMMENT:

As a teacher I know I am more effective during the times we are partners. But how do I know if a child is "with" me in this partnership you speak of?

REPLY:

Good question. By "with" we do not mean in the same room or even at the same activity. We mean genuinely participating with you, not just by your side. Is the child showing he knows what you're doing? Do you feel he is actually being affected by you? Or do you think he couldn't care less that you are there? If he is not with you regularly, in the sense of your feeling he is an interactive part of your class, then he has to build a clear social connection before he can learn from people in ordinary daily contacts.

Self-Assessment
How Are You
Doing?

How much of a play partner is your child? Mark 1 = strongly disagree; 5 = neither agree nor disagree; 9 = strongly agree.

____ 1. He plays in the same activities as I do.
____ 2. He initiates contacts with people.
____ 3. He responds to contacts by others.
____ 4. He actively keeps interactions going.
____ 5. He uses functional and meaningful actions with others.
____ 6. He plays more with people than by himself.
____ 7. He gives you the feeling he is really with you.

Child Goal

5. IMITATE OTHERS

A child's task in learning to be social and communicative is the task of learning to act and communicate in the ways others do. Certainly his task is not to become exactly like others but rather to learn the general rules of how to act in ways that others will relate to and learn to communicate in ways that effectively exchange messages and build relationships. To do this your child needs to pay increasing attention to what you and others do and to attempt to do them as you do. His early attempts may not seem much like your actions and communications. The goal here is for your child's behavior to come closer to yours over time.

Do as others do.

A general rule or goal for your child here is to learn and, less frequently, to "do as others do." Imitating is another term for "doing as others do." Once a child begins to imitate he can use others as natural learning lessons in the daily course of events. That is, your child can learn by imitating you even when you are not intending to teach him something. The child who holds a toy phone to his ear when no one has ever "taught" him directly is an example of a child imitating spontaneously.

One strong social advantage to imitating is the effect it can have on others. The traditional wisdom that "imitation is the sincerest form of flattery" applies to many adults who have long waited for their children to act like them. Imitating is a dependable tool for establishing social links between people. Imitating involves doing something the other person is both able to do and interested in doing. Thus when a child imitates he is likely to maintain the social contacts he needs for learning to communicate.

All this is not to say that imitation is a language goal for a child. We do not want a child to become a responsive mirror image of those around him. We want him to create his own ideas and to communicate them. Imitation, however, is very useful for building new behaviors and for getting the child ready for future symbolic behavior. Just as the child's imitation can symbolize, or stand for, the other person's behavior, it can teach him that words also can stand for things.

Subgoal

a. Attempting to act like others.

Early signs of imitation will come when a child changes his behavior in response to your behavior. Those changes may be very different at first but they may become gradually closer to the way you did things.

You will discover that the more you match your child by doing something he can do, the more the child will try to imitate you. And, generally, the more childlike you are and the more you wait for the child to do something, the more his behavior will become like yours.

Subgoal

b. Imitate when directed.

When a child is beginning to socialize or when he is learning a new task, it will benefit him to follow directions to imitate. However, care should be taken so the child does not depend on your directions to imitate others.

Subgoal

c. Imitate immediately and spontaneously.

When a child is attending to what you do, he has more of your cues to use in trying to act like you. Another advantage of immediate imitating is that you are then able to show him what you did again, thus offering him feedback and another model for him to try at just the time he is attending.

Subgoal

d. Imitate after the fact.

In this kind of imitation, often called deferred imitation, the child acts like you did but some time after you did it. An example is the child who takes the vacuum from the closet and pretends to vacuum, even changing the attachments when moving from rug to wood floor. He might imitate the machine by making a humming sound. Here the child is imitating by following his memory of your vacuuming. Similarly, a child needs to learn to "do as others do" often long after he sees or hears it happen.

It's Your Turn

COMMENT: I try to get Phyllis to imitate but she keeps turning away.

REPLY: When children do not imitate us, we check ourselves on a few things. First is matching. Make sure you are doing something she can do and is interested in. The second important thing is waiting. Make sure you give Phyllis enough time and that you show that you expect her to respond. She may still think you will do it for her. Third is imitate and wait. We find imitating the child is a dependable way to get her attention.

COMMENT: Wait? When Julius and I play, about all he does is imitate. He rarely does anything on his own. How do I get him to do something else?

REPLY:

Wait. You may be encouraging him to imitate when you immediately respond to him. He may be in a habit of imitating, knows that it works and that he doesn't need to do the extra work of initiating on his own.

When your child imitates, wait for something different, any changes at first. This will teach him he will get more of your attention if he does something of his own. Julius knows much more than he is doing. Waiting when he imitates will do a few things: give him the time to do more; let him know that new things will get more from you; show you that he can do more than you expected; and make him feel more competent and motivated to be social.

Self-Assessment:
How Are You
Doing?

How much does your child imitate you? Mark 1 = strongly disagree; 5 = neither agree nor disagree; 9 = strongly agree.

_____ 1. My child generally tries to act like me and others..
_____ 2. He imitates when I ask him to.
_____ 3. He imitates on his own.
_____ 4. He imitates actions.
_____ 5. He imitates communications.
_____ 6. He imitates things he saw at another time.

ADULT STRATEGIES

What you can do.

What can you do to become a play partner with your child? The overriding goal is for you to become the kind of person that your child will stay with and learn from. To build a social habit with your child, we encourage you to learn four general strategies that will help your child learn from you in your daily contacts. These strategies require no special education, because parents do them naturally with young children. Try to understand why each strategy is important so you gradually begin to make them a more natural part of the way you are with children. You can learn these strategies as you play and live with your child.

6. PLAY IN CHILDLIKE WAYS

Adult Strategy

Act and
communicate like
your child.

In childlike play, both you and your child play in ways he can do. The major job here is yours. You need to observe your child closely, then act in many ways as he does. It may seem strange to both of you at first, but soon you should be getting him to stay more and he should be showing that he enjoys you. Many parents and teachers report that learning to play like their children seems wrong at first. But then they report that child play is the best way to really connect with the child and know what he knows. Only when we know something about what the child is thinking and what motivates him will we know how to move him from his world to ours.

To adults, play means different things. We recommend a very open kind of play to help a child communicate. It can include any activity with people, either with or without objects or toys. This kind of play has no rules or jobs to get done. For many children, it's a major accomplishment just to focus on being in one place and attending to one person. Consequently, let's make this very important task as easy and successful as we can.

Later on, when your child is regularly playing and communicating with people, playing games with rules or for specific learning will be appropriate. For now, though, remember that the only job is to get your child in a social habit. That is why we strongly discourage any focus on jobs or goals that could create failures and discourage the child from staying with you. Your measure of success will be how frequently, how long, and how many different activities you keep him in, really playing together with you.

Substrategy

a. Play in the same activity as the child.

The more you and your child are attending to and doing the same thing, the more you will have shared experiences. Then those shared experiences will help both of you to "read" each other and do things that fit the other's interests and abilities. Consider any activity, like a game, book, or car ride, as if it were a topic of a conversation. The more each of you are actively into the activity, the more easily you will build.

Substrategy

b. Play as the child does.

Consider anything safe that the child does as play, and then be as much like him as you can. It may seem embarrassing at first, so try it alone with the child for a while. You can show him new things, of course, but be sure you do them in ways he can do now. Think of a play activity as your child's first conversations, only without words. Just as you want your adult partners to stay in the same conversation with you, you will need to stay in some of your child's activities with him so the two of you eventually have something to communicate about.

Substrategy

c. Play as much or more than talk.

Adults are often more in the habit of talking than playing. At first your child will learn more from your childlike play than your talk. This strategy seems very difficult for most adults, who think their job is to "tell children what to do." We thought so too but now we have learned that we get much more from children if we play more and talk less. Playing with your child will show you what makes most sense to talk about with him. When adults talk they often do so from their distant world of thoughts. When you play closely with your child, your talk is more likely to be understood and motivating to him if it focuses on his world, and that means he will be likely to learn from you.

Substrategy

d. Be more interesting than the child's distractions.

Most children are going to seek stimulation, and understandably so. They often prefer stimulation that allows them to interact and get results, instead of stimulation they cannot control. Novel and interesting changes also engage them. Ask yourself: Are people or things more stimulating to my child? A child's lack of attention to an adult may well relate to how interesting he finds that adult. Since you want your child to communicate, a major task is to learn to become more interesting, at times, than the physical world. Just as your child must stay and

Complete with your child's fun.

play with things to learn about them, he must also stay with people. We recommend that adults be animated and let the child have effects on them as he does on toys. The more you are a flexible toy to your child, the more he is likely to learn to act and communicate like you. Compete with the objects in his world; do not let wood and metal and cloth win over you. He needs you more than he needs them; they will not help him build communicative relationships.

Other Guidelines for Keeping Childlike Play Going

1. Start with anything safe and socially acceptable that your child does.
2. Watch what he's doing first.
3. Then quietly join in his activity.
4. Keep your talking down and your actions and sounds up; in fact, being silent may sometimes help you both focus on the play.
5. Try to be like your child. Move when he moves; sound when he sounds.
6. When in doubt as to what to do, imitate your child. You will get his attention and may start an interaction going.
7. When acting like your child, change what you are doing slightly, then see what he does.
8. Give him time to do things on his own.
9. Be sure you and he are in the same activity.
10. Try to do only about as much as your child does; remember to balance your actions and his.
11. Make yourself more interesting than the things that distract your child. This means being inventive—even being silly is effective.

The bottom line is: *Keep him there a little longer than he usually stays.* In new activities, keep him only briefly to give him a successful introduction to them. We often hear, "But what if he doesn't want to stay?" Our answer is a question: What do you do when he objects to going to school, or to supper, or to bed or to taking medicine? You see to it that he does it, don't you? Once you come to believe that playing with you is as important or more important to your child than school, supper, bed, or medicine, you will find yourself able to physically keep your child with you and use your personality to make him enjoy the time with you.

Keep him a little longer.

Other Considerations

As adults we are generally conditioned to believe that to do something we must do it "right." Then we have children who often do not do things "right," according to our adult expectations. Now we are recommending that you play in any way you can, with no attention to right and wrong. That's confusing, isn't it? Consider this: If your child is not staying in meaningful play with people now, it actually doesn't matter what he does as long as he stays with people. If you have a problem with this idea, it may be because you are not sure that your child can learn best from the people closest to him.

Every time you or your child contact each other, you can show him a little piece of being a communicating person. With some children, we are not sure how much they will eventually communicate as we do. But at least these children can often develop playful relations with people to give them a more enjoyable life.

Children learn on the run.

Think of all the things you want your child to learn. Make a list. If you consider that list carefully, most of those things are ones that are learned from regular interactions that take place at home if the adults are willing to play in the child's world. We realize that the world may make you expect that only trained teachers can do that. A major part of this program is to show you the easy and valuable ways your child can learn from you and anyone else close to him.

COMMENT:

This all sounds good, but I am just not a childlike person. It's not natural and I don't enjoy playing like a child. [We hear this comment from teachers, therapists, parents, and many other caregivers.]

REPLY:

You are certainly not alone. Many adults feel the same way. So the dilemma is this: You don't like to be childlike but your child will learn more from you if you keep childlike exchanges going with him. Perhaps your ideas of being playful and childlike are too limited. Anything can be playful. It's normal to find many child games boring, so make whatever you do like doing playful and involve your child in it. Change what you do with games and objects. The point here is not to do anything in particular but to keep your child with you so that he learns to enjoy staying and learning with people.

Here's another thought for parents and professionals who don't like being childlike. It will take much more work for you to influence your child if you aren't someone he enjoys and wants to be with. And the older he gets, the harder it will get. Bite the bullet, as they say, and gradually become more childlike. You may learn to enjoy it when you see how it affects your child. And, like it or not, you'll find it makes things easier for you now and will prevent years of difficult times with your child.

COMMENT:

I am a nurse working with acutely and terminally ill children. Can I become a play partner with all my other duties?

REPLY:

Maintaining positive relations with hospital staff and family members during medical crises is thought by many to be very supportive of physical improvement.

Describe yourself on a 1 to 9 scale (1 = never; 9 = frequently).

_____ 1. I play like my child does.
_____ 2. I join in the things he does.
_____ 3. I play as much as or more than I talk with my child.
_____ 4. I make myself more interesting than my child's distractions.
_____ 5. I feel confident I can keep him playing with me.
_____ 6. I have to physically keep him with me.
_____ 7. I give him time to respond and to do things on his own.
_____ 8. I imitate things he does.
_____ 9. I notice him doing things I do.
_____10. I enjoy playing with him.

7. COMMUNICATE IN WAYS CLOSE TO THE CHILD'S (MATCHING)

Communications come from a child's actions and sounds. A child does not just talk all of a sudden. Before he talks, he will interact with others by using any movements or sounds imaginable (Bullowa, 1979; Siegel-Causey, Ernst, & Guess, 1988). And adults may best help the child communicate not by talking a lot but by making the kinds of movements and sounds the child makes. If you ask "How should I communicate with my child?" we would answer "By doing things you think he can do."

Remember, in this first program, we do not want you to try for communication but only to build a strong play partnership with real staying power. Your child will learn to understand you long before he learns to communicate as you do. Therefore, it is important that you communicate in ways he can understand and then remember. It appears that children understand and remember communications that include some of the ways they communicate and that may also show them a little step higher. For example, when a child falls down, a parent can move with the child and say "boom" or "oh-oh" or something similar that shows him another way to make his action more communicative.

For a child, learning to communicate means learning to become more and more like the people around him. Children develop in small steps, from random to meaningful movements, then to intentional communications, and on to words and conversations. The more you are in tune with what your child can do and the more you act in ways he can act successfully, the more your child will be able to do what you do, becoming more like you and others.

For children who communicate little, the long stretches of talking that adults frequently direct at them may be completely meaningless. To a child beginning to communicate, a long string of words may be like the sound of a jet overhead on a clear day—just noise. When we can't understand something, we are not likely to stay in contacts that barrage us with it. Once we see the little steps to communication, we begin to realize that doing less with our children is better than doing more. Indeed, our years of personal experience with parents and professionals leave us with a basic operating rule: "Do less so the child does more."

Substrategy
a. Communicate in ways the child can soon do.
You can probably teach your child one of two lessons: to stay and learn from you or to go off on his own. The first you accomplish by doing things that show him a next step, the second by acting in ways he cannot succeed at. Try to train yourself to predict what your child can do next in activities; then do those things and see if he tries them. After a while, you will learn to fine-tune yourself as you play so that you regularly show your child a next step you think he can do.

Substrategy
b. Respond sensitively to the child's actions and sounds.
Be sure your child's casual actions and sounds get your friendly attention because they are his first ways to communicate. Your child needs to learn that actions and sounds can have effects on people. Anything is helpful at first. Your child is likely to stay attending to you more if he sees he has some control over you.

Many children act as though they expect no personal rewards for their behavior. And many adults tell us they think they should wait for words before responding much. Warm attention to your child's subtle behaviors is like fertilizer to flowers. We often encourage adults to "fertilize the flowers and not the weeds." In terms of play, this suggestion means that if you attend to those little behaviors that could become communicative and ignore the behaviors that are unproductive or annoying, your child may do more and more things you can shape into communication.

Substrategy
c. Use gestures, sounds, and words like the child.
If your child is not regularly talking now, make yourself comfortable communicating with sounds and movements similar to his. The closer you are to your child, the more he is likely to link up with you and try to communicate as you do. It takes

practice. But once adults see their child staying more with them and acting more like them, they forget how silly they once felt and gradually become secure that in acting that way they are helping their child progress.

Substrategy

d. Occasionally show the child the next step in talking.

Look at one of your critical jobs as showing your child a next step he can do. This goes for talking as well as playing. Once in a while, talk just a little more than your child so he can try your model. We do mean once in a while, not all the time. Just try it frequently enough so the child can get in the habit of trying to talk as you do.

Substrategy

e. Keep communication going back and forth.

Every time you communicate you give your child an opportunity to learn. The more you match your child and wait, the more he is likely to practice communicating as he can. Accept any attempts at first; now is the time to get anything going back and forth, not to expect anything perfect. Your child must have the spontaneous habit of interaction before he will have any place to learn to communicate. The more your child interacts, the more likely it is that he will communicate.

Substrategy

f. Show you expect the child to communicate.

Come to realize that any behavior can communicate or send some information. Then begin to look for the interesting and subtle ways your child could be communicating. Give him time and show him with a look of anticipation that you expect something and will accept what he can do without judging or correcting him. In time, just giving him that face will trigger him to try to communicate. Soon it comes easy because you get so much back for doing so little.

Substrategy

g. Imitate the child's actions and sounds.

Your child knows best the things he does, and he is interested in them enough to do them. So when you imitate him you are doing both what he can do and what he wants to do. You are speaking to both his capabilities and his motivations at the same time. Consequently, imitation is not only likely to get and keep his attention but also to make him feel good because you showed that you accepted what he was doing.

It's Your Turn

COMMENT:

You tell me to do things my son Jackson can do but I want him to do things that I do. Am I wrong?

REPLY:

No. Of course you want him to do things you do. So do we. But Jackson will first learn to do your things only in those little steps he can do. Think of a staircase with you at the top and your child at the bottom. You want him to get to the top so first you go to his level and show him how to take the little steps he needs to get to where you are. If you think of the staircase with your own behavior at the top, you may be more motivated to match what he does because you know he can then be on his way to being like you. Waiting at the top of the stairs or at your adult way of acting may only frustrate and lose him.

COMMENT:

In my classroom my assistant teacher and I teach children to imitate many things. Is matching the same as imitating?

REPLY: Yes and no. Imitating is only one way to match a child. And it is a very valuable way to interact because it shows a child the important rule to "do as others do." But we don't want him to be just a parrot. We need to show him new things to do, but they must be at the level of activity or communication he can do. Think of matching as being the kind of person your child can be. Matching is more a way to be with your child than a technique for doing particular things. A teacher in a class for infants at risk recently noted that the more she acts like her children, the more they interact and communicate. "When I act like my adult self, the babies are often quiet and not attentive, but when I act like them they jabber and play and even actively keep me with them."

COMMENT: I am a classroom language consultant. I think I am matching the children. The teachers enjoy it. But how do we know if my matching is working?

REPLY: It may take a while to see effects if the children are not in the habit of seeing and hearing things they can do. Waiting is one very important strategy; it gives them the chance to respond. We have found that matching and waiting with expectation is a very effective combination for getting a child to respond. The waiting should be silent, and you will need patience to give the children plenty of time to do something. Neither you adults nor the children are used to having you wait. At first, you will be impatient with the silence, and some children may wait for you to do all the work as you have done so often before. But keep telling yourself, "They need time and space to respond, and we cannot keep doing things for them."

Matching and waiting will be important strategies all the way from learning to play to learning to communicate and have conversations. Even in our own best adult conversations, we match and wait. Try to make this pair of strategies a habit and you may find your children interacting with you more and becoming more like you. Eventually the teachers you consult with will find that they are getting more teaching done with matching. Then your consulting will be a success.

COMMENT: When you first showed me how to match the children in my class, I felt it silly and not what a teacher should do. With practice, I found that matching made me a much more effective teacher. When I matched the children, they paid more attention, responded more, and tried to act more like me. Another advantage of matching is that it applies to all my children. I just remember "Do something he can do."

REPLY: We have realized that matching is a natural help in all relationships. Adults as well as children stay and enjoy relations more when partners do what they can do and care about.

Self-Assessment:
How Are You
Doing?

Describe yourself on a 1 to 9 scale. (1 = never; 5 = occasionally; 9 = frequently)

____ 1. I use movements and gestures like my child's.
____ 2. I use sounds like my child's.
____ 3. I use words like my child's.
____ 4. I show him a next step in talking.
____ 5. I respond to him with things he can do.
____ 6. I match him in my casual contacts.
____ 7. I communicate to my child's interests.
____ 8. I find that matching gets more from my child.
____ 9. I feel comfortable matching my child.

8. COMMUNICATE ABOUT IMMEDIATE EXPERIENCE

Certainly one of the major concerns adults have regarding children with delays is the way they communicate. Parents and professionals need to realize that what they talk about may actually help or hinder a child learning to communicate. Adults often say, "I don't know what to say to children." Then we find that the more shared experiences they have with children, the more natural their language is to the situation. In the beginning, children definitely need certain kinds of language from us rather than other kinds. If we remember that actions become thoughts and thoughts become words, our job as adults may be clearer. The closer you are to your child's action world, the more obvious will be the words he needs to learn.

Talk about visible people, actions, objects, and locations. At first, a child needs you to use words that describe his experiences as he is engaged in them. You may do your child a real disservice by forcing on him school language like the alphabet and adult words like mistake, instead of using words such as fall and hug, which encode his sensorimotor experiences, or words such as want and go, which encode his nonverbal communications. Children need us to allow them to have their own language because it fits their own logic and motivations well. Children can best be children by serving out their childhood fully (Erickson, 1963), not rushing into an adult world (Elkind, 1987).

You can help your child get the most out of his experiences by showing him how to communicate about his world, not the world of school and adulthood that he may never master if he does not learn to master his current world first.

a. Talk about visible people, actions, objects, locations, and feelings.

Your child will learn language and communication about things that have personal meaning for him. Often a child's actions are his first meaning. Consequently, try to create a tight link between your child's thoughts and actions; show him there is a simple way to communicate about the people, actions, objects, locations, and feelings that impinge on him and that he voluntarily takes control of. You can help him see the close relationship between his actions, thoughts, and words. They are all aspects of the same experience. By talking his action world, you can show him that words are becoming a natural part of those experiences.

b. Put words on the child's actions.

Act like a walking dictionary. Let your child know there is a word that goes with his most interesting actions. Do not make him say it; just let him take in the word at the precise moment he's attending to the action. This strategy seems to help children recall and use words more easily than giving them words describing adult interests.

c. Avoid academic and adult words.

We too want your child to succeed eventually in school and the adult world. But before school words will be useful, your child must be a frequent communicator. Academic words such as colors and numbers do not describe his most common experiences and are rarely useful in communicating for relationships. Adult words are likely to confuse your child and discourage him from communicating. If your language does not mirror your child's experiences and nonverbal communications, it may have little meaning for him. You may discover you are talking to yourself and having no learning effect on your child.

Substrategy

d. Keep your child on his or her topic.

By a topic, we mean any theme or string of related ideas, such as a visit from Grandma or putting toys away. Many children bounce from one action or idea to the next. To learn language a child must see how ideas go together to build a new idea. To do this he must stay in an activity and link actions together into new events. For example, if you and your child are playing house, keep him in a series of actions such as going to dinner, eating, and cleaning up. A child can learn to stay playfully on a topic long before he talks. Then when he talks, he is ready to use language for conversation and many other forms of communication.

Substrategy

e. Train as a second language.

Consider your child's gestures, sounds, and unclear words as his own language, foreign to many people. Then translate them into your language. When he points to a light and says "uh uh," say "light." Show him your words for his own communications. If we think of adults and children as communicating in different languages, we can understand the need to translate his attempts into our words, just as we would with a new foreign-language-speaking friend.

It's Your Turn

COMMENT:

But I want to get my child ready for school. I want him to learn numbers, the alphabet, and the words they expect in school. I want him to fit in.

REPLY:

You raise an issue that is very common and very important to parents and preschool children as well. It is understandable to want such things. However, we know many children who know their alphabet, numbers, and colors but do not use their language to build relationships. They have "good boy answer" language but very little "people language." Remember, the purpose of language is not to have it like storage in a computer but to use it as a tool to learn and socialize. Much of the language used today in school is more for book work than people work. Unless your child has language for his own personal, social, and functional uses, it may not matter how much school language he has. Your main question should not be "Does he have the words he needs for school?" but "Is he communicating about his experiences?" If the answer to the second question is yes, then when numbers, letters, and other such concepts become part of his natural experiences he will naturally communicate about them too.

COMMENT:

David has hundreds of words and he initiates as well as responds with them. The problem is that I can keep him on an idea only very briefly. He talks—then he's gone. Is this a problem? One of the people who worked with him told us he has an attention disorder.

REPLY:

Yes. Not staying on a topic is one of the major problems we see in children learning to talk and also in older children with learning problems. Often adults are so relieved to hear any speech at all that they let the child get into a hit-and-run habit of using language. Then the child has few opportunities to learn more language. Help him by saying just a little more about what he has said, then wait and keep him there to say a little more. Make it a game, not a job. You may need to gently hold him there very briefly to show him that staying and talking can be enjoyable.

Another reason to keep him on a topic is to spur his cognitive development, helping him to learn how much more there is to know about things than their names. Many children we know can name everything in sight but can really talk about very little. Note, too, that your style of talking may influence whether David stays on a topic. If you are primarily directive, with questions and commands, he may not want to stay, especially if you're always the one to choose the topic. On the other hand, if you talk with a nonjudgmental style that allows David to participate, he is more likely to stay on topic and, more important still, learn more language. Be sure not to think that it is inevitable that David flits in and out just because he has been labeled as having an attention disorder. You can help. You can have control over his attention if your talk is child-based, matched, and social rather than adult, distant, and directive. If he attends elsewhere, take it as a message that you should become more interesting to him than his distractions.

Describe yourself and how you talk to your child on a 1 to 9 scale (1 = never; 5 = occasionally; 9 = frequently).

_____ 1. I translate his sounds and gestures into words.
_____ 2. My words to him are ones he has a lot of use for.
_____ 3. I talk about the people and things he knows.
_____ 4. I talk about the actions he does and sees.
_____ 5. I talk about his feelings.
_____ 6. I talk about my feelings and experiences.
_____ 7. I avoid words he has little communicative use for.
_____ 8. I keep him on a topic.
_____ 9. I get him onto new topics.

9. COMMENT MORE THAN QUESTION OR COMMAND

The primary goal of this first program is to help your child stay in playful contacts where he learns to actively be with people primarily for social enjoyment. Because the important job here is not to learn anything specific to test your child's knowledge but simply to want to be with people, you need to be very careful about the reasons you communicate with him.

Many adults we have known seem to be in the habit of asking questions and giving commands to delayed children. Even when these questions and commands get little cooperation, they seem determined to continue. Questions and commands seem to put the child on the spot, test him, and often deal him failures rather than the successes that will motivate him to stay with people. These controlling ways of talking, while certainly appropriate at times, also have the disadvantage of getting away from the child's frame of reference and thereby increasing the chance of losing his interest, participation, and learning.

a. Use open-ended statements and replies.

To us, an open-ended statement is a comment on what is happening with no requirement that the child do something. For example, to a child who fell down, say "You fell down" rather than "What happened?" The comment "You fell down" leaves him open to say whatever he feels and may let you get into his thinking. Comments like this also show the child what he could say the next time he falls down.

Often children feel under the gun to answer a question or comply with a command. This feeling distracts them from getting into an activity completely. Remember, talk is not the goal now—there's plenty of time for that later on. For now, use your talk to show your child what both of you are doing and feeling. Remember to keep matching your child's talk at his level and just a step ahead.

Substrategy

b. Give the child freedom to say anything.

By commenting without demands, you will tell the child that all you want him to do is participate, not to say or do anything in particular. When you comment on his action you may be coming close to his thinking; eventually he may try to communicate in the same way. Your child will feel free to communicate about anything if you make sure you do not correct him or respond by making work for him, as you do, for example, when you ask him to repeat or clarify.

Substrategy

c. Allow the child successes.

We hope you will come to appreciate that a success for your child at this time is simply staying with you in play. Your friendly response is his reward. He will not need you to say things like "good boy" or "good talking." In fact responses like this easily become rote and artificial and often put a stop to any interaction you have going. Your job is to keep the interaction going.

Your child will know he is succeeding if you simply accept what he does and show him respect by doing something like it. Success for your child has probably been doing what he can do independently, but now he needs successes with people. To grow, a child need not learn to do anything new with people until he can do in people play what he already knows as he plays alone. And why do we care if your child has successes with people? Because successes with people help him feel safe and good and, most important, competent. Unfortunately, for many delayed children, chances to feel competent are few and far between. A child who feels competent will try more so that successes increase the likelihood that a delayed child will stay with people and make a habit of it. On the other hand, failures, as when a child cannot answer your question or comply with your command, may discourage him from staying or starting up with new people. The point here is that you have your child's successes in your control. There is no avoiding it—you either give him successes or you don't. If you simply respond sensitively to his little actions and any new surprising things, you will soon learn what he needs to do next and how you can encourage him to do it. Just remember: When a child is learning to be social, a success is any behavior he does with people and any new behaviors.

Substrategy

d. Avoid corrections or discouraging feedback.

Tied closely to helping a child have successes, this recommendation is simply a warning that, for a child with a long history of failures, corrections or any feedback suggesting what he did was wrong may drive him away from the necessary person-to-person contacts he needs. Of course, you certainly do not intend to drive him away from people when you get him to do it "right" or when you otherwise let him know that what he did was not enough. Nevertheless, be aware that you may be doing just that very effectively in spite of your motives. Until your child has developed a strong habit of social play, it is successes, not failures, that will get him into that habit.

Substrategy

e. Avoid testing or focus on right and wrong.

When getting your child into a habit of people play, forget about right and wrong (except for unsafe or socially abusive actions). Rather than saying "Is he right or wrong?" get into the habit of saying "Is he doing it with people?" Think of your exciting job now as helping your child begin to do with people all the things he can already do by himself. This change alone would be a major developmental step toward communicating. Once he is a social person, you will have many opportunities to show him the right steps to new things. What is more, only if he becomes a social person will you have those opportunities.

It's Your Turn

COMMENT:

How can I teach my child to communicate without using a lot of questions and directions? Aren't those the ways all of us were taught?

REPLY:

Excellent question. This is a belief of most parents and professionals we know. But there are a few problems here. First, many assume that a child learns to communicate in the same ways that we learned math and reading in school. Not so. We did not first learn to communicate in school or by being taught in traditional academic ways.

We first learned to communicate in relatively stress-free interactions with people we liked and experiences we enjoyed. When we started school we already had the communication skills to help us use what the teachers taught us didactically. This is a critical point. Before school will work well, your child must be an interactive and communicative person. Your child, who is just learning to communicate and be conversational, needs an entirely different kind of teaching. In fact, he may very well learn to communicate more as you teach him less—teach, that is, in the old-fashioned, question-and-answer, do-as-I-do habit.

To begin to understand this, try a little experiment. Play or have a conversation with your child. Then switch between periods of a teaching style with questions and commands and periods of a social style of open-ended comments with no questions or judgments. Keep repeating this sequence and watch what happens. It has been our experience that children interact and communicate less when we use the teaching style and more when we use the social style. Be aware that you may feel anxious when you first cut out your teaching attempts, especially if you believe the only way to teach is to direct. But be patient and let your child's increased cooperation reward and encourage you to become more a play partner and less a teacher with him.

COMMENT:

We run a day care center for infants and toddlers and we believe our center should help the children socialize and not be a skill-training school. We screen our staff in terms of how playful and nondemanding they are. We find that some applicants simply want to be bosses more than partners.

REPLY:

Good for you. We find that teachers and children need many options. We're pleased you are providing a social option.

Self-Assessment: How Are You Doing?

Describe your style of communication with your child on a 1 to 9 scale (1 = never; 5 = occasionally; 9 = frequently).

_____ 1. I make open-ended statements and replies.
_____ 2. I give my child freedom to say anything reasonable.

_____ 3. I allow my child successes.

_____ 4. I limit my questions and testing to a minimum.

_____ 5. I avoid corrections or discouraging feedback.

_____ 6. My attitude toward talking is more playful than getting a job done.

_____ 7. I am more concerned with my child staying with me than being right.

CONCLUSION

In this chapter we have attempted to set the stage for you and your child to get together and stay together playfully. Everything we will cover in the remaining chapters depends on how well you stay playfully with each other. We have found that, with a great number of parents and professionals, only after they establish a play partnership with a child can the goal of building skills of interaction, communication, language, and conversation flow naturally.

Sample Resources for Becoming Play Partners

What Are the ECO Resources?
ECOScale: Becoming Play Partners
ECO Tutor: Becoming Play Partners
ECO Link: Becoming Play Partners
Conversation Routine
IEP/Problem Solver
ECO Practice Plan and Record

WHAT ARE THE ECO RESOURCES?

The *ECO Resources* are tools that introduce and expand upon the **ECO** program for professionals, parents, and other adults. At the end of this chapter and the next four chapters (each of which is devoted to one **ECO** competency), you will find a sample of each of several key *Resources*. Complete sets of the *Resources* and the **ECO** forms are available from the publisher.

ECOScales

The *ECOScale* shown at the end of each chapter presents those interactive goals, child goals, adult strategies, and problems that are involved in that **ECO** competency. It can be used to identify strengths and limitations of the adult, child, and interaction; plan the next steps for both child and adult; and follow progress in home, school, and elsewhere. The complete *ECOScales*, including a Competency Profile and an Interaction Profile, are available from the publisher.

ECO Tutors

The *ECO Tutors* are guides to each major item (interactive goal, child goal, adult strategy, problem) on the *ECOScales*. At the end of each chapter, you will find the *ECO Tutor* for the major Interactive Goal for that competency. For example, the *ECO Tutor* included in this chapter is for item 1, "Becoming Play Partners."

ECO Links

The *ECO Links* are also part of the *ECO Resources*. There is one for each competency. Use these handy lists of questions to evaluate your partnership with your child and to remind you of things to keep in mind as you work on your goals, strategies, and problems.

Use the *ECO Links* to:
1. Learn how to become a partner with your child.
2. Evaluate the partnership between you and your child.
3. Evaluate your own interaction with your child.
4. Identify problems in your partnership.
5. Learn how to communicate with your child.
6. Learn what to avoid doing and saying.

Conversation Routines

The *Conversation Routines,* also a part of the *ECO Resources,* are a sample of exchanges adults and child can have during typical activities. For many situations, there are both a preverbal and an early verbal conversation routine. Each competency chapter includes one sample conversation routine, designed to help illustrate how to develop the appropriate skills in natural living and learning environments.

Use the *Conversation Routines* to:
1. Show examples of successful and unsuccessful partnerships.
2. See how potential problems can interfere with growth.
3. See how to make everyday events into opportunities for social learning.

IEP/Problem Solvers

Problem Solvers provide a resource for use in developing Individualized Educational Plans and Individualized Family Service Plans. Each chapter includes one sample *Problem Solver.* They begin with a description of a child and a significant adult with specific goals and problems. A typical brief dialogue follows, along with a sample IEP form that could be filled out for the child. However, rather than the usual format, this form focuses on two people: child and significant adult. It allows for the specification of interactive goals, child goals, adult strategies, and problems. It also includes specific activities for practice.

Use the *Problem Solvers* when you first identify problems in the interaction (rather than child goals). They can be used the way they are written, adapted for specific adult–child pairs or situations, or used as guides to creating new partnership plans. Remember that every adult-child partnership is different, and their needs will vary. Most plans need to be revised constantly, as the pair changes together. These plans should be fine-tuned just as the adult and child fine-tune themselves to each other.

Practice Plan and Record

The *ECO Practice Plan and Record* is a two-page form with three major parts. Each chapter includes one sample, filled out for an adult and child pair.

The first part is the Practice Plan. The Practice Plan is a prescription for overall goals and strategies and component objectives, as well priority problems to work on. It also includes space to list activities to use in practicing new skills, both on a regular, planned basis and in spontaneous interactions.

The second part is the Partnership Calendar. It is used daily to rate the progress made by both the child and the adult on the activities specified in the Practice Plan.

The third part is the Partnership Diary. This is a tool used by the adult to record progress, problems, reflections, and any relevant comments.

BECOMING PLAY PARTNERS

1. Become play partners.
   a. Be actively together.
   b. Play with the same focus as the other.
   c. Do about as much as each other.
   d. Play and communicate like the other.
   e. Share directions and decisions in play.

2. Lack of playfulness
   a. Little enjoyment of or interest in each other.
   b. Minimal sensitivity to each other's emotions and motivations.
   c. Minimal affect or expressiveness.
   d. Stressful or task-oriented activities.
   e. Focus on right or wrong.
   f. Minimal spontaneity.
   g. Limited use of active playful movements.

3. Directive, controlling style
   a. Takes majority of turns.
   b. Little waiting.
   c. Controlling atmosphere.
   d. Ignores child behavior.
   e. Disregards child's motivation.
   f. Lack of sensitive responding.
   g. Control of topic choice and direction.
   h. Overuse of questions and commands.
   i. Behavior more like that of a teacher than a partner.

4. Stay with others in play.
   a. Play in the same activity as the adult.
   b. Use actions to initiate as well as to respond to others.
   c. Actively keep play interactions going.
   d. Use functional and meaningful actions with others.
   e. Play with others rather than alone.

5. Imitate others.
   a. Attempt to act like others.
   b. Imitate when directed.
   c. Imitate immediately and spontaneously.
   d. Imitate after the fact.

6. Play in childlike ways.
   a. Play in the same activity as the child.
   b. Play as the child does.
   c. Play as much or more than talk.
   d. Be more interesting than the child's distractions.

7. Communicate in ways close to the child's.
   a. Communicate in ways the child can soon do.
   b. Respond sensitively to the child's actions and sounds.
   c. Use gestures, sounds, and words like the child.
   d. Occasionally show the child the next step in talking.
   e. Keep communication going back and forth.
   f. Show you expect the child to communicate.
   g. Imitate the child's actions and sounds.

8. Communicate about immediate experience.
   a. Talk about visible people, actions, objects, locations, and feelings.
   b. Put words on the child's actions.
   c. Avoid academic and adult words.
   d. Keep the child on his or her topic.
   e. Train as a second language.
9. Comment more than question or command.
   a. Use open-ended statements and replies.
   b. Give the child freedom to say anything.
   c. Allow the child successes.
   d. Avoid corrections or discouraging feedback.
   e. Avoid testing or focus on right and wrong.

ECO Tutor

Interactive Goal: Becoming Play Partners (Nonverbal)

What Is It?	When adults and children join together in a friendly, action-oriented activity, we consider this a play partnership. The partnership should have a synergy of its own, building from the input of each person toward a mutual activity that results in more than the sum of their combined input.
What To Look For	To decide if you and your child have a play partnership, first look for a feeling of togetherness and friendliness. The two of you should play on the same activity, building a routine that includes both familiar and creative actions. Both persons need a similar amount of action input to create a balanced partnership in their play together.

LESS LIKE THIS

Nick: (Takes a block from his mother).
Mom: "Good, you took the block, now take this one."
Nick: (Takes it.) "Aha ah ah."
Mom: "See what I'm doing with my blocks? I'm building a block tower." (Builds a tower with some blocks.)
Nick: (Takes his two blocks and claps them together.)
Mom: "Come on, why don't you try to build. You're making too much noise."
Nick: (Reaches over and knocks over his mother's block tower.)
Mom: "That wasn't very nice."

Why Less?

Nick and Mom both play with blocks, but the togetherness ends there. Mom builds with her blocks, while Nick simply takes blocks from his mother on command. Later he destroys her work, causing her disappointment. The two do not have fun together. Mom takes over the role of "boss," commenting on the "goodness" or "badness" of Nick's actions. She tells him things to do, using long sentences, communicating far more than he does in the interaction. The balance a partnership requires is never established.

MORE LIKE THIS

Nick: (Takes a block from his mother.)
Mom: "Mine" (Points to herself, and holds up another block.)
Nick: (Points to himself and holds up the block he took.)
Mom: (Taps her block against Nick's, laughs.) "Whee."
Nick: (Laughs, picking up another block.) "Oo oo."
Mom: "Hey." (Picks up another block, extends both toward Nick.)
Nick: (Takes his two blocks, knocks them up against Mom's.)
Mom: "Bang, bang." (Knocks her blocks against his.)

Why More?

Here Nick and Mom are playing in sync toward each other, creating a feeling of togetherness. They laugh and follow each other's lead, eliminating the need for a "boss." They create a game from their play, building from the initial action when Nick takes a block from his mother toward a mutual block clapping activity. Action and communication input from each partner is balanced to create an activity with a friendly, reciprocal spirit.

Why Is It Important?	Children must share a common world with adults before they can learn how to socialize or communicate with others about that world. Becoming play partners across a range of activities provides places for both the social and communicative learning to occur.
	Adults who practice creating routines with children can also enhance the child's feelings of belonging and success. A child can use what he knows in such routines, so successful exchanges with others should increase his motivation to do things with others. These experiences expand the world he can share with his adults and peers and ultimately provide more social and communicative practice for the child.

Concerns and
Possible Problems

Play partnerships can easily become repetitive and redundant. Remember play routines should take from the input of each partner to create a routine that interests them both and goes beyond the input of each partner.

Many adults do not value play partnerships and fail to see these partnerships as a central factor in building the child's social and communication skills. Adults often become too concerned about the child's communication without bothering to build play partnerships. Consequently, the two have little to communicate about. Togetherness and friendliness work better as first goals to building a play partnership. A child may participate in many routines before he communicates within any of them.

Other adults may confuse parallel play with play partnerships. Playing on the same activity does not automatically create a play partnership. Neither side-by-side play nor child participation on command creates partnerships. A play partnership needs more; look for a friendly flow and a sharing between the partners.

**ECO
Link**

Becoming Play Partners
HOW YOU AND YOUR CHILD PLAY TOGETHER

*HOW DO YOU
AND YOUR
CHILD PLAY?*

1. Do you and your child play spontaneously as well as in specific activities?
2. Are you actively together in play, doing the same things?
3. Do you play for enjoyment more than to get a job done?
4. Is your play balanced? Do each of you do about as much as the other?
5. Are you matched? Do the two of you play and communicate like each other?
6. Is your play more friendly than stressful?
7. Are you playful across natural learning activities such as caretaking, teaching, leisure, and daily routines?

*HOW WILL YOU
KNOW IF YOUR
CHILD IS YOUR
PLAY PARTNER?*

1. He will frequently and voluntarily try to play with you.
2. He will stay in extended play and try to keep you there.
3. He will try to act and communicate like you. You will clearly be influencing him.
4. He will often prefer playing with you rather than alone.
5. His play will change; it will become more assertive, functional, and meaningful.
6. He will pretend with you, even creating stories.

*HOW WILL YOU
KNOW IF THERE
IS A PROBLEM
IN YOUR PLAY
PARTNERSHIP?*

1. Playtimes will be too rare and short-lived for much natural learning.
2. One of you will dominate the activity, doing most of it and controlling its choice and direction.
3. You will mismatch your child, doing and communicating in ways he cannot match.
4. One of you will become easily distracted.
5. Play will not be enjoyable or interesting.
6. You will feel a need to make it more work or school than play.
7. You will mainly talk as your child plays; thus there will be no joint activity.
8. There will be little give-and-take between you; play will be more side-by-side than genuinely together.
9. Your playfulness will not extend beyond playtime.

*HOW CAN YOU
BUILD A PLAY
PARTNERSHIP
WITH YOUR
CHILD?*

1. Realize that play is the necessary work of a child; play is his learning.
2. Realize that playing with people is how children learn to communicate.
3. Be childlike through matching; act and communicate in ways your child can.
4. Be sure there's a true give-and-take; your child must give to you as well as get from you.
5. Be playful in caretaking, teaching, daily routines.
6. Get into the habit of keeping your child a little longer than usual.
7. Follow your child's lead, helping him feel competent and not dependent on you.
8. Show your child new ways to play.

HOW SHOULD YOU COMMUNICATE AS YOU PLAY?

1. Be balanced; let your child do as much as you.
2. Be responsive; communicate to your child's interests and behaviors.
3. Be more nondirective than controlling; comment more than question and command.
4. Make communicating a fun part of the play.
5. Communicate about your experiences together.
6. Communicate and expect something; practice communicating for a response rather than at the child with no expectations.

WHAT SHOULD YOU AVOID DOING AND SAYING?

1. Taking actions that are too complex for your child.
2. Communicating in ways that are too complex for your child.
3. Controlling the activity or otherwise allowing him to be passive.
4. Giving any judgments, criticism, or other signals of failure.
5. Questioning and commanding.
6. Testing the child or focusing on right and wrong.

PEOPLE CONTACTS: After School Chat Preverbal Level

Make the natural events in your day into opportunities for friendly, social conversations with your child. Consider these contrasting examples. Try to avoid limited contacts such as the one on the left. Try to find something you can share with your child, as in the example on the right. Turn just another routine into a joint activity in which your child can stay and learn with you.

LESS LIKE THIS

Adult: "Did you have fun at school today?"
Child: (Looks in the refrigerator for a snack.)
Adult: "Can mommy help you get something to eat?"
Child: (Takes out a banana; starts to eat it while walking into another room to turn on the television.)
Adult: "Sesame Street is on now."
Child: (Continues to watch Sesame Street, which is already on.)
Adult: "You like that show, don't you?"
Child: (Imitates some body movements the characters on the show have modelled.)
Adult: "Wow, you can do what they do, can't you?"

Avoid These Problems:
Low Interactive Participation,
Mismatch

The adult and child in this example never make contact. The adult TALKS AT THE CHILD; the child continues on his own activities. The mother should have noticed the child's willingness to do what he can do with others, which he demonstrated by imitating the television characters. Instead, she continues rambling on in long sentences that he never responds to.

MORE LIKE THIS

Adult: "Hi!" (Waves to child as he gets off the bus)
Child: (Waves to mom.)
Adult: "Hungry?" (Points to refrigerator.)
Child: (Opens refrigerator, points to apple.)
Adult: "Yum, apple." (Gives it to C)
Child: (Begins eating apple, takes Mom by the hand and into the television room.)
Adult: (Turns on television.) "Wow, Sesame Street."
Child: (Shakes head, "yes.")
Adult: (Imitates some movements of the characters.)
Child: (Joins Mom; looking at her and laughing.)

Try These Strategies:
Respond to the Child,
Match Child Communication Progressively

The adult models messages with gestures and single words or phrases to MATCH THE CHILD'S COMMUNICATION PROGRESSIVELY. She RESPONDS TO THE CHILD by following his lead into the telelvision room, yet keeps him interacting with her by doing what he can do, like IMITATING THE TELEVISION CHARACTER.

VARIATIONS:
Getting together after any separation, such as being with grandma, having a babysitter, or coming back from errands while Dad watches the child.

IEP/
Problem Solver

Preverbal
CHILD GOAL: Show a Variety of Actions
PROBLEM: Lack of Playfulness
(limited use of active playful movements)

Kevin's mother is worried about his limited use of words, so she spends time every day with him working on flashcards. They sit at the kitchen table together. She puts two cards on the table, and she asks him to pick the one she names. He gets most of them right. When he gets it right, she tells him to say the name of the object in the picture. Sometimes he tries; sometimes he doesn't. She has noticed that he almost never uses these new words in his everyday life around the house, and she wonders what else she could be doing to get him to use what he knows.

Mom:	"Can you pick out the picture of the radio, Kevin?" (Sets out a picture of a radio and a train.)
Kevin:	(Points to the radio.)
Mom:	"Very good. Now, say 'radio' for Mommy."
Kevin:	"Ra-r-o."
Mom:	"Not quite, but a pretty good try since you didn't say it at all yesterday, right?"
Kevin:	(Smiles vaguely.)

Later that day:

Mom:	(Washes dishes in the kitchen.)
Kevin:	(Draws with crayons at the table.)
Mom:	"What are you doing, Kevin?"
Kevin:	(Points to his picture.)
Mom:	"Nice job!"
Kevin:	(Gets out of his chair and pulls at Mom's apron for attention.)
Mom:	"What do you want, Kevin?"
Kevin:	(Points to the radio.)
Mom:	"Do you want the radio on, honey?"
Kevin:	(Shakes his head yes.)
Mom:	"You know how to say that word. You said it for me this morning. Say 'radio.'"
Kevin:	(Points at the radio and pulls at her.) "Ah."
Mom:	"Okay, you can have it on, but you should use your words."

ECO | **Partnership Plan**

The **ECO** Partnership Plan contains those elements of an Individual Family Service Plan (IFSP) or Individual Education Program (IEP) that specify **ECO** goals and objectives to enhance a child's social and communicative development. Refer to current ECOScales for present levels of development and performance and for new goals.

Child Name: __Kevin__   Birth Date: __12/24__   Parents: __David and Jill__

Date of ECOScales: __7/12__   Examiner: __J.M.__

Present Levels of Development and Performance

Noninteractive; preverbal level

Child Goal

Use action in a functional, meaningful way

Objectives

Use action appropriate to a variety of play

Use a variety of action

Partnership Goal

Become Play Partners

Objectives

Be actively together   Play and communicate like the other

Priority Problem:

Lack of Playfulness

Subproblem

Minimal spontaneity

Limited use of active, playful movements

Adult Strategies

Play in childlike ways   Play as much or more than talk

Substrategies

Respond to Kevin   Respond to actions as messages

Communicate in ways close to Kevin   Comment more than question or command

          Use gestures/sounds/words like Kevin's

Practice Activities
People Only

Sound imitation exchanges

__1-2__ Times a day   __2-3__ Minutes each

People and Things

Car and truck, books, blocks

__2-3__ Times a day   __2-3__ Minutes each

Daily Routines (practice one a day)

Bathtime

__1__

Spontaneous

ECO | Practice Plan and Record

PRACTICE PLAN
Refer to current *ECOScale* for goals; see other *ECOScales* for old goals to maintain.

Interactive Goal Become play partners (Kevin and Mom)

Objectives _____

Priority Problem Lack of playfulness

Child Goal Stay with others in play

Objectives Play with others rather than by self | Use actions to initiate as well as respond

Adult Strategies Communicate in ways close to Kevin's; Communicate about immediate experiences
2) Respond sensitively to Kevin's actions and sounds

Targets to Decrease Kevin: Brief, deadend contacts — Failing to attend to shared activity
Janet: Stressed/task-oriented activity — Communicating in ways Kevin can't do
— Too many academic and adult words

Practice Activities

People Only Exchanging funny actions & gestures
Peek-a-boo

How Often 2 Times a day | 2-3 Minutes each
Where

People and Things Cars & trucks | Rocking a baby doll
Tossing bean bags

How Often 2 Times a day | 2-3 Minutes each
Where

Daily Routines (practice one a day) grocery shopping – dressing – bathing – bedtime

Spontaneous Salt and pepper your strategies across the day. | Make interactions/communications a habit.

PARTNERSHIP CALENDAR

Week	MONDAY	TUESDAY	WEDNESDAY	THURSDAY	FRIDAY	SATURDAY	SUNDAY
1	3 2	4 3	4 3	2 2	3 3	OUT OF TOWN	4 3
2	4 3	3 2½	3 2	4 3	4 4	3 2	5 4
3							
4							
5							

How to Use the Calendar

1. Select one goal each for child and adult. Observe one planned activity a day.
2. After observing, rate child and adult (you or someone else) on the goals listed in the Practice Plan. Use a 1 to 9 scale:
   1-2 = no evidence   3-4 = little evidence   5 = some evidence   6-7 = increasing evidence   8-9 = strong evidence
3. Rate the child (c) in top half and adult (a) in bottom half of each cell. Be sure to practice across many activities. Try some of the following; check the ones you practice.
   People only: ✓ sounds ✓ actions __ conversations   __ your choice _____
   People and things: ✓ toys __ books __ games __ your choice
   Daily routines: __ getting up ✓ dressing ✓ bathing __ meals __ TV __ car ✓ bedtime
   ✓ shopping __ visiting __ household chores __ your choice _____

ECO | Practice Plan and Record

PARTNERSHIP DIARY

Watch your progress and help your habits grow. Quickly, comment on how interactions with your child went today. Say anything: progress, problems, ideas, changes. Mention both child and adult occasionally.

Week 1

Monday
I feel strange using just a few words when I talk to Kevin.

Tuesday
Maybe I'm getting better, but I don't see much difference in Kev. He only interacts with me for brief periods, then turns away.

Wednesday
Same as yesterday!

Thursday
I really felt like "teaching" today + it usually makes a difference with Kevin! He really turned away from me quickly when I started talking about colors.

Friday
We're improving together. I had to keep my ECO plan next to me when we played, though, because I need to keep reminding myself.

Saturday
Out of town on Sat. - visited Ruth. Kevin played with me more than before.

Sunday
I didn't have to refer to the plan! It's getting easier to "match" but it's hard to think of things to do that don't "quiz" Kevin. Those were almost the only times we spent together before.

Week 2

Monday
We're still working — I have a hard time seeing changes in Kevin.

Tuesday
Today I saw a change in both of us — a negative change. Seems like Kevin would rather play alone.

Wednesday
I had a hard time matching and Kev had a hard time staying with me for very long.

Thursday
Kevin playing with me has a lot to do with what I say when we play. The more I tell and do, the more he pulls away & does less.

Friday
We both had great days today! I did less but kept him with me more — and he did more — even new things!

Saturday
My friend Beth was in town and every time I played with Kevin I asked him his colors, numbers, or letters to try to show Beth how much he knows. But he just kept turning to his toys.

Sunday
Yesterday was an eye-opener for me! Today I really felt like Kevin and I were together. I wish Beth could have seen us today.

Extra Hints to Remember
When you play with Kevin, say one thing close to his level — then wait silently for him to take a turn. Be sure your comments relate to what he's doing — not to "getting something done."

5 | *Becoming Turntaking Partners*

SOCIAL
social
PLAY
play
TURN
TAKING
taking
COMMUNICATION
unication
LANGUAGE
guage
CONVERSATION
rsation

Once a child and adult are regularly staying in enjoyable play together, it is time to learn turntaking. Turntaking means many different things to people. For the purposes of learning to socialize and communicate, turntaking means the general habit of give-and-take. Even infants and their mothers have the habit of turntaking as early as the child's first few months (Brazelton et al., 1974; Goldberg, 1977; Kaye, 1979). And yet there are many children who do not seem to have this critical skill. They rarely initiate contacts, stay with others, or show the basic human rule of "give in order to get" (Field, 1980b; Jones, 1980; Bruner, 1988). And their caregivers seem to get little from these children to encourage them to sustain the interactions the children need for learning. Taking a turn may be one of the most powerful motivators children and adults have to begin and sustain stable relationships.

Ping-pong, not darts.

One notion that helps many people understand turntaking is the comparison between ping-pong and darts. Turntaking is like a ping-pong game in which each partner takes a turn and then waits for his partner to take his turn. Ping-pong requires matching in that each hit the ball in a way that the other can return. Each partner has a turn and expects to keep the game going. In darts, there is only one person and a board, and the person throws the darts at the board. The point here is that a child will learn more if he is more like a ping-pong partner than like a dart board or a dart thrower.

Every turn is an opportunity to learn.

Turntaking is nothing new to most adults. In most of our friendly relationships we see an easy give-and-take in which each person does something and then waits for the other to respond. Then the second person does something that is somehow related to what the first person did, and waits for something back. That's turntaking. Look around and you'll see it everywhere. While one person may occasionally do more than the other on a turn, these imbalances usually even out. Imagine how limited your social life and learning would be if you did not regularly take turns with people. Then imagine how much richer a social and learning life your children would have if they habitually took turns. If someone regularly dominates the turns and you feel little chance to have your say, you probably avoid that person if you can. In the same way, children avoid a person who takes most of the turns. By so doing, however, a child loses out on learning from that person. Likewise, if the child dominates interactions by taking most of the turns, he may effectively drive away just the person he needs for natural learning. Do you ever feel you or your child are driving each other away?

The goal of turntaking in the **ECO** program is to help you and your child interact in ways that encourage others to become social learning partners with him or her. In our experience, easy, balanced, turntaking relationships are uncommon among many children with developmental delays and even among many nondelayed children (Field, 1980b; Greenspan, 1985; Lewis & Rosenblum, 1974; MacDonald

& Gillette, 1987; Waterson & Snow, 1978; Young, 1988). Often the contacts are too brief for much learning, and either the child or the adult is doing too much or is doing things that do not keep the other engaged. However simple it may sound, turntaking is an indispensible skill that both the child and adult must learn if their natural interactions are to help the child communicate.

The kind of turntaking we are referring to here can be misinterpreted in many ways. Turntaking here refers to people-to-people interactions, doing something directly to or with a person in a way that relates to what that person is doing. When a teacher tells a boy to "wait his turn" on the slide or says "it's not your turn yet, you tell your story after Carlos," that kind of turntaking is very different from the interactive turntaking discussed here. This sequential kind of turntaking may contribute to social order or politeness but not directly to building interactions between people. The terms back-and-forth or give-and-take or reciprocal better identify the interaction central to the turntaking we mean. Each person is responding to and affecting the other.

Unless the child and adult are in a well-practiced habit of turntaking, the child is unlikely to learn much from others. And, if we accept the assumption that children become social and communicative only to the extent that they interact with others, then turntaking becomes a primary way children and adults can teach and learn from each other in daily living contacts.

Turntaking stimulates a natural learning process that may be viewed as an interactive loop. That is, the adult takes a turn in the form of any movement or communication, waits expectantly for the child to take a turn in some form, and reciprocates with feedback that relates in some meaningful way to what the child did. The loop is sustained when the child takes another turn, related in some way to the adult's turn. The interaction loop continues as long as each person maintains the interaction with turns that help the other participate. Each turn is an opportunity for the child to learn something from the adult and for the adult to learn not only more about the child but also how to spontaneously teach him something. Notice in your own good conversations how this give-and-take loop becomes an easy habit. As with good friendships, the goal with developing children is to keep the interaction going because partnerships are enjoyable, not to get a job done.

What each person does on his turn is not necessarily important, as long as it is something related to what the other did and keeps the interaction going. You may be saying, "But I don't want interaction. I want words, ideas, conversation, 'success'!" A key principle of this ecological model of communication development is that without regular social turntaking and sustained interactions, much of the cognitive play and language teaching may be lost. Both the child and the adults he interacts with regularly must be motivated and committed to interacting in an intimate and extended give-and-take style.

Professionals and parents regularly report that, while a child learns some things in school and at home, he or she often does not use that knowledge in the larger world. The knowledge is not used to build relationships and to continue to learn. It is as if the child's knowledge is stored like money in a bank but is not used to improve the quality of his life; as if you had a great deal of money in an account but no checks or passbook to withdraw it. So too with many children: Turntaking can be the key to help the child show what he knows and build communication

Turntaking means give and take, back and forth, reciprocal.

You can take turns doing almost anything.

Turntaking makes your teaching worthwhile.

and conversations with it. In more technical language this problem is called a failure to generalize what has been learned (Harris, 1975).

Our own experiences with a wide range of children reveal that they seem not to know how to maintain interactions that would allow them to practice and benefit from their newly learned skills (MacDonald, 1989; see research chapter, this book). Perhaps more importantly, adults who are important to these children do not realize how absolutely necessary they are in showing the child how to use his knowledge and how to become more and more like them. Consider the unfortunate situation in which parents and teachers work diligently to teach the child: They know that he does know what they have taught him; but when he is faced with educational, social, or vocational challenges, he fails to show others what he knows and avoids interactions he needs for further learning. We have seen how painful it is for those parents and professionals to see the child lose the benefits of the learning because of a lack of give-and-take relationships.

For the child who often avoids learning, turntaking provides constant opportunities to show what he knows and to practice new skills within the context of safe, friendly feedback. If you are familiar with children with delays, you may be aware of the often-devastating gap between competence and performance. That is, many of these children, when viewed in practical and academic contexts, act as if they know much less than they do. The child's success in the social and vocational worlds may depend less on what he knows than on how he uses that knowledge to build relationships. Our experience with adolescents and adults with delays suggests that often their inadequate social and communicative skills, more than their knowledge, interfere with living and working in communities. It appears that knowledge is only as good as the social skills for using it and turntaking is a critical social skill.

How often have you said, or heard a parent or teacher say, "I know he can do that but he just won't right now." In our years of working with parents and children, we have come to believe that these pleas are valid descriptions more than biased parental claims. Two primary assumptions of the **ECO** program are, first, that most children can do much more than they usually do when interacting with people and, second, that they communicate much less than they know. One benefit of turntaking is that it helps the child and his adult(s) build a habit of reciprocal interaction that then becomes both the place for the child to show his knowledge and the process for his learning more.

Do you have to plan and prepare for turntaking? No. In fact, if you plan it too carefully, it may become just another job that you have to do, rather than a natural habit. Try to "salt and pepper" your daily life with turntaking contacts that keep you and your child with each other just a little more. Your child is more likely to learn to communicate and socialize if his turntaking is reinforced occasionally and unexpectedly rather than at predictable lesson times. Too many children perform in expected lessons but not in the real-life contacts they need. That is perhaps the greatest dilemma in education—lack of generalization.

While natural opportunities for turntaking are everywhere, it may take a while to see them as such. There are some reasons you contact your child that particularly lend themselves to turntaking contacts for learning and socializing. Consider each of the following times as opportunities to keep your child with you. Copy this list and write down the times you try to take turns. Eventually, this can help you make turntaking a natural part of your way of life.

Opportunities for Turntaking

Expressing feelings	Making requests
Getting information	Giving information
Giving affection	Making physical contact
Seeking permission	Getting attention
Giving attention	Getting help
Giving help	Playing with toys
Playing with people	Playing with books
Teaching	Disciplining
Any chance for contact	

A first important
question is not
"What did he do?"
but "How many
turns does he take
with me?"

If slowly but steadily you keep your child in a little more turntaking on each of these opportunities, he will learn the important lesson that *people are to stay with and enjoy, not only to use.* But remember, you must contact him for social reasons, not just wait for him to contact you. You need to show him how social and valuable little contacts can be. A good way to start is by responding to what your child is doing, because he is already interested in the event and therefore more likely to stay. To get turntaking contacts going, contact your child for social, friendly reasons, like playing and expressing feelings, more than for instrumental reasons, like teaching, directing, or controlling him. Social contacts are usually longer and involve less stress than instrumental contacts, which are often resolved in short meetings that offer little learning. With creativity, you can use the guidelines discussed throughout this book to make even instrumental contacts into rich interactions for learning. But remember that it is the friendly, social contacts your child will need to develop relationships and to use his knowledge in the world.

In sum, turntaking is a highly efficient way to learn many things, including communication, language, and friendships. It is a basic building block for conversations. Without turntaking, a child is unlikely to build relationships for spontaneous learning and friendships. A major advantage of turntaking is that it requires extremely few cognitive skills, little preparation, and few materials (even infants habitually take turns). The need for turntaking never ends; that is, a child does not learn turntaking and then go on to more important things. Rather, he learns turntaking and then uses it as a primary technique to learn other things. We know parents and professionals who, once their child takes turns in play, forget the need for turntaking when communication begins. Turntaking is an indispensible tool for learning from people. Without these skills, the child will lose the contacts that can teach him, and his adults will miss out on easy opportunities for natural teaching. Think of turntaking as the weave that holds people together for learning and friendship.

It's Your Turn

COMMENT:

My 4-year-old with Down syndrome, Kaitlin, and I play together several times a day but other times we seem to have little to do with each other. But my 2-year-old, Craig, and I are always doing something together back and forth. What's the problem?

REPLY:

In our time with children we try to look for "missed opportunities" and we look at everything the child does as an opportunity for a little interaction. We call this "salt and peppering" your child's day with people contacts; they are absolutely necessary for her to learn from people.

The accompanying table gives you some examples of how to make a child's casual actions into interactions that can help her be more social.

Ways To Get Interaction Started

Child Action	Adult—Missed Opportunity	Adult—Interaction
1. Dianne walks by Dad, who is watching TV.	Keeps watching TV.	"Gotcha!" Grabs Dianne.
2. Karen staring out window as adult walks by.	Keeps walking through room.	"Ooh, birdie." Points and goes over to Karen.
3. Jeff passes through room as Mom is unloading the dryer.	Keeps unloading the dryer.	"So soft." Holds out a towel for Jeff to touch.
4. Joannie sings to herself while taking a bath.	Continues to bathe Joannie.	Hums a bit of Joannie's tune and then waits expectantly for a response.
5. Frannie walks through the kitchen while the babysitter is making soup.	Keeps stirring the soup.	"Soup!" Shows Frannie the soup in the pan.
6. Leo picks up items in a cart while grocery shopping.	Silently takes items out of Leo's hand and puts them back into the cart.	"Ooh, chilly!" Touches a cold item that Leo is holding.
7. Johnny curiously looks at a new vegetable on his plate.	Keeps eating.	"Yummy yams!" Points to the vegetable.
8. Noelle grabs for a leaf while taking a walk with her teacher.	Keeps walking; no comment made.	"Ooh, pretty leaf." Lightly touches the leaf.
9. Chris and an adult are outside as a plane flies overhead.	No comment made; just looks up.	"Oh—plane!" Points to the plane.
10. Annie and her older sister walk past a mud puddle.	Guides Annie around the mud puddle.	"Oh, muddy!" Grimaces and points at the puddle.

Interactive Goal

10. BECOME TURNTAKING PARTNERS

There are four guidelines you can easily follow as you interact with your child to see if you are acting like turntaking partners. Again, we do not mean strict "every-time-possible" turntaking. What we do mean is that you and your child are getting regular practice staying in turntaking across your many roles and activities, such as caretaking, play, leisure time, household routines, and touching.

a. Keep interaction going back and forth between the two.

Ask yourself if you and your child have an easy, back-and-forth style in your interactions. If not, does one of you consistently do the most? In a back-and-forth interaction, both you and your child are living signals for the other to notice frequently, respond to, and stay with. As we will discuss throughout this chapter, matching and waiting are powerful ways to start or rekindle a back-and-forth interaction (just as they were powerful ways to involve your child in playful interactions). Another key is for both of you to be motivated by the same activity and to be reciprocal; that is, you each should act in ways that are meaningfully related to what the other is doing or communicating, not just rotely participating without sensitivity to the other's turns.

b. Share in choice of activity.

As in interactions between adults, you and your child are more likely to build a partnership if each of you has a personal investment in the choice of activities and the focus of the interaction. Successful partnerships seem to depend on each partner being free to contribute from his or her own interests. While you may feel that you know what is best for your child to do, you might find two important points helpful. First, children seem to learn most efficiently in activities based on their own interests, at their own pace. (In fact, don't we adults learn a lot that way?) We have regularly observed that children stay in interactions much more frequently and actively when they have some choice of what to do and how to proceed. Second, while you may think you are interacting with your child for his benefit alone, we find that the most productive adult-child relationships we see are ones in which the adult is participating for her own benefit as well as for the child's. However committed to a child an adult is, it is unrealistic and perhaps unhealthy to expect the adult will interact solely for the child's sake. And, most importantly, there is no need for adults to sacrifice their enjoyment because the interactions that are the most cognitively and socially productive seem to be the ones in which both the adult and child participate for their own natural motivations and for their own benefit. In other words, if you genuinely enjoy yourself, your interactions will last longer and your child will learn more.

c. Initiate as well as respond.

This issue may sound like it's too obvious to mention; of course, you might say, people will both initiate and respond if they are together. Nevertheless, our consistent observations tell us that in many interactions, one person is usually the initiator and the other, the responder. These roles often look like they are part of the person's definition of his or her role and responsibility. While the adult is often the initiator and the child assumes the passive, responsive role, we do also see the roles shifting to an initiating child and a following adult, but it is the passive habit that can be disastrous to a child's learning and socializing.

It is important to remember that by initiating, we mean contacting a person for your own social or instrumental reasons; by responding, reacting to what the other person did. Initiating and responding can take any form of movement or behavior at all. Thus there is rarely any reason for you and your child both to not initiate and respond when you are together. The major barrier to such a balanced interaction seems to be the adult's or child's belief that only certain kinds of behavior deserve to initiate or to be responded to. Anything a child initiates can be one more step to becoming social and communicative.

Subgoal
Action turntaking is important

d. Give as well as take with action.

It should be very helpful to you to be aware that back-and-forth turntaking is not enough. To build a turntaking relationship, both you and the child must actively give something of yourselves. This does not mean simple, rote movements or just giving something to the other or getting something back. It is too easy to get into routine and socially meaningless turntaking in the name of doing something together. The purpose of turntaking is not to pass time together but to get both adult and child involved in being genuinely together in an activity as a dynamic unit, a partnership. When we observe an adult and a child, we ask if they are primarily spending time together or sincerely building a partnership that is increasingly motivating to each of them.

It's Your Turn

COMMENT:

How can I be my child's most important teacher? I've never gone to college. I just take care of him. I don't teach him.

REPLY:

Don't let anyone fool you; you are a lot more important than you think. You may not deliberately try to teach your child, but he learns from watching you and interacting with you. In fact, there is evidence that we learn much more in easy give-and-take with each other than when one person tries to teach. Think of all the things your child knows that no one specifically taught him—holding a telephone, words, mannerisms, and much more. Every time you and your child take turns, someone learns something.

COMMENT:

I know many adults who do a poor job of taking turns with me. Is turntaking important only for children?

REPLY:

Turntaking is a source of problems between adults as well as children. In most of our friendly relationships we see an easy give-and-take between another person and ourselves. Without this turntaking, we would have little or no social life or opportunity to learn from others. When someone regularly dominates the turns, you feel little chance to have your say and you probably feel like avoiding that person if you can. People who are shy and submissive may need to learn turntaking in order to become more assertive and benefit more in relationships.

COMMENT:

I am the director of a preschool. The students are very good at taking turns as they play in a game and wait for snacks. But they rarely interact with the teachers or each other otherwise. Is turntaking going to help them?

REPLY:

As a director, you should be concerned. While their cooperation helps them stay in order and makes the teacher's life easier, it is definitely not the turntaking they need to learn to be social and build communicative partnerships. Let's discuss what turntaking for communication is not. Taking turns at play or in the cafeteria is important for order, but it's very different. Turns in this sense are taken to sequence events rather than to build interactions. When the children learn to take turns in casual contacts and in their other curricular activities, you are likely to see much more evidence of learning. And as a director, isn't that what you want?

Becoming Partners with Children

I am both a mother and a teacher. I know turntaking is important, but it sounds like we should spend all our time going back and forth, back and forth with our children. What about our time? Don't we need a break?

REPLY:

Of course. Nothing should be done all the time. You are just as important as your child, and you need to be yourself and be by yourself just as your child does. What we encourage is that you gradually contact your child a little more and, when you do, keep him in an easy, give-and-take exchange. That way he can learn that people are to stay with, learn from, and enjoy. If this becomes stressful for you, relax, be yourself, and come back again after you have some time of your own. Instead of asking "Am I doing it all the time?" ask "Have we taken turns recently?"

Self-Assessment
How Are You
Doing?

Rate the turntaking patterns between you and your child. Use a scale of 1 to 9, where 1 = disagree strongly and 9 = agree strongly.

____ 1. My child and I have an easy give-and-take style with each other.
____ 2. We take turns with actions.
____ 3. We take turns with communications.
____ 4. We stay interacting for longer turns that a month ago.
____ 5. I believe my child learns when we take turns together.
____ 6. My child voluntarily stays interacting with me.
____ 7. We interact just to enjoy each other.
____ 8. We make turntaking out of jobs we must do.

Interactive Problem

11. LACK OF ACTIVE TOGETHERNESS

When beginning the **ECO** program, we encourage professionals and parents to put on hold attention to all apparent child and adult problems until the child and adult are regularly staying together. No matter how wisely designed your treatment plan is, it will succeed only to the extent that the child habitually stays with people and that people do what they need to keep the child actively interacting with them. Often adults will say, "What do you mean, keep my child with me? She's always with me." Active togetherness means much more than merely being together.

In the song "She's Leaving Home," John Lennon told us about being actively with others when he wrote about an isolated woman who was "leaving home after living alone for so many years." Do you ever feel alone even when you're with your child? How much of your child's time with others involves real contacts? Children and adults appear to learn from each other to the extent that they are actively engaged in back-and-forth contacts that have a genuine effect on the other. As Lennon observed, living together does not necessarily mean that much is happening between people. Many adults have told us they never thought that actually interacting with their children was important, as long as the children were safe and happy playing alone. These parents, and teachers and other caregivers who hold the same view, grossly underestimate the importance of their own intimacy to the child's development.

Play is the work of a child.

One of the most careful scholars of child development, Jean Piaget (1952), reasoned elegantly that play is the most important work of the child. He argued that a child's sensorimotor activities and their effects shape what he knows. Bruner (1977) went a crucial step further as he demonstrated that, while child play alone develops problem solving and other cognitive functions, a child also needs social play in the form of joint activity routines for communication development and social learning. Joint activity routines are interactive events in which the child and adult maintain a give-and-take relationship in which each reciprocally affects the other. Such routines yield both a common social knowledge as well as the skills to learn from new people in spontaneous contacts.

A few guidelines may help identify the nature and extent of the togetherness problem. When neither person attempts much to keep the other person engaged, the two may appear indifferent or even opposed to staying together. A casual glance may make it seem they are together, but a careful look reveals they are not staying on the same activity or directing their behavior toward each other. Often this problem reveals itself in frequent interruptions of the interaction that prevent sustained learning or attention to a theme. Similarly, the interaction is often characterized by "dead-end" contacts—brief interactions that stop before they go very far. The less continuity there is, the less learning and forging of a relationship will there be.

An imbalance between the amount and kind of things each person does with the other can also interfere with active togetherness. If the adult does much more than the child, she is likely to lose the child's interest and participation. In fact, if she does too much, the child may follow the message that he is not expected to interact.

Much of a child's learning depends on genuinely doing things with others. Several researchers have observed that young children seem to learn and communicate more if they are in regular back-and-forth routines where both adult and child are attending to and acting on the same event or idea (Kaye, 1979; Lewis & Rosenblum, 1977a, 1977b; Stern, 1985). Others have observed that when adults and children do not spend much intimate, mutually rewarding together time, emotional and learning disturbances result (Greenspan, 1985).

We realize that more together time is difficult for most parents and teachers. Most parents and teachers we know feel overwhelmed with simply managing the basics. We respect their concern that more time with one child means not enough time with another child or a spouse. But, in fact, turntaking can be successful without interfering with daily routines. Turntaking needs to become a part of those routines, a way to help the child learn more in them. We propose that turntaking allows us to use our time more efficiently and to get more rewards from the children. Therefore, look at the specific problems below not as criticisms (after many years we too still fall into these traps), but as signals that you need to relax, to do less, and to get closer to your child. And yes, it is true that these problems are inevitable and necessary some of the time. We do not expect you to stop being an adult, only to be more with your child sometimes.

Subproblem

a. Limited give-and-take style.
Do you sometimes feel you are giving to your child and getting little in return? If you do, the major problem is even more serious because the rest of the world accepts only a child who gives as well as takes. Some parents and teachers we know act as though their job is only to give to the child, no matter what the child does. *We very strongly disagree.* As a human being, each child has a responsibility to give to others to the extent he or she is capable. And what is the responsibility of parents and teachers if not to help children build as relationships with others

Guide for Using Turntaking to Make Activities Interactive

Activity	Making it interactive	Examples
Balls	Play catch, roll/bounce back and forth, throw in hoop or back and forth.	Throw, bounce, in and out of container, up in air.
Toy cars/trucks	Take turns pushing back and forth. It's best to use one car, or child may play alone.	Push, crash together, spin wheels, turn around.
Blocks	Build a stack of blocks together and take turns.	Stack, clap together, push, in/out hide.
Ring stack	Take turns stacking and removing rings. Johnson & Johnson puzzle is good because no order is required for stacking.	On/off, push back and forth, blow air, or look through ring.
Books	Take turns pointing at pictures, turn pages (family albums, pictures).	Point to pictures, turn pages, open/close, pass back and forth.
Puzzles	Take turns putting pieces in.	In/out, turn pieces around, pass back and forth.
Pegboard	Take turns putting pegs in board.	In/out of board or can, roll, hit together, dump.
Dolls	Pass back and forth doing different actions each turn.	Hugging, rocking, walking, sitting, combing hair
Drawing/writing	Use one sheet of paper and one pencil or crayon; take turns marking the paper.	Random marks, scribbles, circles, lines.
Toy telephone	Pass receiver back and forth; take turns dialing, talking; some kids work better with a receiver without a phone.	Listen, talk, dial, hang up, hold to ear.
Musical toys	Gather horns, drums, shakers, etc., and take turns picking out and playing, passing it to each other.	Hit, shake, pound, blow, clap together, laugh.
Bubbles	Take turns passing wand back and forth, blowing bubbles on your turn.	Blow, in/out of bottle, pass back and forth.

Guide for Using Turntaking to Make Activities Interactive

Activity	Making it interactive	Examples
Toy work bench	Take turns hammering pegs down.	Pound, turn over, pass hammer back and forth.
Hats	Take turns putting on; use one or more; put on each other.	On/off, look in mirror, pass back and forth.
Toy bank	Take turns putting change in a bank.	In/out, open/close, pass money to partner.
Sand	Take turns using various utensils in the sand.	Pour, scoop, dump the sand.
Making faces	Take turns looking into a mirror making funny faces.	Open/close/cover eyes, ears or mouth, laugh, smile, blow.
Body movements	Take turns performing various body movements; works best sitting across from each other.	Arms up, clapping, shaking hands, jumping up and down, wave bye-bye, touching head, standing.
Objects in box	Take turns moving objects from one box to another (dolls, blocks, balls, etc.).	In/out.
Connect four game	Take turns putting checkers in the frame (don't worry about the rules of the game now).	In/out.
Flowers	Plastic or silk, take turns putting into can or vase.	In/out, pass back and forth.
Toy steering wheel	Pass back and forth; take turns turning wheel and beeping horn.	Turn, beep.
Face, head, hands	Take turns.	Cover eyes, ears, make noises, squeeze noses, stick out tongues, open/ close eyes/mouth, pop cheeks with air, lick lips, hand over mouth.
Busy box	Push back and forth; each partner gets a turn to work one item before pushing to other.	Push, turn, open/close.

Are you giving and
not getting much?

that are as healthy and independent as possible? If your child does not learn to give to others, he will develop extremely limited relationships. No matter how much we teach him, a child will have few places to use what he learns if he has no social relationships.

We know adults who seem to think, "What could my child possibly give me?" The issue is not getting anything in particular from your child but getting something—attention, affection, a small attempt at learning. A substantial first step is learning to be willing to take anything back from your child. At first, accept any little movement, sounds, or words; gradually your child will get in the give-and-take habit and begin to give you more and more. So many parents and professionals have said to us, "I never thought about what I get from my child." Think about it. So much depends on it.

Subproblem

b. Domination of activity by one partner.

If one of you—you or your child—is doing most of the action or communicating when you are together, your child is probably learning very little. In order to learn, your child must have countless chances to take turns and see you take turns. Have you ever seen an adult talk in a continuous stream to a child? What did the child do—sit passively or attend elsewhere or even leave? We adults must learn to play and talk with a child, not at him.

*Is one of you
running the show?*

Think of interacting with a child as having the choice of two games: darts or ping-pong. In darts, one person takes several turns that are not directed to the other person, so that each plays at the board but not directly with the person. In ping-pong, there is a real give-and-take, where the players share turns and each turn is closely related to what the other does; the activity is reciprocal. If you find yourself or your child doing most of the interaction, try to make your time more like ping-pong.

*Don't make your
child passive.*

If adults dominate turns regularly with a child, that child is likely to become passive and expect to be allowed to do little with people. Do you ever see children who act as if they were saying, "Why bother, no one pays attention? Besides, everything will be done for me." The phenomenon of "learned helplessness" is well-documented in animals, and, in our experience, it is also a too painfully frequent habit with children. If you do too much for your child, he may learn to be helpless because you reward him for it. When you dominate turns you are shutting the door to any chances for your child's to learn with you. After many years of practice, we still have to be careful not to do too much. Some children almost beg you to take their turns for them. We must not get hooked into such helpless routines but must gently and firmly give them their turns.

Subproblem

c. Interrupted exchange of action.

*Make your interactions
more like ping-pong
and less like darts.*

When one person in an interaction dominates turns, he interrupts an information flow between the two, preventing a partnership and frustrating the other person. We encourage adults to watch themselves with children and assess the degree to which each person is free to participate on his own terms. Each person usually wants to have many chances to continue a line of action or thought, with the other person participating.

Subproblem

d. Lack of sustained contact.

Many parents and professionals are actually surprised that one of our major goals for them is to maintain more and longer contacts with their child. They genuinely seem to not believe that critical learning occurs in unexpected places. The one-shot, dead-end contact between children and adults is so epidemic that many adults see no problems with it. Of course, there are appropriate times for brief contacts and even for each person to have time alone. But ask yourself how often you see children with delays stay in an exchange with an adult longer than a couple of turns back-and-forth. One of our primary assumptions is that children's learning and socialization depends to great measure on the quantity and quality of truly interactive time with people. If you accept this, then the goal of increased, sustained contact should make considerable sense to you.

Avoid dead-end contacts.

Subproblem

e. Failure to stay in mutual activity.

Although parallel or side-by-side play is productive at times, be careful not to conclude that that kind of time together is enough. Staying on a mutual activity is essential for many kinds of learning. By mutual, we mean that the child and adult are personally engaged in doing something similar with the same things. Only to the extent that the two are in a partnership will they be affecting each other. Of course, such mutual activities can occur briefly throughout the day; they should not be thought of only as planned activities.

Learning together comes from doing things together.

It's Your Turn

COMMENT:

I thought my responsibility was to protect my child and let him play freely alone. He's always safe and free to be a child.

REPLY:

Certainly ensuring your child's safety and freedom to explore are part of your duties. Through playing alone, your child will develop some cognitive skills, but it is through give-and-take interactions that your child will learn to communicate and to become social partners. Many adults we know expect children to learn to communicate by themselves, but that is not possible. Unless your child prefers to be with others actively, not just side by side, his chances to become an habitual communicator may be slim.

Self-Assessment:
How Are You
Doing?

Rate your active togetherness with your child. Use a scale of 1 to 9, where 1 = strongly disagree and 9 = strongly agree.

_____ 1. Our time together is more side by side or parallel than genuinely together.
_____ 2. One of us is usually the giver; the other, the taker.
_____ 3. One of us usually dominates the activity.
_____ 4. Our interactions rarely continue very long.
_____ 5. We rarely stay doing the same thing together.

Child Problem

12. LOW INTERACTIVE PARTICIPATION

While we may think of communicative relationships as based on ideas and words, children find the beginnings of relationships in any actions that can be shared. Infants begin to interact as they and their caregivers move and make sounds back and forth in any ways available to them. When faced with children who are not interacting or communicating as well as we would expect for their age, we must remember that children must begin by interacting if they are to learn to communicate. The problem of low interactive participation is an extremely serious one, one that can undermine all the efforts of home and school to make a child social and communicative. It is critical for a child's caregivers to realize that every interaction is an opportunity to become social and communicative; conversely, the less the child interacts, the less he will learn to socialize and communicate.

It is easy for many adults to see a child play primarily alone and say, "He seems happy and I know play is good for him, so I suppose he'll come to me when he's ready to communicate." This widespread view that interacting with people is optional and not critical for a child may be one of the most pervasive problems facing a child with delays. Regular frequent and sustained interactions must become a habit if any delayed child is to become a social and communicative member of society.

Interaction is not an option; it is a necessity.

Subproblem

a. Low activity level.

To become social, a child must be active. A passive or lethargic child will give others few opportunities to interact with him. Other people will have to initiate to a child who may be sending signals to not interact. Every action of a child is an opportunity to learn and a potential signal for others to interact. Your relationship with your child may be unintentionally telling him that doing little is acceptable, particularly if he is accustomed to being cared for and not being expected to participate.

Subproblem

b. Purposeless or random actions.

Frequently we see children move with no apparent reason or no relationship to what others are doing. A basic principle of the **ECO** program is that every action or sound of a child can become an interaction and a communication if others react as if it were. Consequently, be aware of your child's seemingly meaningless behaviors; with care you can make them interactive by gently showing the child how to do them with you. The more you enter your child's world, act like him, and wait for him to participate, the more likely your child's behavior will become social and meaningful.

You can make your child's meaningless behaviors meaningful.

Subproblem

c. Playful but not social behavior; plays on own activity.

A disturbing sight is a number of children playing alone, with their caregivers assuming that the children are learning all they need. While playing alone is essential for many reasons—cognitive skills, self-esteem, among others—playing and interacting with people is essential for learning to be social and communicative. While playing alone, a child may be learning a great deal, but for that learning to become communicated and useful in relationships, he must practice and express it with others regularly. The kind of modeling and fine-tuning a child needs to continue learning is available mainly in interactions that are matched and responsive and that allow him freedom to act on his own motivation.

Solo play is not enough.

Subproblem

d. Passive style.

A pervasive problem that concerns us in our work with children is the passiveness that children with delays display with adults and peers alike. Throughout this book we propose that these children are victims of "learned helplessness"; that is, they have learned that interacting often faces them with impossible tasks, while acting

Beware of a passive child.

helpless allows them to maintain the status quo. Although the status quo may not be great, it is comfortable and the children have no good reason to change.

Passive children often send a signal to others not to approach and certainly not to expect much new. Unfortunately, passive children often reward caretakers with compliant behavior and little time-consuming resistance. A child who is passive is a child who is not participating in learning and frequently is not showing the extensive knowledge and skills he may have. Our goals with passive children are that they interact, physically prompted if necessary; that they learn that not only is interacting possible but also that it will provide rewards; and that they follow their own motivations.

Subproblem

e. Lack of give and take with actions.

It is understandable that some adults view communicating as the place for children and adults to build a give-and-take social habit and playing as the child's world to explore alone. But once adults realize that communications come from actions, they come to see the value of building a give-and-take habit with any actions available to the child. Consider that every time you interact back and forth with a child, you are showing him the way to communicate and to build conversational habits.

Subproblem

f. Same actions over and over.

Children whose actions, alone or with others, do not regularly change may be in developmental trouble. Children who drop endless checkers into a can, make identical movements to music, or perseverate in other ways are unlikely to be learning either cognitively or socially. Regardless of the reasons for this behavior, it is not productive and it may not represent what the child is capable of doing. Through turntaking a child learns to act and communicate with people in a give-and-take format that teaches new behaviors and that the new behaviors will be more productive than old ones.

Subproblem

g. Failure to keep attending to shared activity.

Inadequate and wandering attention is certainly one of the most frequently reported problems of children. It is essential that children with delays stay in interactions if they are to learn. Language meanings are learned through shared activities, as are the social rules for communication.

Success breeds attention.

While attention is a vast issue in learning and is discussed elsewhere in this book, a few points can be noted here. We have found that a child is likely to attend with others to the degree that (a) the child is successful, (b) the adult matches the child's interests and abilities and allows the child to participate through waiting and expecting, (c) the adult and child both have the opportunity to take the lead and control the event, (d), there is a sense of enjoyment rather than work or testing, and (e) the child has a sense that the event actively belongs to him and that he is not placed in a passive role.

Subproblem

h. Brief or deadened contacts during activity.

In the busy world of home and classroom, it is reasonable to have a brief contact that gets a job done or solves a problem, then move on to another task. Parents and teachers alike report that it takes no noticeably extra time to keep a child for one or two turns in interactions that are laced through daily routines and leisure time. With the notion that any interaction is an opportunity to communicate, we stress to adults the critical importance of teaching their children that extended interactions must be a way of life if they are to build communicative partnerships. Beyond the complex types of learning to communicate, we consistently return to a general recommendation for building interactions to "keep the child back and forth a little longer."

It's Your Turn

COMMENT:

When Jose was a baby, I felt I got a lot from him. We had the playful back-and-forth time you talk about. Now that we know he is delayed in movement and speech, I feel I need to keep giving to him, but it's not as enjoyable as before and I get bored. Jose doesn't respond much to me now.

REPLY:

It's natural to want to give as much as you can to a child with delays. Jose will learn to the extent he can participate. He needs you to give him time. Do something he can do; then wait silently for him to give you something back. Think of your job as a parent as preparing Jose to become an accepted partner with others. To do that he must be in the habit of giving as well as taking, so you must wait and expect him to give to you. This requires not only practice but a conviction that Jose must give in order to get socially and communicatively in society.

Self-Assessment:
How Are You
Doing?

Rate the interactions you have with your child and the child's interactive participation. Use a scale of 1 to 9, where 1 = strongly disagree and 9 = strongly agree.

_____ 1. My child and I interact mainly to get needs met.
_____ 2. My child dominates our time together.
_____ 3. I dominate our time together.
_____ 4. Our contacts are very brief, one or two turns.
_____ 5. I'm giving much more than I'm getting with my child.
_____ 6. I do not see how turntaking helps my child learn.
_____ 7. We take turns but only on my child's terms.
_____ 8. I have to initiate contacts if we have any.
_____ 9. We do not enjoy interacting with each other.
_____10. My child's actions have little purpose.
_____11. My child plays by himself but not with others.
_____12. My child acts passive when with others.
_____13. My child does not play back and forth.
_____14. My child does the same things over and over.
_____15. My child attends little when with others.
_____16. My child stays only briefly in interactions.

CHILD GOALS

Any behavior can
become a
communication
. . . but it must
become social first.

Almost any behavior a child can do can help him learn to communicate and use language. But before they are helpful, those behaviors must first become social, that is, done with people. Turntaking is one major way a child's behaviors become social. As a child takes turns, he learns how to behave in new ways for new reasons, based on the feedback he gets from the turns of others.

We want to stress the importance of realizing that even your child's most casual or simple behaviors mean something to him. Through turntaking, you can help him make those behaviors meaningful to others. Perhaps the only struggle we have with many parents, students, and professionals comes in helping them realize that children almost never start by doing anything "right." Whether it is a sound, a movement, a play action, or a word, children begin with little movements that only resemble the goal we have in mind. We stress that, at first, our goal is merely a great variety of action and that every movement is a tool your child can combine with other movements to build something meaningful. Again, think of your job as helping your child up a great, long staircase. Observe the little things he does at the bottom stair and then be at the next step so that he can get there.

Another surprising finding is that any action, movement, look, or sound can become a communication if we show the child he can get our attention with it (Bates, 1976). The more actions your child makes, the more different turntaking interactions you can have with him, and the more he can learn.

Child Goal

Your child needs the IRS:
Initiate
Respond
Stay interacting

13. SHOW A TURNTAKING PLAY STYLE

When a child shows a turntaking style of play he shows an awareness and willingness to give and take. He may appreciate the relationship between giving and getting. He shows he takes the responsibility in interactions to give as well as get. He knows the rules of turntaking. And while he may often not take turns (when he is acting passive or dominating interactions), in general he shows he will stay in more and more extended back-and-forth interactions. Moreover, he shows that he recognizes both the other person's right to participate and his responsibility to do so. A striking thing about this turntaking style of play is that a child can have it in his first year of life (Bullowa, 1979; Kaye, 1979). Another is that, even in later life, turntaking enables people with and without delays to build the relations needed for learning and friendship. Interaction, to be helpful, must be a two-way street, with both partners initiating, responding, and staying for more.

a. Use actions to initiate as well as respond.

We know many children who respond whenever contacted but who rarely initiate or start a contact. In turntaking, we make sure that we are not always initiating. Instead, we make ourselves interesting enough that the child starts the contact. We wait silently, showing the child we expect something. We are very careful not to allow the child to be passive, but we also realize that he is more likely to continue in a contact if it is motivating to him. What you and your child do is less important than finding something you can do together regularly.

b. Imitate others.

Perhaps a major goal for any child with delays is to become as much like normally developing children as possible. We know many children who act oblivious to what others do. For those children, learning to "do as others do" is an important goal for most learning and most certainly for communication. Unless a child uses others as models for new behavior, we can expect little progress.

Thus, we are concerned that children get in the habit of imitating the movements and communications of those around them. By imitation, we mean attempting to do what others do. It is unreasonable to expect we can "teach" a child all the play, work, and communication he needs. But if he learns to imitate others, he can learn many of those things by practicing them in spontaneous contacts.

Turntaking offers an optimal way for a child to learn to imitate. Through turntaking the child's attention is focused on the adult, making it more likely that he will imitate the way the adult performs. The adult then has the opportunity to give the child immediate feedback, showing the child again how to do it. When imitation of action or sounds is the major goal, we engage children in enjoyable turntaking games.

Beware of parrots.

Keep one general caution in mind. By imitation we do not mean direct, exact parroting of what we did. Instead, think of imitation broadly, as meaning to try to do something that another did. When you look for your child's imitations, look for any attempts resembling what you did. Be aware, though, that imitation is only one way a child should respond; he should respond with his own creative behavior as well.

Subgoal
Responding on his own is essential.

c. Respond in ways other than imitating.

As noted above, we do not want a child to act like a parrot, doing only what he sees others do. We want him to create from his own motivation as well. A child may become more willing to respond in his own ways if you respond to the things he does in positive, supportive ways that encourage him to continue doing them. If a child feels he is free to respond in his own ways, without criticism or sense of failure, he is more likely to show his own self in his responses. Be sure that your interactions with your child do not make him feel he did not succeed or live up to your goals.

Subgoal
Keeping it going is as important as doing it.

d. Keep play interactions going.

A child needs to learn not only how to take turns but also that he has the right to actively keep others interacting with him. If you show him that you expect him to stay and that staying will be enjoyable, he should learn many ways to keep you and others playing with him. Remember, if you assume the role of a play partner, rather than a director or controller, he will come to expect that he, too, should keep interactions going.

A child can keep an interaction going in many ways. He can show he expects you to stay. He can signal your turn. (Many of our children will take our hands or faces to keep us going when we are distracted from an exchange with them.) Once you establish the routine of turntaking, you will feel a rhythm that tells you "my turn, his turn, now mine again" and so on. Think again of playing a ping-pong game. After you hit the ball, you don't stop and think about whether you should continue the interaction. You automatically poise to await your turn. In the same way, your child needs to learn that being with people does not mean dead-end contacts but a balanced, back-and-forth exchange of turns in a routine that becomes an almost automatic physical habit.

Subgoal

e. Be spontaneous; enjoy play with the other.

It is not enough that your child takes turns obediently like a good little soldier. The purpose of turntaking is to build in the child a habit of enjoying interaction with others. Without genuine enjoyment and active interest, it is not reasonable to believe that your child will pursue on his own the interactions necessary for him to learn to communicate and have friendships. Many parents and professionals have reported to us how difficult it was to believe that enjoying people was more important for their child's communication than learning to make sounds and words correctly. However, once their children came to enjoy being play partners more and being students less, the adults found themselves more in contact with their children. And now they have also found that their children are learning from them as well.

f. Take turns reciprocally.

Not only does the child need to take turns but to take them reciprocally. By reciprocal, we mean that your child should do not just anything when you take a turn but should do something related in some way to what you do. For example, if you put your hat on, a reciprocal turn for your child might be to put his hat on, or to grab your hat, or to say "let's go," but not to lie down or to say "I saw Sam today."

When a child is beginning to take turns, he may do anything, because he's just getting the knack of making back-and-forth contacts. At this point, we try to base our turntaking so much on what he is able and likes to do that we soon expect him to take turns related to our turns. We show him how by making certain our turns relate meaningfully to his.

g. Show a sense of give-and-take.

When a child knows that he has to give as well as take, he has travelled a long way on the road to being a socially acceptable person. Without a habit of give-and-take, communication is unlikely to develop. More important, unless they give and take, children with delays may drive away most of the people they need for learning to communicate. Turntaking provides an easy, clear way to teach give-and-take. We begin by doing things the child can do easily and chooses to do.

COMMENT: I am a special educator responsible for training students for careers as teachers. These students expect to be teaching special skills. Do you really mean that it does not matter at first what a child does in turntaking? Isn't it important to avoid encouraging children to do wrong or immature things?

REPLY: That's a very common concern of educators, students, and parents alike. Consider two critical things. First, a child will stay and learn from us to the extent he has successes with us. The goal at first is to keep him actively with people; otherwise most social learning may be lost. Second, no one does everything "right" at first. Unless we accept little steps to the right way, he may never get there. In fact, let's be concerned about what is developmentally a reasonable step to the goal we want. You are probably quite familiar with teachers' incessant complaint that their students will not stay with them. Success-based interactions help many adults we know to keep children with them so they can learn new things.

COMMENT: I am a home teacher of delayed infants. I enjoy imitating the babies because they attend to me more and cooperate better on difficult tasks. Some of the parents tell me it looks silly and they cannot come to do it.

Enjoyment and spontaneity count.

Subgoal

Turns should make sense.

Subgoal

It's Your Turn

REPLY:

Good for you. We have a general rule for a child who is either not attending or not cooperating: When in doubt, imitate. Many times we can only wonder what a child knows or wants. When we imitate him, we are matching both what he knows and what he wants to do. Best of all, it is fun to watch the child's surprised reactions and the way in which he is drawn to stay with you. While we ordinarily try to imitate a child's desirable behaviors, there is at least one exception: crying. As long as the crying has no real basis in pain or fear, we cry, as closely as possible to the way he cries. The children we know rarely continue crying for long, and they often enjoy us getting into their worlds. As a home teacher, you might impress on parents that children must learn the habit of doing as others do and the principle that imitation is a readily available way to help build the habit. You can also educate them to the need for keeping the child interacting and the value of imitating as a way to do that.

COMMENT:

A number of children in my classroom imitate very well, but that's about the only way they respond. No one wants to be with a parrot who gives nothing of his own ideas. What can I do?

REPLY:

To answer you in a word: nothing. That is, wait for something else, for anything other than what you did. Children may continue to imitate you if you respond immediately, even when it is with a reprimand. If you are doing something new for the child, then imitation may be a very appropriate learning strategy. However, if the child can do something appropriate on his own but is just taking the easy way out, you can silently wait with anticipation for something more. He may soon learn that easy imitations will not get him far with people.

COMMENT:

I can help my 3-year-old in turns at home but when we're out shopping or visiting, I can't seem to get more than a hit-and-run exchange with him.

REPLY:

Take a lesson from Terese, who reported the same thing with Daniel, her 4-year-old with Down syndrome. She said, "I had it. I decided he had explored enough. So I decided to keep him in a shoe store looking at shoes with me for 3 minutes. He stayed and even imitated things like 'daddy shoe, mommy shoe.' I'm learning that turntaking can work anywhere when I put my mind to it."

Self-Assessment:
How Are You
Doing?

Evaluate your child's turntaking play style, using a 1 to 9 scale where 1 = strongly disagree and 9 = strongly agree.

_____ 1. My child initiates contacts regularly.
_____ 2. My child responds regularly when contacted.
_____ 3. My child interacts with a wide range of activities.
_____ 4. My child imitates others even when not asked.
_____ 5. My child takes creative turns, ones of his choosing.
_____ 6. My child genuinely enjoys back-and-forth interactions.
_____ 7. My child understands that he has to give in order to get.
_____ 8. My child actively keeps me in interactions.
_____ 9. My child actively interacts, doing things in new ways.

14. USE ACTIONS IN FUNCTIONAL AND MEANINGFUL WAYS

If ACTIONS become THOUGHTS and thoughts become WORDS, as Piaget (1952) eloquently argued, then the more actions a child has and uses socially, the more thoughts and words he is likely to develop. One of our first questions when we assess a child is, "What is he doing?" We assume that the more a child does the more he knows, and thus the more he has to communicate about. In our work, we take care to point out to parents and professionals the child's actions and sounds that often go unnoticed. These are the seeds of future communications. The more sensitively we notice a child's little actions and sounds, the more likely the child is to make them again and perhaps even to make them more like our own.

Therefore, when an adult tells us, "I can't think of what to do with my child," we say, "First look at what he is doing, follow his lead, and then do something that keeps him doing his things with you."

a. Use a variety of actions.

A disturbing sight is a child who plays in the same ways with many objects. He must learn that different things require different actions, but he must not be taught to do things in the "correct adult" ways at first. Any new action, if safe, is good for learning. You can encourage your child to explore actions and sounds by playing around with changing them yourself. If a child is to learn the countless combinations of actions and sounds he needs to become a communicator, he must learn that it is not only acceptable but necessary to experiment fully with the actions and sounds he already has. Therefore, interact with him in ways that increase, rather than decrease, his attempts to make action and sounds with you. Keep doing whatever you do when your child continues to act and sound, and consider reducing what you do when he reduces his actions and sounds.

b. Show functionality and meaningfulness of actions.

Only after your child can perform a range of actions and sounds randomly or with little apparent purpose should you begin to look for purpose and meaning in his behavior. A child is likely to perform actions meaningfully if he has already explored these actions freely and discovered personal meanings and uses for them. The more meaningful his actions, the more ideas he may have. And it is his playful ideas that may be the easiest things he can first communicate about.

It is important to realize that it does not matter so much if your child uses things in the right way as that he tries to do something purposefully. Here is another skill to observe. We often begin playing with a child in the old ways he plays with things, so that he attends to us, and then we gradually show him new ways. A child who uses a knife as a spoon does have a meaning in his actions. We might use the knife the way he does, then show how it can cut. Then we may give him something that can be cut and hold up the knife. Not only does he learn a new meaning this way, he learns a way to communicate about cutting.

c. Use actions symbolically; make one thing stand for another.

We are often excited when a child imitates or—better yet—shows pretend-play. Eventually we hope for words or gestures and signs, which are symbols. A symbol is anything that stands for or represents something else. So when a child takes a paper as a blanket for putting her doll to bed, she is showing symbolic behavior. She can make the paper stand in for a blanket, just as words will later stand for other things.

If we allow anything to be a symbol for anything else, however unexpected, children enjoy the game and often stay for more. Surprises appear to be reinforcing for many children; they stay and signal us to do more. We find that we can keep a child taking turns by doing a variety of symbolic play even when the child is not yet symbolic in his own play. As a child eventually begins to use old actions for new meanings, he is freed from his learned set of skills and can multiply them. Then his interactions become more flexible, communicative, and rewarding to both him and his partner.

Subgoal

d. Use actions appropriate to a variety of play.

Ask yourself this question: Does my child have the physical skills to do what I am expecting him to do? In our daily routines or enthusiastic play, we often find that we do things a child could not try to do. We are several steps ahead of him on that learning staircase. Once you attend carefully to your child's skills, you can begin to match your level of behavior to his. Then when you are doing things he can do, you are likely to find him staying with you longer and trying to do what you do.

It's Your Turn

COMMENT:

Joni always wants to be with me, but she seems satisfied doing old things that don't seem to go anywhere. Should I be satisfied with this?

REPLY:

No. Unless Joni is changing and doing more meaningful things with her play, she may be getting little more than self-stimulation. Certainly it cannot be very rewarding for you. People are not likely to stay interacting with a boring companion. With children like Joni, we begin by waiting for "something, anything, new." It may be a real effort for Joni to change; so be sure to show her a next step that she can do, then wait. You may have to wait beyond her old actions, showing her she will get more if she gives more. Remember any change should be supported, then carefully show her new ways.

COMMENT:

I just don't know how to play. I don't play with the things Willie does; how is it that he should play?

REPLY:

Don't be concerned about the "right" way to play. Children learn by exploring and experimenting; follow his lead, watch him, and then explore and experiment yourself. Be sure you are genuinely playing too, not just showing him how. The more you get into making play of your time together, the more new things will come to you. Just be sure you change what you do and do things Willie can do.

*Self-Assessment:
How Are You
Doing?*

Use a 1 to 9 scale to assess your child's everyday actions. Let 1 = strongly disagree and 9 = strongly agree.

_____ 1. My child plays with a wide variety of objects.

_____ 2. My child plays with the same object in more than one way.

_____ 3. My child uses objects functionally.
_____ 4. My child plays meaningfully with many things.
_____ 5. My child likes pretend-play.

ADULT STRATEGIES

How can you
become a
turntaking partner
with your child?
What can you do to
help your child be
socially interactive?

To get your child into a turntaking habit, you will need to give him time and show him you expect something. You will also need to do things he can do and to be more interesting than the things distracting him. Beyond these strategies, it will help if you come to believe that your child must stay in back-and-forth interactions in order to learn from others. In observing hundreds of adults with a wide range of children, we have known few who believed in the importance of their children staying in interactions with them. One-shot and one-sided contacts often seem enough to satisfy the immediate needs of both adult and child. The longer-term needs for learning and socializing seem to be ignored.

How can you help
your child be
interactive through
turntaking?

Consequently, if we had to recommend only one tactic to help a child socialize and communicate, it would be "keep the child interacting with you." Unless you increase your turntaking and keep your child with you more, the specifics may not matter much because they will have no place to grow. Keep your child interacting. You will get to know him better and you will learn what you can do to help him communicate and learn from others.

The first specific strategy we need to discuss covers a very important **ECO** principle: maintaining and balancing turntaking.

Adult Strategy

15. MAINTAIN AND BALANCE TURNTAKING.

A first step in becoming turntaking partners is to come to believe that your child will learn from you and others easily if you do two basic things: maintain and balance turntaking. Maintaining turntaking simply means keeping your child in little, back-and-forth exchanges as a natural course of your time together. The longer you go back-and-forth when you interact, the more your child learns. If you see every back-and-forth contact as another chance to communicate, you will settle into a relaxed habit of actively keeping your child with you.

Balancing turns means trying to make sure that each of you do about as much as the other. Of course, it is appropriate to do more than your child at certain times, such as when you are feeding, helping, and comforting your child. But even in those times, your child is more likely to attend to you and learn from you if he has a chance to take his turns.

Substrategy

a. Initiate contacts.

Contact your
child just for the
sake of it.

In a busy world, we are often grateful when our children let us alone. Many parents and other adults respond well to their child's needs, but they do not often make contacts just for their own sake. Initiating contacts with your child is important because unless you show him that small, casual contacts are desirable to you, he may not come to value them. By contacting your child only when there is a specific need, your child may come to see contacts with people as tied to immediate needs and not as having value for their own sake. Furthermore, there will simply not be enough of them to build a social habit.

You may say, "I don't know what to contact him for." You don't have to have a reason. Why do you contact a friend? Often just to be with him or her. Contact your child just to show you care and to let him know that contacting others is important. After all, that's how we make friends and learn. When watching television, for example, you could point and laugh at a character and then wait for your child to respond. Some parents allow their delayed child to walk right past them without a comment, yet they tell us they would not allow their other children to avoid a contact.

Substrategy

b. Respond to the child's contacts.

Get into the habit of responding often when your child contacts you. It need not take more than a moment. Try to respond when you see your child doing little things, such as looking out the window or mumbling to himself, even if they are trivial or meaningless to you. Again, do not worry about the correctness of what he's doing, as long as it is safe and socially acceptable. Now is not the time for concern about "right and wrong"; now is the time for back-and-forth exchange. Be sure to respond simply and positively, in a way that encourages him to come back for more. Don't forget that your responses will teach him to do more with people and eventually to do those things to communicate with you.

Sensitively respond in ways that get him back.

Substrategy

c. Keep the child doing more.

While most children do not need to be physically kept for another turn, some do. Do not be reluctant to be physical in keeping your child for a couple more turns. Realize that if he avoids staying with you, he is avoiding learning. Just as you do not let him avoid school or rest, don't let him avoid staying with people. Beyond holding him with you in a friendly but secure way, you can also keep him with you by being more interesting than his distractions, by doing things he can already do, and by showing him you expect him to do something. Become the kind of person that he wants to stay with and expects to succeed with. Children seem to stay in turntaking if they know they will succeed and be accepted.

Unless he stays, he won't learn from you.

How long should he stay? It is important not to overdo it. Staying in turns must not mean a lot of work or loss of good times for the child or you. Staying together a long time is not the goal. Instead, staying just a little longer than usual will become a social habit for both of you if it happens often and unexpectedly. This is the rule we use in our work: When one of you begins to lose interest, keep the child for one or two more quick turns. Then let the child off to his own choices. In this way, your child will learn that staying a little more with people lets him get to do what he wants. This lesson is critical if a child is to become socially acceptable.

Being social takes lots of successful practice.

Substrategy

d. Expect the child to stay.

Once you believe in the lasting importance of your child staying in contacts, you will regularly begin to expect your child to stay, just as you expect your friends to talk. And once you realize that your child owes you attention and contact, you

Go for one more
turn than usual.

will no longer shrug it off when he ignores or leaves you. You probably do not accept giving without receiving in your other relationships, so do not accept it with your child. If you do, he may become just the kind of person you avoid in your social life. The major goal is to help your child act in ways that encourage others to accept him into their worlds. People are accepted to the degree that they are able to give as much as they get.

Substrategy

Do as much as your
child and wait.

e. Balance turns with the child.

In healthy relationships people usually want the chance to give as well as take. Two common problems with children with delays are being passive and doing much less than they can. When adults do considerably more than their children, the children may become passive and miss countless opportunities to learn. Balancing things means allowing your child as many chances to take a turn as you allow yourself. Be sure your child learns that, in most cases, he will have both your attention and the time he needs to participate. On the other hand, if your child dominates the interactions, show him he must allow others their turns. You may actually have to intrude into his flow and show him that you will take your turns when due. Balancing turns means no less than teaching the child the respect that people deserve, without which he will not be allowed into the social relationships we want for him.

It's Your Turn

COMMENT:

In the real world, I don't see a lot of even one-for-one turntaking. If I did that with my child, I'd feel like a robot. It seems unrealistic to me.

REPLY:

Thanks for saying that. Whenever we stress something like turntaking or matching, many people get the message to be "do it all the time, or else." That kind of stress is the last thing you need when you have a child with special needs.

You're right when you say that you rarely see one-to-one turntaking in natural relations. What you do see is frequent give-and-take exchanges in which both adult and child take part, each initiating and responding, each having many chances to have his "say" and respond sensitively to the other. Infants and parents probbably do more one-for-one turntaking than anyone else; whenever you begin a new skill you begin simple and easy. That is what we are encouraging you to do. Not all the time, but frequent back-and-forth exchanges will help your child be more attentive, more experimental with people, and more acceptable to others whom he needs for many kinds of learning.

Don't pressure yourself to take turns perfectly; there's no such thing. Rather, ask yourself a few questions: Is my child staying with me longer than he used to? Is he giving as well as taking, at least more often than before? Am I keeping him in casual interactions for more turns as time goes on? In terms of what to do in the turns, fit it into your life. If you're tired or busy (often both), don't think about it; just keep him for a couple of turns doing absolutely anything. Don't make it a job; make it fun with no "right and wrong"; that way each of you will be more likely to come back to each other. And, remember, that is where your child will learn to communicate.

COMMENT:

What do you mean by "balance turns"? I have 12 children in my class. Not the best juggler could balance anything in my class.

REPLY:

Again, as in the last question, think "Are interactions more balanced than before?" Actually, you can record how often children initiate, respond, and how many turns they stay. Remember that balanced turntaking is useful for learning almost anything but meditation. The more your child genuinely interacts with you, the more he will learn many things other than communication. Turntaking will help your children socially use the things you teach them. We hope you come to see interactive turntaking not as another job but as a way to get many of your other jobs done. Remember, your job as a teacher is not just to get a child to learn but to get him to use what he learns with people. That's what maintaining a child a little longer in turns is for.

Self-Assessment: How Are You Doing?

Rate the following statements on a scale of 1 to 9 where 1 = never or very poorly, 5 = occasionally or fairly well, and 9 = always or extremely well. Do this over time so you can watch your progress.

_____ 1. I initiate contacts with my child.
_____ 2. My child initiates contacts with me.
_____ 3. I respond to what my child does even when he's not directing it to me.
_____ 4. My child responds to what I do, even if I do not direct it to him.
_____ 5. I am comfortable keeping my child for more turns.
_____ 6. My child tries to keep me for more turns.
_____ 7. I regularly expect my child to stay interacting.
_____ 8. My child expects me to stay interacting.
_____ 9. I take my share of turns, no more or less.
_____10. My child takes his share of turns, no more or less.

Adult Strategy

16. MATCH THE CHILD'S BEHAVIOR

Researchers widely support our regular observation that children learn more easily from tasks they are likely to be able to do (Hunt, 1961; Mahoney, 1988; Piaget, 1952; Vygotsky, 1962). While this may sound like common sense, we regularly see adults do something in play or communication that is far beyond the child's reach. Then we also see the child fail to try and develop a habit of avoiding interactions.

Matching is perhaps the most effective strategy you can use with your child, regardless of his level. By matching we mean acting and communicating with your child in a way that he can do. Consider again the image of a staircase with your skills at the top and your child's at the bottom. To show him the next step, you must get to his step or a little step above his. There you do something that he can do and that he shows some interest in. What then? Wait. Think of MATCH AND WAIT as one extremely effective, natural teaching package for helping your child do more, stay with you, and become more like the people around him.

Of course, some of the time you will simply want to be your adult self. Go ahead. Just keep in mind that the more you can act like your child, in natural give-and-take, the more he is likely to learn many things from you (such as how to communicate). Think of matching as fine tuning yourself to your child's skills. Bruner (1983), a widely respected child psychologist who has studied how children learn to think and socialize, has concluded that parents and other caregivers can help a child communicate by providing a certain kind of personal support. The support he has recommended is a playful turntaking habit in which the adult regularly does things that the child can already do but that also challenge him a little.

Matching means being the kind of person your child can become.

Educators know that they succeed more when they give a child a task within his capabilities (Hunt, 1961). But when the task is the social one of mastering what another person does, we adults often forget the basic learning principle of matching. When your child's social or communication development concerns you, then the task to be matched to the child is another person. You need to learn to fine tune yourself to your child's actions and communications so that he can learn from you. Beware not to expect to see immediate effects every time, because sometimes your child may store the action and use it later. The more directly you relate your action to your child's actions, the more likely your child is to use it in the future.

Matching allows the child to be competent

The rule-of-thumb in matching is to learn to "be the kind of person your child can soon be." Remember that when you are together you are always teaching your child something, like it or not. The more that your child is able to do what you do, the more natural a learning and communicating partner he is likely to become.

Substrategy

a. Act and communicate close to the child's level.
Remember to match your physical movements, play activities, and communications. We know adults who can easily play the way their child does but who communicate far differently. They find it difficult to decrease their output of words and increase their sounds and movements to match the ways their child communicates. It's important to realize that matching does not always mean doing less than you usually do. Matching frequently requires doing more, making more of the natural sounds and movements that are the child's critical steps to communication.

Look and sound like your child.

If you fail to match your child's developmental steps, whether unclear sounds or gestures or signs, you may discourage him from making those important next attempts. You don't have to be a slave to your child, matching all the time. But you should begin by matching him when you want him to stay with you. And observe then how much more he gives you than when you mismatch or fail to respond.

Substrategy

b. Use actions and sounds similar to the child's.
If you come to see your child's individual sounds and actions as a chance for you to show him a next step or a step just learned, you will soon get into the habit of doing what he can do. However uncomfortable or silly it feels at first, we find we get much more from a child if we do his actions and make his sounds. This way, children attend more and realize they can have successes with you. Once you become a signal for success to your child, he will be willing to stay and do a little more.

Substrategy

c. Use communications similar to the child's.
We have already recommended that you play like your child. Now we want you to pay attention to the ways he communicates, that is, sends messages or receives

information. You can greatly help your child by using actions and sounds he has, regardless of how much sense they make, in your attempts to communicate with him. Then you can show him the next step.

Substrategy

d. Respond to some child actions using matched communication.

Almost any behavior can communicate something. When your child does something, communicate about it to him—using his level of communication. He may be more likely to communicate about something he just did if you show him an easy way to communicate about it. Feel free to communicate with actions or sounds if that's where your child is.

Substrategy

e. Respond to some communications using matched action with communication.

Respect your child's natural interest in the easier and more concrete actions rather than verbalizations. When he communicates, try to respond with actions and movements that help him attend to your communication. When you unite action and communication, the child may see your meaning more clearly. Think of your whole body, movements and sounds, as a lesson for your child.

It's Your Turn

COMMENT:

I am the father of an autistic-like six-year-old boy, Alex. My wife tries to get me to do this "matching" with him. I have to be honest. Acting like my child is embarrassing. I am uncomfortable doing it and it just seems wrong.

REPLY:

We know many people who say the same thing. Once you come to believe that your child will learn from you to the extent you do things he can do, being childlike will feel more natural. You have the choice. You can feel comfortable acting like an adult but get little from your child, or you can match your child and get the reward of his increased interactions with you. You might try this experiment: Practice moving back and forth from matching your child to acting very adult-like. Do this on the same activities, and observe what your child does in each case. If your child is used to being passive, it may take a while for him to do more when you match him, but give the experiment enough time. You'll be impressed with the results of matching. Let the reward of your child's increased behaviors be the focus; it should gradually distract you from your sense of discomfort.

COMMENT:

As a language therapist I found it hard to match at first. Now my problem is helping teachers and parents keep doing it habitually. Any ideas?

REPLY:

Matching is often hard for adults—perhaps, in part, because it is similar to being in a foreign culture. To be effective with children, we must be able to shift readily from an adult culture to their culture. And we must learn how to build a staircase of skills between our world and theirs. You need to educate the people you serve to the reality that children develop in small steps, steps that can be increased gradually through matching. To make matching reinforcing, show the teachers and parents how much more children make of these developmental steps when they match than when they mismatch and act adultlike. The point here is to show them that matching frequently gets more from the child of what the child should be doing than adult models get. Let the child lead you into an interactive style.

Self-Assessment:
Matching

Rate the following statements on a scale of 1 to 9 where 1 = never or very poorly, 5 = occasionally or fairly well, and 9 = always or extremely well. Do this over time so you can watch your progress.

_____ 1. I act in ways my child can do.
_____ 2. I communicate in ways my child can do.
_____ 3. I change my behavior if my child does not respond.
_____ 4. My behavior shows my child what to do next.
_____ 5. I feel more successful when I act like my child.

Adult Strategy

Wait silently with expectation.

17. WAIT, SIGNAL, AND EXPECT

Adults often move, think, and communicate much faster or in larger pieces than children do. Realizing this helps us to see how difficult we make it for the child to take his turn. Waiting is one of the first, but most difficult, strategies adults must master. Here is a rule we find extremely effective for both spontaneous and intentional contacts with children: "Take one turn, then wait silently for your child to take a turn."

In adult conversations, we rarely wait when a partner stops talking or interacting. Some powerful social rule seems to compel adults to fill the silence immediately. We have observed that most of the times we allow ourselves to wait silently are times of strong negative or positive emotion. Consequently, adults need to realize that every time they fail to wait with a child, they deny him an opportunity to learn. You would never think of eating your child's food every time he was slow to eat. Yet your child needs opportunities to interact almost as much as he needs food.

The time you wait is the time your child can learn.

When adults fail to wait, their dominating behavior actually appears to suppress the child's attempts, even convincing him that no one values what he can do. Waiting shows the child that adults value his behavior enough to give him time to do it. Once adults do learn to wait, they are often rewarded by seeing the child do things they did not know he could do. Many children have hidden talents that they will show you if you wait and give them the time they need to process and deliver.

What does it take to wait effectively?

Waiting is often difficult for adults because taking an extra turn without waiting is so easy, almost reflexive. Add to this the child's physical or cognitive difficulty in taking his turn, and it is clear why waiting requires extra effort for adults. One notion that may help is to realize that a child needs to act in order to learn; listening to you is not enough. Consequently one rule may help you wait: "Communicate for a response." A vital reason to communicate is to get a response, not only to plug in your information.

Communicate and wait for a response.

a. Allow sufficient time and cues for the child to take a turn.

Substrategy

How long should I wait? This frequent question has no single answer. Watch your child carefully to see if he is considering a turn. If your child is used to you doing most of the work in an interaction, he may wait you out at first, expecting you to do his turn. The child often has to work a little to take a turn, and he might welcome your saving him the work. But persist, and let him know he has to do something to get something.

Wait until something happens.

The child must
see you expect
something.

b. Wait silently, showing anticipation for the child's turn.

Even when you play a game with a child, you should wait silently. If you talk when it is your child's turn, he may not take his or you may not attend to what he's doing. Your face and body should not be silent, but alive with expression, eagerly expecting something and showing you will accept what your child gives. With arms out or eyes wide, you can show him that you genuinely want something from him. By waiting, you show, too, that you respect the pace at which he is able to give it to you.

c. Signal and prompt when necessary to keep the child interacting.

After waiting long enough to judge that your child may be stuck, you can gently signal or prompt a turn. Signalling can involve pointing or any exaggerated movement for getting him back into the interaction. Prompting involves actually assisting him in taking a turn. We find that usually only a little physical prompting is necessary to get turntaking resumed. We regularly find that children dislike being physically controlled and will cooperate in order to avoid being prompted. Just a signal that you might prompt him is enough to stimulate his turns. More positively, your child simply does not know what to do on some turns and a gentle, friendly prompt may show him how.

d. Signal and prompt for your own turn when the child doesn't allow it.

You may find that adults are not the only ones who dominate interactions. Once a child gets on a roll, it is as difficult to maintain a good interaction as when an eager teacher or parent runs the show. You need to let your child know that you need your turns too. Be sure not to allow your child to become the kind of person who dominates others' time without giving them a chance to interact. Remember, one of our major goals for any child is to be accepted into some society of people who share with each other. Ask yourself, "Is my child the kind of person who shows respect for others' rights to take a turn and waits for them to do their part?" You may think it inconsiderate to interrupt your child's string of turns, but it is more unfair to teach him socially unacceptable behavior.

If your child keeps taking turns, insensitive to your part in the interaction, then signal your turn by pointing to yourself or by intruding with your turn. Signal your child to wait with an extended palm, or even gently restrain him from another turn until you've taken yours quickly. Teach the important lesson that others will accept him only if he is fair and allows them to participate. Some children we know stay on their own track, with no apparent concern for what others want. If such a child learns to take turns with others, he will not only give them what they need but may also find himself more widely accepted in society.

It's Your Turn

COMMENT:

My problem is that when I do wait for Kamala, she often starts to leave or does something off the topic. Does she have an attention disorder?

REPLY:

Begin by convincing yourself that Kamala must stay with you some of the time. Then gently keep her there for just another turn or two before you let her go. She will learn that she can have her way if she stays with others.

But keeping her is not enough. Before you assume the attention problem lies in your daughter alone, consider that she may naturally go to the things she finds most interesting and leave the boring ones. You need to be more interesting than the things that distract her. We hear so much about attention disorders, but we seem to ignore the powerful likelihood that many children fail to keep attending because we or the tasks we give them just do not motivate them to stay. If you play a rigid teacher role, we predict your child will show more attention problems than if you carefully explore the kinds of things that do keep her attention.

COMMENT: I am generally uncomfortable in silence with people. When I wait with my child, I can hardly tolerate the silence. I feel compelled to talk or do something for my child.

REPLY: You are certainly not alone. While silence may be golden, it is also disconcerting. As you wait, there's plenty to do; watch your child with genuine interest. Use the quiet time to get to know him better—his movements, interests. Take a new look at him. You may see some things that will help you know what to do next, to entice him to stay with you.

COMMENT: I am a language clinician. One day in a classroom I was waiting several times for a child to take her turns. Our principal observed for a while and then asked me later, "Why were you doing so little? Shouldn't language people talk a lot?" I suspected that words alone would not convince her that what looked like nothing was an important part of treatment. So I asked her to observe me again. That day I switched from waiting for several turns to dominating the turns. She even tried to wait with the child. In both cases, the child interacted more when we waited. Now I hear the principal encouraging teachers to "wait a little more."

REPLY: Great work. Want a job?

Self-Assessment:
Waiting

Rate the following statements on a scale of 1 to 9 where 1 = never or very poorly, 5 = occasionally or fairly well, and 9 = always or extremely well. Do this over time so you can watch your progress.

____ 1. I wait silently for my child to take his turns.
____ 2. I am comfortable waiting for my child's turns.
____ 3. My child interacts more when I wait.
____ 4. I can keep my child a little longer when he wants to leave.

Adult Strategy

18. IMITATE AND ANIMATE

After more than 20 years of working with children with delays, we keep relying on one strategy when a child is not interacting with us: imitation. When we imitate, rarely do we fail to get the child's attention, and often he begins interacting again. Remember that imitating means doing anything (safe, that is) the child is doing. Imitation is one of the most extensively documented strategies parents use to maintain their infants' play (Brazelton, 1974; Greenspan, 1985) and preverbal communication (Bullowa, 1979; Siegel-Causey, Ernst, & Guess, 1987). Although imitating a child appears to facilitate social play, it also supports his cognitive development and strengthens his motivation to cooperate with people.

Often we adults feel at a loss for what a child does know and what motivates him. Nothing seems to work. Because the child does know his own behavior, imitating creates a big advantage because we are then doing something he already knows how to do. Thus we are setting him up for success. Since imitating him involves doing something he knows, we are matching his thinking. And if we assume he is motivated to do what he does, then imitating him is also doing something he likes to do. Of course, our goal is not to follow him around like a parrot, but rather to keep him with us and gradually do more independent things.

We often scatter our imitations throughout our time with children to help them practice unfamiliar forms and learn new ones (Peter, 1983; Snow et al., 1984). We find that by spontaneously doing imitation routines, the children experience successes that motivate them to be with people and come closer to our ways of doing things than when we put ourselves into student-teacher roles.

Substrategy

a. Show the child to do as others do.

Imitation is flattering.

We frequently see children ignoring the people around them; they appear to have little value for doing as others do. We are not interested in a child rotely imitating what he sees and hears. But we do want him to begin to operate by the indispensible rule of natural social learning: "Do as others do." That is, he must learn to follow the spontaneous models of people around him. There is simply not enough time and energy to teach him directly all he needs to know; he must learn from his incidental contacts with people.

We expect that, by our imitating a child, he will come to imitate us, or generally act in the ways we do. It can be a genuine pleasure to get back from a child some of our models for him, perhaps because "imitation is the highest form of flattery." For the same reason, imitation may be a critical skill that helps the child become motivating to others.

Substrategy

b. Play in childlike ways.

Playing like a child involves much more creative and enjoyable activities than imitation alone. We have found that, when we are more playful and childlike, our children are more likely to attend, stay, and change in our direction. We know many parents, teachers, and teachers in training who, at first, were quite reluctant to become childlike. Their excuses included "embarrassing," uncomfortable," "inappropriate," "wrong," and even "a waste of my education." But once they realized that their being childlike stimulated their children to give them more and to progress faster, they grew to enjoy it and carry it out with confidence and inventiveness. Many came to feel that being childlike was not just a responsibility, but was actually fun. It even made them friends with the children. Some adults feared they would lose the control they thought they needed as professionals, but just the reverse happened. When they became childlike they were more motivating to their children than when they assumed adult roles, and so the children would do more for them and try to act like them.

Substrategy

c. Act and vocalize with animation.

Do you ever wonder why cartoons are so popular with children? They are usually playful, of course, but another important quality is being unpredictable. They show the world in surprising ways, and children often pay more attention and enjoy it more when unexpected things happen. When we display exaggerated and unpredictable sounds and movements, children attend and participate more than if we act reserved. Being animated is one way to be more interesting than the child's distractions.

Substrategy

d. Imitate some child action and sound.

One effective way to get into your child's world is to imitate him. He will be pleased and you will have a better sense of what he is and is not doing. Imitating him actually brings his world into your physical experience, making it easy for you to interpret your children's experiences as if they were yours. The more you feel of what the child experiences, the more you can know how to keep him with you.

Substrategy

e. Show relaxed enjoyment.

Being fun and interesting will probably work best if you are relaxed and not intent on getting some job done. After all, the point of being animated is to be more fun and interesting to your child than all the distractions around him. Be the kind of person you probably like to be with—one who accepts what you do, follows your lead, makes few demands, and gives you freedom to do what you like at times. Relaxed does not mean anything goes, however. Keep your child interacting. Being relaxed and enjoyable works much more effectively than force to keep a child interacting and genuinely participating.

Self-Assessment:
How Are You
Doing?

Rate the following statements on a scale of 1 to 9 where 1 = never or very poorly, 5 = occasionally or fairly well, and 9 = always or extremely well. Do this over time so you can watch your progress.

_____ 1. I imitate my child's actions.
_____ 2. I imitate my child's communications.
_____ 3. I am more interesting than my child's distractions.
_____ 4. I keep my child attending to me when he becomes distracted.
_____ 5. When I imitate him, he stays interacting more.
_____ 6. When I am animated and playful, he stays more.

CONCLUSION

After hearing so much about turntaking, you may be wondering when we get to communicating. We have found that once adults and children are taking turns now and then throughout their days, each becomes more sensitive and responsive to the other. Thus the stage is set to allow communications of many kinds to develop. As you begin reading upcoming ideas on communication, do not put turntaking behind you. You will find that what you have learned about turntaking will help you interact and communicate with your child in ways that should make it easy and enjoyable for him to communicate with you. You will also learn that turntaking allows your child the practice and feedback he needs to become a habitual communicator.

Sample Resources for Becoming Turntaking Partners

ECOScale: Becoming Turntaking Partners
ECO Tutor: Becoming Turntaking Partners
ECO Link: Becoming Turntaking Partners
Conversation Routine
IEP/Problem Solver
ECO Practice Plan and Record

BECOMING TURNTAKING PARTNERS

INTERACTIVE GOALS

10. Become turntaking partners.
    a. Keep interaction going back and forth between the two.
    b. Share in choice of activity.
    c. Initiate as well as respond.
    d. Give as well as take with action.

INTERACTIVE PROBLEMS

11. Lack of active togetherness.
    a. Limited give-and-take style.
    b. Domination of activity by one partner.
    c. Interrupted exchange of action.
    d. Lack of sustained contact.
    e. Failure to stay in mutual activity.

CHILD PROBLEM

12. Low interactive participation.
    a. Low activity level.
    b. Purposeless or random actions.
    c. Playful but not social behavior; plays on own activity.
    d. Passive style.
    e. Lack of give-and-take with actions.
    f. Same actions over and over.
    g. Failure to keep attending to a shared activity.
    h. Brief or deadend contacts during activity.

CHILD GOALS

13. Show a turntaking play style.
    a. Use actions to initiate as well as respond.
    b. Imitate others.
    c. Respond in ways other than imitating.
    d. Keep play interactions going.
    e. Be spontaneous; enjoy play with the other.
    f. Take turns reciprocally.
    g. Show a sense of give-and-take.
14. Use actions in functional and meaningful ways.
    a. Use a variety of actions.
    b. Show functionality and meaningfulness of actions.
    c. Use actions symbolically; make one thing stand for another.
    d. Use actions appropriate to a variety of play.

15. Maintain and balance turntaking.
    a. Initiate contacts.
    b. Respond to the child's contacts.
    c. Keep the child doing more.
    d. Expect the child to stay.
    e. Balance turns with the child.
16. Match the child's behavior.
    a. Act and communicate close to the child's level.
    b. Use actions and sounds similar to the child's.
    c. Use communications similar to the child's.
    d. Respond to some child actions using matched communication.
    e. Respond to some communications using matched action with communication.
17. Wait, signal, and expect.
    a. Allow sufficient time and cues for the child to take a turn.
    b. Wait silently, showing anticipation for the child's turn.
    c. Signal and prompt when necessary to keep the child interacting.
    d. Signal and prompt for your own turn when the child doesn't allow it.
18. Imitate and animate.
    a. Show the child to do as others do.
    b. Play in childlike ways.
    c. Act and vocalize with animation.
    d. Imitate some child action and sound.
    e. Show relaxed enjoyment.

ECO Tutor Interactive Goal: Becoming Turntaking Partners (Verbal)

What Is It? — Turntaking partners are people who habitually interact with each other in balanced and reciprocal ways. They are balanced in the sense that neither person does a great deal more than the other, at least at times. Similarly, each person gets to take the lead and genuinely influence what the other does. The key is not precise turntaking, but a habit of keeping interactions going gradually longer and in more situations as the child develops. The primary goal, then, is to "keep your child in an interaction for one turn longer than usual." When you consider every additional turn as a chance to learn to be social and communicative, the goal of keeping interactions going should become naturally motivating for you.

How To Become Turntaking Partners
— Interactions go back and forth between the two.
— Partners share in the choice of activity.
— Both partners initiate as well as respond.
— Both partners give as well as take with actions.

The first step in becoming turntaking partners with children is to appreciate, at a deep level, that your child needs such relationships to develop social and communicative skills. Infants and parents do it in the first months of life. Almost every child we know can do it if he has willing adults. A second step is to be rewarded by maintaining your child's contact regardless of what he is doing. Once you are willing to stay interacting at your child's level, he will likely stay and learn with you. A third step is to realize that turntaking is not a task but a way to be with your child. As a turntaking partner, you will see your role as teaching your child to give and take, not only to take. While you will not feel turntaking is necessary all the time, you will regularly ask yourself questions like: Am I getting from being mommy as well as giving? Are we staying in longer interactions? Is our time together an easy give-and-take or a strained push and pull?

LESS LIKE THIS

Kyle:	(Dumps tin men out of bag.)
Uncle:	"You've got lots of men there. You have old men. I see some little boys. Where are the girls?"
Kyle:	(Makes two men march.)
Uncle:	"Where are they going?"
Kyle:	(Marches to the couch.)
Uncle:	"I think they're on a battle front. Wonder if they'll win the war."
Kyle:	(Marches up the couch.) "Up, up."
Uncle:	"I still don't know where they are going."
Kyle:	(Lays the toys down, making the sleep sign.)

MORE LIKE THIS

Kyle:	(Dumps tin men out of bag.)
Uncle:	"Wow."
Kyle:	(Gives uncle some of the toys.)
Uncle:	(Makes two toys march.)
Kyle:	(Follows uncle's men with his own; points to couch.) "Up."
Uncle:	(Leads the march up the couch.) "Up we go."
Kyle:	"Up go." (Lays men down; makes a hand-to-head signal for sleep.)
Uncle:	"Time to sleep." (Snores.)
Kyle:	(Snores; pops up.) "Up, cereal."
Uncle:	"Breakfast for the men."

Why Less?

In the Less Like This example, Kyle and his uncle show little partnership. They both react to the toy men but they are on their own separate tracks. Their turntaking is either very brief and not reciprocally related to each other or the uncle dominates the talk. Each seems to be playing or talking to himself. The uncle's turns are unlikely to teach the child much since they miss the child's activity. They operate on two topics, one playing the game, the other talking about the destination.

Why More?

In the More Like This example, Kyle's uncle is playing directly within the child's play world. Kyle rewards him by paying him more attention. There is an easy flow with each person getting as well as giving. Neither person dominates the activity or ideas. Each shares the control and initiates and responds fairly equally. In this partnership, staying interacting seems more important than getting any job done, as in the first example.

Turntaking partners are more likely to be regularly learning from each other than people in imbalanced relationships. In society, your child will build friendships and learn from others to the extent he can give and take with them. Children with delays often stay briefly in interactions, missing a world of opportunities for learning and companionship. If your child is a turntaking partner with you, he is more likely to know how to do it elsewhere. If your child communicates less than he knows, turntaking is a powerful skill for him to show what he knows. Turntaking is not something to learn for itself. It is an easy way your child can learn many things, especially people skills.

Exact one-to-one turntaking is certainly not feasible or desirable all the time, but it is a useful way to get interactions going. In a turntaking partnership, the goal is to average a give and take, where each person has substantial opportunities to interact. Without regular social turntaking and maintained interactions, all the value of cognitive play and language teaching may be lost if both the child and his significant people are not committed to interacting in intimate and extended give-and-take ways.

ECO Link

Becoming Turntaking Partners
HOW YOU CAN HELP A CHILD LEARN TO INTERACT

HOW DO YOU AND YOUR CHILD INTERACT THROUGH TURNTAKING?

1. When you and your child interact, do you use a back-and-forth style, rather than a one-sided style?
2. Do each of you take a turn and then wait for the other?
3. Do you try to keep the other person interacting with you?
4. Do you regularly give as well as take with each other? Are you both initiating as well as responding?
5. Do each of you share in the choice and direction of your interactions?
6. Do you take turns with both actions and communications?
7. Do you take turns in various settings, such as caretaking, learning, play, spontaneous contacts, and daily routines?
8. Do your interactions feel more like a ping-pong game than a darts game?
9. Do you feel you are getting from your child as well as giving to him?

HOW WILL YOU KNOW IF YOUR CHILD IS BECOMING INTERACTIVE?

1. He will frequently initiate contact with you.
2. He will wait for you to take turns with him.
3. He will regularly respond when you contact him.
4. He will initiate and respond about equally.
5. He will stay in interactions and actively keep you for more.
6. He will give to you as well as get from you.
7. He will take turns in play, caretaking, learning, and daily routines.
8. He will imitate you as well as act on his own.

HOW WILL YOU KNOW IF THERE IS A PROBLEM IN YOUR INTERACTIVE RELATIONSHIP?

1. One of you will be passive and unenthusiastic in interactions.
2. One person will regularly control and direct the interactions.

HOW CAN YOU BUILD STABLE INTERACTIONS THROUGH TURNTAKING?

1. Begin by believing that your child needs to stay in interactions and to give as well as get.
2. Do one thing and then WAIT with anticipation for your child to take a turn.
3. Clearly show that you expect your child to take a turn, and believe he will.
4. Accept any appropriate behaviors; keeping him there is more important than getting a particular response.
5. Often you may need to wait longer than you think you can; your child needs time and expects you to do things for him.
6. Signal and physically prompt his turn if sincere waiting fails.
7. Follow your child's lead; respond to his interests.
8. Avoid pressure or control; realize they will drive your child away.
9. Initiate and respond to your child about equally.
10. Match your child's actions and communications; be sure you do what he can do.

11. Be more interesting than the child's distractions.
12. Build a habit of keeping your child for "one or two more turns."

HOW SHOULD YOU COMMUNICATE IN TURNTAKING?

1. Respond carefully to what he says or does.
2. Use comments more than questions and commands.
3. Talk about what is happening between the two of you.
4. Use words that he can use in his natural communications.

WHAT SHOULD YOU AVOID DOING AND SAYING?

1. Taking several turns in a row.
2. Doing or saying things your child cannot do.
3. Making any attempts to control, like questions, commands, or trying to get a job done.
4. Believing that giving to your child and talking to him is enough.
5. Letting your child go after brief contact.
6. Failing to appreciate your child's little turns.

<table>
<tr><td>Conversation
Routine</td><td>**PEOPLE CONTACTS: Taking Turns with Body Movements and**
Facial Expressions Preverbal Level</td></tr>
</table>

Make the natural events in your day into opportunities for friendly, social conversations with your child. Consider these contrasting examples. Try to avoid limited contacts such as the one on the left. Try to find something you can share with your child, as in the example on the right. Turn just another routine into a joint activity in which your child can stay and learn with you.

LESS LIKE THIS

Child: (Holds foot in the air.)

Adult: "Stamp your feet." (Uses a stern face.) "Stamp your feet like me." (Stamps feet.)

Child: (Makes a nasty face.)

Adult: "Come on. Take your turn." (With a look of frustration.)

Child: (Drops foot and touches the floor with a look of frustration.)

Adult: "You finally stamped your feet, didn't you?"

Child: (Looks at his foot and waits.)

Adult: (Shakes hands.) "Now I want you to shake your hands. What are those?" (Touches child's hands.) Hands. Now shake yours." (Uses commanding expression and tone.)

Child: (Holds one of his toes, with a look of defiance.)

Avoid These Problems:
Child's Passive Style,
Adult Disregards Child's Motivations,
Adult Acts More Like a Teacher than a Partner

The adult appears to want more from the child than he can give. Each contact ends in disappointment, since the adult does not tune into the child's motivations. Their facial expressions match, but hardly motivate each other to keep interacting. The adult asks the nonverbal child to name his hands, something he is not capable of doing. She appears unwilling to enter her child's world, while the child appears unable or unwilling to enter hers.

MORE LIKE THIS

Child: (Holds foot in the air, with a look of delight.)

Adult: (Holds her foot in the air with a surprised expression) "Wow."

Child: (Looks at adult and smiles.)

Adult: (Smiles back and waves) "Hi!"

Child: (Reaches both hands toward the adult) "Ooo ooo."

Adult: (Grabs both of child's extended hands) "Ooo ooo ooo."

Child: (Releases from adult, stands up, begins to walk away.)

Adult: (Holds child by the hand, then shakes it, making eye contact and smiling broadly.)

Child: (Shakes hand back, imitating the broad smile.)

Adult: (Points to the floor where the child had been sitting.)

Child: (Sits back down and waves to the adult, smiling.)

Try These Strategies:
Imitate and Expand Child Behavior,
Perform Activities the Child Can Do,
Physically Prompt When Necessary,
Signal, then Wait for Desired Behavior

The adult begins wisely by following the child's lead. Their vocal and facial expressions add to the excitement of this simple exchange. Using a PHYSICAL PROMPT but no verbal command, the adult regains the child's waning interest. The POINTING SIGNAL returns the child to his former state of attention.

VARIATIONS:
Exchange any movements or expressions such as making funny faces, kicking feet, mussing each other's hair, moving tongue from side to side, or using funny vocal sounds.

IEP/
Problem Solver

Early Verbal
CHILD GOAL: Use a Variety of Actions
PROBLEM: Low Interactive Participation

(passive style)

Lisa responds to her teacher whenever the teacher asks her to say something or asks a question. The teacher considers Lisa the "Model Child" in the classroom. She sits quietly at group and stays on her mat. She does not disturb the other children by touching them or their toys. While this child's behavior seems beyond reproach, the teacher does not know what Lisa's interests are, because she rarely does or says anything unless she is told to.

Lisa:	(Sits quietly in her chair and looks at a book.)
Teacher:	"Lisa, go and get a piece of paper."
Lisa:	(Gives the teacher the paper; then returns to her chair.)
Teacher:	"Lisa, what did you just give me?"
Lisa:	"Paer."
Teacher:	"Can you say the whole thing?"
Lisa:	"I get paper."
Teacher:	"Good talking. Can you say, 'I gave you the paper'?"
Lisa:	"Yes."
Teacher:	"Okay, say, 'I gave you the paper'."
Lisa:	"I give paper."
Teacher:	"That's better. You are a pretty good talker."
Lisa:	(Returns to her chair and book.)

ECO | Partnership Plan

The **ECO** Partnership Plan contains those elements of an Individual Family Service Plan (IFSP) or Individual Education Program (IEP) that specify **ECO** goals and objectives to enhance a child's social and communicative development. Refer to current ECOScales for present levels of development and performance and for new goals.

Child Name: ___Lisa___ Birth Date: __6/6__ Parents: ___David and Jill___

Date of ECOScales: __9/12__ Examiner: _____

Present Levels of Development and Performance
Playful but minimally interactive; early verbal level

Child Goal
Use action in a functional, meaningful way

Objectives
Use a variety of action   Use action symbolically

Use action appropriate to a variety of play

Partnership Goal
Become Turntaking Partners

Objectives
Keep interaction going back and forth between the two
Initiate as well as respond   Give as well as take with action

Priority Problem:
Low Child Participation

Subproblem
Passive style   Brief or deadend contacts

Low activity level

Adult Strategies
Maintain and balance turntaking   Keep Lisa doing more

Substrategies
Match Lisa's behavior   Use actions and sounds like Lisa's

Imitate and animate Lisa   Imitate some of Lisa's actions/sounds

Practice Activities
People Only
Imitation Games

__1-2__ Times a day   __2-3__ Minutes each

People and Things
Old Maid card games   Doll house, doll play

__1-2__ Times a day   __2-3__ Minutes each

Daily Routines
(practice one a day)
Picking up toys together

Spontaneous

ECO | Practice Plan and Record

PRACTICE PLAN
Refer to current *ECOScale* for goals; see other *ECOScales* for old goals to maintain.

Interactive Goal Become turntaking partners (Laurie and Becky—teacher's assistant)

Objectives _____

Priority Problem Low interactive participation

Child Goal Show a turntaking play style

Objectives Keep play interactions going | Take turns in ways related to Becky's turns
Take turns in war

Adult Strategies 1) Maintain & balance turntaking 2) Match Laurie's behavior 3) Wait, signal, & expect
Play in childlike ways – Act & vocalize with animation – Act/communicate in ways close to Laurie

Targets to Decrease Laurie: 1) Interrupted exchange of action 2) Lack of sustained contact
Becky: 1) Dominating activity 2) Taking majority of turns 3) Use words when Laurie mainly uses actions

Practice Activities

People Only Exchanging funny faces | Looking at each other in mirror

How Often 1-2 Times a day | 2-3 Minutes each
Where

People and Things Rolling car | Bouncing a ball
Rocking baby's cradle

How Often 1-2 Times a day | 2-3 Minutes each
Where

Daily Routines Snack time — Putting coats on
(practice one a day)

Spontaneous Salt and pepper your strategies across the day. | Make interactions/communications a habit.

PARTNERSHIP CALENDAR

Week	MONDAY	TUESDAY	WEDNESDAY	THURSDAY	FRIDAY	SATURDAY	SUNDAY
1	1 1	1 1	2 2	2 1	2 2		
2	2 2	2 2	3 2	3 3			
3							
4							
5							

How to Use the Calendar

1. Select one goal each for child and adult. Observe one planned activity a day.
2. After observing, rate child and adult (you or someone else) on the goals listed in the Practice Plan. Use a 1 to 9 scale:
   1-2 = no evidence 3-4 = little evidence 5 = some evidence 6-7 = increasing evidence 8-9 = strong evidence
3. Rate the child (c) in top half and adult (a) in bottom half of each cell. Be sure to practice across many activities. Try some of the following; check the ones you practice.
   People only: __ sounds ✓ actions __ conversations __ your choice funny faces/mirror
   People and things: ✓ toys __ books __ games __ your choice _____
   Daily routines: __ getting up __ dressing __ bathing ✓ meals __ TV __ car __ bedtime
   __ shopping __ visiting __ household chores __ your choice putting coats on

ECO | Practice Plan and Record

PARTNERSHIP DIARY

Watch your progress and help your habits grow. Quickly, comment on how interactions with your child went today. Say anything: progress, problems, ideas, changes. Mention both child and adult occasionally.

Week 1

Monday
I tried fewer turns but Laurie turned away as quickly as she always does. Then I had to take care of other things and I didn't get back to her.

Tuesday
By the time I get the baby and cradle set up, we hardly have time to play. I felt really rushed so I did too much of the talking.

Wednesday
I saw a difference today in Laurie and in me. She stayed for about 4 turns, which is LONG for her.

Thursday
I felt like I was matching Laurie, but she didn't stay with me for long.

Friday
Another pretty good day, like Wed. It's very hard for me to say less, tho. Whenever Laurie is quiet I feel I should say something.

Saturday

Sunday

Week 2

Monday
I've been trying to imitate some of Laurie's words and sounds. She keeps interacting when I do this, but how can she be learning anything?

Tuesday
Maybe I'm concentrating too hard on the activity and what I'm supposed to be doing. Laurie seems like she'd rather play alone.

Wednesday
I actually think I matched and waited successfully! Laurie said "dog," which I've never heard her say before.

Thursday
What a day! When Laurie was getting her coat on, we just started throwing her mitten around. It wasn't planned at all, but it felt so natural for both of us. She stayed almost 5 minutes and said

Friday
things like "down," "mine," "mitten," "you," "out." It was wonderful and I wasn't even really trying the way I have been.

Friday / Saturday
We were really both together today at snack time. We just made silly faces back and forth about 5 times. I was the one who had to end it!

Sunday

Extra Hints to Remember
When you act or communicate at Laurie's level, give her time to respond.
Wait silently and with anticipation for her to take her turn.

6 | *Becoming Communicating Partners*

SOCIAL PLAY
social play

TURN TAKING
turn taking

COMMUNICATION
communication

LANGUAGE
language

CONVERSATION
conversation

Any behavior can communicate. That is, anything you do can get someone's attention, send information, or communicate many things. You and your child are sending messages all the time, even when you do not realize it (Bates, 1976; Watzlavick, et al., 1967). This chapter is concerned with what a child needs to do to become intentionally communicative and what you can do to get him into a communicative habit. Before we begin, you must understand that, in discussing communication, we do not mean just talking. Long before your child talks habitually, indeed in order for him to do so, he will be in the habit of sending and receiving messages of all sorts—movements, faces, sounds, and expressions so subtle and delicate that they are difficult to describe. He will also be staying in interactions with you (if you let him) mainly for the rewards of the give-and-take that comes from communicating with you.

Among most of the families of children with disabilities we've come to know, communication is not simply the major hope shared by parents and professionals, but the inability to communicate is the major barrier between the child and success in friendship, school, and vocation. Despite an almost universal concern for communication development among parents and others, communication before speech has been given very little formal attention in school or therapy (Newson, 1979; Peck, in press; Siegel-Causey, Ernst, & Guess, 1987; Sugarman, 1984). We know many parents who wait, push, and hope for their child to talk even as they fail to establish habitual communications involving those nonverbal movements and sounds their child can do. Thinking that "speech is the only way," they miss widespread opportunities to build preverbal communications that children need before speech. These adults act as if they cannot enjoy their child or have a relationship with him other than as a caregiver *unless the child talks.* We also know many adults who learned to have rewarding and progressive relations with whatever sounds and movements the child has available.

We see many potentially rich and rewarding relationships fail to get off the ground because adults do not know what to do to become a part of the child's current communicative world. No matter how strange it seems at first to get into a nonverbal communicative world, this step is necessary if adults ever expect the child to move into their communicative world. When parents and professionals whom we know have learned to communicate in the child's world, they report less loneliness, greater effectiveness, and more genuine desire to be with the child. They also report a more interactive child who begins trying their ways of communicating.

Here is one idea that may help you use and appreciate this chapter.

> Most of communication is not talk; talking is the result of much friendly, playful practice in communicating without words.

Think of communication as the most powerful way your child can have some control over his environment, including you. Then understand that, if your child fails to have much control over others with whatever he can do, he may retreat from people and seek what small control and rewards he can alone, even if those isolate him socially. Your child, just like us, is motivated if he is successful and will avoid valuable experiences if they offer him little success and control.

For a child who is primarily nonverbal, success is having effects on others, not talking in the ways adults want. If you hold out for words with a child, he may experience so much failure and so little enjoyment in communicating that he avoids communication—and therefore learning and friendship—except when he needs something.

> Avoid the rush to words.

A child becomes communicative as you allow him to have effects on you. Because your child learns to communicate to the extent that his current behaviors have effects on you, you are in a powerful position to show him how to communicate. Simply by responding to things he does, you can show him that his behaviors can affect you. This means that you can have control over which of his behaviors become communications by treating them as such (Bates, 1976). This chapter offers some guidelines that can help you help children communicate.

Jenny is 22 months old. Her parents feel she rarely communicates. Her mother reports that Jenny regularly plays in her crib with a toy hanging over her. Often, when her mother entered the girl's room at naptime, she saw Jenny reaching up to the toy. This led her mother to wonder if reaching looked like a signal to get up. Following that idea, the mother began to respond to the girl's reaching to the toy by picking her up as if she were sending the message, "I want up," even though she knew Jenny was really reaching to play, not to communicate. After a few days of this pretend-communication, the mother found that, when she entered the room and Jenny's arms were not up playing, Jenny immediately reached up excitedly. Now she was clearly communicating something like, "Get me up." Her mother showed her how to communicate by regularly acting as if her play behaviors were communicating. The point of Jenny's story is that you and other adults close to your child have the power in your daily contacts to help stimulate communication. As long as you accept the child's current behaviors and let them have rewarding effects on you, you can help your child communicate.

Remember, though, that the goal is not just to get your child to communicate now and then in dead-end contacts for need or for show. The goal is a habit. The previous two chapters examined skills that both you and your child must have in order to build a communicative habit. In other words, do not think of playing together and turntaking as skills you are finished with. They are your child's tools for learning communication. A child learns to communicate on his own only if he learns it playfully and by staying in the basic kinds of reciprocal turntaking exchanges essential to any healthy social relationship.

In this chapter, we examine a series of skills that unite children and adults in associations that support learning how to communicate. For many adults, these skills appear to generalize and become a part of their lives only when both the child and adults develop certain attitudes. Learning the skills will help you develop the attitudes discussed here, but we encourage you to work on developing these attitudes as well as the skills.

To become an independent communicator, a child needs certain beliefs and attitudes about himself and the world. Children who regularly communicate in many social contexts appear to operate by the following beliefs.

"I can have control over people as well as things."
"People will accept what I can do, so I will not fail if I try to communicate."
"People want information, affection, and any healthy communication from me."
"People will be in my world and show me the ways to communicate next."

To become a natural communication partner who will help your child communicate, you may find that the following attitudes give you the support you need.

"The adults closest to the child can help him communicate best."
"Therapists and clinicians can assist parents and teachers but cannot do the job alone."
"In every contact we have, I am teaching my child either to communicate or not to communicate."
"The ways I communicate have profound effects on how my child communicates."
"My child must communicate without words long before he regularly talks."
"The more I communicate like my child, the more my child will learn to communicate like me."
"I can have a rewarding relationship with my child even if he is not communicating as I would like."

It's Your Turn

COMMENT: Do you mean every little thing my child does could become a communication?

REPLY: That's the way it happens. Those little behaviors of your child that you pay most attention to are likely to be some of his next communications, especially if your attention is matched to what he can do and responsive to his interests. Beware that you do not attend to unpleasant behaviors, as they might then become his strongest communications.

Just as important, your own movements and sounds will communicate to your child, sometimes more effectively than even your words could. More than your words can, your little movements will tell your child how you feel. To support your child, your subtle communications must tell him you genuinely accept him and want him to keep communicating with you.

19. BECOME COMMUNICATING PARTNERS

In helping a child learn to communicate, the major goal is to build an environment in which the child and significant people in his life have a habitual, communicating partnership, a life filled with a continuing exchange of messages. In this partnership, they will communicate not only to solve a crisis or satisfy a need, but because they believe that is what people do with each other.

Children need partners to learn to communicate.

Contrast this notion of a "continuous exchange of messages" with a smattering of brief, dead-end contacts that fail to show the child how to keep communications going. In a continuous exchange, the child and adult learn to be reciprocal, meaning that each person responds sensitively and meaningfully to the other's communication. If you learn to give back to the child something that motivates him, he will more likely give you back something meaningful.

Thus, the goals in the preceding chapter on turntaking are absolutely essential to building communications. We know parents and professionals who learned playful turntaking with their children but then reverted to their old dominating, directive, adult-oriented ways of communicating when their child began to communicate. Unfortunately, the loss of control, motivation, and fun of a turntaking relationship seems to drive the child away from learning to communicate with his adults. We are also concerned about the effects of this loss of interaction on the child's self-esteem and confidence in being a competent communicator.

Keep the turntaking habit in communication.

One word that says a lot about developmentally productive communication with children is exchange. The goal for you and your child is to begin an *exchange* of ideas, so that each person is affecting the other, taking the other's message with respect, and giving back something of himself that also relates to the other's communication.

Begin to see your child as a communicator whether or not he talks.

You will likely become communicating partners with your child only when you *see him as a communicator and regularly expect him to communicate.* Often parents say something like this: "Now I see what I'm doing. I would never let my normal 3-year-old pass by me and not communicate but I let my delayed child do it all the time." Yes, we realize that children may very effectively teach others not to expect them to communicate. They give little and fail to live up to age expectations, and their adults allow them. To begin to overcome that, you can first accept any and all ways he communicates with you and then help him stay communicating with you.

Begin to see the mere presence of your child as your signal to communicate with him. It is virtually impossible to keep a highly social child from communicating at the sight of another human being. That should become a goal for your child: to communicate whenever he sees another person. We want children to regard people as more than tools to help them or direct their behavior. Those roles are far too limited to help a child become a communicating partner with others. A child needs to contact and stay with people because communicating with them is its own reward. Only when the social rewards of communication become naturally motivating to the child will he develop social and learning relationships.

To learn more about the extent to which you are a communicating partner with your child, ask yourself about the following issues. Discuss them with family and professionals.

Subgoal
Communicate back and forth with each other, not at each other.

a. Keep communication going back and forth between the two.

There needs to be, at least some of the time, an easy, turntaking exchange between you and your child. If one of you does too much, you may lose the other. Remember, it is much less important *what* the two of you communicate than that you *keep communication going*. Again, think of communicating as a ping-pong game, in which one of you hits the ball (communication) to the other, the other hits it right back, and the first keeps the volley going. Think of communicating as keeping the ball in the air back and forth. The longer you keep the communicative volleys going, the better the result. Your child will learn more. You will learn better how to communicate with him. And better yet, he and others around him will begin seeing him as a communicator.

Subgoal
Each of your should have your own say.

b. Initiate as well as respond.

Many of us will continue a relationship only if we have both the chance to initiate our own ideas and the time and attention to respond to the other's communication. A child may appear not to initiate because he and the adult are not really participating in the same activity; the more you share experiences the more reasons for initiating the child will have. Initiating can be any kind of attempt to communicate, and a response need not be a full communication but simply any reaction that relates to your communication.

Subgoal

Communicate more for friendship than for control.

c. Exchange messages that have a social more than an instrumental focus.

We find that if we communicate only to direct or to get something we want, these communications are short-lived and neither the child nor the adult learns much. On the other hand, when we communicate for low-stress, social reasons (such as to play, share information, or make things happen together), the communications last much longer and are more fulfilling. And surprisingly, the child often tries to do more and usually shows he is learning more when the contacts are social rather than directive or controlling through questions and commands. Adults need to make more communication nonjudgmental, inviting, and relatively free from stress on getting a job done.

Subgoal

d. Make each communication understood by the other.

By this we do not mean totally intelligible speech, but simply that the adult attempts to communicate like the child, using a variety of communicative styles rather than relying on adult speech only. The child will often attempt to help the adult understand by changing his communications to accommodate the adult. There should be a general reciprocal fine-tuning, by which each person changes in ways that keep the other communicating.

It's Your Turn

COMMENT:

Until I learned how easy turntaking was, I thought I had to sit down and teach Louie to talk. Now we babble and grumble and make movements back and forth while dressing, eating, cleaning up; it's a part of us now and Louie is communicating more on his own and more like me.

REPLY:

Once you discover that communicative turntaking gives you more of your son than you got before, it becomes as natural as breathing and makes you feel very successful.

COMMENT:

I was raised in an atmosphere where "children should be seen and not heard." My dolls were my partners, not my adults. Then I tried to be partners with my delayed 3-year-old and his 6-month-old sister. It worked. I'm still a parent and authority at times, but I see them learn more this way. Now I'm trying to teach other parents about being communicating partners. There seems so much to learn. Parents seem to need one thing to remember to keep them on track. Is there one recommendation I can give them to help their children communicate?

REPLY:

Keep your child communicating with you. Unless adults see communicating as something that continually goes back and forth, all the other recommendations may fall flat. When your child knows his role is to stay communicating with others, he will naturally learn more mature communication, more language, and more conversation skills.

Self-Assessment: How Are You Doing?

Rate yourself on a scale of 1 to 9 where 1 = never or very poorly, 5 = neutral, and 9 = always or very well.

_____ 1. My child and I exchange messages regularly without words.
_____ 2. My child and I exchange messages regularly with words.
_____ 3. Communication goes both ways between us.
_____ 4. Our communication exchanges last longer than a few months ago.
_____ 5. Each of us starts a communication as well as responds.
_____ 6. We communicate more to be together than to get a job done.
_____ 7. We understand each other more than a few months ago.

INTERACTIVE PROBLEMS

Be sure to expect your child to communicate.

For many children with developmental delays, one barrier to learning to communicate seems to be the failure of adults to expect him to do so. When children fail to communicate in the ways and at the times adults first expect, those adults report that they stop expecting the children to communicate much. This lack of expectation is not just a state of mind for the adults: It shows up in reduced communicative contacts, increased caregiving, and a general pattern of ignoring all but the child's most obvious communications. In short, those parents and professionals do not view the child as a "communicator" beyond his efforts to get his needs met. We have regularly seen adults treat children as if they were not communicators and the children then appear to fulfill that prophecy. This pattern is most disturbing when the same children communicate with us in a variety of ways in a clinic. When we wait and show that we expect these children to communicate, they often show a range of communicative attempts. In those cases, many of the adults expressed surprise or refused to consider the child's attempts as acceptable communications.

The Knowledge-Communication Gap

Does your child communicate as much as he knows?

Another problem is to think that a child knows only what he communicates. Once we are in a playful relationship with a child, we nearly always find that he knows much more than he communicates. We call this the "knowledge-communication gap," and one of the first jobs any parent, teacher, or friend has in building a relationship with a child is to bridge this gap. This is best accomplished not so much by helping the child to communicate new things but by helping him to communicate what he already knows. Ask yourself, "How much more intelligent and socially acceptable would my child be if he simply communicated what he knew?"

You may already know your child communicates much less than he knows, but wonder how to show him a way to communicate that knowledge. Adults often forget that any behavior can communicate. Therefore, they miss many opportunities to let a child's behaviors affect them in ways that would make the behaviors into communications. When we respond to the child's displays of knowledge by showing him how to communicate them, we may be helping him store that knowledge and make it socially useful.

Almost equally problematic is the attitude that if a child knows something, he will communicate it when he needs to. Thus, many educators and parents try to teach the child knowledge with little attention to whether he has the motivation or communicative skills to use that knowledge. This attitude seeks to have clinical and educational work focus on implanting knowledge rather than showing the child how to use it communicatively. We simply do not find children communicating much of the knowledge they are taught, perhaps because they have been taught to store it but not to communicate it. Our clinical model makes the first task in building communication to show the child how to communicate what he already knows, not to teach the child new knowledge.

A Reminder about Turntaking

Two other problems we observe as children learn to communicate are turn dominance and dead-end contacts. Although we discussed these earlier, they merit our continued attention here. Adults who learn to take turns and extend back-and-forth exchanges in play often forget these critical rules when the child begins communicating. Without allowing the child to take his turns, by waiting and signaling, and keeping him in longer exchanges, the adult greatly restricts the natural learning opportunities the child needs. Consider every extra turn as a practice and consider your child needing a stream of practice just as he did when he learned to walk. Is your child getting as much practice communicating as he did walking? Every adult turn is either a model to show the child how to communicate or to provide feedback on how the child did. Similarly, every child turn is an opportunity for him to practice his communication. If a child is in mainly dead-end exchanges, ones that last only briefly, he is unlikely to learn that communication is used for developing topics and relationships.

Beyond these problems in attitudes and interactive style, we are concerned with early attention to two global problems: low communicative participation and mismatch.

It's Your Turn

COMMENT:

REPLY:

How can I expect my child to do something I know he cannot do or has not seen?

The simple fact of it is that we cannot know for sure what a child can or cannot do. If we have not seen him do something, it may mean only that we have not provided the support he needs to do it. The idea is to show your child that you expect "something" but not necessarily something particular. When you expect something from your child you show him respect. When he feels respect and acceptance, he is more likely to communicate with you. If you act like you know

---

Margin notes:

First step; communicate what he already knows.

Knowledge grows when communicated.

Your child's first step is not new knowledge but to communicate what he already knows.

Just like walking, communicating requires steady practice.

what he can and cannot do, you are severely restricting him. You will probably send him discouraging signals that will reduce his contacts with people.

COMMENT: For years now as a principal, I have seen students in my school communicate much less than they know. With teachers in the classroom, they communicate all kinds of things. Then with other professionals, especially those with tests, they act like they do not know much. It is very frustrating to me, and I am afraid it hurts them a lot. What can be done?

REPLY: Parents tell this sad story all the time. The one thing that can be done is to show children how to become communicating partners with others, not the passive, uninterested victims that others may see now. Unfortunately, you cannot do this alone. A child cannot learn to be a communicating partner alone any more than you can clap with one hand. You, as a principal, can work to build communicative partnerships as a regular part of your curriculum. You may find that the students will show more learning from other curricular areas. Your teachers must learn to be partners who match, respond, and stay communicating with the children.

COMMENT: It almost sounds like you are saying that, for some children, communication is more important than knowledge. I want my child to learn in school and therapy. Doesn't learning mean knowledge?

REPLY: By communicating, a child will acquire more knowledge because he will get both practice and feedback on his activities. Without communicating, the child's knowledge will have little use. We agree with those theorists who claim that the primary purpose of education is not to implant information but to teach children how to learn on their own. Once a child is communicative, he begins to pursue his own education and follow his own motivation, which is his most powerful source of learning. Once adults see how the child is learning through communicating, they realize what a powerful role they have as communicating partners. Think of communicating as socially active learning.

COMMENT: We have a 2½-year-old nonverbal boy. My husband says he's waiting to get close to him until he talks. I say he should start now.

REPLY: A child learns to communicate in his closest relationships. By the time your child learns to talk, your husband will have missed many wonderful opportunities to build a solid relationship with your son. And your son will not have had the extra models and stimulation provided by his father's input. Encourage your husband to get involved with your son now.

Child Problem

20. LOW COMMUNICATIVE PARTICIPATION

Usually when communication disorders are discussed, we see terms such as *language, phonology, semantics*, and *syntax* (Bloom & Lahey, 1978; Lund & Duchan, 1983). All these terms refer to verbal communication. Rarely do we see much concern for the rate and active participation of the child in preverbal communication. Similarly, when we ask parents and professionals about the child's communication, we usually do not get an estimate of how often and how long the child communicates. Instead, they report the number of words and their intelligibility. Our concern here is that we frequently observe children in a variety

The less your child communicates the less he learns.

of play, caregiving, and learning situations and see very little evidence of the communication that we know they are capable of. If a child can communicate, why doesn't he?

Subproblem

a. Limited frequency of communication.

Ask yourself if communicating seems to be a natural part of your child's interactions with others. Is it a habit he uses as regularly as you do, or something he does only occasionally? When you estimate how much he communicates, be sure to note whether others are communicating regularly and allowing him to participate.

Do not encourage your child to avoid communication.

When adults hold the attitude that "a child should be seen and not heard," a child who communicates little may be encouraged not to communicate. For the child to whom communication does not come easily, that attitude is likely to be a devastating problem. Some adults tell us children have the right to not communicate if they don't care to. Do they mean that children have the right not to learn? Thinking of communicating as the most generalizable learning tool affects your decision to allow children to communicate only as much as they wish to. You would not allow a child to avoid school, and we must not let him avoid communication—the preverbal child's school out of school.

Subproblem

b. Infrequent initiation.

A child who communicates on his own is likely to be more highly motivated to communicate than one who regularly waits for others to make contact. The child who initiates is also more likely to be seen by others as a communicator, thus increasing the likelihood that others will engage him in regular communication. Adults we know have told us that they assumed their children did not want to communicate because they did not start many communications. Consequently, these adults respected the children's right to be alone. In the name of communication

A motivated child initiates.

development, a child no more has the right to be alone most of the time than other children have a right to avoid school, dinner, or sleep. Parents and professionals alike need to realize that a child will not likely go far in learning to communicate if he does not initiate contacts frequently. A related problem for the child who does not initiate is that we are unlikely to know his concerns and intentions, the very links we may need to build communication with him in his own world.

Subproblem

c. Infrequent responses.

While we see more problems in initiating than responding, most children we know often fail to respond when others address them. When a child with delays fails to respond to people, he is risking the serious danger of turning them away, thus turning away chances to learn how to communicate. When looking at a child's responsiveness, be sure to observe what the adults are doing. Do they allow

Do not allow your child to ignore you.

responses? Are they following the child's interests? Are they stressful and controlling or are they inviting and accepting? Are they communicating in ways that the child can try to model?

Subproblem

d. Repetitive or meaningless use of gestures, sounds, or words.

On first sight, children often seem to be communicating to us. A closer look might reveal that they are using conventional gestures or words but are not intentionally sending messages. They may talk often but not communicate. Occasionally the child's communication appears to be directed to a person, but is repetitive beyond reasonable use. Children with autistic features often use words but show no evidence of intentions or expectations of a response. Even with many children who are not autistic, we find we must ask the twofold question: How much language does the child show, and how much of that language is used to communicate intentionally?

Subproblem

e. Communication too instrumental; focus on getting needs met.

Let's look a little more closely at the problem of "instrumental," or needs-oriented, communication. Consider the number of things a child needs. Then consider the number of potential ideas a child and you can share. Ideas seem to greatly out-number needs. Nevertheless, a great many children communicate mainly to get needs met or to manipulate others. Not only are these instances relatively infre-quent, they usually require only brief communications. Thus instrumental com-munications appear to be insufficient in number to help a child build a com-municative habit. Beyond that problem, few people seem willing to build rela-tionships with people who mainly want to use them to satisfy their needs. Again, a habit of reciprocal give-and-take appears to be ideal for building and maintain-ing communicative relationships.

Subproblem

f. Failure to attend to shared topic.

"Attention disorders," which go by a variety of names, are clearly problematic for many kinds of children. Those children act as though they are completely free to move in and out of topics with others at will. And their adults seem almost to agree with them, allowing them to leave before much of a topic is developed. The more a topic is developed, the more the child learns to communicate. A critical feature of resolving this problem is to become convinced that the child absolutely needs to stay longer and longer on a topic and that, to keep him on a topic, you need to be more interesting to the child than his distractions.

It's Your Turn

COMMENT:

Do you mean to say that if my classroom of children simply communicated what they already know, they would look smarter?

REPLY:

Absolutely. But we could say the same for all of us. For children with delays, this idea is important because society (adults, peers, teachers, etc.) will judge and accept them on the basis of what they communicate, not what they know.

COMMENT:

But as a teacher and mother, I have always thought my job was to impart new knowledge to children. Have I been wrong?

REPLY:

Most teachers and clinicians we know tell us they were trained just as you say: to teach new knowledge to children who have the social and communicative skills to use that knowledge in life. But if you want your teaching to have any sustaining effects, you must attend carefully to whether your children are communicating habitually and decide whether what you teach them is something they can use and care about in life.

In fact, many child development theorists argue that our primary job is not to teach facts, but to show a child how to learn. We contend that it is through com-municating with us about his knowledge that the child learns more. In our own clinical work, parents and teachers often say, "I didn't know he knew that. How did you teach him?" They're surprised when we say that we did not teach him the knowledge, but simply let him communicate it by matching, waiting, and sensitively responding to his interests.

COMMENT: I have a day care center for about 20 delayed children and I see very few of the children ever initiating to adults or peers. That's one of my major goals. Why don't they initiate?

REPLY: Since this is a pervasive problem with children with delays, there is certainly no easy answer. The **ECO** model is an attempt to help adults bring children more into an interactive world. A big part of that attempt involves initiating. To initiate, a child must think of himself as a communicator and feel that he is allowed to initiate. A child will initiate if adults and peers are inviting and doing things that interest him. He will continue to initiate if he regularly has success when he does so. A success to a child is not always what it is to us adults; for a child a success may be simply being accepted and responded to warmly. Certainly, if a delayed child is accustomed to being corrected or given more work when he initiates, he will do it less. Ask yourself which of the following rules reigns at your day care center: "Do something" or "Do the right thing." If it is the former, the children will almost certainly initiate and learn more.

COMMENT: No matter what I do, my child rarely responds to me. All the adults around him complain that he ignores them.

REPLY: We see this same problem frequently. Much of this book is an answer to your question. For now, consider this: You may be the one who is not responding to him. Often adults who say the child is not responding actually mean that the child is not responding the way they want. Be very careful to attend to your child's little responses to you. They are the seeds for the more mature ones.

COMMENT: I always believed my son Mac would communicate when he needed to. He's 4 now and has been diagnosed with severe learning disabilities. Then we had Joshua, and I am astounded at how much he communicates at only 11 months. Now I think Mac should be communicating more than just for his own needs.

REPLY: Many parents and professionals feel that children will communicate when they are ready, and that works with many children. But for children with developmental delays, it is the responsibility of adults to catch the little signals and get the children to be habitual communicators, no matter how they can do it. Do not wait for words. You must accept and support communicative attempts that you may not understand or appreciate. You should not allow Mac to not communicate. Our view is that Mac does not have the right to not communicate any more than he has a right to not learn. Consider every period of time your child avoids communication as playing "hooky" from the most important learning he needs—learning to be a communicating person.

Self-Assessment:
How Are You
Doing?

Rate yourself on a scale of 1 to 9 where 1 = never or very poorly, 5 = neutral, and 9 = always or very well.

_____ 1. I do not expect my child to communicate much.
_____ 2. My child knows much more than he communicates.

_____ 3. I communicate with my child mainly to serve his needs.
_____ 4. My child gets little practice communicating.
_____ 5. He rarely initiates or starts a communication
_____ 6. He rarely responds when others communicate to him.
_____ 7. He communicates the same things over and over.
_____ 8. He communicates mainly to get his needs met.
_____ 9. He communicates mainly about his own interests.

Adult Problem

21. MISMATCH

As we have stressed in the two last chapters, matching is fundamental to any communicating partnership. Children will learn to be social and communicative in part to the extent that they have others who regularly communicate in ways they can do. We have consistently found in our work with children that the more different our communications are from the child's, the less the child participates, and thus learns, with us. Here are some specific instances of mismatching in communication.

Subproblem

a. Limited use of childlike actions.

Communications come from actions.

Getting a child to communicate requires making connections that he can perform and understand (Kaye, 1980b; Snow & Ferguson, 1978; Stern, 1985). Since many children appear quite centered in their own physical and motivational world, we are more likely to get them to communicate if we enter that world. Many adults seem extremely resistant to being childlike. Instead they put on children the burden of coming into a difficult, unfamiliar world if they are to communicate. It is distressing to see a child try to communicate with an adult who holds an adultlike stance, effectively sending this message: "I'm doing it right and you had better come to my world if you want me." We have found that when adults do become childlike they are often astonished at how easy it is to keep the child communicating. Parents who are first teachers and nurses are particularly rewarded by their child when they change their role from an adult authority to a communicatively matched partner.

Subproblem

b. Little use of communication that the child can use.

Often we communicate with children for our own reasons. We assume that our communications are good for the child as well. Just a little thought will tell you that children communicate very differently than we do. Ask yourself "Am I communicating in ways my child is likely to use?" Consider that every time you communicate you are showing your child how to communicate. If you are communicating in ways he cannot match or in ways inappropriate for him, he may miss opportunities to communicate effectively.

Subproblem

c. Main use of speech with nonverbal child.

The roles adults take with children seem to strongly influence their communicative relations (Bruner, 1983). Parents and professionals we know generally see their role as the talker who narrates as the child plays. Because communication is based on shared experiences (Watzlavick, Beavin, & Jackson, 1967), this mismatch of talk and play does not allow either to have intimate knowledge of what the other is intending to communicate. Such a pattern also seems to tell the child, "Your job is to play, mine is to communicate," thus running the serious risk of leading the child to believe that he is not supposed to communicate.

Subproblem

Sounds before words.

d. Words but not sounds used with a sounding child.

A child is likely to communicate with a wide and changing range of speechlike and nonspeech sounds before he regularly uses words. Adults who use only words with such a child may not be helping the child develop a strong repertory of sounds. We find that when we use a combination of sounds like the child's and just a few words, the child stays communicating with us and gets more sound practice than when we use only words. If we do not communicate in ways the child can, he may sense failure rather than the encouragement that comes with models he can do.

Subproblem

e. Use of word combinations beyond the child's expressive capability.

Adults frequently tell us they communicate in sentences far above what the child can do because the child understands them. Some of them even report that professionals have told them to "bathe the child in language." In communication, as in bathing, too much will drown your child. As we have urged in the last two chapters, adults must realize they need to communicate not only to be understood but, just as importantly, to show the child how to communicate next. If adults take an "all or none" view of talking, they fail to see that children need adults to carefully bridge sounds into words and words into combinations.

Subproblem
Mismatching child's interests.

f. Failure to talk about the child's activity or interests.

Another way to mismatch is to communicate about things that do not motivate the child. Of course, at times we must show the child how to communicate outside his own world. However, we frequently see adults totally missing the child's current thinking and losing the child's participation. To help a child communicate, we must make a meaningful link not only to what he is doing but also to what his intentions are.

It's Your Turn

COMMENT:

I know that the more I communicate like my child, the more he communicates and tries to communicate like me. But it's hard for me. Is there some way to remember?

REPLY:

Think of a staircase with you and your child on different steps. Imagine you are showing a 16-month-old girl how to climb stairs; if you are mismatched, you might place the girl on the first step and then run up 12 steps and say: "Come on, Suzi, let's do it!" Of course you would not do such a thing. But it is common to see adults do very similar things in communication. For example, with a primarily nonverbal child who gestures and sounds, adults often do not match the child but rather say things like "Oh, you found your tinkertoys. I hope they aren't wet; they get stuck when they're wet." Such talk is very much like running several steps ahead of a child on a staircase. So, when you are tempted to do much more than your child can do, visualize the two of you on that staircase and get yourselves on similar steps.

Rate yourself on a scale of 1 to 9 where 1 = never or very poorly, 5 = neutral, and 9 = always or very well.

____ 1. I am uncomfortable communicating like my child.
____ 2. I believe I should act like an adult with my child.
____ 3. I prefer talking to playing with my child.
____ 4. I see sounds and movements as baby talk that I should not do.
____ 5. I explain things in full sentences to my primarily preverbal child.
____ 6. I talk mainly about my interests with my child.

Child Goals

22. INTENTIONALLY COMMUNICATE WITH OTHERS

Even children with language need to learn to communicate.

We often hear parents and teachers say that their child communicates. When we look at the child more closely, though, we sometimes find that he sends occasional messages of need but he is far from having a communicative habit. We also see some children talking to people or to themselves but not in a way that builds relationships. It is common to hear adults say that a child with autistic features or behavior problems "has a lot of language." Too often, we find that the child is not actually communicating much with that language. Thus, even if a child does speak, we cannot automatically assume that he is habitually communicating with it. Try to look for the important difference between "having language" and "using language regularly to communicate." Even a child with language may still have a lot to learn about communication.

Expect new communications.

Be concerned that your child communicates more and more. Parents and professionals alike tell us they get satisfied even with their child's most limited, nonsocial attempts to communicate when they consider their earlier doubts about whether the child would ever communicate. In their view, "something is better than nothing"; perhaps they accept too little. Learning and socialization require a child to get into the habit of communicating whenever people are near, not just in times of need or distress. Frequent, regular communication is what makes a child be perceived as a communicator by those who have the power to help him communicate. We regularly encourage adults to not be satisfied with the same communications all the time. Expect new and different communication, just as you expect new ideas and information from your own friends.

"Read" your child's little communications.

Unlike adults who are too satisfied with their child's communications, others fail to see many of their child's communicative attempts. These adults think of communication as sounds and words, and so they ignore other critical movements and sounds that are their child's basic building blocks for communicating. When an adult fails to respond to a child's little communications without words, the child goes elsewhere for his entertainment. In those instances, both adult and child are missing critical opportunities for learning to communicate. Further, remember that first communications can be any behaviors, even when the child is not clearly intending to communicate. You do not have to see your child's intention to communicate. If you simply respond to him as if he were communicating, your responses may in fact tell him that these behaviors can communicate.

Keep in mind throughout this section that the interactions discussed in the last two chapters must still be building. Communications will develop only if playful interactions are maintained. Here are some specific expectations you can have of your child's communication.

Subgoal

a. Use nonverbal messages alone.

It is essential to realize that children will regularly communicate nonverbally, with sounds and movements, long before they use words. In fact, become convinced that your child's words come from nonverbal communications. Just as buds become flowers, gestures and sounds become words. Since any behavior can communicate, we need to treat children's behaviors as if they were communicating. Why? Because one way to show a child how to communicate is to let his behaviors have communicative effects on you. Nonverbal communications are a rich resource for knowing how to communicate with a child and for knowing when and what words to give him to move from nonverbal to verbal productions.

Subgoal

b. Use nonverbal messages with verbal messages.

Often it is difficult to see and hear a child's subtle communications. Ask yourself how he conveys information, shows his intentions, tries to affect others, shows you he knows something. The answer to these and similar questions will help you gauge your child's communications, even if he doesn't seem to be intending to communicate. Think of it this way: If you know that your child knows some specific thing, he has communicated that knowledge to you, whether intentionally or not. Train yourself to see and hear the many little communications we often miss when we are waiting and hoping for fully mature communications. No matter how crude and immature you think your child's subtle communications are, he is unlikely to develop the communicative habit he needs unless you accept what he can do now. To get what you want for him, you must come to see and hear his small efforts so you can support and build them.

Subgoal

c. Balance initiations and responses.

Do you know children or adults who respond to you but who rarely initiate on their own? Or someone who initiates frequently when it is his idea but hardly ever responds when you communicate? Building relationships requires both, and your child must learn to both initiate and respond.

Your child must communicate both from his ideas and yours.

Initiating allows your child to have some control over his time with you. Children seem to be more likely to stay communicating if they have some choice of direction in the exchange. If your child is to learn to initiate, he must feel you will give him time and attention and will follow his lead at times.

Your child also needs to learn to respond when you communicate, not just with rote, unthinking behaviors like nods of the head or pat words like "uh uh," but with communications that gradually become more related to your communication. At first, allow any safe responses, then begin looking for an increased variety and better fit to your message.

In short, your child must initiate to keep motivated to communicate; he must respond in order to keep others motivated to communicate with him. Once your child is doing both, he will have more opportunities to learn and he will be perceived as having a sense of give-and-take.

Subgoal

d. Imitate as well as respond in other ways.

Because we care about how others affect a child, one of our first questions is whether or not he imitates. If a child is in a habit of doing as others do, he has an important skill for learning how to communicate in spontaneous daily events. Children seem more likely to try to imitate others who do things they can already do, that is, that match their current abilities.

Imitation is one of the first ways we look for a child to communicate new ideas or in new forms, such as speech. Imitation games are enjoyable ways tous daily events. Children seem more likely to try to imitate others who do things they can already do, that is, that match their current abilities. Imitation is one of the first ways we look for a child to communicate new ideas or in new forms, such as speech. Imitation games are enjoyable ways to get you and your child into one world, where your communications can really connect. Watch what your child imitates; those imitations can tell you which of your communications he is able to do.

For all that imitation is an important skill in learning, it is not a final goal. Consider two cautions about imitating. First, be sure you are not satisfied with imitation by itself for long. A child also needs to be encouraged to respond from his own ideas, not to adopt a parroting habit. Second, if you think your child can do more than imitate, wait silently, with anticipation, for a little while after he imitates you. This helps to show him you expect him to do something on his own.

Subgoal

e. Maintain communicative interactions.
The habit of communicating once and then leaving the interaction can be difficult to break *but it must not be accepted*. Most all other learning will be wasted unless children maintain communications.

Keep the child communicating for one more turn.

In our experience, a large percentage of people with disabilities act as if they do not value or understand how to maintain communication with others. We speculate that many of these people have a history of failure to communicate in the ways others do or want them to do. Regardless of the cause, when a child fails to show an interest in keeping a communication going, he actively discourages others from staying in an interaction with him.

Keeping communications going back and forth is critical for social and communication development. It really does not matter much how a child communicates, in movements or words, clearly or with difficulty, if he does not *stay communicating* with people. It is frightening to realize that countless children appear to have a firm self-image of themselves as "one shot" responders or initiators, not as people who stay in interactions. Whether this dangerous habit began with their disabilities or the management approaches used by adults, it is difficult to change because the adults may also define the child as a dead-end communicator. Dead-end communications teach a child little more than how to satisfy his immediate needs or the demands of others. Dead-end contacts do not help a child learn how to relate to others. Avoid being satisfied if your child only responds and initiates but does not stay in increasingly longer turns communicating. Get into the habit of keeping him for one or two more exchanges.

Subgoal

f. Exchange messages with ease.
Your child needs to do more than just give or take from you in communications; he needs to exchange ideas meaningfully. A reciprocal exchange is one in which each person communicates in ways that relate to what the other person has communicated. Your child needs to accept your communication and respond in a way that lets you say, "He heard me. I connected." Is your child taking what you com-

municate and giving you back a part of himself that makes sense? The beauty of exchanging messages is that each person's later messages change and develop and reflect your influence. That's when the child is learning to communicate.

It's Your Turn

COMMENT:

I was always taught to communicate only when there was something important to say. Now it sounds as if you want my child to communicate regardless of whether he really has something to say. Can you help me?

REPLY:

For a developing child who communicates little, every communication is an important one. When a child is beginning to communicate, two things are important: *practice* and *anything*. The important thing for a beginning communicator to do is do anything and do it frequently. A child's first communications will not have messages that seem "important" to you unless you realize that any first steps he can do are the most important things he can communicate to you. If you wait for or only respond to messages that are important in adult terms, you will probably be ignoring your child and discouraging him from building a habit of communicating in any way he can. Try to convince yourself that, for a child who is learning, any communication is important.

Self-Assessment:
How Are You
Doing?

Rate yourself on a scale of 1 to 9 where 1 = never or very poorly, 5 = neutral, and 9 = always or very well.

_____ 1. My child usually communicates whenever people are around.
_____ 2. He initiates or starts communications regularly.
_____ 3. He responds to communications regularly.
_____ 4. He imitates others' communications.
_____ 5. He communicates with sounds and movements. He stays communicating for extended turns.
_____ 6. He communicates with ease.
_____ 7. He communicates much more than he did a few months ago.

Child Goal

23. COMMUNICATE NONVERBALLY

Even when highly verbal adults communicate, much of the full meaning of the messages lies in the nonverbal communications, not in the words (Watzlawick, Beavin, & Jackson, 1967). If someone says "hello" to you, you may respond by asking "What are you so happy about?" on one occasion and by asking "What's wrong with you?" on another. The nonverbal behaviors such as intonation, posture, and facial expression create messages that go far beyond the word "hello."

If nonverbal communication is so important to those of us whose verbal skills are developed, consider how critical a child's movements and sounds are to him. Learning to see and hear your child's communications without words is a most important job in helping him become a social and communicative person. The more you notice and respond to these essential building blocks, the more likely you are to build them into more communicative exchanges with your child.

Here are some of a child's skills in developing nonverbal communication.

Subgoal

Encourage creative and communicative use of movements.

a. Use a range of gestures, sounds, and movements that send a message

Again, remember that any behavior can communicate. At first, your child must learn that any of his behaviors will be accepted as communications. This means that you must accept as communicative many more behaviors than just the speech-like sounds and words that many adults limit their children to.

Think about it. Every movement and sound that your child uses with you could become a word or a sentence someday. Consider your child's sounds and movements as the places where words come from, as infants that can become children (words) and later adults (longer verbal messages). As with infants, we need to nurture these tiny expressions and help them to mature.

We have learned to appreciate the richness possible in nonverbal communications when we observe parents and teachers with enthusiastic children with cerebral palsy. These children, eager to communicate, can communicate a dictionary of meanings with movements and sounds that no one but very familiar people could interpret.

Subgoal

Look for idiosyncratic then conventional communications.

b. Send clear messages without words.

You probably understand your child's nonverbal communications much more readily than strangers do. Many parents and teachers we know can read a rapid flash of movements and sounds that convey nothing to us. It may be helpful to consider two kinds of communications, conventional (usual) and idiosyncratic (special). Your child's conventional communication includes all those messages that most strangers would understand and accept. Your child's idiosyncratic communications are ones that only you and other close people understand and accept. Because you know your child's motivation and ways of communicating, you are likely to understand much more than strangers.

The most important goal is for a child to develop any communications, even if only you understand them. Think of his next task as making his idiosyncratic communication (that is, the one only you understand) more conventional, i.e., understood by strangers. Do continue to encourage new idiosyncratic communications all along, however. Once you understand these new messages, you can help him make them closer to ones strangers understand. Throughout this growth, do not consider unclear messages as mistakes or problems. It is absolutely natural for children to begin communicating in rough pieces.

Subgoal

See your child's nonverbal vocabulary.

c. Express a range of meanings without words.

If nonverbal communications are the source of words, then we want a child's gestures and sounds to communicate those meanings we hope he will someday speak. But what meanings can a child first communicate? The answer lies in those things that he both knows and has a reason to communicate about. Children's first words appear to describe those people, actions, objects, locations, and feelings that are important enough to share with people. Consequently, when you respond to those nonverbal communications, just translate them into words. Then you can help him by communicating to him a range of people, actions, objects, locations, and feelings that are alive both to him and to you.

Subgoal

d. Communicate nonverbally for both social and instrumental reasons.

Just as children need to communicate a wide range of meanings, they need to communicate for a wide range of reasons. How often do you see children communicate only for instrumental reasons like demanding and rejecting? Children like these appear to see communication as mainly for getting, not for giving or exchanging. We have seen too many people with disorders who communicate mostly for survival reasons rather than for reasons that unite people in relationships. Communicating for social reasons results in contacts that seem to last longer than contacts for instrumental reasons. It is essential that we help nonverbal children see the great range and rewards of communicating for social reasons, like information, affection, attention, and the enjoyment of sharing experiences.

Subgoal

e. Be assertive with nonverbal messages.

Not only do children need to communicate without words, they need to be assertive about it. They need to let others know that they do, in fact, communicate and that they will not take a back seat just because they do not talk like others do. In order to assert himself, your child needs your help; you must carefully reward his nonverbal attempts. Make him feel important and worth attending to. The more you support him now, the more self-respect he will develop, and the more he will be able to develop communication on his own. Try to put aside your understandable urge to go for words. Convince yourself that one of your important jobs with your child is to build up his nonverbal communication world. Tell yourself that by doing that you will be preparing him for speech and language.

It's Your Turn

COMMENT:

It just feels wrong to communicate with a child without words when I want him to talk. I can't see myself doing it.

REPLY:

We often hear that. Our experience has been that a nonverbal child will stay communicating with us more if we communicate in his ways and a little above. Giving him something he can do seems to motivate him to do more; the more motivated he is to communicate with us, the more likely he will stay to try to communicate with us in new ways when we progressively match him. Again, visualize the developmental staircase that your child needs your careful help on. You must be within his reach if he is to successfully use you to get from sounds and movements to words and beyond.

COMMENT:

Sometimes, as I watch Chico play alone, he is happily playing with sounds and gestures that make him look like he is communicating. What he's doing has no meaning to me. Could these sounds and gestures be important?

REPLY:

Yes, they are as important to later communication as seeds are to flowers. They are important for practice as well as for signalling to others as to how to communicate with him. Those sounds and gestures that are part of his being playful for a child can build his first conversations, if you follow them and let him know they can be tools to keep you interacting with him.

COMMENT: In our classroom, playing with sounds and gestures, with no judgments, has become a regular activity. One child takes his turn, then another child imitates him or puts a word on the communication. We try to help the children become more responsive to their peers' little behaviors that may have been ignored before. Then the children try miming other children. Very playful and long turntaking strings ensue.

REPLY: That's very creative and speaks to a problem we see in many groups of children with delays; they rarely respond to each other spontaneously just for the fun of it. Our primary recommendation to teachers is that they increase the interactions within the classroom. Often we suspect that children do not respond to each other because the adults do not. Adults in classrooms often initiate and direct the children rather than respond to them, which would support the children's personally motivated communications. We have a deepfelt concern here—that many opportunities for relationships and communicating are missed if adults are not committed to fostering interaction that stems from the child's own motivations.

Self-Assessment:
How Are You
Doing?

Rate yourself on a scale of 1 to 9 where 1 = never or very poorly, 5 = neutral, and 9 = always or very well.

_____ 1. My child communicates with sounds.
_____ 2. My child frequently communicates with movements.
_____ 3. I believe that communication with sounds and movements is needed before words.
_____ 4. My child communicated with sounds and movements more than he did a few months ago.
_____ 5. My child's nonverbal communication works for him.
_____ 6. My child's nonverbal communications are understandable to strangers.

Child Goal

24. BEGIN TO COMMUNICATE VERBALLY

We are finally to the topic of talking, and we're half-way through the list of competencies. We understand the patience it takes for parents and professionals to wait to talk. We hope the discussions so far have shown you many goals to be excited about on the road to verbal communication. But again, there is an important caution to be heeded here. Once your child begins using words, it is not the end of nonverbal communication, turntaking, or playful interactions. It is absolutely critical that you still join in your child's nonverbal interactive world because *that is where his new words will come from.* Turntaking is still the tool to give a child both practice and the important feedback he needs. Think of this as a garden. Just because you get a few early peas, you do not quit watering the other vegetable seeds underground.

Subgoal

a. Show a range of words or signs.
A child will build relationships largely to the extent that he shares experiences with others. We have mentioned several times that many children we see communicate much less than they know. If we think of words and signs as symbols of knowledge, then we can begin to see where a child's new words can come from.

Once you get into interactions with the child, his personal knowledge can then become social knowledge. The more intimately interactive you are in your child's world, the more you will know about what he knows and the better position you will be in to give him words that match his thinking and motivations. Then ask yourself, "What does my child know that he's not communicating?" The answer will lead you to giving him words for those experiences.

Subgoal

b. Express a range of meanings.

Talk about the meaning he has in plan and nonverbal communication.

As with nonverbal communications, our concern with verbal communication is that the child is communicating an ever-increasing range of meanings or ideas. If he has some words and he has more knowledge, he can probably begin to use new words for that knowledge. Again, we want him to be able to use words for most of those pieces of his knowledge that he both cares about and has communicative use for. The child who communicates only a limited range of meanings will likely have a similarly limited range of social relationships. As you carefully observe your child, you will be able to identify not only his current words, but meanings he has that he soon may be ready to turn into words. You will also identify when he's using the "same old words" and use that observation as a signal to give him new words for the same experience. In order to successfully engage people in conversations, your child will need not only words but words that are creative and interesting. Your child needs to become a wordmaker in new situations—not just a talker.

Subgoal

c. Show both social and instrumental reasons.

Children who communicate mainly for instrumental reasons, that is, to get their immediate needs met or to manipulate people, seem to have less need to expand their vocabulary than do children who communicate for social reasons, for example, for information, affection, or play. As we noted earlier in this chapter, instrumental communications appear relatively short-lived compared to social communications, which support longer exchanges and require more creative language.

Subgoal

d. Send clear, understandable messages.

Certainly one of our goals in verbal communication is for the child to send clearer messages. At the outset, we want to stress that the messages should be "clearer," not "perfect" or "adult." The more you are in tune with your child's current ways of talking, the more readily can you show him the next steps he can do. There are at least three things you can do to help your child become clearer. First, you can help him make his "solo" words, ones no one understands, into "idiosyncratic" words, ones understood by you and other people who are close to him. The second task is to help your child change his current idiosyncratic words so other people can understand them. And the third task, perhaps a surprising one, is to help him put into words, even initially unintelligible forms, things he is currently thinking or communicating without words. The point here is that the road to intelligible speech is not a clear freeway, but involves many steps that can be made if adults have the attitude "Am I understanding a little more?" rather than "Is he talking right?"

Subgoal

e. Show conviction and assertiveness

We have known children who communicate so passively and with so little enthusiasm that, regardless of the richness of their language, their lack of convic-

Shows he means
what he says.

tion seems to interfere with developing communicative relationships. In fact, we even find ourselves losing interest in conversing with them. If we lose interest, how many opportunities to learn further is the child losing? In effect, the child must be his own public relations specialist. Ask yourself how well your child communicates the conviction that he belongs in the exchange and knows what he is doing. The communicative world requires active, confident participation. And we have found that such confidence is something that can be developed even in people with considerable delays.

It's Your Turn

COMMENT: My two granddaughters are 2½ years old. They have about 10 words that I can make out. I try to get them to stop their baby talk and put 2 words together. They turn away when I tell them to talk and not babble.

REPLY: First, realize that words will come from those sounds you call baby talk. Encourage them by showing them a word for their sounds and gestures. Watch carefully how the girls communicate together; you will see what they know and what behaviors are successfully working between them. And, better yet, you will learn how to communicate in their world.

COMMENT: How can my son Benji communicate with conviction or confidence if he has only a few words?

REPLY: If he has accepting partners he can be confident communicating with any behaviors. He will feel confident communicating to the degree those communications are successful. One value of matching is that it makes success more likely for the child.

Self-Assessment:
How Are You Doing?

Rate yourself on a scale of 1 to 9 where 1 = never or very poorly, 5 = neutral, and 9 = always or very well.

_____ 1. My child uses a range of words [signs] to express himself.
_____ 2. My child uses more words [signs] than he did a few months ago.
_____ 3. He expresses a range of meanings verbally.
_____ 4. He expresses more meanings than he did a few months ago.
_____ 5. My child uses words for more than only instrumental meanings.
_____ 6. My child uses words for social reasons.
_____ 7. He expresses himself clearly enough that strangers could understand him.

Child Goal

25. MAKE SELF UNDERSTOOD

For a developing child, making himself understood involves more than articulating well. The more you and your child share joint experiences, the more understandable he will be.

Subgoal

a. Use body language to clarify messages.
Frequently, we understand one child better than another, even when the child who is harder to understand is the one with more language. The difference, we think,

lies in the clarity of each child's body language. Body language can be so effective a method of communication between children and their caregivers that it actually may interfere with learning the communication that is more conventional and understandable to outsiders. Observe whether your child's body language helps you understand him more than it helps others. Ask yourself if your child deliberately uses body language to help others understand him. Gradually teach yourself to read your child's body, but be careful not to accept old attempts when simple waiting would get more from him.

b. Change the message to accommodate the listener.
It is a positive social and communicative sign when a child recognizes he is not understood and when he actively changes his communication to make himself more understood. Your child might articulate more slowly, speak more loudly, increase attention, or change in any of many other ways to become more effective. Often if you simply wait silently for your child, he will learn which changes help. Children may perseverate on old, easy ways; they may keep those old ways because they serve a purpose and get for the child what he wants. However, since change comes slowly for many children with delays, it is less important for a child to communicate as adults do than for him to learn when to change his communication and how to come closer to productions that will be more easily understood and accepted.

c. Repeat the message when there is no response.
When your child repeats your messages, he is practicing your sounds, intonations, and other features precisely at the time he is attending to the message. We can assume that the more motivated he is to attend to the message, the more effect his practice will have in changing his own messages to be closer to yours. Children repeat what we say more readily if we are matching them and waiting for them to do something.

Communication requires more than words.

Subgoal

Change when not understood.

Subgoal

It's Your Turn

COMMENT:

How long should a child keep communicating without words?

REPLY:

Forever. Just as you and I communicate much of our intentions with intonation and gestures and body language, so will your child. If you are asking how much preverbal communication is needed before a child speaks or signs regularly, there is no clear answer. It seems reasonable that the more messages a child communicates without words, the more ready he is to transfer these meanings into words. Our concern is that children develop a communicative habit and that others treat them as communicators, with the expectations and opportunities they need to learn from others.

Try to seek the relationship between a sound or gesture and a word. Think of the word as the product or result of the sound and gesture. The more sounds and gestures your child uses to communicate the more likely he will develop words to talk about the same things he communicated without words.

Think of communication development as a pyramid. At the bottom are all the experiences your child gained by himself and in interaction with others. Above these

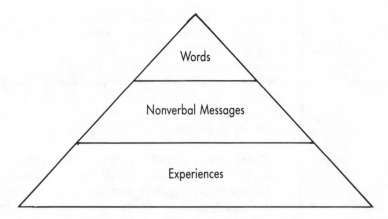

are the nonverbal communications that come from these experiences and interactions. Above the nonverbal communications are the child's words. More words require a larger base of interactions that underlie more nonverbal communications.

COMMENT: I have a few children in my class who communicate with gestures and sounds but have shown no progress with words for 3 years. What should I do?

REPLY: Keep communicating with them. Be careful not to consider yourself or the children failures if they do not develop speech. Many children, for physical, psychological, or undetermined reasons, may never use speech as their major way to communicate. Let's be very careful not to exclude them from the communicative world. Many persons with disabilities are in this dilemma, including adults with delays and others with physical injuries.

Our main concern is that you set up the classroom environment so that the children use the communication skills they have. That environment must include people who match, wait, expect, and keep the children communicating. Children and adults can develop rewarding relationships with nonverbal communication, especially if we do not hold out speech as the only goal.

While nonverbal communication may be the future of some children, consider another reason for not seeing progress toward speech over 3 years. Often we see adults fail to build on the child's nonverbal communication. They wait for speech like a gardener waiting for flowers but not fertilizing or watering seeds in the soil. Gestures and sounds are like those seeds; unless they get attention, they will not blossom. Unless your children are encouraged and stimulated to communicate in the early ways they can, they are likely to communicate less over time. Consequently, words have no base to develop from. Remember the pyramid—the more nonverbal communications you and the children share, the more likely the words will come.

COMMENT: My son communicates all the time but no one understands him. When I stop and show him the right way to talk, he tries hard to make the sounds right, but he hardly ever succeeds. I find myself obsessing on having him make the right sounds.

REPLY: We have known many parents and professionals in just your predicament. Think about this—it is absolutely natural and appropriate (even biologically correct) for a child to start making sounds in many ways different from our sounds. That is the way sounds develop. Therefore, in many cases what is *right* for an adult is *wrong* for a child developmentally. What this means is that it would be developmentally wrong for your child to make sounds in the way you think is the "right" way.

Give your child credit that he is still trying. His continued motivation to change is a promising sign. Some children avoid communicating when they are corrected or made to feel they failed. Just keep your child communicating more and more with you. Then you can show him how to communicate more clearly by matching him and showing him his next steps.

COMMENT: I understand everything my daughter communicates—her body language, sounds, even long strings of words. The problem is that no one else does, not even my husband or her teacher. Now professionals are saying she knows a lot less than I know she does, because they cannot understand her. Why can't they see and hear her through my eyes and ears?

REPLY: First, because they don't have your eyes and ears. Almost every parent and long-term teacher we know feels the same way. We see this as a very natural result of child-rearing. A young child needs an adult, usually mother, to build a special communication system with. The two have their own "language." Child movements that baffle everyone else are readily understood by the mother, who has a lot of experience watching and interpreting. Unless parents and children have this special language, a child may never get into seeing communication as a rewarding activity. This special "language," then, has helped the child become communicative, but it has also become an obstacle to the child communicating in the world at large.

The first step is to be sure the child enjoys communicating and is well into the habit of it. Try to realize that you have done a good job thus far. Your child is communicating in part because of the special language you have built together. Now your job is to wean both of you from that special language you have and prepare her to communicate with others.

One notion we use is the "stranger test," which is really a way of observing, thinking, and responding. When you're with your child, ask yourself which of her communications a stranger would understand and accept. Then try to get into the habit of responding immediately to those communications you think strangers would understand and waiting silently and expectantly when you think strangers would not understand. Gradually your child will learn which of her communications are more acceptable than others. Since you understand everything she communicates, it appears that you now reward her for all of her communications, so that she is not learning which ones to change. While you are not doing anything wrong (you do have her communicating and can take a lot of credit for that), it is time to move on. Realize that your communicative attention is a very powerful tool, and use it to let her know when to change.

COMMENT: I am responsible for training day care workers in a city school system. Many of them seem overly concerned with the articulation of their 2- to 4-year-olds. I tell them that preschool children shouldn't speak "perfectly," but they still want to do something. I see some of them drill the children on sounds; I'm afraid that will interfere with their play relationship. Any ideas?

REPLY: Congratulations on your concern. Certainly in day care play should reign over perfection. In our 20 years of working with unintelligible children, we have developed a specific style of communicating that can often elicit more intelligible communicating without driving the child away. We respond to an unintelligible child in several ways—imitate, wait, emphasize, translate. Each of these strategies has its own function, so we vary them according to how they get a child to stay and try again.

Self-Assessment:
How Are You
Doing?

Rate yourself on a scale of 1 to 9 where 1 = never or very poorly, 5 = neutral, and 9 = always or very well.

____ 1. My child uses body language to clarify his messages.
____ 2. He changes his message when not understood.
____ 3. He tries to communicate more like others.

ADULT STRATEGIES

In any contacts with you, a child can learn either to communicate or not to communicate. Parents and professionals usually greatly underestimate the power of their casual contacts in helping or interfering with a child's learning to communicate. Your child learns from you especially when you are not intentionally teaching him. Watch your other children and ask, "How did they learn from me? Was it all teaching or was it more like closely matched living?"

A child can learn to communicate in any interaction.

Before we discuss specific strategies to help children communicate, let's examine some attitudes that seem necessary. Without these attitudes, you may use the strategies so mechanically that they fail.

First, understand that your child's communications will increase and become central to his daily life to the extent that they grow out of his interests, not those of others. Thus, think more of your child's learning than of your teaching. When he has a playful, interactive relationship with people that focuses on his interests and his internal motivations, he will be ready to communicate.

Communicate about your child's interests.

Many adults are trained to believe that their own interests are more important than the child's. This can be a devastating belief for both the child and the adult. It harms the child because it shows disrespect for exactly those things that his motivation and cognitive level predispose him to learn and generalize. It harms adults because it almost guarantees the child will not participate with them enough to learn much. Once you genuinely believe that following your child's interests is the best way to get him into the habit of communicating, you will also see him following your lead and communicating more like you.

Communication develops best from your child's interests, not yours.

Realizing that your child's communications develop better from his interests than from yours will help you change your view of what communication is and where it begins. Communication is your child's expression of his own ideas and interests in any form possible. A child needs to communicate first *without words*. We adults are so used to thinking of communication in terms of words and sentences that we often ignore the sounds and movements children must make before they will talk. Think of a staircase with words and sentences at the top, and many kinds of sounds, movements, and other signals on the steps below. Just as a child cannot get to the top step without taking the steps leading up to it, he will not use words habitually until he habitually uses many different nonverbal means to communicate. Accepting this principle may seem easy, but it takes determination for adults to pay attention to those little behaviors we have often considered unimportant.

A third important attitude is that you are your child's best communication teacher. You cannot avoid teaching him—either you teach him how to communicate or how not to. Once you understand that any child behavior can communicate and that all your contacts are teaching him something, you should find the following strategies logical and helpful.

26. MATCH CHILD COMMUNICATION PROGRESSIVELY

Communicating in ways close to your child's ways may seem unusual, even incorrect, at first. But if you watch parents with infants, you can see how natural and effective matching is. A growing body of research now supports the conclusion that, in the infant's first year, adults regularly change their communications to match their infant's level (Lewis & Rosenblum, 1974). These changes appear to allow the child to get into the habit of communicating in the first year (Kaye, 1980b; Stern, 1977; Trevarthan, 1977). If the adults around him do not match his level, it is much more difficult for the child to learn to act like other people do. Matching provides the child something that he can physically do and cognitively process and that motivates him through the success it offers.

However, our experience with many young children suggests to us that adults give up and retreat to adult ways if a child fails to give them what they expect or does not regularly respond when they communicate. Then we see a mutual stand-off. The more adults act like adults, the less the child communicates; the less the child communicates, the more the adults expect the child can't communicate, and proceed to act more like adults. The pattern continues this way. It is a cycle that isolates child and adult further and further. The finding that infants can learn to communicate when adults carefully match their ways of acting (Bates, 1976; Mahoney et al., 1986; Stern, 1985) has led us to explore the effects of matching on older children with weak communicative habits. While research never actually proves causes and effects, there is substantial research evidence that matching children's communication results in greater communication and more willingness to stay in communicative interactions (MacDonald & Gillette, 1988).

Studies of parent-infant interactions are useful because they document the great variety of ways adults can match children's behaviors. Three reviews of parent-infant interaction (Haslett, 1983; Siegel-Causey, Ernst, & Guess, 1987; Snow, 1984) have analyzed more than 50 studies. They support the observations that (a) caregivers alter their behavior to fit their child and (b) those changes facilitate the child's rate of and interest in interacting and communicating. While these studies do not predict more rapid language development, they do strongly suggest that caregiver strategies do help build the kind of relationship that is likely to support a habit of social interaction. While many terms are used for these changes (including the popular motherese), we have chosen matching as a general term to refer to those attempts to come closer to the child physically, communicatively, linguistically, and motivationally.

Match: The more you communicate like your child, the more your child will communicate like you.

When you match your child, you are doing something he can do. This process functions with adults, as well. Consider what you do when someone talks "over your head" or says so much that he loses you. You certainly do not learn much and, more importantly, you probably avoid communicating with him in the future. Be careful this does not happen to your child too much; the most harmful thing for his communication development is to get in the habit of avoiding people.

Substantial clinical and research evidence now confirms that children learn a task best when it is at their ability level or a little higher. Not only will a child learn more from you if you do things he can do, he will be more motivated to learn with you (Deci, 1975; Mahoney, Finger, & Powell, 1985). If we do things too far below the child's level to challenge him, he will not participate (Hunt, 1961). On the other hand, if what we do is too difficult, the child will expect to fail and may get into a habit of avoiding such learning situations (Hunt, 1961; Peck, in press). Consider the notion of "learned helplessness"; by mismatching a child we may be teaching him to have failures with people; that is, we may teach him he is more helpless than he might find if we matched him.

The task to learn in communication is people.

Much of the research on task learning has been conducted with learning tasks in school settings. However, we have found that the matching principle may have even more profound effects on learning to communicate in natural interactions. If we agree that a child learns best if the tasks are at his level and slightly higher, then the question for learning communication is: What is the task to be mastered? To learn to communicate, the child's task is clearly another person and his communication. Just as a child cannot solve a puzzle meant for adults—a puzzle with too many pieces—you also must not be too difficult a puzzle to him. Because *you* are your child's task when it comes to communication learning, you have ultimate control over the basic communication tasks he faces. No longer do you have to look outside yourself for teaching tools. You always have them with you.

Are you too much for your child to learn from?

Earlier in this chapter, we likened learning to communicate to learning to climb a staircase. Picture yourself with your child near the bottom of the stairs. Your child is looking to you for ways to get to the top or, for now at least, to get somewhere. At first you run up to the top all at once and say "come on up" (similar to talking for a long time to a child with a few sounds). But your child is not even trying, and in fact is leaving the situation. You realize that he needs to crawl before he can walk, so you go up again, crawling all the way (similar to the way we make sounds and actions far beyond what the child can do). You tried to match him by crawling instead of walking, but you still did more than he could, and again you lost him. But you don't give up. You learn how to progressively match him: first doing just what he is doing, such as reaching for the next step. Then you show him another small step, like lifting your leg as you reach. And when your child makes another try, you respond acceptingly and show him still another step. And he stays learning with you.

Fine turning and progressive matching.

Bruner (1983) calls this process "fine tuning." He has suggested that spontaneous communication development requires a *Language Acquisition Support System* (1983), an environment provided by caregivers that assists the child in becoming social and communicative. The more that environment is matched to the child's physical, motivational, and cognitive skills, he argues, the more the child will learn from the adult. According to Bruner, the habit parents have of fine tuning their physical and communicative behavior to their infant's immediate performance allows the child to be social and communicative. This is not what we usually consider "teaching." Fine tuning, or progressive matching as we call it, can occur regardless of whether you intend to teach something or the child intends to learn something in the interaction. Thus, ask yourself about how matched you are in every contact and how likely your child is to be learning from you. And remember that your child can learn a great deal from you without your deliberately teaching him.

When we progressively match, we are showing a child a next step in learning. For communication, we need to see how words are the next step from sounds and gestures. Frequently when we observe young children, we are struck by the private language they have with a parent. Parents, and sometimes professionals, close to a young child tell us, "I know what he means, but no one else does." Older children with delays often have a similar communication system. Looking at your child as someone speaking a foreign language, his own special language, helps you see that your task is not to teach him "language" but to teach him "your" language. The task becomes a matter of "second-language training." Picture a Spanish-speaking child, Lupe, in an English-speaking home. The child points to a bright light and says "luz." Immediately, an adult might say "light," giving the child an English word for his Spanish word. When traveling in a foreign country, how often do we create nonverbal signs when attempting to communicate? And the native attempts to train us in a second language by giving us local words for our gestures. Second-language training is a valuable way to think of matching both the child's communicative level and his intentions. It is one form of progressive matching, because we communicate in ways the child can do and, at the same time, show him a next step as well.

A final word about matching: While it is among the most powerful strategies we use, we do not mean for you to become compulsive about it. Surely we want you and your child to become better matched. But we know that a relationship must have two satisfied people. You cannot successfully live totally for your child. There must be enough times when you are your adult self. Do not feel guilty for being adult around your child, as long as there are other close times when you match your child so that he can learn from you.

The Matching Staircase

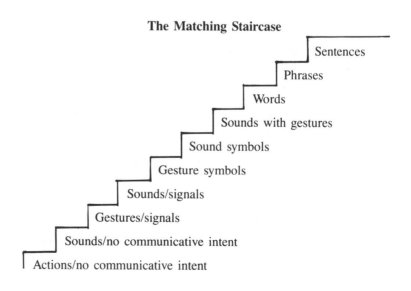

Sentences
Phrases
Words
Sounds with gestures
Sound symbols
Gesture symbols
Sounds/signals
Gestures/signals
Sounds/no communicative intent
Actions/no communicative intent

Assessing the Match Between You and Your Child.

Use the matching staircase to rate the forms you and your child perform with each other. Use ratings of 1 to 9 for each form (1 indicates not at all; 5, a moderate rate; 9, a constant use of that form). Use the profile to help guide where you are and how you can match your child.

Let your child's communication guide how you communicate.

Use the following matching strategies in your casual contacts with a child. With a little practice, you can learn to weave them into the very ways you live and work with a child, in play, in school, or anywhere in the community. The strategies should help you form a closer bond with children, one that keeps children communicating with you and becoming more like you.

Substrategy

a. Provide an effective model for the child's communication.

Consider everything you do with your child as something he might learn to do. We call this "modeling" (Bandura, 1977)—doing something that your child attends to and learns how to do. Just as your child learns to push the vacuum, hold the phone, and make certain facial expressions by watching you, he can learn to communicate like you. As long as you match his level and get his interest, he is likely to act more like you. You will know if your modeling is effective if your child attends to you and tries to do something as you did it. Understand that modeling need not mean you are deliberately trying to teach your child. Modeling can occur naturally and still be effective when you intend no particular result with your child.

Substrategy

b. Communicate close to the child's expressive level.

Observe your child to better understand his current level of communication. It may be "clear speech sounds but unclear single words," "gestures and nonspeech sounds," or "body movements and a few words, except longer sentences when with toys and books." Don't worry. You won't be perfect, because he will change over time and situations. But with that level in mind, try to shape your communication to his and try one step above part of the time. Beware of the easy habit of talking at the level your child understands; he may nod or otherwise show he understands and that can keep you satisfied for a while. Remember you need to communicate not only to be understood but also to *show him how to communicate*. Matching shows him how he can now communicate. In fact, be careful not to continue your adult level of communication just because your child understands it. We know many children who understand much of our complicated language but rarely communicate any of those ideas. When we match the same children they often communicate more.

Substrategy

c. Use nonverbal body language and sounds that are at or slightly above the child's expressive level.

If we accept the premise that verbal communications are based on a broader set of nonverbal communications, it is also important to show your child new, more mature, nonverbal ways to communicate. Your child needs to learn expressions for surprise, exasperation, and other emotions that play critical roles in communication. Often the words are not the critical feature of the message. If all a child hears are words and sentences, he may fail in his attempts to match. Worse, he may also fail to develop the nonverbal habit essential for full language to develop.

Substrategy
d. Use words and word combinations (or signs) that are at or slightly above the child's expressive level.

You can do many things to match a child's words. For example, you can give him new words at the same level (e.g., when he says, "that's a banana," you say "long and yellow"). Or you can show him a sentence for his words (e.g., he says, "dog bark outside," and you say, "doggie is barking outside"). The strategy is to show the child a new way to talk, one that is within his productive reach. Think of these as two kinds of matching: horizontal and vertical. In horizontal matching you give the child new words at the some level. This shows him new meanings or words he can use while he is still at the single-word level. In vertical matching, you show him how to combine words or make sentences out of current words.

Substrategy
e. Up the ante occasionally for improved response.

Many children with delays experience so many interpersonal difficulties that they are inclined to take the easy way out. For example, we have known many children with Down syndrome or cerebral palsy who communicate much less frequently and less maturely than we know they could. If we wait silently for them to do more, they often show a considerably improved response. Sometimes we have to signal them to do more, or even prompt them with part of the response, again waiting for them to do more. There is a name for this process of responding to an immature communication with a period of silence and then signalling if necessary. It's called "upping the ante," a card-playing analogy Bruner (1983) used for the process he observed in mothers with infants. With this strategy, adults are teaching children that they get quicker attention from the world if they communicate in newer or more mature ways than they usually do.

It's Your Turn

COMMENT: Why should I change the way I communicate when my son understands everything I say? I feel so good when he understands; I want to keep it up.

REPLY: Good question. We know how rewarding it is to be understood. You keep communicating in adult ways because it works for you. But is it working for your child? The reward for your communications should not be just passive understanding. Let's think a bit now about the reasons we want to communicate to a child. Certainly, being understood is one reason. But another extremely important reason is to show your child how to communicate. Every time you communicate with your child, he may learn to communicate as you do. Try to get into the habit of thinking, "Can my child communicate the way I am communicating? How can I communicate so he can do something like me?" Then match your child and communicate in ways that get more mature communication from him.

COMMENT: I feel silly when I communicate like my child. I know he communicates more when I do it, but it still feels wrong and childish. My husband teases me when I match my child.

REPLY: There is a big difference between childish and childlike. For years you have probably believed in only one way to communicate. Be patient with your feelings. Watch and listen to what your child does when you match him. We suspect he will do more and enjoy your company more. Enjoy the success your child is achieving. What others think will begin to pale in comparison to the rewards your child can give you for giving him something he can do. Even your husband might begin matching if he sees your child giving you more for it.

Self-Assessment:
How Are You
Doing?

Rate yourself on a scale of 1 to 9 where 1 = never or very poorly, 5 = neutral, and 9 = always or very well.

_____ 1. I communicate with actions like my child's.
_____ 2. I communicate with sounds like my child's.
_____ 3. I communicate with words like my child's.
_____ 4. I communicate with phrases like my child's.
_____ 5. I communicate in ways my child can probably soon do.
_____ 6. I show my child how to communicate next.
_____ 7. I am comfortable communicating at my child's level.
_____ 8. My child communicates more when I match him.
_____ 9. I think my child needs a professional to learn to communicate.
_____10. I think I need a professional to help my child communicate.
_____11. I feel I should talk to my child like an adult.
_____12. I think I should talk to my child like another child.
_____13. I think my child can communicate better than he or she usually does.
_____14. I think I can help my child learn to communicate.

Adult Strategy

27. RESPOND TO THE CHILD

Many adults expect children to learn to communicate on their own. They believe it will "come in time." Others believe that children with learning problems can learn only when intentionally taught by professionals. Most parents do not realize that every time they respond to their child (however "insignificant" his actions or communications may seem to them) and every time they fail to respond, they are influencing how he communicates. In other words, your responses to your child's movements and sounds are the rewards that teach him what to do more often. Again, your responses are like fertilizer to flowers; if you are warm and matched, they will make your child grow. If you ignore these little building blocks, your child may try less.

If you expect and accept only certain kinds of communications, each of you will be discouraged from trying to communicate with the other. When children and adults respond only to old established communications, the adult does not support the child's spontaneous attempts or show him how they can communicate next. Neither child nor adult seems to feel any control over the other. The child may come to believe that what he can do is not enough, and the adults may come to feel they cannot get the child to communicate.

Respond to new
little behaviors.

One way we work to break this vicious cycle is to adopt the habit of responding to anything the child does, as long as it is safe and inoffensive. We respond in a matched way, positively and supportively, then wait silently while we allow the child to keep communicating with us. We respond to the child's actions and sounds and words, no matter what they are, because these are intrinsically motivating to the child (Bronfenbrenner, 1979; Hunt, 1961; Mahoney et al., 1986). Again, it is not what or how your child communicates that matters most; it is that he communicates often and stays for longer and longer turns with you.

And one surprising way we have found to get a child to communicate is to pretend he already is. Bates (1976) has carefully recorded how parents first treat play behaviors as if they are communications. For example, if a mother says "want up" to a child reaching up to play with a toy, the child may learn to reach up to get her mother's help.

Respond as if your child were communicating.

Responding to the subtle things your child does can also help him learn to respond to others that way. Once he begins responding to others, they will be naturally motivated to stay communicating with him. Remember, a primary goal of this approach to building relationships is to help children and adults stay interacting together for more time on more topics. The more staying and interacting together, the more learning occurs.

Even after some training, parents and professionals need more help in learning what exactly they should respond to. Observe yourself and answer these questions: "What am I doing that results in my child responding to me? What am I doing that results in my child not responding?" Your answers can become a practical list of what you can do and what you should try to avoid. In the same way, look at the other side and ask these questions: "What does my child do when I respond to him? When I do not respond?"

How Do You Respond to Your Child's Behaviors that Could be Communicative?

Come to believe that formal teaching is not the way to learn to communicate. Once your child is in the habit of communicating, formal teaching may help shape him up. Until then, he needs you and other close people to support him in his first communications. Think of your responses to your child like those of a gardener who must regularly fertilize the flowers and vegetables but not the weeds. Every time you respond to your child, in effect, you are making his communication more fertile, actually making it grow. Every time you ignore his actions and communications, they wither, like an unfertilized flower. Like the gardener, you do not have to fertilize every single behavior. But a regular habit of responding is necessary to help a child communicate so habitually that he will be soon learning spontaneously.

Fertilize the flowers, not the weeds.

What behaviors should you not respond to? Even casual attention may strengthen inappropriate or lazy communications. Adults frequently wonder "Why does he keep acting that way when I keep explaining why he shouldn't?" Or they say, "I keep telling him to use his words and not just sounds. Why doesn't he?" Therefore, unless the child's behaviors put someone in danger (in which case we must attend to them to stop them), we try to ignore any socially undesirable or clearly immature behaviors. You can safely ignore the child who says "don't" to many things or answers "uh uh" to a hundred questions, and wait for something better. You will not hurt the child; you will show him that the world will only give him more if he gives more. We know how difficult it is not to respond to a child communicating to us, but we find that truly ignoring inappropriate behaviors not only stops them but often results in the child finding more appropriate or mature ways of communicating. Often the child is already competent to do more, but will continue his easier ways if they work for him. Again, fertilize the flowers, not the weeds.

Substrategy

a. Respond immediately to actions and all forms of communication.

Years of research in studying how people can affect others' behaviors (Skinner, 1957) show that our responses are much more likely to strengthen ("reinforce") a person's behaviors if we respond immediately to those we want to occur again. At first, we want our children to strengthen any actions or sounds that could develop into communications, and as that occurs, to learn more and more mature communications. Build a strong base of actions and sounds in a stable habit of interactions back and forth, and communication will evolve.

Many adults seem unaware of those small actions that are the seeds of their child's communication. Until your child is communicating, respond quickly, watching and listening carefully to what he does when you respond in certain ways. Soon you will learn to respond almost automatically to keep your child communicating with you and to get slightly more mature communications. Let your child show you the way: Increase your responses that get more; decrease those that get less. Just as the gardener plants and waters many seeds to get a few plants, you will find that by sensitively responding in a matched way to your child's actions and sounds, some of them will flower into meaningful communications.

Substrategy

b. Respond to some actions as if they were communications.

An important finding in recent years has been that almost any action can send a message (Austin, 1962; Watzlawick, Beavin, & Jackson, 1967). We all know this intuitively, as when two people say "hello, nice to see you" to us and we know that only one of them is really glad to see us. We see that one-word greeting as two different communications because of the differences in intonation, facial expression, and body language.

As we saw with the story of Jenny in the crib earlier, you can encourage your child to make his spontaneous actions into meaningful communications if you respond to them as though he were communicating something. Adults have countless opportunities in homes and classrooms to help a child make simple actions into intentional communications. Let your child's behaviors have clear, meaningful effects on you and you will see him use similar behaviors later to get those same effects. That's communication.

Substrategy

c. Show sensitivity to the child's intentions.

Once your child is responding, you have the power to strengthen or weaken those communications by learning to "read" him. By reading your child, we mean observing him and interpreting his needs, desires, and interests at the moment. The

Read your child's intentions.

more accurately you read your child's intentions, the more you can tailor your response to get him to respond. If you see your child frown when you say, "Eat some carrots," you can say something like, "Oo, yecchy carrot. Eat just one." Here you have shown him you understand him and have modified your goal to accept only one carrot. An extreme example of misreading is to deny or reject the child's intentions. For example, a child tries to leave a therapy room and the adult says, "You don't want to go. You want to stay with me." If you habitually misread the child's intentions, he may become confused about his intentions, mistrust yours, or simply avoid communicating with you.

Substrategy

d. Follow the child's lead as you communicate.

A child is more likely to genuinely hear your communication and respond to it if it relates to what he is doing or saying. This does not mean communicating about his interests. But, for a child who is not assertive about communicating, perhaps neither confident nor regularly successful, when you follow his lead you enter both his cognitive and motivational worlds. Thus you make communication easier and more interesting for him.

Substrategy

e. Respond at least as often as you initiate.

If you have a positive and emotionally attached relationship, your attention is likely to reward and build your child's communications. A child needs to learn that his little attempts at communciation, however primitive they seem to you, can have clear effects on others. You can help him here by responding to many attempts in ways that keep him communicating. At times, your response can be carefully matched to show him a next step; at other times your responses can be whatever comes to you. The issue here is to help the child get into the habit of communicating increasingly more with people.

It's Your Turn

COMMENT:

I have three children. My 4-year-old twin boys, Alex and Sean, are delayed, with autistic tendencies. My 6-year-old daughter, Julie, is bright and social. Before training, I thought I was responding to them all the same. But when the clinician began responding to the boys, I realized that I had missed seeing many things they were doing. I had been responding to their words but to very little else. One thing that really helped was imitating each of the boys for a minute or so. After doing it a few times a day for several days, I got to know exactly what they were interested in doing. And they stayed with me so much longer. The most exciting thing was that they began responding to me. They had rarely ever done that before.

REPLY:

We have heard many such stories. Parents and teachers often have no idea how important a child's little, spontaneous behaviors are for building communicative relationships. Acting just like a child tells your whole body what the child is. You need to feel what the child is, not just think about it, if you are to become a finely tuned communication partner.

Self-Assessment:
How Are You
Doing?

Rate yourself on a scale of 1 to 9 where 1 = never or very poorly, 5 = neutral, and 9 = always or very well.

_____ 1. I respond to his actions.
_____ 2. I respond to his gestures.
_____ 3. I respond to his sounds.
_____ 4. I respond to his words.
_____ 5. I respond to his negative behavior.
_____ 6. I respond only when he directs his behaviors to me.
_____ 7. I pretend he is communicating to me.
_____ 8. I respond by imitating him.
_____ 9. I respond by matching him (doing something he can do).
_____10. I respond by questioning him.
_____11. I respond by correcting him.
_____12. He responds more to some of my communications than others.

A FINAL NOTE

Communication develops best in a partnership between two people who value each other, who avoid controlling each other, and who want to continue their relationship. Some believe that words and the language of words will evolve naturally from such communicative relationships. In cases where language does not come easily, words and language can become a priority. The next chapter discusses some ideas and directions to foster language. But when language fails, always return to the principles in this chapter on nonverbal communication. Whenever you are in doubt, return to the simpler kinds of communication you have learned about here. These will strengthen you with successes and show you the language that is appropriate for your child.

Sample Resources for Becoming Communicating Partners

ECOScale: Becoming Communicating Partners
ECO Tutor: Becoming Communicating Partners
ECO Link: Becoming Communicating Partners
Conversation Routine
IEP/Problem Solver
ECO Practice Plan and Record

BECOMING COMMUNICATING PARTNERS

INTERACTIVE GOAL

19. Become communicating partners.
    a. Keep communication going back and forth between the two.
    b. Initiate as well as respond.
    c. Exchange messages that have a social more than an instrumental focus.
    d. Make each communication understood by the other.

CHILD PROBLEM

20. Low communicative participation.
    a. Limited frequency of communication.
    b. Infrequent initiation.
    c. Infrequent responses.
    d. Repetitive or meaningless use of gestures, sounds, or words.
    e. Communication too instrumental; focus on getting needs met.
    f. Failure to attend to shared topic.

ADULT PROBLEM

21. Mismatch.
    a. Limited use of childlike actions.
    b. Little use of communication that the child can use.
    c. Main use of speech with nonverbal child.
    d. Words but not sounds used with a sounding child.
    e. Use of word combinations beyond the child's expressive capability.
    f. Failure to talk about the child's activity or interests.

CHILD GOALS

22. Intentionally communicate with others.
    a. Use nonverbal messages alone.
    b. Use nonverbal messages with verbal messages.
    c. Balance initiations and responses.
    d. Imitate as well as respond in other ways.
    e. Maintain communicative interactions.
    f. Exchange messages with ease.

23. Communicate nonverbally.
    a. Use a range of gestures, sounds, and movements that send a message.
    b. Send clear messages without words.
    c. Express a range of meanings without words.
    d. Communicate nonverbally for both social and instrumental reasons.
    e. Be assertive with nonverbal messages.

24. Begin to communicate verbally.
    a. Show a range of words or signs.
    b. Express a range of meanings.
    c. Show both social and instrumental purposes.
    d. Send clear, understandable messages.
    e. Show conviction and assertiveness.
25. Make self understood.
    a. Use body language to clarify messages.
    b. Change the message to accommodate the listener.
    c. Repeat the message when there is no response.

ADULT STRATEGIES

26. Match child communication progressively.
    a. Provide an effective model for child communication.
    b. Communicate close to the child's expressive level.
    c. Use nonverbal body language and sounds that are at or slightly above the child's expressive level.
    d. Use words and word combinations (or signs) that are at or slightly above the child's expressive level.
    e. Up the ante occasionally for improved response.
27. Respond to the child.
    a. Respond immediately to actions and all forms of communication.
    b. Respond to some actions as if they were communications.
    c. Show sensitivity to the child's intentions.
    d. Follow the child's lead as you communicate.
    e. Respond at least as often as you initiate.

ECO Tutor

Interactive Goal: Becoming Communicating Partners (Preverbal)

What Is It?	Communicating partners actively and frequently share ideas with each other. As they share messages, the two create a common ground which includes input from each to develop the partnership. How they exchange messages often becomes more important than what the two talk about. To become a successful communicating partner, consider developing a relationship with the child as the main goal of your message exchanges with him.
What To Look For	To decide if you and your child have a communicating partnership, look for a spirit of togetherness and friendliness. Additional ingredients will include a balanced amount of input from each partner, a sharing in the responsibility of initiating contact with each other, responding to contact with the other, and maintaining the message exchange.

LESS LIKE THIS

Tom: (Plays with his cars on the floor.)
Dad: "What are you doing there, son?"
Tom: (Continues with his cars.)
Dad: "You look like you're having a good time."
Tom: (Looks up briefly and smiles.)
Dad: "I thought so. Can you give Daddy a car?"
Tom: (Gives Dad the car.)
Dad: "Wow, what a good boy! I used to love to play with cars when I was a little kid. You're just like Daddy, aren't you?"
Tom: (Nods his head "yes" and smiles.)

Why Less?

Dad mainly talks; Tom mainly plays. This pair does not have a communicating partnership. Tom plays a responsive role each time he communicates. His compliance tends to keep his adults satisfied that he participates with them as a communicating partner, yet he only responds, and only in the most limited manner possible. Dad will need to communicate less and play more, while his son will need to do the opposite in order to establish a communicating partnership.

MORE LIKE THIS

Tom: (Plays with his cars on the floor.)
Dad: (Lays down across from him.) "Vroom, vroom." (Pushes a car to Tom.)
Tom: (Laughs and takes the car, pushing it back.)
Dad: "Go." (Pushes it quickly to him.)
Tom: "Oo oo." (Pushes it back, laughing.)
Dad: "Wow." (Makes the car crash into the couch.)
Tom: "Wow." (Expresses enjoyment on his face.)
Dad: (Expresses enjoyment on his face.) "Fun."
Tom: (Places the car in Dad's hands and laughs.)
Dad: "Oo car." (Pats it to express concern.)
Tom: "Oo oo." (Pats it too.)

Why More?

Dad responds to Tom by joining him at play with cars. They exchange similar actions and messages. Dad matches the way Tom communicates, using gestures, sounds, and facial expressions as his primary methods of communicating. He progressively matches Tom by adding an occasional single word. Eventually Tom may begin to use these single words as well. In the meantime they can continue to establish a habit of mutual enjoyment and message exchanging that will help them develop a relationship, whatever Tom's eventual communication skills might be.

Why Is It Important?	Your child needs to establish a habit of regularly communicating with others, though he may not yet use words. Skills like responding to others as well as initiating and maintaining contacts can be fostered now, so that your child can experience the enjoyment communicating with others can provide. A child who enjoys communicating will do so more frequently; the more he communicates, the more opportunities he will have to learn about how to deal with the world and the people in it.

Strategies That
Can Help
— Respond to the child.
— Match the child's communication.

Concerns and
Possible Problems

Adults who live or work with handicapped children often push too hard for words, forgetting that all behaviors can communicate. Even if the child does eventually learn words, he may not have the communication skills to contact others, respond to others, or maintain interactions with them. These important communication skills do not require words and should be the focus of communication training for every preverbal child. Other times, adults may initiate to the child, yet fail to respond to the child's subtle initiations. Treating a child in this way may inadvertently teach him not to initiate with others. Adults who treat the child's behaviors as communications increase the child's desire to contact others.

Avoid dead-end contacts whenever possible. Little social or communication learning takes place with a hit-and-run communication style. Your child can experience what it's like to participate in an ongoing message exchange even without words. Later, he may be able to participate more fully in a conversation because you have laid the groundwork for this skill in his preverbal communication experience.

**ECO
Link**

Becoming Communication Partners
HOW YOU CAN HELP A CHILD LEARN TO COMMUNICATE

HOW DO YOU AND YOUR CHILD COMMUNICATE TOGETHER?

1. How often do you communicate together? Is communicating a habitual part of being together?
2. Is your communication balanced? Do each of you communicate about as much as the other?
3. Do each of you communicate with similar sounds and gestures? Are you nonverbally matched?
4. Do each of you communicate with similar numbers of words? Are you verbally matched?
5. Do each of you communicate about similar ideas? Are you cognitively matched?
6. How effective are your communications? Do you get each other's messages?
7. Do your communications together help build a relationship between you?
8. Is your communication together enjoyable?

HOW WILL YOU KNOW IF YOUR CHILD IS YOUR COMMUNICATION PARTNER?

1. He will habitually communicate as a natural part of being with you.
2. He will both initiate and respond communicatively about equally.
3. He will voluntarily communicate as well as when you want him to.
4. He will balance his communications with yours, and rarely take a passive or dominant role.
5. He will change his communications to be more like yours and to be understood.
6. He will be sensitive to your communications as well as assertive of his own.

HOW WILL YOU KNOW IF THERE IS A PROBLEM IN YOUR COMMUNICATIVE PARTNERSHIP?

1. You will communicate too little for it to become a habit.
2. One of you will communicate much more than the other, thus limiting the other's chances.
3. Your communication will focus on getting needs met or jobs done.
4. Your communications will not be matched in terms of difficulty or ideas.
5. One of you will control the communications by initiating most contacts and directing them with questions and commands.
6. Your communications will often be ineffective, either in being understood or in getting responses.

HOW CAN YOU BUILD A COMMUNICATIVE PARTNERSHIP WITH YOUR CHILD?

1. Understand that language comes from nonverbal communications.
2. Enjoy communicating and make it more like play than work.
3. Balance communications; take turns by communicating once and then waiting.
4. Match; communicate in ways your child can do and about ideas meaningful to him.
5. Progressively match; show your child how to communicate messages in higher forms, like sounds that become words and movements that become sounds.
6. Respond to even the most subtle communications, encouraging more.
7. Communicate mainly for social reasons, rather than to get something done.
8. Be effective; fine-tune your communication to one that keeps the child voluntarily with you.

1. Communicating much more than the child without waiting for his turns.
2. Communicating in ways the child cannot do (ability mismatch).
3. Communicating outside the child's interests or understanding (cognitive mismatch).
4. Accepting immature communications when he can do more.
5. Communicating to control the child, as with many questions and commands.

**Conversation
Routine**

DAILY LIVING: Bathtime Preverbal Level

Make the natural events in your day into opportunities for friendly, social conversations with your child. Consider these contrasting examples. Try to avoid limited contacts such as the one on the left. Try to find something you can share with your child, as in the example on the right. Turn just another routine into a joint activity in which your child can stay and learn with you.

LESS LIKE THIS

Adult:	"Honey, hold this toy while I wash you up, okay."
Child:	(Takes the toy and splashes it around.)
Adult:	(Tries to wash the child's back.) "Don't move around too much. Mommy can't do a good job."
Child:	"Oo oo oo." (Pushes a rubber duck through the water.)
Adult:	"You like your duckie, don't you." (Keeps washing child.)
Child:	(Keeps playing.)
Adult:	"You can make him go, go, go, can't you?" (Keeps washing.)
Child:	(Keeps playing.)

Avoid These Problems:
*Adult Mismatches Child,
Lack of Active Togetherness*

The adult seems tuned to the child's world, but the child is not likely to perceive it. Her words are far above his level to use or perhaps even understand. Additionally, her actions do not relate to what she talks about; an ACTION-TALK MISMATCH.

MORE LIKE THIS

Adult:	"Ooo-washie-washie." (Washes child's back, then gives him the washcloth.)
Child:	(Takes the washcloth and washes his little duck.) "Wa-wa."
Adult:	(Takes the cloth back.) "Wash." (Washing her child's face.)
Child:	(Dunks the duck in the water.) "Wa-wa."
Adult:	(Imitates the child's action on the duck.) "Wash."
Child:	"Quack, quack." (Puts the duck up to his mother's face.)
Adult:	(Mom waves to the duck.) "Hi, duck."
Child:	(Waves to mom.) "Aiya."
Adult:	(Waves to child.) "Hi you!"

Try These Strategies:
Match Child Behavior, Imitate and Animate

Mom gets her child washed while providing him with some turntaking and communication training. They move from the topic of washing up to the social topic of saying "Hi!" because the child takes the initiative. The mother follows his lead through imitation with expansion as well as animation. Despite the limited use of verbal communication, they conduct an animated social exchange without requiring the child's use of words.

VARIATIONS:
Washing up any time of the day, or other related caretaking routines.

IEP/
Problem Solver

Early Verbal
CHILD GOAL: Communicate with Others
PROBLEM: Adult Mismatch

Donnie can talk, but his mother out-talks him ten to one. She thinks that the more she talks to him, the more he will talk back—someday. So far she sees few results from her efforts. She remains hopeful because everywhere she looks she reads that she should "bathe the child in language" and then the child will talk more.

Mom:	"This tree is lovely. It has wonderful green leaves, and a shiny bark. I think we should find a leaf and take it home. Maybe we could put it in wax paper and iron it. That way we can keep it for a long time. Doesn't that sound like fun?" (Picks up leaf and shows it to Donnie.)
Donnie:	"Wif." (Grabs a leaf from the tree).
Mom:	"Good. I'm glad you like leaves. Why don't you take this one and put it in your back-pack."
Donnie:	(Takes the leaf from his mother and opens his mouth to talk, but she takes over.)
Mom:	"You'll have to use your good zipper skills on this backpack, I think. I think you can zip jackets better than these tricky backpack zippers. I'll sit and watch you. Let's see how you do without any help."
Donnie:	(Struggles with the zipper, then glances at Mom for help.)
Mom:	"You need help, don't you? Here, give it to Mommy. I can zip real well. You can watch me and maybe the next time we go out leaf hunting you can do it yourself. Are you watching carefully?"
Donnie:	(Shakes his head yes.)
Mom:	"Good. I'm glad you think you can. Remind me to check you on that next time. Okay?"
Donnie:	"Okay."

ECO | *Partnership Plan*

The **ECO** Partnership Plan contains those elements of an Individual Family Service Plan (IFSP) or Individual Education Program (IEP) that specify **ECO** goals and objectives to enhance a child's social and communicative development. Refer to current ECOScales for present levels of development and performance and for new goals.

Child Name: ___**Donnie**___   Birth Date: ___**2/9**___   Parents: ___**Lou and Ginny**___

Date of ECOScales: ___**4/16**___   Examiner: _____

Present Levels of Development and Performance
___Noninteractive but minimally communicative; verbal level___

Child Goal
___Intentionally communicate with others___

Objectives
___Balance initiations/responses___   ___Use nonverbal and verbal messages___

___Maintain communicative interactions___

Partnership Goal
___Become Communicating Partners___

Objectives
___Keep communication going back and forth___   ___Initiate as well as respond___

Priority Problem:
___Mismatch___

Subproblem
___Level of word combinations too high___

___Little use of communication Donnie can use___

Adult Strategies
___Match Donnie's communication expressively___

Substrategies
___Respond to Donnie___   ___Respond to all forms of communication___

___Comment more than question, command___   ___Use open-ended questions, replies___

Practice Activities
People Only
___At the park___

___1___ Times a day   ___3-5___ Minutes each

People and Things
___Schoolhouse___

___Connect Four, dominoes___

___1-2___ Times a day   ___3-5___ Minutes each

Daily Routines
(practice one a day)
___Watching TV together___   ___Picking up toys together___

Spontaneous

ECO | Practice Plan and Record

PRACTICE PLAN
Refer to current *ECOScale* for goals; see other *ECOScales* for old goals to maintain.

Interactive Goal Become communicating partners (David and Dad)

Objectives make communication understood
by The other

Priority Problem Low communicative participation

Child Goal Communicate more frequently with others

Objectives Balance initiation and responses   Imitate as well as respond in other ways

Adult Strategies 1) Become play partners   2) Match David's communication progressively
Communicate close to David's level   MATCH — use words just above David's level

Targets to Decrease DAVID — Limited frequency of communication   Infrequent imitation
Practice Activities JARED — Using word combinations beyond David's level   Communicating in
ways David can't do

People Only Tickling   Exchanging body movements/words

How Often 2 Times a day   2-3 Minutes each
Where

People and Things Put baby in & out of bed   Stack blocks

How Often 2 Times a day   2-3 Minutes each
Where

Daily Routines
(practice one a day) Grocery shopping   Changing diapers

Spontaneous Salt and pepper your strategies across the day.   Make interactions/communications a habit.

PARTNERSHIP CALENDAR

Week	MONDAY	TUESDAY	WEDNESDAY	THURSDAY	FRIDAY	SATURDAY	SUNDAY
1	1 / 1	2 / 1	2 / 2	3 / 3	No time	3 / 3	3 / 3
2	4 / 3	3 / 3	3 / 2	4 / 3	4 / 4	3 / 3	4 / 4
3							
4							
5							

How to Use the Calendar

1. Select one goal each for child and adult. Observe one planned activity a day.
2. After observing, rate child and adult (you or someone else) on the goals listed in the Practice Plan. Use a 1 to 9 scale:
   1-2 = no evidence   3-4 = little evidence   5 = some evidence   6-7 = increasing evidence   8-9 = strong evidence
3. Rate the child (c) in top half and adult (a) in bottom half of each cell. Be sure to practice across many activities. Try some of the following; check the ones you practice.
   People only: __ sounds   ✓ actions   __ conversations   __ your choice _____
   People and things: ✓ toys   __ books   __ games   __ your choice
   Daily routines: __ getting up   __ dressing   ✓ bathing   __ meals   __ TV   __ car   __ bedtime
   ✓ shopping   __ visiting   __ household chores   __ your choice _____

ECO | Practice Plan and Record

PARTNERSHIP DIARY

Watch your progress and help your habits grow. Quickly, comment on how interactions with your child went today. Say anything: progress, problems, ideas, changes. Mention both child and adult occasionally.

Week 1

Monday
I found it impossible to match David! I really feel he understands when I talk to him in sentences.

Tuesday
I'm doing a little better with matching him, but it isn't easy. It's hard to say how David did because I concentrated

Wednesday
I used a few two-word sentences and David repeated each of them!

Thursday
Starting to feel more natural — but I'm worried about doing the best thing for David.

Friday
Got home late from work. No time.

Saturday
We stacked blocks together, and David repeated some of my sentences, but also said a few original ones on his own. I think it is because I'm doing what he can.

Sunday
Same as Saturday

Week 2

Monday
Just read over the "extra hints" at bottom of this page. Tried matching and waiting — it really helped David. He used more original sentences than usual.

Tuesday
I felt myself using too many words, but not as many as I used to.

Wednesday
David was real passive, did not initiate much. Not sure what I did wrong.

Thursday
Today was better. I concentrated on using words that David may soon be able to use. He repeated some of them.

Friday
Great! We put a baby in and out of bed. And both of us did about as much as the other — and said about as much.

Saturday
It just does not seem like David initiates as much as he responds.

Sunday
Felt pretty good about our interaction at the grocery store. David really said things to me while we shopped, I think because I said things to him that were at his level — not above it.

Extra Hints to Remember
David mainly lets others communicate for him and when he does communicate it's mainly to respond. Adults need to communicate once at David's level, then WAIT for a response.

7 | *Becoming Language Partners*

SOCIAL PLAY
social play

TURN TAKING
turn taking

COMMUNICATION
communication

LANGUAGE
language

CONVERSATION
conversation

Language is perhaps one of the primary concerns you have with your child. You want him to talk or sign and to come to use language more like you do. This chapter discusses how you can use your language to help your child develop his. The term language has different meanings to people with different needs and perspectives. Traditionally, language has been viewed as the system of rules that governs humans' use of symbols to communicate for a wide variety of purposes (Bloom & Lahey, 1978). In the **ECO** model, we view language as an interactive system of exchanging symbols, such as words or signs, that are commonly accepted in a culture. Thus, we begin by recognizing language as evolving from intimate, joint activities based on motivations and knowledge shared by two people.

Language learning is a partnership.

Language does not emerge from a vacuum; it comes from a child's relationship with parents, peers, teachers, and other close people. We view learning language as a partnership between two people who habitually interact with each other in balanced, playful, and mutually responsive ways, and we always involve at least two individuals, a child and parent or a child's teacher or caregiver, in planning how to influence a child's language. That is, when we address the problem of a child's language, we always involve both the child and those persons in regular language partnerships with him. This chapter builds on the issues in the previous three; we see language as evolving directly from the interactive and communicative relations discussed earlier.

Again, this chapter focuses on an interactive two-person view of children's language development, that is, development of meanings in words and concepts. Our concern is how adults and children can interact in ways that naturally allow the child to put his meanings and experiences into words and topics. This approach to language evolves from our own clinical and research work with language-delayed children (MacDonald & Blott, 1974; MacDonald & Gillette, 1985a, 1985b; MacDonald & Horstmeier, 1978), as well as the rich base of knowledge on semantic development, (Bloom, 1973; Brown, 1973; deVilliers & deVilliers, 1978; Leonard, Bolders, & Miller, 1976; Lucas, 1980; Nelson, 1974). A consistent conclusion throughout this work is that children do not learn language through traditional didactic teaching (as in the everpresent "What's that?" approach). Rather, language evolves out of sensitively responsive interactions—the matched, playful, turntaking exchanges that are the core of social development discussed so far in this book. The principles and strategies we have examined in earlier chapters set the necessary stage and actively support a child to learn language spontaneously within daily casual contacts. As a child learns language, those principles—balancing, matching, reciprocity, and stress-free playfulness—remain as critical as before. We have found many adults learn balanced turntaking interactions only to abandon them when they view the current job as teaching language.

It is often difficult to convince parents and professionals that a child is either learning language or actually not learning it in every contact with others. "I wasn't trained," we are often told. "I'm a teacher, not a speech therapist." "I pay taxes for someone to do that." However, once parents and teachers begin to build these intimately matched and responsive interactions, they quickly realize that only they really know the child and can capitalize on that intimacy to show him language at just the right times.

The critical activity for learning language, then, is any joint interpersonal activity, that is, an event in which you and your child are both actively involved and genuinely together. These events will often be frequent and momentary, not requiring any extra time or change in your daily routines. The more you are together, the more you will intimately know what your child knows, what he cares about, and what he wants to communicate about. This is the time when your easy, stress-free comments will help your child talk about his world. Joint activities with a child do not take hours out of your everyday life. We have found the most effective joint activities are not long ones, but frequent, brief contacts where there is a genuine link between you and your child. Once the child is talking habitually, the joint activities can be little verbal contacts that code some experience the two of you share.

How many close joint activities do you have with your child? Picture yourself and your child as two circles. When the circles are totally apart, neither of you is doing anything with the other. When you are with your child, try to move the two circles closer together, by joining in each other's activity, even if just momentarily.

Ask yourself what your joint activity score would be in a normal day, across all of your activities with your child and in a few specific activities. That is, when you are together, to what extent are you doing the same things together, genuinely being affected by each other? Rate yourselves on a scale of 1 to 9, where 1 = totally apart in communication and activity and 9 = mutually engaged in and responsible to the other's activities and communications, with the numbers between showing differences. In Figure 7.1, (a) illustrates no togetherness in activity or communication, (b) depicts some joint activity but considerable time spent apart, and (c) shows two partners acting and communicating in the same activity most of the time.

Figure 7.1

a. Mom and child attend to different activities with no communication

b. Mom and child occasionally attend, act, and communicate about the same activity

c. Mom and child attending, acting on, and communicating about same activity

Does your child have more language than he communicates?

Many people—teachers, testers, peers, and others—will judge a child's knowledge or intelligence by his communications in unfamiliar circumstances. Frequently we see children placed in classrooms for autistic children on the basis of their communication in an unfamiliar situation with unfamiliar people. Consider language a measure or reflection of the child's knowledge. A major problem for many children, therefore, is what we call *the language-communication gap,* the finding that many children communicate much less than they know. Not only do we commonly see a child who understands much more language than he expresses, we also see in his sensorimotor and interpersonal behavior a wide range of knowledge that he rarely communicates. Nevertheless, judgments that determine his school placement and his acceptance into social circles are regularly made on the basis of the language the child communicates, not the knowledge he has.

This knowledge-communication gap is useful in indicating the kind of language that is most appropriate for your child to learn. We operate on the premise that we learn something new most effectively in the context of something we already know. This principle, that "new forms evolve from old content" (Slobin, 1973), leads us to a practical rule: "Teach new language for current knowledge." Thus, a basic principle that guides our own clinical practice in teaching language is: "Focus on helping the child to talk about those things he already knows." We are saddened when we see a child fail to learn new language because it does not capitalize on his current knowledge, especially when he will readily communicate new words for things he already knows. *It is undeniably unfair to say a child does not have language or can not talk on the basis of failures to teach him words for things outside his knowledge, motivation, or practical use in communication.*

Setting Goals for Learning Language

In selecting language goals in the home or school, it may be helpful to reflect on the question, "Why does a child need language?" Although the answers may seem too obvious to discuss, we know many children who have been taught language that does not serve their needs. We recommend that you help your child learn language that fulfills several needs. There are several reasons a child may need language in different situations.

1. *To show what he knows.* When a child begins to talk, he is coding his own knowledge. In so doing, he defines himself to the world as someone who can tell us what he is thinking. Thus, being able to show what he knows gives him a new role in the world, informs others more about him, and shows them how they can relate to him. In terms of a child with language delays, this first need suggests that we must show him words for those things he already knows. Once he learns that language is a powerful tool to express his knowledge in addition to helping him understand others, he will soon begin to use language creatively. Language will then become a tool for creating new knowledge as he uses its rules to regularly generate new combinations never heard or used before.

2. *To communicate with others.* The language we encourage in a child should be communicatively useful to him. Isn't all language communicatively useful? Many language goals established for children in school and therapy appear to be more concerned with academic knowledge than daily communication. We must ask ourselves regularly if the child is likely to want to communicate with the language we want him to learn. While we would like a child to learn academic language for concepts such as color, numbers, letters, and size, we doubt that he will be able to use them in communicating his way into a social life. How can we expect the child to generalize what he has learned if we focus on teaching him language that is rarely useful in his commerce with the world? Unfortunately, children often act as though language is something they use only in response to questions and commands, an impression perhaps based on the way they were taught and currently use their language. Even worse, a child who sees language as questions

Marginal notes:

What language should a child first use? Language about what he already knows.

Language exposes knowledge.

Language is for communication.

and commands may see it only as a tool for others to use to tell him what to do. Thus, it may contribute to his development of "learned helplessness."

We know two children, Aaron and Steve, who have language for the alphabet, complex numbers, even to read words like *watermelon* and *antifreeze,* but appear lost when communicating about toileting, affection, and functional information sharing. There is often excessive concern with ensuring that a child *has* language and less concern with *using* it. Unless we provide a child with communicatively useful language, he is not likely to engage in enough conversations to learn more language through natural communication.

3. *To build relationships.* The language a child needs to build a relationship depends on those joint activities he has with some other person. Every relationship has its own vocabulary. Motivation is the key here. A child is more likely to talk about events that, in themselves, motivate him to talk (Olson, 1980). Some adults want their child to learn to talk for school and etiquette. Because we believe that an academic, adult-oriented focus may discourage a child from developing a habit of using language, we encourage language for playful relationships long before we teach language that may not show him how to initiate and build those relations in which he can learn language spontaneously.

Language is for uniting people.

Identifying Words for a Child to Learn

We have a simple, practical rule we use to decide spontaneously what language to encourage the child to use. We simply put words on the child's own wordless communications. When interacting with a child, we view his nonverbal and unintelligible communication as his known language, and we view our job as translating his language into ours. Thus, the task of language teaching no longer requires a separate curriculum. The child's own communications provide us with an immediately available answer to the questions, "How should we talk to our child so that he learns language from us?" and "What language should he first learn?"

What language does a child first need?
____ Words to code his knowledge
____ Words to code his communications
____ Words to code his interests
____ Words with high communicative utility
____ Language for communication, not for storage

They come from:
____ Your matched words
____ His communications without words
____ His current knowledge
____ His own interests

Observe your child, and make a list of those meanings he is already communicating. Then make another list of those things that he both knows and cares about. These two lists provide a good estimate of the things your child may be ready to use words to communicate about. They are already a part of his thinking and he shows some interest in sharing them with the world.

What is the child communicating?
_____ hunger
_____ love
_____ frustration

What does he know and care about?
_____ soda
_____ kitty
_____ Sam

It's Your Turn

COMMENT:

I've never considered that what my year-old twins know has much to do with the language they will have. Are you saying that language comes from that knowledge?

REPLY:

Yes. Not only does language come from your child's knowledge, it's the communicative expression of it. Consider your children's knowledge, all those things they show they know when they play, solve natural problems, and make contacts with you. In a manner of speaking, when that knowledge "grows up" it will become language. And you can help transform that knowledge into language by genuinely understanding what they know and care about.

COMMENT:

I am a parent of five children. Every time I've tried to suggest what my children should learn, I get from the school "We'll do it. We're the ones who are trained." I've learned to feel I am "just a mother" and not important to my children's learning. Now, you say I'm my child's "best teacher." I'm confused.

REPLY:

We regret deeply that you have felt unimportant. Few professionals have been trained to know about the first 3 years of development, when early language learning occurs. Teachers usually begin with conversational children who already have learned language and communication at the sides of their parents, most of whom had no formal training to do it. No teacher or professional is likely to replace the time, investment, and intimacy that children have with their parents, and it is only with that time, investment, and intimacy that a child's language is likely to develop and flourish. Getting a first language going well cannot be approached like other school subjects; it must happen through close interactive living.

Interactive Goal

28. BECOME LANGUAGE PARTNERS

As language evolves, keep playing, turntaking, and communicating.

A fundamental principle of the **ECO** model is that children learn language for social use not through direct teaching but by communicating continually in sustained interactions with other people. Thus a child learns language in partnerships with people who use language that is matched to his abilities and interests and who give him matched models of language that he can do. An extension of this principle is that we learn language not to store it for recall but to use it as a natural part of acting and interacting.

Learning language is not an isolated task in itself, then, but a natural extension of the learning we have discussed in preceding chapters. You will need to use the elements of learning to play, take turns, and communicate, discussed in prior chapters, because they are essential to the process of learning language. The goal of staying together in enjoyable play, with no pressure for achievement, also applies directly to language. Maintaining this goal allows the child to express his genuine interests and encourages the adult to match those interests with appropriate and useful language. Unless the child learns language related to his interests, he is unlikely to use it or continue to learn more (Bruner, 1983; Wells, 1981).

Similarly, maintaining the goal of turntaking promotes longer interactions between the child and his natural language teachers, allowing increased practice and feedback with language. Unless your child communicates back and forth with you and others, he will have little opportunity to learn language for those meanings that are most important to him. Further, maintaining the goal of communication provides an ideal source for the child's next words as he expresses current communicative intentions, whether verbal or nonverbal. Unless adults see a child's language as evolving from his earlier communications and unless they support that communication, language may be discouraged. Thus, the strategies for increasing play, turntaking, and communication explored in the previous chapters are essential to maintain because they are the steps on a staircase that lead the child to even higher skills.

The more turntaking, the more language learning.

When the adults closest to a child learn strategies they can use in the most casual contacts, they can help the child use language as a creative, not just passive and responsive, process. When this happens, the adults report that the child begins saying new things that they had never said themselves. When a child first begins to talk, his words seem to come relatively slowly, But when he gets into the habit of talking, it is surprising how fast new words come. Parents often say, "I can't imagine where he learned that," unaware that he learned it from their incidental language during easy contacts. It is difficult for them to believe that language comes less from direct teaching than from the playful interactions and communications they have developed with their child. When parents and professionals come to believe it, they begin valuing their interactions with their child more and come to make them more of a habit. We have observed that as parents and teachers feel more important to the child's language, we see more language from the child.

In helping adults and children become language partners we are concerned with three major goals: first, *to share more and more closely matched ideas and vocabulary*; second, *to share increasingly more mature language;* third, *to share the lead in developing topics.* When adults realize that the child will learn language best if the matched communicative interactions (discussed earlier) are extended beyond the game of toys to the interactive game of words, they are often surprised at how naturally language seems to evolve.

Language: the social game of words.

Subgoal

a. Share a closely matched vocabulary.
Our concern is to help parents and professionals become partners in their child's language development. Because we see learning language as a partnership, we want to know the language goals not only for the child but for the adult as well. In other words, we want to know the general kinds of words that will match the

adult's and child's worlds as closely as possible. To this end, we have devised a simple procedure for predicting what language might be most helpful for the adult and child to be using. The *Interactive Word Bank*, which is shown in Figure 7.2, is a way to identify some of the words a child appears to be ready to express. These include words your child (1) knows the meanings of (is cognitively ready for), (2) cares about (is motivated to express), and (3) can frequently use communicatively (finds socially useful). Children are more likely to learn language that describes what they experience—their knowledge (Brown, 1973), what is interesting for them—their motivation (Mahoney et al., 1986), and those things they are already communicating about—their communicative intentions (Bates, 1976).

Language sources:
knowledge
interests
nonverbal messages.

Use the *Interactive Word Bank* to identify and record several sources of first words. One source is **knowledge about** the experiences and perceptions that are most real for the child, that is, ideas that are most likely to become words. A second source is any of the child's particular **interests** that are most likely to motivate him to remember and use words communicatively. The third source are those **meanings** or messages the child is regularly communicating nonverbally (without words). Thus, the *Word Bank* alerts adults to the kinds of language that may be most logical and useful to the child. The resulting words help adults respond more sensitively to the child's own meanings and intentions, assuming these are the most efficient, communicatively useful, and long-lasting stimuli for the child.

The *Word Bank* also classifies a few different kinds of meanings children begin to talk about. These meanings come from extensive research, in several languages, to identify what normally developing children first begin talking about (Bloom, 1973; Brown, 1973; MacDonald, 1978). This research, and a wider body of literature, are quite consistent in finding that children's first words and sentences comprise a few similar meanings and relationships between words.

Children appear to code their own childhood experiences into a few common classes of meaning: *agent* (a doer), *action* (visible movements), *objects* (something the child acts upon), *location* (places that interest the child), and *feelings* (states of emotion). In our own work with children, we have found that these same meanings also describe the first communications of children with language delays (MacDonald & Horstmeister, 1978). We have also found that, when we chose these meanings as the content for language training for a group of children with Down syndrome (MacDonald & Blott, 1974), the children readily used the meanings as their first words. Thus, the *Interactive Word Bank* encourages you to look for those meanings that seem to be the natural building blocks for a child's early language. Notice that we recognize the distinct experiences of every child; thus we do not suggest the same words. Each meaning can be expressed in a great number of words; this approach gives a child great freedom in building language in his own creative ways.

You can also use the *Word Bank* to match your language to the child's. After you identify the meanings that are important to your child, you will know some of the kinds of things to talk about. Of course, you should talk about many more things than these, but consider these as a guide to the language that your child may be ready for.

Becoming Partners with Children

Figure 7.2
Interactive Word
Bank

	Agents	Actions	Objects	Locations	Feelings
Interests					
Knowledge					
Communications (without words)					
Language (what child says)					
What you want (child to say)					

To use the *Word Bank*, take your time and do one part at a time as a way of getting to know your child better. Learn a little about his meanings by watching him in daily activities in the home or classroom. In the appropriate sections of the *Interactive Word Bank*, record what he knows, what he cares about, and what he communicates and talks about. Observing those things will help you see the kind of language the child needs.

Of course, we do not intend that you carry the *Word Bank* around with you or check it as you talk with your child. Nothing so foreign should come between the two of you when you are talking. The things you are both interested in doing at the time will tell you what to talk about. Instead, refer to the *Interactive Word* Bank from time to time simply to help you remember the kinds of things to talk about. When you are with your child, you can silently ask yourself four questions about him: (1) What does he know? (2) What is he doing? (3) What is he communicating? (4) What do I want him to say? Then, while you interact with your child, try to give him words for each of these four important sources. By doing this, you will be tapping his knowledge, his motivation, his present forms for communicating, and your concerns. The more intimately you know your child, the more easily you will show him the language he needs and will use.

Let the "Word Bank" guide you.

b. Share closely matched structures and forms.

Subgoal

If you view language learning like helping a child up a staircase, gradually showing him something he can do next, you will find talking with your child rewarding and surprising. The more you and your child interact together, the more ideas and experiences you will share, each of which can be put into words. As each of you puts words on your shared experiences, you will have even more experiences. Let those experiences that mean something to each of you lead you to use new words and new grammar. Note that if you let the experiences tell you the new words to use, you will not spend time away from the interaction wondering and thinking about what you and your child should say. If you are genuinely into something together, you will know what to say. Just as you know what to say in your familiar conversations, where you do not think and ponder, let your experiences with your child lead you naturally to showing him new language in a matched way he can do.

c. Share the lead in topic development.

Subgoal

Like any two people, you and your child will be interested in talking about different notions or topics. By talking on another person's topic, we learn more about that person. Learning language requires getting into another person's topics or interest. Consequently, you and your child will each benefit from keeping the other talking about both your own interests. When you follow your child's lead, you learn more about his thinking and interests, and thus you are better able to provide him language he can use. When your child follows your topic lead, he is learning new meanings and intentions that could become new language for him.

Allow both you and your child to take the lead.

Talking about another's ideas has an additional, perhaps more basic value, and that's that it shows the person respect. Because language learning requires keeping two people interacting, it appears logical that the more respect you show your child's ideas, the more he will stay. And since a major goal for any child is to be accepted into interactions in society, learning to stay on others' topics may be a fundamental requirement for being accepted socially.

It's Your Turn

COMMENT:

I am a teacher. Isn't my job to teach my children "new things"? Why talk to a child about things he already knows and understands?

REPLY:

Because communicating that knowledge is the new thing. Having an idea or understanding words is an old skill for many; learning how to express them in words is the major task. Look at your children and identify what they know, then make a classroom goal for each child to communicate in words what he already knows. A few important things will happen. (1) The child will have more successes talking about what he knows. (2) You will be more successful, thus motivated. (3) His increased use of language will strengthen his relationships and others' view of him as a competent communicator.

COMMENT:

I am a teacher with 5- to 7-year-old socially and communicatively delayed children. I used to think that my job was to teach them "my words." Then when I began communicating with words that mapped their experiences, they talked more, began to try my own words, and they stayed longer in casual conversations as well as in class lessons.

REPLY:

And they learned more spontaneously with you.

COMMENT:

How can I be a language partner with my son? I have thousands more words and sentences than Luigi.

REPLY:

Imagine that you are a good tennis player and your 9-year-old wants to learn. How would you be his partner? You would fine tune your movements to ones he could do. Similarly, a language partner is one who matches her language to the child's knowledge, behaviors, and interests. Consider every exchange between you and Luigi as an opportunity to be a partner by matching your words to what he is currently doing and knowing.

Self-Assessment: How Are You Doing?

Rate yourself on a scale of 1 to 9, where 1 = not often or very poorly, 5 = neutral, and 9 = very frequently or quite well.

_____ 1. My child and I talk about the same ideas.
_____ 2. We each take the lead in developing topics.
_____ 3. We both initiate and respond about equally.

Problems that Interfere with Language Learning

Dominating the language   If you believe, as we do, that learning language requires an adult and a child to become partners, you may be alarmed to see children saying little while their adults do all the talking. Not only do we often see adults saying much more than the child, we find that what they say is often far beyond the child's reach in terms of what he can do or is interested in. It feels natural to respond to a quiet child by filling the silence with a stream of talk, and many adults believe that is what they should do to help the child learn. Some professionals even encourage caregivers to "bathe your child in language," apparently unaware that children communicate more when they get messages matched to what they can already do and that they need time to process and prepare messages. Some of these adults seem to have a kind of "black box" theory of learning language. That is, they believe that children need only to hear oceans of language and store it in their minds in order to use it on their own someday. The belief is that the child will somehow, almost by magic, learn to use the language he has heard. While a child who is habitually communicative may sometimes pick up on adult models that are far above his present level, many respected learning theorists argue that the child must participate in order to learn. Bruner (1983) calls this "fine tuning"; Hunt (1961), "minimal discrepancy"; Piaget (1952), "cognitive schematic match," Skinner (1957), "shaping," and Vygotsky (1962), "zone of proximal distance."

Be very careful not to talk too much.

Unfortunately, when adults dominate the talk without waiting, the results may be disastrous for a child's learning. If an adult fails to wait for a child to talk, the child is likely to get discouraged and find something more interesting to do. The child has to participate in order to learn and to stay motivated to become a genuine talker. If your child is learning language, there should be few things that are more interesting to him than talking with people.

Few things should be more interesting to your child than talking with people.

Again, the same habit of turntaking that helps your child become an interactive participant with others is now necessary for you to show your child you will also give and take with language. Remain on guard against the natural habit of dominating time with children that may send children off to operate on their own. Certainly, children need time alone, just as you do, but to learn language, their lives must be showered with frequent, interactive language exchanges.

Academic language problem   Many times a child's entry into school is the stimulus for serious concerns about language delays. Parents and professionals then focus on teaching the child the language they suppose he needs in school, that is, the language involved in academic tasks. We have known far too many children who could recite their numbers, letters, colors, and other academic concepts, and some of them could even read. But the language these children used in natural communication, for playing and building attachments, was so meager that it isolated them socially.

Much "school" language has little communicative use.

The pressure that parents and professionals report for a child to succeed is understandable. Parents frequently say things like "If only he can get into that school, he will become like the other children." We absolutely share those goals with parents, but we often differ on how to achieve them. Parents who pressure their children to learn "school" language, but who spend little time keeping them in playful conversations about their own interests, are likely to end up with the "black box" language we mentioned earlier. The child may be able to recite what he has been taught, but he will not use language to build the friendships he needs or learn all the language that happens naturally in children's daily activities.

Elkind (1987) has discussed a range of problems resulting from teaching children skills before they can use them; he has referred to the "circus tricks" that young children can perform on call while they lack many of the creative and social skills they need to learn from their own natural motivations. Using Elkind's notion of "circus tricks," we encourage parents and professionals to help children learn language that can emerge regularly from their own activities, and not to have the child learn language as a primarily responsive "show and tell" skill. Allow your child to learn how to learn language naturally and enjoy participating in that learning as a partner.

Language for communication before language for school.

29. LOW VERBAL AND PRAGMATIC SKILLS

Child Problem

There are as many definitions of language delay as there are definitions of language and communication. In our interactive approach, we are concerned about a child's language skills when they appear to interfere with his interpersonal relationships or his social, educational, or vocational development. We regularly ask a few questions about a child to get a perspective on both his language potential and his actual use of language. Remember, too, that language develops not in the child by himself, but as a function of his interactions with people. Thus, a child may have a severe language delay in some contexts but much stronger language in others. Just as you have different language skills in different situations (friendly, punitive, demanding, exciting, and so on), so does your child. In view of this, be very careful that your child is not defined as severely language delayed, for example, when it may have been the situation that suppressed his potential. We are concerned when we hear children use much more language playing by themselves than in interactions with others. We are concerned that the interaction is making the child's language look more delayed than it actually is.

Is the situation making your child look more language delayed than he is?

Before discussing more specific problems we see in children's early language, there are four general problems that seem to make it more difficult for a child and adult to readily learn language together.

The cover-up problem   The gap between a child's knowledge and his language can be the heart of the problem. A first question we ask is this one: To what extent is your child talking about what he knows? If you could possibly make a list (don't try it) of everything your child knows and then check off those things he communicates, you might find he still needs words for some very important pieces of knowledge. A great many parents of children with delays lament the fact that their children show all kinds of knowledge very creatively in their play and daily living. The problem is that they show little of it when they talk. Another problem for those children is that they do not seem to know they should talk about their experiences. While many children use words as common tools, just for interacting, many children with delays seem to limit their use of words, and use words only to get things.

Is language hiding knowledge?

Thus, a language delay that particularly concerns us is seen in children who do not use language as a natural part of their time with people and things. These children often respond to us with talk but do not, as most young children do, use talk as another tool for play and personal contacts. Consider the consequences when a child uses language minimally, even in situations where he could talk much more. Kenny, a 6-year boy with Down syndrome, showed considerable creative and academic language but only *if we initiated the contact*. Otherwise, he was virtually mute. His parents said he talked at home more than they expected. At school, his teacher and therapist considered him a model child, never talking out of turn and always answering them with words, though often just the words they had taught him. In his time by himself and with children, however, Kenny never used words to show others the interesting child he really was. In this case, then, the problem clearly lay not only with Kenny, but with the many adults who, "pleased with his gains for a *retarded child*," did not see how his life could change if he made his language as much a part of his personality as his compliance was.

In the case of Kenny, we were fortunate to intervene. We took away the pressure of questions and commands (see next chapter for more) and allowed him time, freedom, and support for speaking his own ideas, to show that encouraging him to initiate with others and to share his knowledge made him appear not only much more intelligent but more personally rewarding as a conversation partner. We have known many other children whose passive approach to communication covered up much knowledge and prevented many social relationships. Thus, we feel that the term *language cover-up* describes these cases more accurately than does *language delay.*

The cognitive mismatch problem Language is apparently more effective if it relates to what the other person is thinking and his or her level of thought or cognition. Certainly if someone talks to you about something you know little about or something far off your track of thinking, you feel it. Consider what may happen when a child hears language that is so adult-like he cannot attempt it or language so far from his current thinking that he ignores it. We have observed a great number of adult-child pairs in which the adult's language regularly mismatches the child's abilities and experiences; the result is often a noncommunicative child or one who tries to withdraw from that learning opportunity.

Talk about your child's ideas.

Consider 2-year-old Jeff's father, who was concerned that he must teach his son. So he explained carefully how trucks, and dishwashers, and elevators worked. He was cognitively mismatching the boy's simple actions—pushing a car, imitating the sound of a dishwasher, and pointing at the elevator light. Once the father followed Jeff's actions and intentions with words Jeff could understand and that described what Jeff was doing, the boy stayed interacting and attempted to use appropriate words.

The language-as-a-job problem When we have observed nondelayed children beginning to talk, they do it less as a job than as an extension of their spontaneous play. It is as though many of the playful acts are sprouting language. They don't stop their actions to talk but talk as a natural part of those actions and their associated intentions. When language develops as a part of what the child already knows and cares about, it is likely to develop much faster, simply because the child is more likely to do those things than things adults want.

We are greatly concerned, therefore, with language-delayed children who use language mainly to respond to others or to get some basic needs met. Note that when we put the child in these "talk-only" contacts, we have removed him from the natural, action-based contexts that generate language for children. It may be like judging how a child swims by observing him in a bathtub rather than a swimming pool. On a numbers basis alone, the child just does not have enough experiences with practice and feedback to learn language as a habit. Further, language is not self-motivating for children like these. Unless language becomes rewarding in itself, children may be unlikely to do the work it takes to develop the habit of talking. These children appear to operate by the rule, "Language will come from others, not from what I care about."

Language learning is a living, not a job.

Children and adults alike must realize that a habit of language learning comes only when the child has control of what to say and when adults support and respond to his choice of language. Thus, language learning must become a natural part of your child's life just as his play is. In the same way that making a job out of a child's play encourages him to leave us, making work out of talking can also bring about unfortunate effects. A final point is for us as adults to be realistic. A child has thousands of chances to talk about his knowledge every week. How can we expect the few times when we deliberately try to teach him to talk to be more effective than all those natural opportunities he has? Once parents and teachers come to see that their child's natural times are when he learns best, they see how much more they can get from him.

"Communicatively useless" problem Though we rarely see it mentioned, we frequently find another problem in children with a wide range of diagnoses—the view that language is something to "have" rather than to use. Thus, parents and other adults are often proud and satisfied with language-delayed children who know their numbers, alphabet, TV jingles, and other academic or adult language. We, too, want children to succeed in school and vocations. However, we have serious concerns for children whose language is limited to the academic or adult worlds.

What would he use the words for?

Abe, age 5 and variously described as having attention deficits and autistic tendencies, is considered a "good" student, reporting most of the language taught him. While Abe occasionally uses his language socially, he seems to prefer reciting words, perhaps in the direction of a person, perhaps not. He even reads and spells. In fact, one day when his mother said, "Time to go," Abe replied, "D-A-D-D-Y," spelling the word.

Abe illustrates a rather extreme case of having language that is, for the most part, communicatively useless. But we have found that many other children, children whose social skills are stronger than Abe's, seem stuck with a similarly academic vocabulary. They are often unrestrained in showing off their school language but at a loss with simple words for conversation. A related concern when a child's language is limited largely to such "book" rather than "people language" is that his language may be not merely communicatively useless but may actually interfere with developing social relationships. People expect language to be directed to them and related to a joint topic.

It's Your Turn

COMMENT:

If I am a language partner with my preschoolers, what are they giving me? Isn't partnership a two-way street?

REPLY:

Good question. When you look closely and interact, your preschoolers are giving you the curriculum you need to teach. What they know, care about, and communicate nonverbally is precisely what you need to know to guide your language and to determine what language they need next.

Self-Assessment:
How Are You
Doing?

Rate yourself on a scale of 1 to 9, where 1 = not often or very poorly, 5 = neutral, and 9 = very frequently or quite well.

_____ 1. My child's language is a good mirror of what he knows.
_____ 2. Learning language seems more like work than play to my child.
_____ 3. Language learning seems more like work than play to me.
_____ 4. My child and I are in a habit of talking with each other.
_____ 5. Other people consider my child a "talker."
_____ 6. My child's language is more useful for school and learning than for casual conversations.
_____ 7. I am more concerned about language for learning than for interacting with people.

Subproblem

a. Narrow range of vocabulary.
When an adult waits for a child to begin to talk long after the expected age, a few words from a child can satisfy that adult for quite a while. We understand the relief that comes with the first words. However, these children soon begin to say the same things over and over and use the same words for a variety of intentions. To a degree, this is natural. However, the goal is not for the child to use words occasionally, when pressured to do so by others or by his needs, but rather to communicate habitually about his experiences, his interests, and the concerns of those close to him.

A few words go
a long way.

Fortunately, research into child language provides clear direction for the kinds of meanings we can expect children to talk about first. The *Word Bank* (discussed earlier in this chapter) can identify strengths and weaknesses in a child's early language. We consider a child to have a problem in his vocabulary development under the following conditions. First, if a child is not expressing in words the meanings he has a history of communicating *without* words, we are concerned that he is not learning the most likely candidates for words. Second, if the child is not regularly talking about his immediate experiences, we are concerned that he is not viewing language as playful tool. He is not using language to code his experiences symbolically and therefore cannot effectively expand his general knowledge base for further learning.

A practical test for this problem is to ask yourself, "What new words is the child using?" This leads to the question: What is an appropriate range of vocabulary? Often we see children do little more than label what they see. The research can help here. A child speaking in one- to three-word utterances should be talking about his experiences in terms of the five meanings of agents, actions, objects, locations, and feelings that are relevant to him. His words should be extensions of his actions, perceptions, and thoughts. Consequently, it is not important that your child use any words in particular, as long as he talks about those five meanings.

Subproblem

Stuck at single
words? Wait
for more.

b. Use of single words more than phrases or sentences.

We often hear of children who seem "stuck at single words," although they clearly know and communicate much more than those words reflect. Adults need to take care that they are not reading the child's total communication as conveying much more information than the word itself. When we suspect that a child who is in the single-word habit can say more, we try to do two things. First, we wait, letting him know that we expect more and that others will give him more attention if he gives what he can, that more will get more. A little waiting often shows us the child had much more language than he was using; putting out new words takes effort that a child may not make if we accept his old ways. Second, we talk to him in matched ways, using his meanings (agent, action, object, location, feeling) to guide how we talk, and keeping our talk within a range the child can do.

Subproblem

"Gimme" language
is not enough.

c. Speech used mainly to get or manipulate.

Unfortunately, many children use language as a tool to satisfy their needs rather than as a tool to build relationships. Questions like "Dat?" and commands like "Gimme" are very common, as are specialized words to solve a host of problems. Even at later stages, we see some children using only a little language, primarily for instrumental purposes. Two problems exist here. First, if a child's use of language (or the kind he hears) is limited to instrumental reasons, he is unlikely to get into the extended conversations he needs to build a language for social learning. Second, because questions and commands can usually be answered with a few words, many children seem to have language that is limited to short exchanges, where little of the child's knowledge is expressed. Beyond the social fact that people do not prefer conversations with demanding children, communicating mainly for needs gives the child severely limited opportunities to build language.

Subproblem

Assert your ideas.

d. Lack of assertion; mainly verbal imitation.

We know many children, at a variety of developmental levels, who have language but at times rarely use it. These children will usually respond to a speaker, often with imitations, but otherwise act mute. A fundamental problem with these children is that, though they show language in school tasks and on command, they do not view themselves as "talkers." This kind of self-image is more than a personality trait. We feel it is at least partially a result of being treated in a controlling, directive manner. A child under these restraints becomes an "answer man," not an assertive speaker and communication partner. Beyond missing a world of learning opportunities, the problem with a nonassertive speaker is that he is constantly signalling to potential communication partners that "I don't want to talk." Those people, in turn, respect the child's right to be alone, and the child remains severely language delayed.

Like so many other problems, this one may occasionally have its origin in other successes. When he is first talking, a child will imitate much of what we say. This is a success because the child is at least talking, even trying to talk like us. But success can soon become excessive if the child's major mode of communicating is imitating others. Adults often allow the imitative pattern to go on too long, letting the child merely imitate them instead of urging him to give some of his own ideas. As with many other problems of "language-delayed children," it is essential to view this not as inevitable but as the child's clever avoidance of doing more difficult things. And his adults unintentionally but effectively aid his escape by continuing to support his immature ways of talking.

Subproblem

e. Difficulty finding words to say.

Each of us, at times, feels we just can't find a word to say. *Word-finding difficulty* is a term often used to describe children with language delay. Descriptions of this problem often refer to a child trying to think out a word. With many children we know, the task of finding what to say may relate to the task of linking what he is doing to what he is saying. It is unclear exactly when a child should regularly talk about things from just his thoughts and not his actions. The more involved we are in an activity with children, the less word-finding difficulty they seem to have. Thus, while we hope that children will eventually talk from their ideas, without activity props, we believe that too many children with delays move too soon from joint activities to purely verbal conversations.

Let his actions find his words.

Another of our concerns with so-called word-finding problems is that the child is having trouble finding words for an adult's choice of ideas, not his own. It is clear that the less motivated a child is to talk the more he may appear to have word-finding problems. The problem may well not be in word finding but in not looking for a word at all. Word finding may also relate to "word giving." If adults communicate with the child in matched ways, with words the child can perform, he is more likely to be able to remember the words for those events.

Subproblem

f. Minimal pragmatics.

Pragmatics here means getting things done with talking. In order to learn a language system he can use on his own, a child needs to use a variety of purposes, such as friendship, information, practice, control, and so on. A child will be severely limited in his social and educational development if he does not learn to use language for reasons far beyond satisfying his needs. We will examine this more carefully in the next chapter; for now, let us focus on one critical reason to talk that is often overlooked: to communicate. Too often we assume that, if a child has language, he is using it to communicate. Our observations of many kinds of children do not uphold that assumption. Many children communicate by themselves or at others with little apparent intention to communicate. Often we see adults also talk without waiting or expecting a response. Consequently, we are not joking when we ask, "We know your child has language but is he communicating?" The problem is so marked across homes, classrooms, and clinics that we strongly urge professionals and parents to put aside their goal of teaching any new language until the child is in the habit of communicating his current language for social, friendly purposes.

Talk for many reasons.

Subproblem

g. Lack of topic development.

This problem is related to what may be the most basic goal of the entire **ECO** model: to keep the child interacting. No matter how much language a child has, it may be of little benefit if he does not use it to stay in interactions. Frequently, parents and professionals successfully build playful interactions, keeping the child there. But when language comes, that fundamental goal—keeping interactions going—gets lost. Adults resume the controlling role that discourages the child to participate. Because the child again has little control, he again leaves the interaction. If children in homes and schools are ever to build relationships with their language, their adults must stop being satisfied with language limited to brief dead-end contacts, language that shows the child little more to do with what he already has.

Keeping a child on a topic may be the most effective way to teach a host of educational goals. Unless a child can build conversational topics with others, the knowledge he gets in school and home may be virtually useless. Unless adults become convinced that the reason for language is to build relationships, the child is likely to be relegated to the unfortunate state of knowing a great deal but not knowing what to do with it.

h. Speech hard to understand.

Subproblem

Many children communicate more effectively with nonverbal attempts, tugging on you, gesturing, and many other creative gyrations, than with words or signs. Understanding speech is a two-way process. First, a child may continue to communicate unclearly if those ways work for him; consequently, adults need to be sure a child's new attempts are more successful, that is, get more attention, than the immature ones. So a second way that speech understanding is a two-way street is that the child is likely to speak more clearly if his adults and peers speak to him in matched ways he can do. If a child says "wa ai i" for "want ice cream," he may be more likely to learn a clearer way if we say to him "Want ice cream?" rather than saying "What kind do you want, strawberry is your favorite." As throughout this approach, the more adults are aware that a child is learning language from them in every exchange, the more they will give the child a next step he can do.

It's Your Turn

COMMENT:

Just how much language should a 5-year-old child have? Mitchell used to be very autistic-like, avoiding people and paying little attention to things. Now he plays with people, enjoys communicating often, and keeps showing us new words. His grandparents say he talks enough, his teacher disagrees, his therapist is pleased with his progress, his playmates talk much more than he does, and I am confused. When is it a language problem?

REPLY:

One question is "language for what?" Apparently, Mitchell's language is enough for his relationship with his grandparents; they may not expect much. His teacher may see the gap between all he knows and what he communicates with words; she may see that he can do more. His therapist appears to see progress; she is wise to be optimistic on the basis that often the best way to predict future changes is to follow recent changes. Mitchell's recent changes show where he is cognitively and socially moving.

Rather than asking "Does Mitchell have enough language?" ask the following questions:

- Is he changing? Is he showing new words and more use of old words over time?
- Is his language effectively communicating with others?
- Does he have enough language to keep you and others interested in being with him?

A language problem is different for every child. A language problem exists to the degree a child's language keeps him from communicating his knowledge, building relationships, and learning.

COMMENT:

I am a mother of three children—14 months, 28 months, and 40 months. The oldest is severely delayed both in language and motor skills. He is beginning to talk a little, but less than the younger ones. I am now realizing that I'm a good language partner with the younger two; I talk like them and about the things they do. But with the oldest, I feel a real need to teach him language that will make him look smart. So he knows his numbers, alphabet, and names for every little body part. But he hardly talks with any of us at all.

REPLY: We see this a lot. However simple it sounds, we strongly recommend that you communicate with the oldest more like you do with the youngest. Use language for fun, with no pressure for doing things he does not need now. You may be setting him up for failure. And like all of us, he may be avoiding talk because it means work and failure. Use language that describes his interests and that he can use as he plays in friendly contacts. Rather than trying to make him look "smart," become committed to making him look and be "social." Unless he's social, he's unlikely to become usefully smarter.

COMMENT: I am a principal of a school with infant and preschool classrooms; many of the children are developmentally delayed. I used to feel successful when the children could recite numbers and label their body parts. Once I realized all they showed was school talk, I became concerned. My question is: Most of us were trained to teach school language, not the casual talk of conversations. I feel we need to do more.

REPLY: What you say is a concern of many administrators, teachers, and parents who see children use language in their lives little more than other subjects like math or geography. The problem seems to be this: A majority of teachers and therapists were trained to work with the child who has the kindergarten skills of social conversation. Such children are expected to use their social skills to apply what we teach them to their world. And here's the rub. Many of our children with delays do not have conversation skills; consequently the school language we teach them is stored and unused. What we hope you move toward is a curriculum that establishes social communication habits before teaching language and other skills that the children will not use without the conversation skills that are evident in most 2- and 3-year-olds.

COMMENT: My family has been so pleased that Tyrone finally talked, they accept the same old sounds and words now. When do I know he's ready for new words?

REPLY: If Tyrone *can* talk, he can talk more. He is ready to talk more when he shows he knows the meanings of things and when he communicates many messages without words. Look to the section on Adult Strategies in this chapter for ideas. For now, realize that since talking is new to your son, it is somewhat difficult. If your family responds to the easy ways he communicates, he will not learn that the world will give him more for new ways. Be sure to wait and show you expect more; then give him a word when he tries something new.

COMMENT: What is a good vocabulary? In my class, a few children can talk about all of our lessons, even some know the words to the "pledge of allegiance," but they talk little when they are playing. Then other children have few words for school learning but have enough language to play and solve problems with the other children. Which group has a "better" vocabulary?

REPLY: A vocabulary is only as good as its uses for learning and socializing. We know many children who say what others want but seem at a loss in casual conversations. Since these children do have language for school and job, they definitely can have language for play and friendship. It's up to you and their parents to show the child that people-language is absolutely important. The children who do use language socially have a head start; now they need to learn to be cooperative partners and learn language that, imitatively, is important to others.

Self-Assessment:
How Are You
Doing?

Rate yourself on a scale of 1 to 9, where 1 = not often or very poorly, 5 = neutral, and 9 = very frequently or quite well.

____ 1. My child says only a few things.
____ 2. He seems stuck with single words.
____ 3. He rarely says things on his own.
____ 4. He talks mainly to get something.
____ 5. He seems at a loss for things to say.
____ 6. He rarely stays talking on one topic.
____ 7. His speech is difficult to understand.

CHILD GOALS

What Language Should Your Child Be Learning?

A child could not be directly taught every word he learns. His adults simply do not have the time or energy. He learns language primarily within spontaneous contacts with people, where the goals are living and friendly interacting—not learning language. When the question is "What language does he need?" adults are often concerned that the child learn formal language for school and other accomplishments. If your child is to learn how to develop language on his own, however, he needs entirely different language first.

Child language before school language.

We believe that your major concern about learning language shall be that your child become an habitual talker who makes language a friend and is learning it all the time. Wouldn't it be unfortunate if your child mainly talked about things related to school instead of what other children constantly talk about? We personally know many children who seem to use language more to perform, as in show and tell, than as a natural extension of living with people. If learning language is seen as a task that depends on adults, a child will miss the constant opportunities to learn language as a natural part of interactions with others.

Make language a friend to your child.

And so the answer to the question, "What language should my child learn?" is fundamental: *communicative child language*. We are not concerned here with helping a child store knowledge for academic accomplishments. We are concerned instead about helping him develop language that supports him in becoming so constant a communicator that his natural communications will be his best language lessons.

Communicative child language is the goal.

Thus, both the literature on how children learn language (Hubbell, 1981; Moerk, 1972; Nelson, 1980; Olson, 1980) and our own clinical research (MacDonald & Blott, 1974; MacDonald & Horstmeier, 1978) leads us to conclude that it is the *communicative functions* of language that should direct us in selecting *language goals* in home and in school. All of these efforts conclude that a child develops language to the extent he is in habitual, communicative interactions with a range of people. We encourage you to use the following guidelines for building your child's first language.

1. Build on his own nonverbal communications. As we have said so many times, language naturally evolves out of those things your child is already communicating about without words. Those messages your child sends with gestures or sounds are perhaps the best candidates for his next words. For example, when your child points to get up, signals he wants more, or waves, he is indirectly telling you "Now's the time to give me a word for this!"

2. Make sure your child has a communicative use for the words. If we focus a child's language goals on concepts he has little communicative use for, the language he learns is not likely to survive. Once you come to realize that communication is not only a practical use for language, but is the indispensible process for learning language, you will see that the task of selecting your child's language goal simply involves attending to those words and sentences your child could use frequently in communicating. Ask yourself: "How likely is my child to use these words to communicate in his common interactions?"

3. Provide words for the child's own knowledge. Even when our children are not communicating much, they always know something. As you observe your child closely, you can easily make a list of the things he knows. Those are some of the first things he can most readily learn language for. To motivate you, realize that every word your child uses to show a bit of his knowledge shows him to be more intelligent and offers others another way to link up to him. Be sure that when you give your child a word for his knowledge, you wait, let him take it in, and make some related response. Remember we want him to use language, not just to have it.

Child Goal

30. USE VARIED VOCABULARY

Different words for different things.

Rather than think of a child's communicative vocabulary as a preset list of words he should have, envision it as an ever-expanding dictionary that describes his current knowledge, interests, and communications. Thus, when you are in an authentic interaction with your child, you will naturally see the language your child needs. It will be those things he is doing, caring about, and communicating. Thus this goal of using varied vocabulary refers to how well your child is talking about an increasing range of his experiences. Watch your child in home or school. Make a list (in your mind or on paper) of those things and events your child talks about. Then watch him a week later, and to see if he is talking about any more things. As you watch your child over time, check to see if he is gradually talking about more and more of the things in his world. Remember, he is more likely to be talking about things you are doing with him. Your child's goal in language learning is to be talking about more and more things and events that mean something to him. When you interact, you can make those things more meaningful and more likely to become words.

Subgoal

a. Use a range of meanings: agents, actions, objects, locations, feelings.

Once your child begins talking, he should be using more and more words for experiences that are important to him. Again, some of the most basic child meanings are agents, actions, objects, locations, and feelings. Most children experience several of these meanings in every interaction. For example, when you and your child are at dinner there are probably many important meanings he could talk about: agents such as mom, dad, sister, brother, visitor; actions such as give, eat, spill, pass, sit, stay, do; objects such as spoon, drink, bowl, milk, peas, meat; locations such as here, there, lap, outside, bed, cup; and feelings such as funny, angry, hungry, full, no more, silly, polite, careful, hot.

The great advantage of these few basic meanings is not only that they describe what children care about but that they are the building blocks for early sentences. As you can see from the list above, the words would allow a child to make many new sentences to fit many possible situations. Consequently, a child needs not only to use an increasing number of words but also to spread those words out over the range of meanings that can build sentences and topics.

Child words from child meanings.

Another advantage of approaching language through child meanings is that it directs the natural words a child may best learn next. For example, if a child says "Daddy" while rough-housing, we can help him with new words by putting words on Daddy's actions (such as *hug, swing, fall*), meaningful locations (such as *up, down, around*), and relevant objects (such as *me, foot, shoe*). Any interactive event has a living dictionary available if you just observe and translate the child's experiences into words. Make this an enjoyable game; it will help you find answers to the question, "What should he talk about next?"

Subgoal

b. Imitate and otherwise talk like others.

Of course we want children to talk like others do, as well as to be creative. While imitation can become a dead-end habit for children, it is an efficient way to expand their language. There are many ways to learn to talk more like others talk. The issue here is for the child to gradually use language as others do, first through imitation, then in a variety of creative ways.

Initiate new words.

Parents and professionals report enormous satisfaction when their language-learning children imitate the adults' words, especially when the children do it spontaneously. Imitating an adult's words may sometimes be the first clear indication that a child cares to become like the adult. And these imitations work like compliments to adults, encouraging them to talk with the child.

Like all developing skills, imitations should not be expected to be adult-perfect. Children's own special imitations can often be entertaining, even endearing. When Larry was beginning to talk about animals, one early imitation of "elephant" was "elegant." His parents then enjoyed calling animals with trunks "elegants" and were somewhat saddened when Larry, maturing to "elephant," informed his parents they were saying it wrong. Larry's parents enjoyed talking with him so much that his new words were genuinely rewarding to them. Like all children, children with delays need to know that their new talk will be truly enjoyed, to discover that "talking" is the point rather than "saying it right." Remember that "right" can be "wrong," especially if we expect things the child is not ready for. One advantage of imitating is that it can happen anytime; another is that it can become a reciprocal game in which your child hears that "Talking is good" and "I'll keep doing it with you."

Subgoal

c. Use words nonimitatively.

Eventually your child needs to talk about things as he sees and does them, rather than to wait for others to talk. Too often the children we know seem to see talking as something to do when others initiate it. Not surprisingly, their talk is often based on others' interests rather than their own. Every developing child needs

Use words on his own.

to learn that his talk will be supported. He must not feel that he must say only the "right" things. When a child learns that words are an enjoyable extension of play, rather than a task at which he can fail, his words become extensions of his interests and experiences that are as natural for him as for any normal conversationalist. If he learns that talk is good, regardless of its correctness by adult standards, talking will be more likely to become a natural habit through which he can learn language in any interaction.

Subgoal

d. Use vocabulary appropriate to the topic.

Speak to the topic.

The more a child stays talking on a topic, the more he will learn. Truly effective control in stimulating learning comes not in directing the topic but in guiding the child to what more he can say about the things that interest him. When we begin, we want the child to talk about a topic in any way he can. The point is not to say something in particular but to make sound conceptual links between his words and his experiences. For example, if you are looking at two boys running up and down stairs, there are countless words appropriate to the topic: agents *(boys, brothers, baseball team, friends)*, actions *(run, climb, hurry, trip, fall)*, objects *(stairs, shoes)*, locations *(home, outside, up, down, away)*, feelings *(excited, afraid, happy, hungry)*. An entire curriculum for language learning can often be played out on one activity (or picture of an activity). The question here is a simple one: Are the child's words describing more and more of the topic? Or is the child saying only a little about one topic and then fleeing off to another?

Subgoal

e. Show a sense of knowing how to talk about things.

Child as "talker."

In order to learn language, your child needs to have speech become an integral part of his self-image. He needs to see talking as something he is supposed to do whenever people are around and even when they are not (as a tool for self-play). In turn, it is essential that you clearly show him you expect him to talk. Do not let him operate as a nontalker. Every time he misses a chance to talk with others he misses an opportunity to learn language.

Subgoal

f. Show creativity in speech.

Create with words.

We often hear the same stereotypic lines again and again from a child who has shown us he actually knows more. In a case like this, it almost seems that the child is taking the easy way out. To learn language, children need to be able to talk about the same events in different ways and to use words as a tool to create new stories or whole new worlds. We know children who use language quite creatively when playing alone but then revert to static and inflexible language with adults. We adults must look carefully at what we might be doing to discover why we get much less creative language from a child than he gives himself. Watching a few videotapes of 2-year-old Chris, alone and with his mother, showed a major difference between the functions of talk when they were together and when Chris was alone. With his mother and a clinician, Chris seemed to be trying to "say the right thing." When he was alone, though, his talk seemed to be another toy, a tool he practiced uninterrupted and used to create an imaginary world. Chris, by the way, showed much more language when he played alone than with others.

It's Your Turn

COMMENT:

I am a language therapist; my case load includes many children who use the same few words over and over. I know they know much more, but some have used words like "dat" for "What's that?" or "Give me that!" for years even when I know they know more words. What's going on here?

REPLY: In cases like that, we notice that the old repetitive words usually get a response. Children appear to maintain these words because they work and because they are physically and cognitively easier to do than the new ones for which they have less practice. Our approach to getting new words is to wait after the child says "dat" or "um" for the (umpteenth?) time in a day; we wait and show we expect more, and to many parents' and teachers' surprise, the child often gives a new word, one he had but knew he didn't have to use. Matching, a strategy we use throughout this approach, also helps in these areas. Through matching and waiting, the child gets a model of language he can do. Otherwise a child is likely to rely on tried and true words if he is not hearing models he can do.

COMMENT: My principal is very concerned that we help preschoolers become ready for school; because of this, we have strict language programs for each child. The program focuses on concepts children need to adapt to school—concepts like time, numbers, attributes, and colors. For a few years I have carried out these programs and have been successful. My concern is that there now are several children who have left my classroom who can give all the right labels and answers to school-language questions but who rarely use language to play, socialize, or solve problems on their own. What's wrong?

REPLY: Your concern relates to one of the primary problems that motivates us to write this book; that problem is teaching children language and other skills that they will not be able to use until they are in regular social and communicative habits. For nondelayed children we usually expect that they should become socialized, to learn to enjoy groups and to communicate freely, before we impose on them lessons and concepts that they have no immediate communicative use for. We hear your concern from many therapists, teachers, and parents. Until we become committed to helping children develop a genuinely communicative language, one that serves his current interests, he's unlikely to be successful. School should be a place to help children solve *frequently* occurring learning problems. And perhaps the most frequent language problem a child with delays faces is how to talk about his ideas in a way that engages others in conversations. Recall that many of these children do not appreciate the benefits of talking, as we do. Talk is naturally reinforcing to us, but it is often not so for them. If we want to invite a child into the world of language, one that is not physically and cognitively difficult for him, we had better give him words that he knows, that have frequent communicative use for him and that effectively engage others in conversation. No matter how much school language a child has, with numbers and colors, even reciting poems and songs, he is extremely unlikely to build relationships or learn language on his own. On the other hand, with a communicative child-world language a child can explore and learn more language on his own.

COMMENT: I know I should talk with Lucy but it's so boring. She says the same things over and over. I'm worried she's going to bore others, too.

REPLY: Look at your child's world as hundreds of events and things Lucy can have words for. Don't expect her to learn them out of the blue. Give them to her. Be her "living dictionary," showing her words for those things that matter to both of you. Then keep her a little longer. Every time you're bored with what your child is saying, remember others will be too and will not likely stay with him for learning and friendship. Consequently, when you're bored, give her something else to say, then wait. Keep her there and expect her to try.

COMMENT: I manage a group home with six adults, all language delayed, from ages 18 to 36. They all talk, but some of them seem to say only what they've heard while others use language to make up experiences regularly. I admit to preferring to talk with the latter group. Any ideas?

REPLY: You raise a very important issue. Let's refer to your two groups as the *imitative* and *creative* talkers. From our experience, we feel that imitators are persons who have taken a passive role, perhaps as a function to being exposed mainly to questions and commands. Being regularly directed when and what to say, your imitators may define "talking" as what to do when addressed, not what to do on their own. The *creative* talkers are taking advantage of what language is—a very flexible system for combining ideas in an infinite number of combinations to fit the experience at the moment. Language theorists call language generative—that is, once a person has language exposure, he learns rules that allow him to create novel utterances as the interaction requires.

A final point—while one of your two groups of talkers may talk much more creatively than the other, they may not be very different in language ability. They are different in what they think they can do with language. There are problems of pragmatics that will be addressed more fully in the next chapter.

Self-Assessment: Rate yourself on a scale of 1 to 9, where 1 = not often or very poorly, 5 = neutral,
How Are You and 9 = very frequently or quite well.
Doing?

____ 1. My child talks about many events and things.
____ 2. My child imitates others' talk.
____ 3. My child talks on his own without imitating.
____ 4. My child uses words appropriate to the topic.
____ 5. My child uses words creatively and in new ways.

Child Goal

31. FOLLOW GRAMMATICAL RULES

From an interactive view of language learning, we would predict that children would learn to speak in sentences to the degree that they are in frequent conversations with people who match them progressively, thus showing them the next step to a sentence. The details of grammar, because they do not carry primary information or communicative intent, may easily be lost to a child who is grasping for the meaning from a mismatched adult model. Thus, because grammar may not at first get much communicating done for a child (that is, a nongrammatical sentence may be supported in an interaction as well as a grammatical one) adults concerned about grammar may have to carefully match the child's language with desired models. Grammar itself is unlikely to be differentially reinforced for the child.

Another issue related to grammar is timing. When should a child's sentences be grammatical? At what expense are we willing to correct and direct a child to new forms? Widespread research on children's first language (Bloom & Lahey, 1978;

Brown, 1973; MacDonald, 1978; Resler, 1973) has demonstrated across cultures that normally developing children build sentences according to childbased semantic grammatical rules. These rules, derived from many studies of children from ages 1 to 3, show that children combine words into sentences by combining the first meanings children express. Those meanings are (again) agent, action, object, location, and feeling. Up to sentences of three words children combine these meanings without use of traditional grammatical markers such as tense, plural, prepositions, and articles. Apparently the children communicate those words that carry the primary meanings first. It has been our experience that children more easily build sentences when we model the words they currently have than when we model grammatical changes. For example, children appear to be more ready to say "throw ball" then "the ball." The issue throughout this developmental guide is that habitual communicative interactions must be firmly established before the child is pressured with language goals that might generate both failure on his part and no additional communicative gains for his partner.

Certainly, grammar is an appropriate goal for a child who clearly has a communicative habit such that he can generalize such learning. To reiterate, our interactive view would predict that grammar will be learned within natural interactions in which the adults models are progressively matched to the child's performance and the child's newly learned performance has regular communicative uses and rewards.

Subgoal

a. Follow semantic-grammatical rules in sentences.
As discussed above, a child appears to form sentences most readily by combining words he already has into some combination of the order of the meanings. The accompanying display shows some child word and the first sentences he might make with them.

Words:

Agent	*Action*	*Object*	*Location*	*Feeling*
Mom	throw	ball	here	goodie
Tata	pick	me	up	love

Sentences:
Mom throw
Throw ball
Tata here
Mom love

Subgoal

b. Use pronouns, prepositions, and articles.
It is understandable to want a child to talk "right." However, when an adult pressures the child with one- and two-word utterances to say "the ball" instead of "throw ball" or "put in" and not "put ball," we are concerned. Our concern is threefold—first, articles and prepositions simply do not give additional information to the partner; second, they will probably not get a different communicative response; third, unless the child is a well-established conversationalist, he may be discouraged from communicating if he faces regular correction of his efforts to communicate.

But, as we've said frequently, communication is a partnership and what a child considers necessary for a communicative relationship is of importance. Once a child is habitually communicating with three or more words, it appears developmentally appropriate to stress the pronouns, prepositions, articles, and other grammatical constituents as adults match their communication to the child. Stressing, for example, "she," "the," "in," in a friendly, even repetitively, playful way may keep the child's interest motivating him to change for your positive regard.

Subgoal

c. Use verb tense appropriately.

Again, whether we should be concerned if a child says "I see Joey yesterday" or "I saw Joey yesterday" depends on how well he is a habitual communicator. Once he is genuinely involved in a conversation relationship with someone, that person may safely set herself up to change features such as verb tense. Until then, modeling and stressing the differences may be most effective without directing attention away from the interaction.

It's Your Turn

COMMENT:

Most of the children in my class talk in one- to four-word sentences. Many of them use grammar that bothers me a lot. Their plurals, past tense, prepositions, and articles are either missing or obviously wrong. I feel like sitting them down and teaching them correct grammar once and for all.

REPLY:

For several reasons, we hope you don't do that. Children learn to talk to communicate, not to get A's in grammar. We find that the first task is to get the children so they are in such a strong habit of communicating that corrections and judgments will not discourage them from talking. Perhaps more importantly, children do not normally begin to use plurals, verb tense, prepositions, and articles until they are regularly using three- and four-word utterances. The grammar that children learn first is the rules for how to build first sentences. They do that by combining their first words into multiple-word utterances. We are very concerned that we do not make children feel they are failing when they are getting into a habit of communicating words that are communicatively useful. At first, much grammar adds no new information for a child.

COMMENT:

I am a teacher who pays a lot of attention to books on how to teach language. Are you saying that for a child's first language, we do not need any book to tell us what to teach?

REPLY:

Absolutely. Many school books for language assume the child already talks and stays in conversations. They try to teach language about the world outside the child. All you need to decide the language to teach is your eyes and an active child. Every one of his actions, intentions, and communications will give you exactly the words that he needs to learn. Also, look to yourself and your situation, and then put words on those things that you want the child to attend to as long as they are, at first, communicatively useful for him.

COMMENT:

I am a mother of a 3-year-old girl who plays mostly on her own. I've been teaching her words I thought she needed for school. She will tell me those words if I press her, but I notice she has begun to talk less and less about things I know she has words for. I thought she'd always have the words she once had.

REPLY:

Be very careful. Do not take a child's language for granted. You must encourage your child to use her language regularly if she is to become a habitual talker. She may be getting into a habit where she talks only the kinds of things she thinks you want. And if those are "school" words, she will have less chance to practice them than the words she used to use naturally. We suggest you go back and talk with her about her experiences with no push for any specific words. Once you are a regular reward for her in communication, you can begin to use those "school" words in playful give and take that are a part of what she is already doing.

Self-Assessment:
How Are You
Doing?

Rate yourself on a scale of 1 to 9, where 1 = not often or very poorly, 5 = neutral, and 9 = very frequently or quite well.

_____ 1. My child combines words to make sentences.
_____ 2. My child uses grammar that is appropriate to his language level.
_____ 3. My child is beginning to use pronouns, prepositions, and articles correctly.
_____ 4. My child is beginning to use verb tense correctly.

ADULT STRATEGIES

What Can You Do To Help Your Child Learn Language

The first step in helping your child learn language is to realize that he either learns or fails to learn some language in every contact the two of you have. "How can he be learning language from me when I'm not teaching him?" you may ask. The answer is that a child does not learn language by the kind of direct teaching through which we learned math and science. He learns language through even the simplest exchanges with you.

Talk to your child's
knowledge and
interests.

Your child is more likely to learn language when what he hears fits his knowledge and motivation. A child learns language within the kind of interpersonal relationships we have discussed throughout this book. Because adults are often fairly fixed in their approaches to teaching language, it is helpful to ask, "From what kind of relations does language develop?" First, the more that you and your child engage in joint activities, the more likely it is that you will share meanings that can evolve into words. Put another way, the more the two of you pay active attention to the same thing and communicate about it, the more your child will learn your language. Second, matching is just as important to language as it was to building first communications. The more you use language that your child can use, the more likely he is to do so. Remember, in learning language, more is definitely not better. In fact, in many cases more language on your part may even be worse than no language, because too much language can set up a child for failure. Third, and perhaps most important, your child needs to be in the habit of back-and-forth interactions, where the adult communicates once and then waits expectantly for the child to respond. Too many children with emerging language are talked out of an interactive habit, we believe, when adults dominate the talk and give them little freedom to have their say. Consequently, all the principles for becoming partners discussed earlier in the book apply just as directly to language learning.

Becoming an effective natural language teacher almost requires that you take on four roles, or ways of being, with your child. Just as you take the role of caregiver and nurturer with an infant and the role of nurse with a sick child, you can assume these four roles so that your child learns language as a spontaneous part of your relationship. The more you see yourself in terms of these roles, the less you will have to deliberately try to teach your child. In fact, you will learn that the least successful times may come when you do deliberately teach your child.

First role: *Translator.* When a child learns language he is learning your symbols for ideas, perceptions, or nonverbal communications he already knows. Thus, he is not learning the word by itself but, we hope, your way of communicating about something he already knows in some other form. We have found it helpful to view a child's learning language as translating the child's own special language of movements and sounds and experiences into our more conventional language. Think of your task as one of inviting your child to replace his language with yours. Parents and professionals close to language-delayed children agree strongly that those children do have their own special language. With the idea of two languages in mind, those adults see themselves as translators, or second language trainers, responsible for bridging the child from his language to theirs. A practical advantage of this "translator" role is that adults no longer wonder what language the child should learn, for they use the child's play and communications to lead the way. The adults simply learn to code what the child is immediately doing or communicating, thereby showing him their language at the moment he is most interested in it.

Second role: *Living Dictionary.* Many parents and teachers we know are highly aware of what their child knows and cares about, but they forget this essential information when they wonder what language to teach the child. The adult who plays the role of a living dictionary treats the child's active world as a field of potential words and expressions the child needs to know. It is at the moment the child is involved in an activity that he may be most ready to learn words for those experiences. Thus, in this role, asking, "What language can I be teaching him?" yields the answer, "Say what you see."

Be a dictionary.

Third role: *Communication Coach.* Too often we meet young children who can show they know a great deal of language learned in school, such as entire songs or correct answers to a series of problems. But when we watch them in casual interactions, we wonder where all the advanced language has gone. Many of these children seem to have a rich vocabulary in storage but little available for communication. These children need "communication coaches," adults who give them language that has immediate communicative uses, language that can build relationships. As a communication coach, you can regularly evaluate the language in your child's learning environment. Ask how useful that language is in helping him build a communicative habit. While you may be pleased when teachers praise your child for his work in school, do not necessarily conclude that success in school means success in communicative relationships. Your child may need regular coaching to encourage him to communicate what he knows.

Fourth role: *Story Partner.* Parents and teachers of a child identified as language delayed or nonverbal are understandably relieved when the child begins talking. Too often, however, a little bit of language seems to satisfy them. We must not limit a child to language in brief contacts that go nowhere. We must help children develop topics and use language to see the stories in their lives. When you see yourself as a "story partner," you get into the habit of keeping the child in little conversations. No matter how inconsequential they may seem at first, these little conversations teach the child that language is a tool for creating words, images, and relationships. When a child sees language as conversation rather than just a way to respond or to gratify needs, he can use people as rich resources for further learning. And once you see in your child's contacts the potential for an enjoyable story, learning language can become a recurring highlight to your relationship.

Adult Strategy

32. VERBALLY MATCH CHILD EXPERIENCES AND COMMUNICATIONS

Just as we adults attend more closely to people who talk about experiences we are familiar with and who use familiar words and structures in their language, so do children. One reason for using the specific matching skills discussed below is that they allow the child success in talking and learning more language. If you have experience with children with delays, you know this is no small feat. Success for many language-delayed children is rare, when we define success in terms of the child responding appropriately to your talk, initiating talk with you, and keeping talking exchanges going. The primary reason for matching your child's actions and nonverbal communications with language is to provide him with something relevant and interesting he can do. We have known many parents and professionals who strongly resisted becoming like their children in this way. They felt it was uncomfortable, embarrassing, and even mistaken. As we showed these adults how much more the children did when we matched, they began to realize how much more influence they could have than did we, who were virtual strangers to their child.

Substrategy

a. Use words and sentences related to the child's actions, words, and sentences.
A critical assumption of the **ECO** model is that a child will learn more readily if adults respond to his experiences than if they direct him more to their interests. Thus, the more we fine-tune our language to what the child is doing, what he is communicating at the moment, the more likely he is to learn our language. This notion of "semantic relatedness" (Cross, 1978; Snow, 1978) ties together a child's cognitive and social needs. When an adult links her language to the child's experience, she is increasing the likelihood of uniting the child's attention, interest, and cognitive competence. It appears more likely that a child will learn language that relates to both what he knows and what he has an interest in than to the language children frequently hear that is beyond their knowledge and interest.

Substrategy

b. Respond to the child's nonverbal messages with the appropriate word.
Many adults have reported considerable relief, not to mention success, when they began to treat frequent messages their child sent without words as opportunities to translate them into words. Learning to look at those sounds and gestures as embryonic words made it easier to translate them into words the child could use. Before this training, those adults either ignored the nonverbal messages or quizzed the child for more information, often losing him. After the training, those adults had something positive to do: immediately show the child an appropriate word in *their* language, thereby encoding the child's message at the moment of his greatest interest.

Substrategy

c. Use grammar the child can model.

Often your child may use the same words over and over for the same experiences. For adults who are relieved just to have the child talking, it may be difficult to realize how much more can be said about any event. Watching Sesame Street, for example, a child might say only "Oscar funny" when he sees that character. There is an endless number of ways to talk about Oscar that you can show him: "Oscar the grouch." "I love Oscar." "He lives in a can." "I bet he smells." "He eats garbage." "Garbage is yukky." Again, encourage any adult to get into the habit of being a living dictionary who regularly shows the child another way of talking about an event. The point is not to try to make him say these new words, but to show him another way. This teaches two critical skills for language development: first, to talk about many aspects of a thing; second, to actively learn that every event carries many concepts that are potential words. Work on developing the habit of saying something new to your child.

Substrategy

d. Imitate and animate; expand some of the child's communications.

When we imitate a child's language we do several things. We show him we accept and support his language, and we inform him that we are willing to do what he does, in the hope he will come to do what we do. Imitating a child also gives him a mature production of what he said, at precisely the time he is most likely to register the new way of saying it. Finally, when we imitate a child's words he usually pays more attention and stays with us longer to learn more language than had we talked on our own. Of course, we want more than imitative language; otherwise there would be little progress. To that end, we expand on what the child says by giving him another word or two that adds meaning and is communicatively useful. Expanding is a key element in the general principle of matching that pervades the **ECO** model. However, we are very careful not to expand so much that we lose the child. Always remember the rule for knowing when to simplify your language and make it more childlike: "When your child begins leaving, you begin changing."

It's Your Turn

COMMENT:

I want my child to talk about the world he will have to face, not his own world. Why should he talk about something he knows about?

REPLY:

Before your child will talk about anything frequently he must become a confident talker. Confidence will come from having success talking and developing a strong need for talking. That need is likely to develop only if he feels free to talk about his concerns. An old learning rule is "Begin learning new skills with old familiar content." By giving your child language for his world, you are giving him the power he needs to talk spontaneously from his own experiences. Again, as we said before, children do not conversationally value talk for its own sake, especially children with delays; they learn to value it to the degree it allows them to explore and have positive effects. We have found, over and over, that children who have adults who talk to their motivations are children who stay longer and attempt to communicate more often.

COMMENT:

Until I realized Frank had his own communication without words, I just waited and hoped for words to come. Now every time he points, makes a sound, or acts something out, I translate it into one of my words. He usually pays more attention to me and often tries to do what I did. I'm just not at a loss for what to do now.

REPLY: Yes, and we remember when nothing would satisfy you except words. It was fun watching you begin to "see" a word in many of the things Frank did.

Self-Assessment
How Are You
Doing?

Rate yourself on a scale of 1 to 9, where 1 = not often or very poorly, 5 = neutral, and 9 = frequently or very well.

____ 1. I talk in ways my child can do.
____ 2. I talk about my child's activities and communications.
____ 3. I talk about my child's activities with relevant words.
____ 4. I give my child matched sentences.
____ 5. I show my child a next step in language.

Adult Strategy

33. DEVELOP VERBAL TOPICS

Topic building is story making.

For our children, language must be more than labels for familiar things, calls for needs to be met, and answers to directives and questions. Such language alone leads to little learning and limited relationships. As common as these brief chances to talk may be, they simply do not allow the child to use language as the powerful tool for creating and reporting experiences that it can be. Every time you and your child talk, there is some topic or theme between you: being hungry before dinner; driving into a city of buildings and lights; the traditional report on the school day; playing house; puppets talking about a friend; and so on, ending only after bedtime. Consider the task of building topics to be like creating a story, not an involved one, but one where the child hears and says new words that relate realistically or imaginatively to the topic. Almost any word in the child's active world can build a topic. For example, when a child says "rain" you can exchange words with him like "wet," "cold," "raincoat," "sneeze," "medicine," "dry," and "towel." Topics are not first developed as logical conversations. They start as exchanges of words that express the many meanings of a given topic.

Topics release a child's knowledge.

A topic is any idea that lasts across a number of exchanges. Topics emerge easily when you are genuinely together in joint activities with a child and spontaneously say what you both are seeing and doing. How important it is to keep your child talking about different aspects of an experience, far beyond just labeling things or announcing demands! As we have said several times in this book, we are deeply concerned with the large number of children who communicate much less than they know. The job of showing a child how to build language topics is extremely important to his social and educational future; topic building actually is the job of *releasing the child's hidden knowledge from his quiet self into the world of communication.* We might even consider intelligence as including, in good part, the ability to seek relationships in an experience and to tie them together, thereby creating new knowledge. Thus topic building should enhance a child's intelligence.

Substrategy

a. Share choice of topic with child.

Consider this strategy as an extension of the fairness principle of give-and-take. We want you and your child to give and take ideas and make new language out of those ideas. While it is common to see a child talking only about his ideas, a critically important stage in socialization involves the child's learning that he must respect, stay with, and incorporate what others have to say if he expects them to build relationships with them. This sharing means more than the attitude that "now it's your topic, now it's my topic." Perhaps a more valuable way of sharing topics for learning language is to do it within a broader topic. There the adult can show a child the many avenues of topics that can take off even from the simplest notion. Often a major problem is the child's failure to stay on a topic. We see this when adults are totally following the child's lead. We enjoy catching a child as he is leaving a topic by saying something designed to renew his interest in it. We often accomplish this by doing something unexpected or even silly. This not only keeps the child interacting with others but also shows him a playful way to get more language from the topic.

Substrategy

b. Keep the child on the topic of his or her choice.

Children often act as if they know little more about something than its name or how to request it. A child needs to learn at least two things about language: first, that every word has an endless number of words related to it; second, that words are tools for keeping people with them for further knowledge and companionship. For every extra turn in which you keep your child talking on his topic, he has an opportunity to learn more language and to learn how rewarding talk can be.

To keep the child on his topic means, of course, that you must also follow the child's topic. When you talk about the topic chosen by the child, you also increase the likelihood that he will attend to your language and relate it to his experiences. Again, the principles of matching and waiting apply, because they give the child something he can do and the time to do it. Following the child's choice of talk, you can show him what more can be said about it. In fact, you can show him creative new meanings of even a common event. For example, when a child hugs his teddy bear, rather than just saying "nice Teddy" or "love you," you can re-create daily events for Teddy to participate in. Soon the child will be having breakfast, bedtime, school, and many other topics available from an event about which he used to say only a few things.

Balance: Both follow and take the lead.

Note, however, that you should not overdo your part in following the child. Many professionals and parents have taken this to an extreme, and their children are expected to take the lead all the time. A fundamental goal of the **ECO** model is a balanced partnership. Thus, while it is critical that you frequently follow the child's lead to keep him interested and to match his knowledge, it is equally important that you show him that your ideas are an essential source of his learning language. Thus, just as we discussed in the chapters on play and turntaking, children learn best in a give-and-take relationship. When we are with a child who dominates the choice of topic, we gradually encourage him to stay on our activity or with our ideas, briefly at first and then increasingly more. We do this in many ways— imposing our turn, intruding actions to talk about, and otherwise informing him that we will allow him his ideas but we will also have ours. We do this firmly and gently, knowing that any child who dominates the ideas will not be accepted long in the learning relationships he needs. The child thereby learns a general rule of society: Others will stay on your topics to the extent that you participate in theirs.

Substrategy

c. Keep the child on the topic of your choice.

Language can be a powerful tool for a child to learn about other people. A common regret parents and professionals report is that children with delays often show

The child needs to see your perspective.

little interest in them. If children continue to fail to take another person's perspective, society may well reciprocate and take less interest in the child. It is incumbent on you to make your language and ideas so engaging that your child will become increasingly interested in what you say beyond the necessary talk of caregiving. Often when a child loses interest, the adult seems to say, "Oh well," and shrug it off. Recognize that every time your child leaves your topic successfully, he is learning that he can similarly isolate himself from others. We make it a point occasionally to get the child to stay on our topic one or two more turns than usual, even if it requires us to do or say something less mature than usual. That is, we do not talk like an adult to do this, but make the topic as lively and as closely matched to the child as we can.

Substrategy

d. Build a topic with new ideas and vocabulary matched to the child's level.
In keeping with the entire **ECO** model, we generally strive to use language that the child seems able to use himself. This language matching can take at least two forms, horizontal and vertical. When we match horizontally we use words at the child's quantity or syntax level, but we give him another meaning for the message.

Keep new ideas coming.

For example, when a child says "snow," we might match him by saying "cold," "outside," "wet," or "Santa," showing him how to describe his experience with different words. When we match vertically, we show the child how to say more about the same thing. Again, for "snow," we might match by saying, "it's cold," "snowman," "car gets stuck," or "go sledding." Matching is a very simple way to build a theme. Not only does it show a child different meanings in a context, but it also shows him how to combine those meanings into a bigger picture. For example, when a child who is playing with a truck says, "truck," "woosh," "bump," "up," and "down" separately, we might say things like: "woosh, truck go bump," "truck up my leg," "down my leg, bump, woosh." An entire little comic strip could be enacted to show the child how to add new words and combine old ones to create the story, say, of a truck going up and down a mountain.

Show your child the stories in his life; your words can make them come alive to him. Children with delays should not be seen, either by themselves or by others, as concrete, dead-end talkers. We know a great many children with a variety of delays—including autistic disorders, Down syndrome, cerebral palsy, retardation, deafness, behavior disorders—who have learned to use language in creative, storytelling ways. Engaging a child in make-believe play is one of the easiest ways to explore his often-unused store of knowledge. We are frequently surprised when a child expresses many kinds of ideas and relationships in story play that no one remembers him saying before. We find that the less directive, less judgmental, and more matched the adults are with a child, the more readily will the child launch from topic building into stories.

Substrategy

e. Communicate with a variety of concepts.
For almost everything you and your child talk about there are many other things that could be said to show him how to build a topic and learn more about the ideas at hand. Remember the meanings we have said children usually begin talking about: agents (people), actions (movements), objects (things acted upon), locations (places), and feelings (emotions). These meanings can guide you in keeping a topic going. You can get into the habit of asking yourself: What agent, action,

object, location, or feeling could I tie into our topic in order to build it and get my child talking more?

A little story may illustrate this task of building a topic. Peter is telling his mother about the puppet named Oscar the Grouch. His mother is busy with dinner but remembers to keep him on topic with the five meanings. Notice that she does not use questions, as she wants to show him what things can be said more about Oscar.

Peter: Oscar was sick to his tummy.
Mother: I'm sorry he was sick. (feeling)
Peter: Me too. He didn't cry.
Mother: Good. He should sleep. (action)
Peter: Garbage can is too small.
Mother: He needs a bed. (location)
Peter: Can he have my bed?
Mother: Sure, you sleep with Katie. (location) You'd love that. (feeling)
Peter: Yuk. I sleep with Oscar.
Mother: He'll make you sick. (feeling)
Peter: I don't like it sick.
Mother: You sleep here. Oscar sleep on TV. (people and location)
Peter: Is supper ready?

As with most children, Peter's concerns were easy to keep going by translating them into his important people and the objects he directly affected, his personal locations, actions he experienced, and feelings that his mother knew he could relate to. There was no stress or chance of failure, no job to get done. Under the stress of working with a child with language delay, adults often feel they should try to pull the words out. In the example here, Peter is not unlike many children we know. If we simply comment about meanings that match the child's interests and that are communicatively useful, children stay for your attention, for the success of talking, and for the little surprises.

It's Your Turn

COMMENT: I have four children ages 2 to 8; Meghan, 4 years old, is language delayed with a history of seizures and problems attending. We discovered a way to get Meghan and the 2-year-old, Daniel, to be talking throughout the day. Everyone has a job: to say something about what he sees or does; then everyone available puts a word on it, and then the oldest person puts the words together. We find that just a few words can lead to a story that everyone tries to add words to. The older ones have to be careful to wait as the younger ones get their word in. We often make up quite humorous stories. If someone likes Dr. Seuss, they'd like our family stories.

REPLY: What a creative way to encourage language! Of course, every event is part of a real story and can be used to create stimulating pretend stories. What you seem to have done is to make your home a place where stories are expected, where language is an enjoyable game, not the drudgery many feel. Meghan is fortunate to learn that she can play with language and it can bring her closer to others.

COMMENT: I know when I talk to Henry about his ideas and at his level, he responds and stays more than he does when I talk like an adult. But I can't be a child all the time.

REPLY: Relax and be yourself a lot of the time. You need not match all the time as long as you do it frequently enough for Henry to learn to use your words. He can learn other things, like understanding and your concerns, when you use adult language.

COMMENT: My 2-year-old Juan talks but won't stay in the stories I try to tell him. They are the ones I enjoyed as a child. Why doesn't he?

REPLY: The first stories or topics Juan may stay in are ones he knows himself. Play with him in certain ways, like building something or going somewhere, then tell that story. He will stay on topics more if he personally knows them. You might even act out some of the stories you enjoy; the more he knows them in his actions, the more he may stay with you. One further point. Your life is full of stories—real ones and ones you can make up. Do not rely on books or try to keep your child talking on a topic. Your own personal stories, even silly ones, can help your child value staying in talk with others.

COMMENT: I conduct training programs for professionals and parents new to the task of interacting with preconversational children. Can you put what you've been saying into a list of what to do and what to avoid doing when you want to help a child learn language?

REPLY: The following list is a set of guidelines we use in training parents and professionals and in assessing their progress as natural language teachers.

Use a Child Communicative Language Style

Increase
- Respond to child's ideas and actions.
- Use language that matches child's performance level (showing a next step)
- Use language that is communicatively useful to child
- Be a living dictionary who:
  - Puts words on child's experiences (references)
  - Puts words on nonverbal communications (second language training)
  - Shows new words and combinations for child's messages (thesaurus)
- Use language in a back and forth style
- Keep the child on a topic a little longer than usual
- Keep the child on a topic of his choice
- Shift the child from his world to your point of view
- Accept new verbal attempts without judgment
- Focus more on the child's ideas than his ways of communicating
- Use talk that stimulates images in child, not rote responses
- Make language an extension of your play

Decrease
- Mismatch with adult language
- Talk about your concerns alone
- Make a job out of language learning
- Use academic language
- Use language with little child communicative use
- Allow yourself to dominate topics
- Accept rote or stereotypic language
- Use limited verbal routines with child
- Focus on language form more than meaning
- View language more for learning and storage than communication
- Expect your child to learn language only from school-like teaching

Rate yourself on a scale of 1 to 9, where 1 = not often or very poorly, 5 = neutral, and 9 = frequently or very well.

_____ 1. I can usually keep my child talking on a single topic for more than a couple turns.

_____ 2. I stay on topics that my child chooses.

_____ 3. I keep the child on topics of my choosing.

_____ 4. I can easily add new ideas to build topics with my child.

_____ 5. I have a number of stories going with my child.

Sample Resources for Becoming Language Partners

ECOScale: Becoming Language Partners
ECO Tutor: Becoming Language Partners
ECO Link: Becoming Language Partners
Conversation Routine
IEP/Problem Solver
ECO Practice Plan and Record

BECOMING LANGUAGE PARTNERS

INTERACTIVE GOAL

28. Become language partners.
    a. Share a closely matched vocabulary.
    b. Share closely matched structures and forms.
    c. Share the lead in topic development.

CHILD PROBLEM

29. Low verbal and pragmatic skills.
    a. Narrow range of vocabulary.
    b. Use of single words more than phrases or sentences.
    c. Speech used mainly to get or manipulate.
    d. Lack of assertion; mainly verbal imitation.
    e. Difficulty finding words to say.
    f. Minimal pragmatics.
    g. Lack of topic development.
    h. Speech hard to understand.

CHILD GOALS

30. Use varied vocabulary.
    a. Use a range of meanings: agents, actions, objects, locations, feelings.
    b. Imitate and otherwise talk like others.
    c. Use words nonimitatively.
    d. Use vocabulary appropriate to the topic.
    e. Show a sense of knowing how to talk about things.
    f. Show creativity in speech.
31. Follow grammatical rules.
    a. Follow semantic-grammatical rules in sentences.
    b. Use pronouns, prepositions, and articles.
    c. Use verb tense appropriately.

ADULT STRATEGIES

32. Verbally match child experiences and communications.
    a. Use words and sentences related to the child's actions, words, and sentences.
    b. Respond to the child's nonverbal messages with the appropriate word.
    c. Use grammar the child can model.
    d. Imitate and animate; expand some of the child's communications.

33. Develop verbal topics.
    a. Share choice of topic with the child.
    b. Keep the child on the topic of his or her choice.
    c. Keep the child on the topic of your choice.
    d. Build a topic with new ideas and vocabulary matched to the child's level.
    e. Communicate with a variety of concepts.

ECO *Interactive Goal:* **Becoming Language Partners**
Tutor

What Is It?   Children need partners to learn language. Children learn to talk by being in frequent interactions with people who act like partners in the following ways. They talk with the child about his interests and often let him lead the way. They match the child's language by talking in ways that he either can do or is likely to be able to do soon. They talk a little, then wait, carefully showing the child they expect him to talk also. Because they know it is essential for the child to stay talking with others, they will keep the child talking a little longer than he might usually stay. A language partner is someone who is accessible and willing to frequently take a few seconds for a brief exchange, knowing that it is in those brief exchanges that the child learns that he can be a talker with others who are not yet partners.

What To Look For   A first step in becoming a language partner is to learn where language comes from so you know where to start your partnership. Often parents and professionals know where they want the child to get to but are unclear as to where to start. Your child's language comes from at least three places: first, his knowledge, including his thoughts, ideas, and know-how; second, his motivations, what he cares about and will do something for; third, his communications, what he has reasons to communicate about. You can begin to be a partner who helps your child learn language by talking directly to these three language sources. Practically speaking, this means talking directly about what your child knows at the moment, what he cares about, and what he is already communicating about.

For practice, you can make a list to identify these three targets for your talk.

My child's knowledge	*My child's motivations*	*My child's communications*
grandma	tv	reaches to get up
car	outside	nono for grandpa

Keep the list only to get into asking these questions; then let the answers lead you as to what to talk about. Then talk about those things frequently and casually. Don't wait for special times; children can learn to talk anytime you do.

Strategies That Can Help   Refer to these whenever you and your child are not talking more than before. Translate sounds and gestures into a word.

— Talk in ways your child can match.
— Show your child a next step in talking.
— Use words that are communicatively useful to a child.
— Limit adult and school talk until he has a strong talking habit.
— Keep the talking going back and forth.
— Wait and expect him to talk again.
— Say things you want him to say.
— Limit questions and commands.
— Give him freedom to talk his own ideas.
— Sprinkle brief talking contacts throughout your time with him.
— Occasionally, see how long you can keep him talking as a playtime.

LESS LIKE THIS	MORE LIKE THIS
Rodney: (at elevator) "I wanna push button."	Rodney: (At elevator) "I wanna push."
Dad: "Do you know how elevators work?"	Dad: (Lifts boy up.) "Push the 'up' button."
Rodney: "Are we going up?"	Rodney: (Coming down.) "Mom's up."
Dad: "There are long, thick, wire cables and a powerful motor. That little button makes the motor go and the cables pull the car."	Dad: "She's with Freddie."
	Rodney: "Freddie's leg still sick?"
Rodney: "Mom's upstairs; I wanna push up."	Dad: "His leg was broken."
Dad: "When the light's on, it's being used. The light and the cables and the motor are electronically interrelated."	Rodney: "He has a cat on his leg."
	Dad: "A cast; it's coming off."
Rodney: "Light's off. I wanna push it."	Rodney: "Freddie's leg off?"
Dad: "Do you understand how it works now? Can you explain it to me?"	Dad: "No, silly; the white cast, not his leg."
Rodney: (Jumps up, presses button.) "Let's go, dad."	

Why Less?

While this example is exaggerated, we see many children and adults talking side-by-side but not together. These are times when the child may be missing valuable language learning with others. Notice how mismatched the father was to his son. He talked in sentences far beyond Rodney's ability, ignored Rodney's interests, and used language that was far beyond the boy's current thinking. There was no development or sharing of a topic and no evidence that the father's talk was having any effect on the boy. Unless Rodney has other strong language partners, we would be concerned that he may be discouraged from talking and thus learn less language from others.

Why More?

In this example, the boy and father are fairly balanced and matched language partners. Each takes the lead and the father uses language the boy can do. He shows the boy some next steps in talking but never gives him more than he could try. Notice that they are talking for the enjoyment of being together, not to get a job done, and with little pressure. For this pair, language seems to be a natural part of being together.

Why Is It Important?

While the answer may be obvious now, we know many adults who are not comfortable language partners with children and who do not see its importance, especially for children with delays. Consider some likely consequences if a child does not have language partners. He will depend on catching language on the fly for his learning. Consequently, he may find language learning to be a difficult job wrought with failures. He may not even learn the pleasures and importance that language could hold for him. He will learn not to stay with others for talking, even people who might be good language partners. He will use language to get his needs met and miss countless opportunities for learning friendship. Beyond these disadvantages, the primary reason to become a language partner is that only in frequent, matched partnerships will children get the practice and develop the motivation to become habitual language learners.

**ECO
Link**

Becoming Language Partners
*HOW YOU CAN HELP A CHILD
LEARN LANGUAGE WITH YOU*

*HOW DO YOU
AND YOUR
CHILD TALK
TOGETHER?*

1. Do you talk habitually as a natural part of your time together?
2. Do the two of you use similar words and numbers of words?
3. Do you build topics as you talk?
4. Do each of you talk about the other's ideas?
5. Do you talk for enjoyment as much as for getting things done?

*HOW WILL YOU
KNOW IF YOUR
CHILD IS LEARN-
ING LANGUAGE
IN THE
PARTNERSHIP?*

1. He will put words on his nonverbal communications.
2. He will imitate and otherwise talk more like you.
3. He will stay more with you just to talk.
4. He will talk increasingly more like you do.
5. He will be showing new words and using old ones creatively.
6. He will talk for more and more reasons.
7. He will talk about your ideas as well as his.
8. He will stay talking longer on topics.
9. He will clearly enjoy talking and at times prefer it to being alone.

*HOW WILL YOU
KNOW IF THERE
IS A PROBLEM
IN YOUR
LANGUAGE-
LEARNING
PARTNERSHIP?*

1. Your child will not be in the habit of talking; he will show little use for and interest in talking.
2. Your child will have some "school" language but little communicative language.
3. Your child's language will show few recent changes.
4. He will use words over and over.
5. He will often seem at a loss for what to say.
6. His language will often be imitative, with little spontaneous talking.
7. You will use language that is controlling rather than friendly.
8. You will not talk about his interests.
9. Your language will be too advanced for him to try.
10. You will see talking as more work than fun.
11. One of you will control the topics.
12. Both of you will talk but not develop topics.
13. Your together time will involve little spontaneous talking.

*HOW CAN YOU
BUILD A
LANGUAGE-
LEARNING
PARTNERSHIP?*

1. Use language that has regular communicative use for your child.
2. Be sure to show him how to talk for more reasons than simply reacting to questions and commands.
3. Be responsive to and accepting of his language; make sure it works for him.
4. Talk in ways that show him what to say next.
5. Let him talk; balance your talk with him; wait and give him time.
6. Keep him a little longer on a topic.
7. Match; talk in ways your child can do, about his interests.

1. Talking in ways he cannot do.
2. Talking mainly about your concerns.
3. Making work out of talking together.
4. Telling him what to say.
5. Moving rapidly from topic to topic.
6. Talking about the same things over and over.

Conversation Routine   **ACADEMICS: Teaching Body Parts**   Verbal Level

---

Make the natural events in your day into opportunities for friendly, social conversations with your child. Consider these contrasting examples. Try to avoid limited contacts such as the one on the left. Try to find something you can share with your child, as in the example on the right. Turn just another routine into a joint activity in which your child can stay and learn with you.

LESS LIKE THIS

Adult:	"You sit here, and I'll sit here so we can see each other while we talk about our body parts."
Child:	(Sits down.)
Adult:	"Show me all the parts of your face and tell me their names."
Child:	"This my ears." (Points to his ears.)
Adult:	"Yes, you're right. But they are not really on your face are they?"
Child:	(Looks at adult quizzically.)
Adult:	"They're on your head. What's on your face?"
Child:	"My nose?" (Points to it.)
Adult:	"Yes, that's right."
Child:	"My eyes?"
Adult:	"Yes, what's over your eyes?"
Child:	"I think . . . hair."
Adult:	"Right here . . . points to her eyebrows . . . try again."
Child:	"I think . . . eyehair."
Adult:	"No, we don't call them eyehairs; we call them eyebrows."

MORE LIKE THIS

Adult:	"I see your nose." (Playfully touches the child's nose as he passes.)
Child:	"Me got your nose—beep beep." (Pretends to honk the adult's nose.)
Adult:	"I don't see your ears!" (Holds hands up with an air of surprise.)
Child:	"They hiding under my hair." (Shows them by lifting up hair.)
Adult:	"Sure enough." (Covers child's head with a cloth.) "What else is hiding?"
Child:	"My whole face!" (Pretends to struggle from under the cloth.)
Adult:	"What's on your whole face? I don't see anything." (Laughs to tantalize child.)
Child:	"My mouth, my chin, my eyes and my eyehairs." (Lifts the cloth to point at each one.)
Adult:	"These we call eyebrows." (Points to her own.)
Child:	"They hairs. I feel them."
Adult:	"Eyebrows are made of hair. We call them eyebrows."
Child:	(Laughs and points to them, proudly.) "Me got two eyebrows."

Avoid These Problems:
Focus on Right and Wrong,
Acts More Like a Teacher than a Partner,
Stressful or Task-Oriented Activity

This adult creates a fear of failure in the child by focusing on the "wrongness" versus the "rightness" of his response on the first turn. From then on he hesitates or asks a question for each of his responses. There is no playful spirit between the two. Instead, the adult gives each correct response a judgment such as "Yes, that's right," then moves right along to another question.

Try These Strategies:
Avoid Discouraging Feedback,
Act and Communicate Close to the Child's Level,
Have Social, Friendly Conversations with the Child

The adult discovers what the child knows about the parts of his face through friendly banter. She uses comments more than questions or commands, then waits for the child to show what he knows in response. The adult provides corrective feedback by supplying the appropriate information without using the word "no" or other similar forms of discouraging feedback. The effect of such a combination of strategies helps the child learn rules of conversation along with the academic content that is a part of his lesson.

Verbal

CHILD GOAL: Use Varied Vocabulary to Develop Verbal Topics
PROBLEM: Directive, Controlling, Dominating
(the adult who ignores the child's actions and ideas)

Barbara and her grandmother play school together while Mom works. Grandma likes Barbara to show off to Mom what she has taught her. This demand for a good performance often ends in tears, since Barbara often does her worst work under the pressure of other people's questions and commands. She does better when she can use her own ideas at least half the time.

Barbara: "Look Mom—my milkshake—I make it." (Holds out empty cup to Mom.)
Grandma: "Let's show Mommy how well you can match your colors now after our work today."
Barbara: "No colors. I want go home."
Grandma: "Now look. Here's your nice picture with all of your new colors. Which one do you like the best?"
Barbara: "Yucky place."
Grandma: "Oh, you make Grandma sad." (Makes a sad face.)

ECO | *Partnership Plan*

The **ECO** Partnership Plan contains those elements of an Individual Family Service Plan (IFSP) or Individual Education Program (IEP) that specify **ECO** goals and objectives to enhance a child's social and communicative development. Refer to current ECOScales for present levels of development and performance and for new goals.

Child Name: __**Barbara**__   Birth Date: __**6/18**__   Parents: __**Peter and Marian**__

Date of ECOScales: __**11/12**__   Examiner: _____

Present Levels of Development and Performance

Communicative but minimally linguistic; verbal level

Child Goal

Use varied vocabulary

Objectives

Use a range of meanings (agent, action, object, etc.)

Use vocabulary appropriate to a topic

Partnership Goal

Become Language Learning Partners

Objectives

Share a closely matched vocabulary   Share the lead in topic development

Priority Problem:

Poor conversations

Subproblem

Lack of developed conversational topic

Rigid roles rather than flexible partnership

Adult Strategies

Develop verbal topics

Substrategies

Share choice of topic with Barbara   Match ideas to Barbara's level

Imitate and animate Barbara   Show relaxed enjoyment

Use words and phrases matched to Barbara's

Practice Activities
People Only

Imitation Games

__**2-3**__ Times a day   __**2-3**__ Minutes each

People and Things

Turntaking word games

Book "reading"

__**1-2**__ Times a day   __**2-3**__ Minutes each

Daily Routines (practice one a day)

Cooking, washing dishes

Spontaneous

ECO | Practice Plan and Record

PRACTICE PLAN
Refer to current ECOScale for goals; see other ECOScales for old goals to maintain.

Interactive Goal — Become language partners (Chad. and Mom)

Objectives — _____ _____

Priority Problem — Low verbal and pragmatic skills

Child Goal — Use varied vocabulary

Objectives — Use vocabulary appropriate to topic | Show sense of knowing how to talk about things

Adult Strategies — Develop verbal topics
Build topic with new ideas and vocabulary matched to David's level

Targets to Decrease — CHAD: 1) Minimal topic development 2) Lack of assertion — mainly verbal imitation
CHRIS: 1) Lack of developed conversation topics 2) Communicating about few concepts

Practice Activities

People Only — Greetings when arriving home | Exchanging comments about day's events

How Often — 1-2 Times a day | 3-4 Minutes each

Where

People and Things — Picture book or magazine for "reading" — talking reciprocally about pictures | Card games involving conversation.

How Often — 1-2 Times a day | 3-4 Minutes each

Where

Daily Routines (practice one a day) — Washing dishes | Cooking

Spontaneous — Salt and pepper your strategies across the day. | Make interactions/communications a habit.

PARTNERSHIP CALENDAR

Week	MONDAY	TUESDAY	WEDNESDAY	THURSDAY	FRIDAY	SATURDAY	SUNDAY
1	2 2	3 2	2 2	No time – baby sick	2 2	3 3	3 3
2	4 4	5 5	4 4	4 4	5 5	3 2	4 4
3							
4							
5							

How to Use the Calendar

1. Select one goal each for child and adult. Observe one planned activity a day.
2. After observing, rate child and adult (you or someone else) on the goals listed in the Practice Plan. Use a 1 to 9 scale:
   1-2 = no evidence   3-4 = little evidence   5 = some evidence   6-7 = increasing evidence   8-9 = strong evidence
3. Rate the child (c) in top half and adult (a) in bottom half of each cell. Be sure to practice across many activities. Try some of the following; check the ones you practice.
   People only: __ sounds __ actions __ conversations __ your choice _____
   People and things: __ toys __ books __ games __ your choice _____
   Daily routines: __ getting up __ dressing __ bathing __ meals __ TV __ car __ bedtime
   __ shopping __ visiting __ household chores __ your choice _____

ECO | Practice Plan and Record

PARTNERSHIP DIARY

Watch your progress and help your habits grow. Quickly, comment on how interactions with your child went today. Say anything: progress, problems, ideas, changes. Mention both child and adult occasionally.

Week 1 Monday	Today Chad and I tried looking at a book together, but it wasn't really a "topic." We basically labeled what we saw. Chad mostly said animal names.
Tuesday	I did a little better job of talking about more things myself and pointing out a variety of "concepts" in the books.
Wednesday	Didn't feel we were creating a "topic" today. A lot of Chad's comments aren't related to previous ones.
Thursday	No time today — Chelsea was sick
Friday	I really didn't have too much energy to give Chad. I ended up labelling a lot of pictures in a book while he pointed to them. He said "cow" once.
Saturday	Much better than yesterday! I was more with it. A lot of times I waited when Chad just pointed to a picture without saying anything. Then he sometimes made a comment.
Sunday	Think we're getting into a routine.

Week 2 Monday	Chad was very assertive today. He kept the "conversation" going by continuing to point out pictures on the page and making comments about them.
Tuesday	Today while we washed the dishes we talked about it very naturally. Stayed on one topic about 5 min, then went to related one for 5 min. Maybe because I was doing something natural, it felt like less
Wednesday	work to Chad, so he did more. For a change, I put no pressure on him! Wed — good — same things were happening again today
Thursday	I'm just not as natural with Chad when we're doing a play activity — I try too hard probably.
Friday	Curled up with Chad on my bed and looked at books for ½ hour. We both feel so comfortable, the words just come. Really maintained topic after topic.
Saturday	Felt pressured today — Chad just another "chore to get done." I hope I can eventually make time for stress-free conversations every day.
Sunday	Much better than Sat. But the activity I'm evaluating was very much "on the run." Somehow I just tried to maintain a relaxed conversation with Chad as he put on his coat. Much to my surprise, it took less time than when I tell him what to do.
Extra Hints to Remember	AVOID RIGID CONVERSATIONAL ROLES THAT LIMIT WHAT CHAD CAN SAY ABOUT A TOPIC. TRY FOR A MORE FLEXIBLE, RELAXED PARTNERSHIP WHERE YOU BOTH MAKE COMMENTS. AVOID QUESTIONING CHAD TO GET HIM TO PERFORM.

8 | Becoming Conversation Partners

SOCIAL
social

PLAY
play

FUTURE

TAKING
taking

TURN

COMM
comm

UNICATION
unication

LANGUAGE
language

CONVE
conve

RSATION
rsation

THE PRAGMATICS OF HOW TO USE LANGUAGE TO BUILD RELATIONSHIPS

When your child becomes a conversational partner with you and others, he will be ready for a wide variety of relationships in friendship, learning, and work. The ultimate goal of the **ECO** program is for children and adults to automatically have conversations as a natural feature of their time together.

As partners, you will often talk about the same ideas. Sometimes your child will follow your lead but you will often follow the ideas that motivate him. Just as you learned in becoming play partners (chapter 1), both of you must pay attention to the same topic in a conversation. Likewise, turntaking (chapter 2) is as important as ever: The turntaking rules of give-and-take and waiting are absolutely essential if others are to stay with your child in conversations he needs for learning, friendship, and day-to-day routines.

Another skill you have learned in this program is matching. Like turntaking, matching is fundamental to learning conversations. As we have seen, the more closely an adult acts and talks like a child, and the more the adult communicates about the child's interests and experiences, the more likely the child will stay interacting and learning with the adult. In conversations, we become partners by fine-tuning ourselves to the ideas and forms of each other's messages. In adult-child conversations, the adult does most of this fine-tuning at first, but you can slowly expect the child to read you and to adapt to your forms and ideas at times.

Recall that we talked earlier about the serious problem of children communicating much less than they know. We said that society is more likely to treat and accept such children on the basis of what they communicate than on what they actually know. Unfortunately for these children, a child must show his knowledge in everyday social conversations if he is to build productive and enduring relationships.

Interactive Goal

34. BECOME CONVERSATION PARTNERS

What conversational partners do you prefer?

In learning to be a conversation partner with your child, consider the kinds of people you prefer as conversation partners—people who join in what you do, either through their actions or ideas, and who make themselves accessible to you.

* These partners take turns with you, waiting with interest for your turns and expecting the same from you.

- They keep you with them if the conversation falters, and they respond sensitively to your concerns and changes in your ideas.
- They match or fine-tune their communication to what you can understand and what you are interested in.
- They let you know their ideas and preferences so that you can match theirs.
- Accordingly, they stay on the topics you start and help to keep you on the topics they start.
- Further, they are not always intent on getting a job done or getting something from you. Rather, they exchange ideas with you as much for the pleasure of your company as to learn something from you or to teach you something.
- Such a partner appreciates that many times he comes away from conversations having learned something, and he is pleased when you learn from him as well.
- A genuine partner seldom directs or controls you, nor does she let you do that to her.
- Because this kind of partner both accepts you and expects you to do your part, he or she is a person who affects your life, a person to whom you want to return for more.

Be the kind of person you want to be with.

a. Communicate for social reasons.

Subgoal

A primary goal of **ECO** is to show the child how to build many kinds of relationships. To make conversation become your child's preferred way of being with people, you must first make your conversations *successful* for him. The best way to do that is to make your conversations primarily social, rather than concentrating on getting a job done or testing the child's knowledge. Social conversations exist for the enjoyment of being together, friendly exchanges that accommodate each other and risk little failures.

Move from a directive to a social role.

Parents and professionals are often uncomfortable when they first move from a directive to a social role in conversations. They report feeling that they are getting nothing done. And if their child is delayed, they feel considerable pressure to help him, teach him, and change him. After they get into a social habit, though, by reducing their demands and controls, some encouraging things happen. First, the child begins staying with the adult more, and he begins doing things more the way the adult does them. Not only does he stay longer in exchanges, he frequently becomes less demanding himself, communicating more for social reasons such as commenting, replying, and showing affection. Many adults report to us that they enjoy the child more when their conversations cease to be the tugs of war that directive communications often become.

A child benefits with less commands and controls.

Remember that, no matter how much your child knows, he will only benefit from society to the degree he can have the kind of easy, friendly conversations that society requires. You know the kind of conversations that you enjoy and return to again and again; you know, too, the kind you avoid. Be sure you are showing your child how to be the kind of conversation partner you want to be with. And be sure you are that same kind of partner.

Each conversation is a learning event.

Don't fear that you will deprive your child of learning what he needs if you become a social conversation partner rather than the directive teacher you may think you should be. On the contrary, unless he stays with people in conversations, your child will have far fewer opportunities to learn and few opportunities to use what he knows to learn still more and build even stronger relationships.

Consider, for a moment, how many things you know. Imagine putting on one list all the things you know and use that you learned by direct teaching. Then put on another list all the things you know and use that you learned in casual contacts with people who were not trying to teach you something. Which list is longer? For most of us, the list learned from casual contacts is much longer, especially considering the knowledge we use for friendships, problem solving, and work. The marvel of social conversations is not just that they can happen anytime but that they are such a painless way of learning.

b. Limit instrumental and controlling communication.

When children begin to communicate intentionally they do so for instrumental as well as social reasons (Greenfield & Smith, 1976a, 1976b; Halliday, 1975). Instrumental reasons are those focused on getting something done. Before the end of their first year, many children are requesting and rejecting objects and regulating the behaviors of others (Brazelton, 1974; Bruner, 1983; Stern, 1985). They are also responding to other people's directions and finding many communicative ways to get their needs met. This is as it should be: We do want our children to assert their needs and intentions. Similarly, as adults, we often need to direct and control our children, especially to maintain their safety, their socially appropriate behavior, and their attention and cooperation.

On the other hand, in building a child's habit of conversation, we must be very careful that neither you nor the child communicate mainly for instrumental reasons. Why? Imagine yourself in a strange situation, where another person's contacts with you consist mainly of demands and questions beyond your scope, where the person generally tries to get from you more than he gives to you. It is not likely that you would voluntarily return to that situation unless you really needed something that person had. Too often we see our children in very similar situations (Mahoney et al., 1986; Mirenda & Donnellan, 1986; Prizant, 1983). They have a kind of "crisis language" but very little conversational language. If your child communicates mainly when he needs something, he is unlikely to develop the conversational habit he needs for so much of his learning.

Of course, it would be both unwise and impractical even to try to eliminate all instrumental communications. Your child should build a language for requesting, answering, and otherwise asserting himself as a person with rights and wishes. And you certainly have the right and responsibility to direct and regulate your child with your communications. Our point is simply that a *conversation habit requires much more*.

Reducing questions
gets more but is
difficult at first.

Do not be discouraged if you find it uncomfortable, at first, to reduce your questions and commands. Many adults have told us they genuinely believed that their job was to be directive, especially with a delayed child. After a little practice, though, they found that making easy comments in place of questions and commands encouraged their children to talk more and to stay with them longer. And when a child stays longer in a conversation with adults close to him, he learns.

In our experience, the less work we make for a child in an interaction, the more he stays and the more he communicates.

Subgoal

c. Plays an active rather than passive communication role.

More often than not, children who communicate mainly for needs otherwise play a very passive role in communicating. They may talk if spoken to, but they rarely try to keep a conversation going. We often see the parents and teachers of these children communicating with questions and commands that seem to put the child in the role of responder. The children act as though they are following a hard-and-fast rule: Communicate for needs; otherwise respond only when spoken to. Although these children rarely initiate contacts just for the sake of being with another person, they often have considerable language and a wide range of interests. They seem not to believe that conversation with adults is a desirable, let alone indispensible, part of their development. And too often their parents and teachers tell us they themselves do not view conversations with children as necessary to either of them. Fortunately, once a concerned adult experiences some success in keeping a child in conversations, the adult appreciates the value of conversations for both of them. The more the adult enjoys conversations with a child, the more clearly does conversation become an indispensible tool for bringing together people who have so much to offer each other.

Believe that conversations are essential for social learning.

What helps children and adults take active conversational roles with each other? The most important factor seems to be to realize that social conversations are the easiest and most valuable context for children to establish a pattern of success as an active participant. To begin taking an active role in conversation, the child needs to experience a taste of success as an initiator, and social conversations are freer from the stress of possible failure than are conversations where the child must respond to questions or commands most of the time.

As we discussed in the preceding chapter, adults are often satisfied when a child shows in his responses and school performance that he has a great deal of language. Children are often placed in an academic program largely on the basis of their language ability. Without conversation skills, however, children may appear to be learning little at home and in school. We wonder where children might be placed if the decision maker asked about the child's use of language in conversation rather than about his tested language? When parents and teachers actively engage in social conversations with children, the children also reveal all the valuable things they have learned at home and at school.

It's Your Turn

COMMENT: I know that my child talks more when I don't ask questions all the time, but sometimes I can't think of anything else to say. What can I do instead of questioning?

REPLY: We, too, find it hard to not ask questions. But we keep trying because we also find our children respond more and show more of their own ideas when we comment with little pressure on them. Look at the examples below for ideas on how to comment rather than question.

Alternatives to Questions	
Question	**Alternative Comment**
What did you do at school?	You look tired.
Are your feet wet?	Your shoes look soaked.
Are you full?	We ate a lot!
How old are you?	You look about 7 years old.
Are you cold?	It's chilly in here.
Are you tired?	You look a bit sleepy.
Is it raining?	It looks stormy outside.
Are you finished yet?	You look about finished.
Do you like playing this?	You look like you're having fun.
Are you ready for dinner?	You look/seem hungry.
How many sisters do you have?	I have three sisters.
What's your favorite show?	My favorite show is _____.
Do you like winter?	I like making snowmen.
Do you like cookies?	My favorite cookies are chocolate.
Do you want a drink of water?	I'm real thirsty.
Are you playing with your trucks?	Those trucks are going fast.

COMMENT: With my 6-year-old son with Down syndrome, I used to be obsessive about all the things I needed to teach him. He became very passive and even often avoided me. Once I learned to have little easy conversations with him throughout our casual time together, he stayed with me more and I could see him learn from me. I want to encourage other parents and teachers to see how little conversations can teach so much.

REPLY: Many parents we know also tell us what an easy and rewarding job conversations are compared to the old-fashioned teaching jobs they had assumed were necessary.

COMMENT: Balancing a conversation with my 2- and 4-year-old girls doesn't make sense. I have so much more to say to them than they do.

REPLY: We certainly do not mean a word-for-word exchange. Often you will say a lot more, and that will provide greater understanding for your child. But to help children participate more in conversations, we have more success when we give them a chance by taking a reasonable turn and giving them their turn. We also balance by sharing the topic, sometimes the child's ideas, sometimes ours. The balance can be brief and simple; the point is for your children to learn that communication is a two-way street. Each gives and gets and lets the other do the same.

COMMENT:

I believe that it is important to reason with my children. We have conversations about every little difference of opinion. My husband says I waste a lot of time that way. What concerns me is that he only rarely explains things to them but they seem to go to him for more conversations than to me. What's going wrong?

REPLY:

There are good and bad times for conversation. While discussion is useful in disputes, you do have the responsibility to regulate as you judge best, with no delaying tactics of conversation. Your husband may be doing two things: first, showing your children when conversations are not appropriate; second, insuring that conversations are not mainly negative disputes or sources of antagonism.

Self-Assessment
How Are You
Doing?

Rate yourself on a scale of 1 to 9, where 1 = not often or very poorly, 5 = neutral, and 9 = very frequently or quite well.

____ 1. Conversation is a major way my child and I use our time together.
____ 2. My child and I communicate regularly for social reasons.
____ 3. My child and I communicate mainly to control each other.
____ 4. Only one of us communicates regularly for social reasons.
____ 5. One of us communicates mainly to control the other.
____ 6. Our conversations are more fun than work.
____ 7. Both my child and I participate actively in our conversations.

Interactive Problem

35. POOR CONVERSATIONS

Both you and your child must share the responsibility for developing conversations. It is his responsibility to stay and give, and almost any child can do that. No less will be expected of him in society. While many children with delays may not develop the rich, independent conversations we hope for them, most children can build much stronger partnerships with others than they have. Once a child begins to talk, he can have little conversations with you. A major barrier we help many adults to cross is the belief that easy, back-and-forth conversations with the child are not important. Once parents and teachers realize that their children will learn and build friendships to the extent they become conversational, they begin seeing other problems that interfere with the child's conversations and they work to overcome them.

Subproblem

a. Lack of communicative responding between the two.

There is increasing clinical and research evidence that children communicate more when adults respond sensitively to their nonverbal and verbal behaviors than when the adults direct and control the children (Cross, 1984, 1985; Girolometto, 1988; Greenspan, 1985; Lieven, 1978; Mahoney & Powell, 1988a; Prizant, 1983). Nevertheless, we continue to find many adults who come to our program unaware that the ways they respond to their children's communications can actually help the child learn language and conversation skills. Nor are they aware that ignoring their child's communicative attempts may discourage the child and result in his being less communicative. In discussing the problems with these adults, we find that they also turn away from communicating with their child when he fails to respond to them. With a new awareness, they begin to see how they and their child are

*Sensitive responding
fuels conversation.*

caught in a dangerous cycle of ignoring each other, a cycle that continues to keep their child from becoming a communicative partner.

Subproblem

b. Directive, controlling style.

It is not surprising to find adults in the habit of directing children with questions, commands, and other efforts to control their lives. Some adults seem convinced of the necessity of this approach because the children they teach and care for are much less able than the adults are. A primary principle of the **ECO** model often surprises these adults: Children will learn to communicate and learn from adults to the extent that the adults are responsive and noncontrolling and allow the child successes in his interactions. After several years spent studying parent-child interactions, Mahoney concluded from work with more then 60 families that his "research suggests that a directive, non-responsive style of interaction is relatively ineffective at promoting the development of handicapped children" (Mahoney & Powell, 1988).

A controlling style limits a child's successes.

In our own experience, children seem naturally motivated to act and interact when they are allowed to have successes. Many parents and professionals in our program report they feel a responsibility to direct and control children. They feel that, when they focus on the child's developmental needs, questions and commands are the only way to move the child. The same adults report their genuine amazement when they see the result of simply responding to the child's motivations and then commenting and accepting his participation: The child cooperates and stays longer in conversations.

The problems arising from a directive or controlling adult style can be difficult to counter, perhaps because of the widespread belief that children with delays need highly structured and directed teaching instead of the kind of environment that usually facilitates language learning in nondelayed children (Hunt, 1961; Vygotsky, 1962). In other words, skills such as language and conversation, which are not naturally learned through direct teaching, normally appear to evolve from spontaneous interactions in which partners are matched and motivated (Bruner, 1983; Stern, 1985; Wells, 1981). Recent research supports the importance of the open, nondirective style with delayed children learning language and conversation.

Subproblem

c. Minimal topic sharing.

Doing something together is still as critical for conversations as it was for fostering a child's very first interactions with you. While before, the "something" may have been toys or other forms of play, the "something" now is ideas or topics.

Major attention problem: Topic flitting.

Reports of attention problems among children frequently include descriptions of a child flitting from one topic to another in conversations. Again, adults need to recognize that children need to stay in conversations to learn to be socially acceptable. If adults do not recognize this need or underestimate its importance, they are likely to allow the child to leave the topic or to remain uninvolved in the adult's topics. Often we find that when an adult and child are not on the same topic, they also are not engaged in a joint activity. The more that adults and children attend to and act on the same things, the more they will share ideas and thus share a topic. Moreover, your child is more likely to develop new language if you and he are sharing ideas that you can then expand a little. Think of your conversations with your child as a story. Both of you know the basic theme, and now your task is to show him new ways the story can develop. The more of the story you share, the easier it will be for him to learn new things because of the context or framework into which he can fit the new information.

d. Failure to follow each other's lead.

When you talk about another person's ideas, he or she is more likely to stay in a conversation with you. The same is true with children. When you follow a child's lead, you are getting into his thinking and motivation. When you do not, you are likely to lose his interest. Even if a child is motivated to stay with you, he will find it more difficult to follow you if you do not talk within his frame of reference. Be careful, too, of the message you may be giving him: If you regularly take the lead and ignore his, you may be teaching him that his ideas are not worth a conversation.

On the other hand, take care that you don't allow your child to dominate the conversation with his ideas to the exclusion of yours. Recall that a basic **ECO** principle is to "Give as well as get." In conversations, a big part of giving is talking about what your partner cares about. We find that children are often reluctant to follow our lead in conversations if the interaction is primarily verbal. However, if we couch the conversation in a joint activity, we can start by getting the child to follow our action lead. Then, as we superimpose a conversation on the activity, the child learns to follow our verbal lead as well.

e. Academic or instrumental flow.

If conversations seem like work, our experience is that both child and adult will tend not to make a habit of them. An "academic" conversation is one in which the adult tries to teach the child something she thinks he needs for school. An instrumental conversation is one in which one or both partners are trying to get something done. The problem is that these tasks are too often approached with directive, controlling styles that tend to limit rather than foster participation. This is not to say that you cannot meet these goals through conversations in which the child shares the control and choices with the adult. In fact, we find that responsive, nondirective conversations give a child valuable practice in academic and instrumental tasks.

f. Rigid roles rather than flexible partnerships.

For a child to learn through conversations, the conversations should be open to changes as they occur in each activity. If a child knows that a certain adult always asks him questions, one after another, the child may avoid the adult if he is motivated to relate in some way other than answering a question, e.g., to tell a story. Conversely, a single conversation is more likely to continue if each person can follow the lead of the moment, e.g., get off a "command/reply" track and switch roles by telling a little story or even sitting back and allowing a little monologue to develop. The freer the child feels, within reason, the more we would expect him to stay in conversations and join them on his own.

g. Few reasons for communication.

The more reasons you and your child have to communicate with each other, the more language he will learn and the more socially appropriate he will become. Many children mainly label things and make requests when in need; they are very

The more reasons, the more learning.

predictable and they rarely engage in conversations. Because their limited reasons for communicating make them fairly uninteresting as conversation partners, we would expect others to give them little opportunity to engage in conversations. Whenever a child begins to communicate for a new reason (for example, to make a comment or a reply), he not only takes on another role with people but he also opens himself up to a new kind of learning experience.

Similarly, when adults communicate for limited reasons (to question or to command), they not only limit the kind of language the child can learn from them but they also limit the roles he learns to play. Because conversation is a primary tool for socializing, children—especially children with delays—need us to help them avoid becoming passive or rigid in conversation.

Subproblem

h. Lack of a developed conversational topic.

Brief exchanges are not conversations.

Adults often report that they communicate with their children regularly, but we see little conversation when we observe them. The adult may talk and so may the child. They may share a few turns on a topic but are more likely making parallel comments about their activity, with little relation between the comments. There is little or no building of a topic and no learning more about the topic. It seems they think all that is needed is talk, but not necessarily talk to each other or about any continuous topic.

It's Your Turn

COMMENT: How do you share a topic with a 3-year-old? I can't imagine what conversation topics my son Patrick and I could share.

REPLY: Anything your child does or sees is a potential topic. The more Patrick chooses one activity or a comment, the more likely either could be a topic of conversation. Remember the recommendation to be a "living dictionary." Exchange words that describe your child's activity or comment and you are building a topic. Then add another idea or a new twist to the topic the next time.

COMMENT: I am sure that many experts in child development encourage adults to use questions with children. They draw the child out and lead him to talk about new topics. It seems strange to discourage questions.

REPLY: There are many issues here. First, questions that are genuinely elicited and desired, or ones designed to move the conversation forward, are useful. They will be most useful when the child feels freedom to communicate and direct the conversations as well.

A general concern we have with questions relates to our experiences and substantial research findings that a directive and controlling conversational style, one predominated by questions, appears to lead the child to be passive in conversations. And if we accept the premise that a passive role allows much less language learning and severely limits social development, then a predominance of questions becomes a serious concern.

A primary issue here, as elsewhere in the **ECO** approach, is that a preconversational child, for whom the model is prepared, has distinctly different needs than a child who has a strongly established and resilient conversation habit. Children with delays are often fragile in their social development; too much frustration, failure, and barriers to self-expression can lead a child away from just those spontaneous relationships he needs to become a generalized communicator. It is our persistent impression that a consistent questioning style contributes to that situation.

The questions that concern us are the ones that appear to place the child in a passive, responsive role, not an assertive, interactive role. Some of the kinds of questions that we find are less than helpful, especially if they predominate conversations with children, are the following:

- *Rhetorical questions* are used as fillers with no expectation of a response. An example is "Are you pushing your car?" when it is obvious that the child is doing just that.
- *Nonstop questions* are fired off with no pause to allow a response. An example is "Where did you go? Did you see Jackson? Did you tell him to come in? Don't you know it's suppertime? Aren't you hungry?"
- *Questions that test the child*. Children with delays are often confronted with challenges to show what they know; those questions frequently set up failure and encourage the child to avoid conversations.
- *Motivationally mismatched questions*. These questions require the child to communicate from the adult's point of view and rarely inquire sensitively into the child's concerns.
- *Image-limiting questions* are so specific that they limit the child's ability to respond with his own creative ideas.
- *Cognitively mismatched questions* presume more knowledge or motivation than the child may have. An example would be asking a preschool child "Is that Porsche or a Corvette?" or "Do you know how the elevator works?"

When used occasionally intermingled with comments, replies, and other communications that invite the child to communicate with his own ideas, questions are certainly a useful tool for conversations. However, our experience shows us time and again that many parents and professionals rely on streams of questions to keep a child communicating and rarely allow the child to communicate his own world.

COMMENT: My husband and several relatives try to have conversations with our son Yuri, but they always look like "show and tell" games, where Yuri performs but does not really let himself out. Then they ask me why I think he can have conversations. I know he does with me.

REPLY: You're very sensitive to be concerned. Often adults do not know how to have easy conversations and they resort to making the child do most of the work. What can be very unfortunate here is that those adults will be unlikely to develop intimate relationships with the child. They will miss many of the joys of having a child and the opportunity to contribute to his language and personality development. You may be able to show other members of your family how much more you get from Yuri by having a balanced conversation. If you can get your husband and the others to try strategies such as commenting and sharing a topic, they may find they get more from Yuri, too. Soon they may stop asking you, "How come Yuri does so much more with you?"

COMMENT: How can I teach my children anything if I follow their leads? Don't they need to learn something new?

REPLY: Keep a few things in mind. First, children stay longer with us when we follow their leads. Second, children often learn more readily if they are motivated in the event. Third, often the "new" thing many children need to learn is how to communicate or share what they know with others. We must come to realize that learning facts and skills is not all of learning; learning to be social can make those facts and skills grow and allow the child to fit into society. We regularly find that we can follow a child's idea and still teach him many new things, like staying longer in turns, communicating more clearly, saying new words, and the like. Every action and idea of a child has great potential for stimulating new learning just at the time the child is most ready to learn.

COMMENT: My daughter Mitzie is 10 and has been labeled learning disabled. She can have good conversations about school and house matters but they're all very impersonal. She almost never has casual conversations about her feelings or what's happening at the moment.

REPLY: It sounds like you feel lonely with her and are concerned others will as well. We share that concern about many children and adults who shy away from spontaneous and personal conversations. One important thing to consider is *habit*. A habit is a proficiency that comes from practice. Don't let her drive you away from little personal conversations. Make them totally nonjudgmental but believe, yourself, that they are more necessary to building healthy relationships than perhaps any other habit. Practice, a few turns at a time, but do practice whenever you are with her.

COMMENT: I am both a first grade teacher and a mother of Archie, a 5-year-old boy with Down syndrome. Many consider me an excellent teacher and I sincerely believe that questions are the most effective way to communicate with children in school. Why don't questions work as well with Archie? Can I be right at school and not at home?

REPLY: Certainly. First, your first graders probably have strong conversation habits that will not be discouraged by questions. Your son may not be as stable in those habits and may be discouraged by questions, which signal failure.

Second, one of your primary jobs with your first graders is to get information to them that they can use elsewhere in natural learning and conversations. With your son, your job is more to provide him a safe place for learning conversations so he will use them to learn and to extend that learning to relationships in work and play.

COMMENT: I am a home trainer with preschool disabled children. The big problem I have in helping parents have conversations with their children is the constant comment "I can't think of anything to say." Often I feel the same way. Any ideas?

REPLY: You may not like this answer but here it is: "Stop thinking." When you are thinking "What can we talk about?" you are less able to attend closely to what you and the child are experiencing. Let the child's actions and your shared activity lead the way. Say what makes sense to the immediate situation. Wait for the child to reply, and then say something else that makes sense. *Say what you see and feel and keep him doing the same.* Thinking "What should I do?" does get in the way.

Rate yourself on a scale of 1 to 9, where 1 = not often or very poorly, 5 = neutral, and 9 = very frequently or quite well.

_____ 1. My child frequently does not respond to me.
_____ 2. My child rarely initiates talk with me.
_____ 3. I frequently do not respond to my child.
_____ 4. I rarely chat with my child just for the sake of talking.
_____ 5. My child is very controlling with his talk with me.
_____ 6. I am very controlling with my talk with my child.
_____ 7. We have difficulty having conversations on a topic we share.
_____ 8. My child rarely follows my ideas in a conversation.
_____ 9. I rarely follow my child's idea in a conversation.
_____ 10. Our conversations sound more like jobs to get finished than like friendships.
_____ 11. Our conversations are about the same things, over and over.

Child Goals

36. CONVERSE FOR A VARIETY OF REASONS

Pragmatics is the field that studies what language is used for, what it is intended to accomplish (Austin, 1962). Every major reason for communicating, such as questioning, commenting, and imitating, gives the child another way of learning and being a social person. The fewer reasons for which the child communicates, the less likely he is to learn and the narrower his social relationships are likely to be. Consequently, if you can help your child communicate for more and more reasons, you will be giving him tools with which he can learn more and develop richer relationships on his own. The first step in this process is to communicate for many reasons yourself.

Subgoal

a. Communicate verbally for a variety of reasons.
We seldom think much about why we communicate. However, in getting to know children who rarely communicate to request or comment, or who rarely play or act friendly, we seek to help them communicate for more reasons. While every communication has its own reason, our own studies of children have shown us that children can have problems with three major kinds of reasons: *self-directed, instrumental*, and *social* reasons. These reasons represent those common communicative intentions that researchers have found in children developing language in the first few years (Dore, 1975; Greenfield & Smith, 1976a, 1976b; Halliday, 1975; Piaget, 1952). These reasons also represent those communicative uses that we often find missing, limited, or excessive in our children.

Self-directed communications are those the child makes, apparently to himself, with no obvious intention to contact others or to get something. They are gestures, sounds, and words that accompany his actions rather than sending messages to others. Instrumental communications are those messages a child makes for the primary purpose of getting something, regulating a situation, or manipulating others to do something. Social communications are used primarily to interact with another, that is, to initiate, respond, and maintain interaction mainly for the interpersonal value of the contact itself.

1. Self-Directed Reasons. Your child spends much of his time alone. This is the time to explore and try out new skills, including communication. It is normal and developmentally useful for a child to communicate to himself, even to some degree when he is with others (Halliday, 1975; Piaget, 1952). The purpose of these nonverbal and verbal behaviors is to express oneself rather than to send a message. When a child communicates with himself, he is free to do so without being constrained by the wishes and communicative style of others. He can create and respond to his own images as well as practice a variety of ways to communicate. We know several children who show their most mature language when playing alone. Thus we recommend that you observe your child as he plays alone to see if he is communicating differently than when he is with you. If so, you can begin to join his play, occasionally and very gently, to discover how you might become a part of that play so that he extends his personal communication to you. You may even be pleasantly surprised to discover that your child knows things you did not expect.

Talking to himself is useful at times.

Children appear to communicate for many self-directed reasons, including the following:

- Practice: Self-directed communication allows children to try out their new gestures, sounds, and words without having to be understood. Here a child learns how communicating feels and sounds to him and how he can create new combinations without any pressure to change to fit another's views. We often see children practicing gestures and words others have recently made, sometimes in dialog and sometimes even communicating more than they did in the original situation.

Examples:
"Ababa abab ab baba baba"
"Time for bed; bedtime; time for bed; bedtime; time for bedtime; my time bedtime"

- *Accompany actions*: With some children, actions seem to stimulate communications. It is uncertain whether the actions are helping the communications or vice versa. Nevertheless, children appear to enjoy using communications as if they were another set of toys when they play.

Examples:
Pointing finger and shaking head no (as the dog chews her blanket)
"Oops" (as she falls down)
"Choo, choo, choo" (while pushing a train)
"Now Boo can't come out" (as he closes the toybox)

- *Expressing feelings*: At times, sounds and words appear to be an almost automatic part of many emotions. Without intending to communicate, a child may often communicate interest, fear, pleasure, surprise, and other feelings.

Examples:
interest: "Look" (when seeing a lost toy)
pleasure: "Silly man" (while watching TV)
surprise: "There you are, Max."
ritual joy or excitement: "Car coming, daddy home"
distress: "Owie"
fear: "Mommy!" (when confronted with a strange animal)

- *Delayed imitation*: Another encouraging form of practice is to imitate what the child has heard others say at another time. Parents and teachers can often see what powerful learning models they are when they see and hear their movements and words spoken as the child plays alone. This kind of communication shows that the child can store what he hears and then use it later, perhaps to re-create past images and to play.

"I'm busy; I have to go." (on a play phone)
"You're okay; you're not hurt." (on falling down)

- *Imaginary friend and pretend*: We often watch a child's play in order to discover his interests, as well as those language and conversation skills he has but may not show when communicating with others. In these contexts, the child has control of the entire situation, including all of his conversational partners. Here we can see what conversational roles he chooses. A very passive boy we know took a quite assertive role with his imaginary friends, questioning them, testing them, and giving them orders. The boy's mother reacted in surprise: "He sounds just like me." We find imaginary play an excellent place for us to gently enter the child's world and learn to have conversations based on his motivations and roles he has chosen. Because many children's pretend worlds seem to be very fragile, we are very careful when we do this. If the child senses that the old adult-directed rules are being imposed on him, his pretend world may vanish; and he may resume a more passive, less creative role that is far less helpful in building conversations.

Larry, a boy we know very well, would play in the bathtub and have elaborate conversations by himself. These conversations showed his parents that he knew many things and had many conversation skills that he did not show in conversations with people. Adults who are concerned with children with delays might listen carefully to their child's conversations alone, to identify any ideas and skills that might be emerging. They can then use that information as cues for how to shape their conversations with the child.

"Jackie, it's your turn to take out the garbage."
"I'm gonna dive. Splash. So deep. Out of the water and dry off."
"Let's fly up to the roof. Hold on. Don't fall."

- *Thinking out loud*: At times a child's self-directed communications seem as though he is just thinking in words. He does not appear to be playing, imagining, or commenting on anything in particular. Again, listening carefully to these ideas may give adults insight into when and where they can enter into the child's world. Certainly the child should be allowed to talk to himself without regular intrusions, but his personal communications may also contain valuable ideas for conversations the adult can have with him.

"Grandma's got candy for me."
"No school. Joey push me down."
"Five o'clock. Time to go home."

In self-directed communications, a child may say anything, and it may or may not make sense to adults. Nevertheless, self-directed communication appears to be valuable for two reasons: First, it allows the child freedom to create, without the restrictions of style or the expectations of others; second, it provides others with a window on what the child knows, can do, and is interested in. However, these communications can be a concern if they are the major way a child uses language. In those cases, it is necessary for adults to observe their own communication style to see how they might be restricting the child's freedom to communicate. Ask yourself: If someone communicated with me the way adults communicate with my child, would I have more freedom to communicate alone or with them present? Offer your child considerable freedom and success so he doesn't find self-directed communicating more enjoyable than with others.

2. Instrumental Reasons.   Think of instrumental communications as tools your child uses to satisfy his needs or manipulate others for his benefit. When a child communicates for instrumental reasons he is learning how to assert himself and become more independent. Many children, including children with and without delays, are far too passive with others. In order to establish themselves as individuals who can use language to take care of themselves, children genuinely need to communicate for reasons such as getting help, protesting, giving directions, and asking questions.

The child needs to assert himself, but not all the time.

The other extreme, communicating primarily for instrumental reasons, is an equally serious problem. Instrumental reasons often produce contacts with people that are too brief to build conversations. They also place the other person in the constant role of giving. A common complaint of parents and professionals is that they are always in a giving role with their child. "All I hear is 'gimme, gimme, gimme'." Despite their complaints, too many of these adults actually believe that their only role is to give. Yet when we ask them what kind of eventual relationships they want for their children, they describe friendly, give-and-take friendships. A fundamental **ECO** principle is that *parents and other influential adults must show their children how to give as much as how to get*. If we allow a child to just get from us, using us mainly as tools for his service, we are virtually training him to treat others the same way. The likely consequence of that is very limited conversations, minimal language learning, and even more restricted chances to cultivate friendships.

Following are certain instrumental communications we frequently see and hear.

- *Getting needs met.* It is not easy for an adult to make the transition from attending to a child's needs to allowing the child to serve his own needs. It appears difficult, especially for caregivers of children with delays, to wean themselves from the habit of continual giving, especially when the child becomes less needy. That habit may become a crippling problem if the child develops a pervasive expectation that he will always be helped. Studies on learned helplessness show that people who are competent to do many things can also learn to act helpless when others regularly take care of them. We are especially concerned about children who seem to see themselves as helpless, communicating mainly for help rather than for friendship.

Examples:

"I want some juice."
"Get my blanket."

- *Command and control.* Too often, we see adults act as if they had to respond to all of their child's requests, even quite unfriendly ones. Far too frequently have we observed the scene of a small child ordering his mother around and responding to her compliance with still more orders. Parents and professionals who feel a genuine need to help a child with delays often fall into the trap of helping and complying to the extreme. Worse yet, these adults may in effect be teaching the child that such a controlling style is the way to interact with the world. And they are often alarmed to realize that such a child may become a similar adult, one whom few people in society will tolerate.

Examples:

"No, you pick up the toys."
"Gimme my milk. I want it now."
"I don't want to." (Ad nauseum)
"Do it yourself."
"I can't do it." (often with a persuasive whine)
"Leave me alone."
and the interminable "uh, uh, uh" with persistent pointing.

- *Request objects and actions.* In healthy interactions, it is entirely appropriate for children to ask others to do things, whether to satisfy a physical need or a range of needs related to play and information. We want children to come out of themselves, to initiate contact. Requesting actions or objects is sometimes an easy way to break into social contacts, and they can be successful if the adults show the child how to stay and make the contact into a little longer conversation. The issue is balance—we do not want any child to be primarily a "gimme" person.

Examples:

Requests objects: "Can I have my blue dress?"
"Cookie, cookie ... please."
"Would you get that truck up there?"

Requests actions: "Push me, dad."
"Up."
"Go bye bye."
"Can we go swimming now?"

- *Protest*: There seems to be a fine line between healthy independence and socially inappropriate behavior. While we know some children who protest and argue even when they seem to have everything, we also know too many who are so passive and compliant that they do not protest or assert themselves even in the face of a real abuse of their rights. Consequently, protesting can be a symptom of serious problems with cooperation or a negative attitude, or it can be a healthy statement of rights. Thus we help some adults build a cooperative relationship that eliminates much of the protesting. With others, we work on helping the child to become more assertive and to learn that he must ultimately protect himself from injury and unjust intrusions.

Examples:

Cooperation problems: "No, I don't want to go to bed."
"That's mine. You can't have it."
"No, no, no. I won't do nothin'."

Healthy protests: "No, don't push so high."
"No, I had it first."
"I want to do it this way."
"Don't touch me; I don't like it."

- *Seek permission*: Learning to communicate also involves learning limits and opportunities. A child who thinks he can do anything he wants will have serious problems. Likewise, a child who never explores what is allowable will be very limited. Therefore, seeking permission is a communicative reason that both endears children to adults and helps them discover new worlds. When a child and an adult show respect for each other's rights and territory, the child learns when it is time to seek permission and when he is free to act on his own. Whenever we play with children, we are careful to discover their limits and to show respect by asking permission of them when it is appropriate. We are careful not to overdo it, though, like adults who ask their children for permission on matters only the adults should be deciding. We also do not want to teach the child subservience, so that he asks permission for things he has a right to do on his own.

Examples:

"Can I?" (as he puts a stick in a hole)
"Can I get up?" (to his father reading the paper)
"I did my work. Robbie wants me to go out."

3. Social Reasons.   Social communications are *indispensible tools for building conversations*. In order to become a conversational person, your child needs to learn to communicate just for the value of someone's companionship. He must learn the value and reward of simply giving of himself—whether he gives information, affection, or anything else—for little more reason than to be with you. He needs to learn that the result is to get much more from you than he would get by trying to control and direct you.

Friendship is
enough reason
to communicate.

When a child communicates socially, he does so with little stress or pressure to get a job done or to "say the right thing." Communicating from his own motivations, he is able to set his own agenda. By setting his own agenda, he has much more information to draw on than when he is trying to answer your questions or figure out what you want him to say. He will also respond to your ideas, but more for your social contact than because he feels he has to. When your child communicates for social reasons, he may have other purposes in mind but his primary concern is being with you.

When you and your child engage in conversations for social reasons, he will learn that conversations can be their own rewards because they give him more of you. One of our major goals with parents and children is to help the adults create social conversations out of their children's instrumental communications, as for help or information. For example, even if a shoe needs to be tied or a glass of juice needs refilling, you and your child can make easy comments, replies, and other verbal exchanges that turn the instrumental contact into a social conversation. In this way, your child can learn that the reason to contact other people is not just to get needs met but also to give and take with a partner.

Social
communications
often last longer.

When your child communicates for social reasons, he is free to communicate his own ideas and to create images that lead him to new ways of talking. When we hear adults directing the conversation with a child, questioning, commanding, and otherwise determining what to talk about, we wonder what the child would like to say. At times, we have taken the children and followed their leads in the conversation. And frequently we have seen the child talking more and staying longer in the conversation with us than he did when the adult was directing it. Another benefit of easy, social conversation is that you may hear your child say things you did not know he knew. When a child is free to talk from whatever images he can create with us, he also gives us ideas of ways to keep him in the conversation longer, to keep him learning with us longer.

What are some common ways your child can communicate for social reasons? Social communication involves three main actions: initiating, responding, and maintaining the conversation. Many children either mainly respond or mainly initiate, but do not do both. The responders seem to view communication as something to do only when others talk to them. They can be in a room with you for an extended period and never communicate with you; however, once you talk to them, they respond and end it there. Many other children will initiate, expressing their needs, observations, and even affection, but seldom respond when others talk to them. A third group of children usually respond to us and also initiate, but they hardly ever do anything to keep a conversation going. These children seem satisfied with brief contacts; staying in conversations does not seem to have developed as a natural motivator for them. Children in all three of these groups have yet to become conversation partners.

Given these three basic ways of communicating socially, let's look at some more specific kinds of social communications. The more specific kinds we will discuss come from two sources, literature on the early pragmatics of child communication (Bruner, 1983; Chapman, 1978; Dore, 1975; Searle, 1969) and our own studies in clinical intervention with children whose communication is delayed (Dobe, 1989; MacDonald, 1984; MacDonald & Gillette, 1985a, 1985b; McLowry, 1981; Owens & MacDonald, 1982; Young, 1988). We have selected the communicative purposes described here because we have found them to be useful building blocks for successful conversations. In short, they are the reasons that encourage us to stay in relationships with our children and that may make the children more accessible in society.

- *Commenting*: When a child comments, he is letting us know what he experiences without any pressure to do so. Whether he says, "The dog got out," "I have a headache," or "The slide is wet," his communication gives us a look into the child because it is coming from his own motivations. Because comments show us the child's thoughts and interests, they are valuable signals to us for what to say to him. When we accept a child's comments and build upon them, we find him more likely to stay communicating with us and, in turn, more likely to attend to our comments. We find that, in conversations with children, we often get what we give. If we give mostly questions and directions, we get the same. If we freely comment, with no pressure for particular responses, children seem freer to give us their own ideas in their comments. Note: Be sure to comment in a way the child knows you expect more.

"I got a booboo."
"Baby Thomas is sleeping."
"Raining."
"Spiderman sticks to the wall."

- *Reply*: A reply is a response to a comment or some other communication that does not specify a particular response. The value of replies for a child is that they allow him to say any one of a great many appropriate things when someone comments to him. When a child replies he has the freedom to select from a host of images he may have. For example, when a mother says "Sesame Street

Both initiating and responding are necessary.

Comments: Quiet but powerful tools.

Examples:

Easy, no-stress responses.

is on," a child might reply by saying "I'll turn it on," "I want to play outside," "Let's see Oscar," "Sarah's watching dancing," or "Gramma's going to watch it with me." Generally, all that is required for a reply is that it address the other person's general topic. With children who are just beginning to have conversations, we accept any replies at all (except offensive ones, of course) because our goals are to keep the conversation going and to make it a success for the child. Note: Be sure your replies show you expect a response. Be sure your replies do not stop the interaction.

Examples:

Adult Comment	Child Reply
"You look happy."	"Nonno's here."
"Petey made a picture."	"That's a silly picture."
"I lost my pencil."	"I got it."
"The bus is here."	"I see Maurie now."

- *Imitation*: In trying to understand a child's communication, one of our first questions is, "How does he imitate others' communications?" In order to communicate more maturely, your child needs to get into the habit of communicating as you and others do. This kind of imitation is a later stage of the general skill of "*doing as others do*" that we mentioned earlier in discussing how a child learns to play with you.

Although we certainly do not want a parrot-like child who only copies or mimics others, we find imitating an easy and effective way for a child to keep a conversation going and to practice new words or ideas before he is ready to use them on his own. Imitation is also valuable because it serves as a kind of compliment to the other person. We find many parents, teachers, and peers who are pleased when the child talks the same way they do. Remember to encourage the child to talk in ways that reward others, to help keep with them people who might otherwise not want to communicate with children with slow or limited skills.

Examples:

Adult	Child
"You've got dirty shoes."	"Dirty shoes."
"Look at that big moon."	"Looky, moon."
"Mom's at work."	"No mom work, mom sleep."

As the examples show, your child can imitate some or part of what you say. The point is for your child to be so attentive to you that he not only registers what you say in his thoughts but also practices it in his speech. We hope he will then know something to say later in similar contexts.

- *Nurture*: A child also needs to communicate in order to nurture or emotionally support others. By *nurture* we mean to give attention, help, affection, or concern that reflects another person's perspective. When a young child communicates with warmth to a person in grief or pain, we view it as a strong sign of social development. Children are so often characterized as self-centered and unconcerned about others that we encourage adults to show children how to nurture others and to reward them for it. As many schools of psychotherapy attest, one of the hallmarks of problems in adult relationships is the inability to feel and communicate intimate concern for another's emotional states (Satir, 1972).

"You okay, Mom?" (after Mom slipped on a ladder)

"I'll get the door for you." (to Dad, whose hands are full)

"You look pretty." (to a sister in a new dress)

"I love you, Ta ta."

"Don't cry. Owie get better."

- *Show off*: So often we think of language as meaningful, important for learning. To a child, often the most important thing is to get attention and learn that he can entertain others. Often this purpose of personal expression is missing from goals for a child's communication development. And yet we know how important this reason is for many of us who talk mainly to get noticed and affirmed by others. There is nothing wrong with communicating to get attention, as long as the person also gives attention in return. Attention and affirmation are worthy goals; they seem to be among the most common reasons for beginning relationships.

Examples:

Making a funny face in your face.

"Look, Spiderman. Watch me fly."

"Daddy, look at me." (peeking under his newspaper)

"Would you listen to my spelling words?"

"Hi." (as he looks in your face and waves)

"Look, I'm Pee Wee!"

Subgoal

b. Communicate in socially appropriate ways.

Beyond their having language and using it to learn and develop relationships, we want children to be socially acceptable. Of course, what is considered acceptable will vary across cultures, ages, and the purposes of the situation. For many reasons, children need to learn the difference between polite and rude communications. The difficulty with this skill *is* that it varies. Children need to learn how to shift communicative codes, that is, how to communicate differently with grandma and with peers, as well as to know that they can communicate differently with peers in school, at church, and in horseplay.

Be sure communications are attractive.

Likewise, what is socially appropriate at one age is not so at another. To illustrate, hugging and kissing may be desirable for a 3-year-old who has been socially isolated. However, for a 25-year-old person with Down syndrome the same behavior may well offend others and put him in social jeopardy. While these rules do differ, there is a general rule of "personal offense" that does not change. That is, if a child communicates in a way that personally offends us, we silently ignore it. Then, after a short period of no attention, we give him another way to communicate the same thing without offending us.

Examples:

"Hello, how are you?" rather than "Hi, hi, hi. I love you!" in a loud voice to a stranger.

"See you later" rather than leaving a situation silently.

"Please, may I have more" rather than reaching over another to get some food.

Responding in any acceptable way rather than ignoring others when they address him.

Subgoal

c. Favor social over instrumental communications.

Given that our goal for your child is to develop conversational relationships, not just to communicate to satisfy immediate needs, we hope that over time he communicates more for social reasons and less for instrumental ones. This hope is in keeping with a general goal of the model, to build easy, nondirective, child-based conversations that will make learning language (and many other skills as well) a natural part of his life that he is able to control.

Examples:

"I see the moon" rather than "What's that?"
"I'd like to see that" rather than "Gimme that."
"I'd like you to move" rather than "Get out of my way."

It's Your Turn

COMMENT:

My son Harvey is learning disabled and is not very social at home or school. Making social talk with him is boring. I don't like comics, baseball, or cartoons, and that's all he cares about. What can I do?

REPLY:

Building conversations with Harvey has life-long consequences for both of you. Once you regularly talk about his interests, you will be more able to hold him in your kind of conversations. Think of this: Learning disabled children are often less social than they need to be for friendship and learning. Allowing him to be noncommunicative is allowing him to miss many opportunities to become what he can be. Be creative. Open up to the comics and baseball world. You can find some things there to talk about and relate to your world. Spiderman flies; talk about other flying things. Learn the baseball rules; remind yourself that your child needs you there as much as he needs medicine when he's sick.

COMMENT:

I have a classroom of 5- to 7-year-olds with severe communicative disorders. Three years ago, I thought conversations were out of the question; I was lucky to get single-word answers. I mainly questioned and directed but after a year they were still very noncommunicative. Then I decided that a goal for every child was to have several conversations every day; they could be brief or nonverbal but each child had to take turns communicatively with me or another child. It took some pulling of teeth at first, but I was committed; they were going to interact. Most of the conversations lasted only a few seconds but soon each child learned it was expected of him. They learned that dead-end contacts were not enough; each had to stay at least a couple of turns. What can they learn on one turn? What's happened is that the more developed children are having conversations with each other and are leading conversations showing the less developed children what next to do. And the lowest level children are beginning to initiate. When they do, someone knows they are to respond to any initiation and keep the child interacting by matching and showing him a next step.

REPLY:

Congratulations; you seem to have a commitment to conversation as a valuable tool for teaching almost anything.

COMMENT:

I am a family counselor and a major concern of mine is the lack of easy conversations in families. I regularly hear that children and parents alike make conversations mainly to get something or to lodge a complaint. One thing I prescribe is for families to have a conversation time every day, only for a few minutes if necessary. The only rule is that each person talks about a topic for a couple of minutes with no interruption; then the other does the same. Then they can have their conversation. They need coaching at first, but my families report that their conversations were now based on more information than before.

REPLY: Excellent; in your approach each person participates and learns the other's ideas. A good safeguard against one-sided conversations.

COMMENT: I consult in three schools for developmentally delayed children. Why do so many children communicate just to get needs met? I see very few stay and talk just to be friendly. What can be done to show them the benefits of friendly conversations beyond getting something?

REPLY: Your question raises a major issue that motivated this book. For years we taught language to children but rarely saw them become conversational. We hope that this book offers both an attitude and a style of interacting that could guide you in building conversations.

Reminders for Conversing with Children

1. Believe that conversations are necessary for social and cognitive learning to flourish.
2. Make staying in back-and-forth conversations an absolute goal for every child.
3. Balance your interactions. Be sure the child does as much as you do.
4. Match the child in many ways; give him language he can use and is interested in and show him a next way to communicate.
5. Keep the child for more. "One more turn than usual" is a rule of thumb.
6. Stay talking on his topic; then keep him on your topic.
7. Respond sensitively to his ideas; make him feel genuinely valued.
8. Be nondirective at times; follow his lead and let him follow his images.
9. Avoid failures. Staying in conversations is the goal.

Self-Assessment:
How Are You
Doing?

Rate yourself on a scale of 1 to 9, where 1 = not often or very poorly, 5 = neutral, and 9 = very frequently or quite well.

_____ 1. My child communicates to play by himself.
_____ 2. My child communicates to pretend.
_____ 3. My child communicates to get his needs met.
_____ 4. My child communicates to command and control others.
_____ 5. My child communicates to seek permission.
_____ 6. My child communicates to be friendly with others.
_____ 7. My child communicates to comment on what he knows.
_____ 8. My child communicates to respond to another's comment.
_____ 9. My child communicates to answer questions.
_____ 10. My child communicates to imitate others.
_____ 11. My child communicates to show affection or support.
_____ 12. My child's communication is socially acceptable.

37. STAY IN VERBAL CONVERSATIONS

We hope that, since the beginning of this book, you have understood that a continuing goal throughout every stage is to keep your child with you, in play, in turn-taking, in communication, and now in conversations. We know too many children with considerable knowledge and language but with very limited lives—children who have few conversations, most of which are short-lived. The more your child stays in a conversation, the more he learns, the more attached he becomes to others, and the more rewarding his life will become. Another goal, as your child stays in conversations with you, is to have those conversations change with new topics and with your child's growing interest in your ideas. When that happens, you will then look to him as a conversational partner who can satisfy some of your need to share ideas and to form friendships.

a. Balance turns with partner.

The notion of balancing turns relates to the principle that relationships go better if there is a give-and-take, with neither partner controlling or doing much more than the other. We do not mean turntaking that is rigidly restricted to talking in alternating speeches. We mean balanced turntaking. If your child has learned to balance turns in play with you, he has learned the basic rule of give-and-take, that you must give if you expect to get and you must allow the other person to take his turns. Sometimes we find that adults and children who do very well in balancing turns in play seem to forget to take turns in communicating. One explanation may be that those adults have much more of a habit dominating and controlling communication with children.

Pay careful attention to monitoring your conversations; strive to do less so your child can do more. Take your turn and then wait expectantly for his. The more you do, the more he will learn to play an active role in communicating. The more you respond sensitively to your child when it is your turn, the more he will learn how to communicate with others. Don't forget that having conversations with your child is not only a way of sharing information but a way of actively teaching him how to have conversations with others. Ask yourself, "Would other people stay in conversation with my child if he treated them the way I treat him?"

Do more like this:
Mom: "I'm going to make cookies. Cookie time."
Kate: "I wanna help."
Mom: "We need sugar and the chips."
Kate: "I get the sugar."
Mom: "No, you spill sugar.
Kate: "I get the chocolate chips."

Do less like this:
Mom: "I think I will make cookies today. We haven't had any for quite a
      while. Should we make chocolate or lemon?"
Kate: "I want . . .
Mom: "Oh I know, you like lemon. But Buddy likes chocolate, and we had
      lemon last time."
Kate: "Let's make both."
Mom: "We don't have time. You have your lessons at four."

Look at how much more a sense of participation Kate has in the first dialog. Which of these two patterns of conversation would you want to return to? After years of developing programs with children and their significant adults, two persistent findings still amaze us: first, how much more the child stays and does when adults do less; second, how much more a child is able to do when adults balance turns and wait for him to do it.

Subgoal

b. Follow discourse rules to maintain, shift, and develop topics.

To keep a conversation going, your child must know both how to lead and how to follow. He must be able to stay on your topic, get you to stay on his topics, and shift topics (both his own and yours) without confusing you or losing your attention. A child who dominates a conversation with topics related only to his own interests, or who bounces between several topics without considering the other person's interests, will find few people willing to repeatedly build conversations with him. Your child will need to learn many subtle skills, such as knowing when you want to keep the topic going and when you have had enough. The more the two of you are genuinely into the topic, rather than superficially talking at each other, the better he will know when to shift a topic or maintain it.

To develop a topic, your child must know that everything can be talked about in a great many ways. We are concerned when children have only the same, role-bound things to say about a topic. When all a child says about grandma is "Grandma home," "Grandma sick," and "Grandma brings candy," he is not just missing out on many conversations he can have about grandma; he is actually limiting his relationship with her. Certainly, he knows much more about her; and if others can keep him talking about her, he may be ready for real conversations. A general rule in building a topic is to *add a new idea*; in grandma's case, add "Went to hospital," "Feeling better now," "Doctor gave her medicine," or "Stomach feel better." Each of these new ideas can launch the two of you into another little conversation, which will naturally give rise to another new notion that may extend the conversation about grandma or start a new one. Soon you may be talking about what happens in hospitals or why medicine is only for people who are sick. This natural expansion of topics occurs only if your child views himself as someone who has conversations and can keep others in conversations. Similarly, when you see your child as a conversation partner, you automatically give him new ideas for maintaining topics, and you will look to him for ideas you can follow to create new conversations.

Subgoal

c. Converse in a comfortable style.

A child is likely to choose to enter and maintain conversations only after he has learned they can provide easy successes for him, with little stress or pressure to perform. Again, both children and adults habitually avoid conversations that are designed only to get something done. When children are not comfortable in conversations, they tune them out or avoid them completely, thereby losing opportunities to appreciate or learn from people. Our work with children of many ages has persuaded us that every month without comfortable conversations brings a child closer to defining himself as a person who does not have conversations. The problem too quickly becomes circular. A nonconversational child is defined that way by his potential natural teachers, who are then less likely to pursue conversations with him. We must help a child enjoy being conversational as early as we can.

Subgoal

d. Comment more than question or command.

When a child comments, he is expressing what he knows and cares about. He is not trying to accomplish a task, but rather to offer his ideas. Those ideas are valuable sources for adults to build conversations. Comments show that a child values communication for the social exchange itself. In social living, there are many more opportunities to comment (any event invites a great many comments) than to question or command. Consequently, a habit of commenting allows much more opportunity to learn to communicate than do questions and commands. Comments are also much more acceptable in and supportive of conversations; they allow partners similar freedom. In contrast, questions and commands restrict the partner's freedom and conversational options. A child who primarily questions and commands his partners may be less likely to accumulate and maintain the number of conversation partners he needs to develop language and social relationships.

It's Your Turn

COMMENT:

My son Phillip is 5 and has been diagnosed as autisticlike. He is beginning to talk to me and with me, but he still talks mainly to himself—especially when he's with strangers or in class. My one hope comes from knowing that a year ago he talked to himself practically all the time.

REPLY:

We have worked with many children with such autistic habits. Mitchell, Ben, Jamie, and Alex in particular moved from a habit of isolated, stereotypic, self-directed language to staying in more and more appropriate conversations. While there was no magic formula, a few techniques did seem effective in all these cases. First, their parents and teachers become genuinely committed to the idea that their children must stay in conversations and talk *with* people. The parents also believe that is possible for their sons. We try to help build their commitment by showing them that we can keep the child in conversations. We start by building a give-and-take play base in which the child is gently kept in interactions and taught that he can have successes with people. In these interactions, we prompt the child in order to direct his behavior, using nonverbal prompts at first. Because we see conversation as a natural development from social play, we make sure that the child and adult are having easy back-and-forth interactions in child-world activities before we impose language demands on them. Then the adults learned to respond more to the child's social behaviors (that is, behaviors directed toward the adults) than to his self-directed behaviors. In this process, the adult design the interactions so that the child is successful. Subsequently, the adults match the children and clearly wait for them to participate. They avoid tasks that pressure the child with excessive questions and commands, but they also require the child to stay in increasingly longer interactions. The child learns gradually that social behavior results in more choices and independence than nonsocial behavior.

The commitment to becoming social seems to be the major determinant of success for children with autistic-like tendencies. Regardless of how well adults perform **ECO** strategies, only a genuine commitment is likely to carry them through the persistent difficulties and frustrations that occur when moving a child from a primarily nonsocial world to an interactive world.

COMMENT: My preschoolers communicate for two main reasons—to ask for something or to answer questions. How can I get them to use language for social, conversational reasons?

REPLY: You might set up conversations as a central part of your classroom day. In these, follow the general strategies we have discussed: balance, match, wait, respond, be nondirective, and be emotionally attached. Then you might consider the following guidelines for encouraging children to have social conversations. Remember, if your children now mainly question and command, they could be learning that style of communication from you. If you change your style to include the range of conversation reasons, your children may follow.

- Say what you see (anything can become a conversation).
- Tell him how you feel about it.
- Tell him what it reminds you of.
- Imitate him, then show him new ways to talk about it.
- Make a story about it.
- Do something about it, then talk about that.
- Play with words about it.
- Give him more information about it.
- Tell him how.

And, in every case, wait for him to tell you his ideas about what you said.

COMMENT: My daughter is 5 years old and talks incessantly about only a few favorite things. How do I keep from getting bored with the old, predictable things she wants to talk about?

REPLY: This is a major problem. A first step is to let yourself go, and make the conversation much more like play than like a job or a responsibility to teach something. The only job you have is to keep your child talking with you. Ask yourself how many different ways you can talk about the topic? For example, when your child talks for the hundredth time about the dog biting, let your mind play. Show her new ideas that can become conversations. Maybe you can talk about other animals that bite. Or make up a story about a friendly dog that does not bite. Or set up a problem and make a conversation about it—why does the dog bite or how can we help him to stop biting? Some of these examples may be too simple or too advanced for your child, but the technique isn't. Get beyond the exact topic at hand and make it into a story that interests you. Books are excellent tools for building conversations, as long as you let the pictures lead you beyond the printed story and into new conversations that will encourage both of you to stay.

COMMENT: My son Joshua is 5 years old. It bothers me that he stays in his longest, and most interesting, conversations when he's playing alone. Sometimes he even gets in conversations with strangers that last a lot longer than our conversations. How can I get him to be that way with me?

REPLY: Watch and listen carefully. Use as your guide the way he talks and the things he talks about. Gradually get closer to him at those times, but don't intrude. Just play parallel to him at first. Communicate to yourself like Joshua does. Get closer until you are playing with him. If he cuts down on his talking, back up, keep playing, but make no demands. Joshua may have learned that you control his conversation time and he may quiet down to let you take your role. Don't let him give in to you. Let him know, slowly, that you will let him take the lead and not direct or control him. What we are talking about here is a major shift in your role with Joshua, and it will not happen overnight. The more you play like him, the more you're a partner rather than a teacher to him, the more he will let you into his conversational world.

Rate yourself on a scale of 1 to 9, where 1 = not often or very poorly, 5 = neutral, and 9 = very frequently or quite well.

_____ 1. My child communicates for the same few reasons.
_____ 2. My child communicates regularly to himself.
_____ 3. I communicate with my child for a response and I expect one.
_____ 4. My child communicates mainly for instrumental reasons, that is, to get something.
_____ 5. I communicate with my child mainly for instrumental reasons.
_____ 6. My child communicates frequently for social, friendly reasons.
_____ 7. I communicate with my child for social, friendly reasons.
_____ 8. My child is sometimes willing to have conversations on my topics.
_____ 9. My child and I give and take fairly equally in our conversations.
_____ 10. My child knows how to have socially appropriate conversations.
_____ 11. My child is staying in longer conversations than he did a year ago.
_____ 12. My child is staying in conversations on new topics more than he did a year ago.
_____ 13. Both my child and I are comfortable in conversations with each other.

ADULT STRATEGIES

A fundamental consensus of several recent approaches to child development (Brazelton, 1974; Bronfenbrenner, 1979; Bruner, 1977a; Vygotsky, 1962) is that natural, stress-free conversations provide the critical process by which a child becomes social and communicative. In addition, widespread studies of adult communication styles with children learning language have concluded that adult styles may help determine how quickly children become social and communicative. In a series of longitudinal studies of infants and toddlers with their mothers, Mahoney and his team of clinical researchers (Mahoney et al., 1986, 1988) distinguished between mothers who were primarily directive and adult-oriented and those who were child-oriented and conversational. They found that the mothers of children with the highest developmental scores were highly child-oriented and showed low degrees of control and stimulation. In other words, the parents with the more communicative children were those who *acted like their child, followed their child's lead,* and *established an easy, conversational style* rather than a directive, controlling one.

Thus, as we lay out a broad series of strategies to use in helping children become conversation partners, we urge you to keep in mind the importance of being non-directive and of respecting the child's own abilities to direct his own learning. We have found again and again that making all the right technical moves simply is not enough. If you remain a directive person who controls your child's interactions with questions, commands, and topics you choose, you will still lose your child as the casual, habitual interaction partner he must become. Consider this issue very carefully: It is not easy for adults to become responsive and conversational in a noncontrolling way. You may ask, "How can I teach if I don't act like a teacher?" We can only respond that *if you want to teach your child, you had better not "teach" him.* That is, if you want your child to learn from you in the great many potential contacts the two of you have each day, you had better not put him in the passive student role that many children and adults associate with "teaching."

Always remember that two things must regularly happen for spontaneous learning in your interactions: Your child must have successes that motivate him, and both of you must stay for increasingly longer exchanges. When your attitude is nondirective, your child shares control and is therefore more likely to experience successes (Bronfenbrenner, 1979). And when there is little stress in the interactions, because no task demands to be done, both partners are more likely to stay.

Adult Strategy

38. MAINTAIN BALANCED CONVERSATIONS

The less you try to "teach," the more your child will learn from your communications.

If you have developed a playful relationship with your child, as we have described in the earlier chapters, you should be ready to guide your child naturally into becoming a conversational partner. It is essential that you continue to practice the major strategies that brought you and your child into a language partnership. Remember such valuable strategies as matching your child's actions and communications, waiting and expecting more, and using child-world language. Too often we see parents and professionals forget what has already been successful for them in getting their children to stay with them.

It seems that many adults see conversations as adult activities in which children just don't fit. Therefore, the first strategy is to develop the attitude that conversations are absolutely necessary for your child to develop the social and communicative skills he needs for learning, friendship, and the world of school and work. Work on changing attitudes like these:

- "There's so little we can talk about."
- "We're not interested in each other's ideas."
- "He should play like a child, not sit in conversations."
- "He needs a teacher, not a conversation partner."
- "Conversations interfere with my getting things done."

These attitudes have been evident in many adults we have known. They have not believed that social and communicative skills can be learned effectively only within easy conversations. They also had children who chose to play alone, except for rare times when they were being directly taught. *It is simply unrealistic to expect a child to learn language and all the other skills needed for building relationships if his contacts with people are limited to brief exchanges where he merely gets a need met or responds to an adult's directions.* Such contacts just do not occur often enough, and we cannot expect anyone to learn habits that are mainly directed by what other people want.

Even when we have most success with parents, clinicians, and teachers, we have found that keeping conversations going is a persistent problem. Even for children with quite mature language skills, we continue to encourage one goal: Keep the child for one more turn. Certainly, brief contacts are both appropriate and necessary at times, but they are not sufficient to build relationships. Once adults develop the habit of monitoring how long their child stays in the interaction, they work to keep him a little longer. He then begins to expect longer exchanges, and best of all he takes more responsibility for the conversation.

Substrategy

a. Keep a verbal child talking in a back-and-forth exchange.

The goal here is that, when a child and an adult see each other, they automatically expect not just a one-shot contact but an exchange, something that happens back and forth between them. The adult actively tries to make the contacts reciprocal; that is, going back and forth and sensitively responsive to the concerns of the other persons. In other words, the child directs the contact to the adult and the adult responds in a way that relates meaningfully to what the child said. And the reverse takes place as well; the adult starts some contacts and gets back from the child something related to what she said. As soon as those reciprocal exchanges begin, the adult can keep the child a little longer and build a conversation out of any small exchange.

Be reciprocal.

Be sure you both initiate and respond.

Give each other something back.

Respond meaningfully to the other.

We always try to follow the general rule of *giving the child one more idea*. This builds the conversation slowly, at the child's pace, with an idea that clearly relates to his interests and to ideas he has expressed on one of his recent turns. Children often act as if nothing more can be said on a topic, even when we know from their actions that they know more about it. Watch your child and you will have little difficulty adding a new idea. Simply say what you see that he knows. A second rule we follow is not to wait for a child's words to be perfectly clear before we get him talking about new ideas. The more a child stays in conversations, the more practice and feedback he has to strengthen his sounds, and the more motivating and successful his habit of conversations becomes.

Example:

Child and teacher with book.

Child: "Look at the boat."
Teacher: "Two boys in the boat."
Child: "No. Boy and man."
Teacher: "Yes, maybe that's his daddy."
Child: "Daddy took him fishing."
Teacher: "I don't see any poles."
Child: "They got a net."
Teacher: "Nets get more than poles."
Child: "They got a million."
Teacher: "A million? In that small boat?"
Child: "Maybe ten."

Keep the child for one more turn with one new idea.

One more turn means another chance to learn.

The exchange here was clearly back and forth and reciprocal; each person put in his ideas and then waited for the other to take his turn. Note that the teacher, knowing more, easily took the responsibility of feeding the child with a new idea that both taught him new language and helped him stay longer in the conversation. The new ideas related directly to what the child said and appeared to motivate the child to follow with another comment.

Substrategy

b. Communicate and show expectation for a response.

Do you ever feel someone is talking at you without caring or expecting a response from you? Do you ever do that with your child? We regularly observe adults communicating at a child but not *for* a response. The adult says one thing after another, neither waiting nor showing through signals or intonation that her reason for communicating is to get something from the child. It is not uncommon to hear a parent go on like this: "Oh, you found the dolly. Where was it? I know, I saw it under the couch. Oh, how nice to see the dolly. Let me give her a big hug."

Of course there are times when adults need just to talk; they want or need no response. An example is giving information: "Watch out, that's a big dog." "Up we go. Let's get your coat on." Sometimes a job has to be done and conversations would simply get in the way. However, if a child is constantly exposed to talk that does not expect him to respond, he may learn that it is perfectly acceptable to let others do all the talking.

To develop the habit of communicating for a response, think of your conversations as a ping-pong game, not a game of darts. Adults sometimes act as if their job is to talk at the child, the way a player throws all the darts at a board, rather than to get back a response to what you gave, as the two people do in ping-pong. Follow the same rules of turntaking and matching we have discussed many times here. Say something the child can both do and understand, then wait silently with a clear look of expectation on your face and a tone in your voice that says you expect a response.

If your child has not been responding to you much, you may have to wait a while at first. And be sure to accept any kind of response at first. Children often respond first with a change of face, or with a gesture or a sound. Accept it; if he's pressured to say something "right" he may withdraw. You may have actually taught him that he need not respond and that you will do all the talking for him. Give him successes for any response at first, and then you can gradually begin cueing him to give you more of what he can do.

c. Share the conversational load with a verbal child.

We are more likely to stay in conversations when both people are sharing their ideas. If we always have to initiate the topic and keep the conversation going with our ideas, we soon withdraw. On the other hand, if the other person regularly controls the topic and ignores our ideas, we are likely to go to someone who will show us more respect. So, too, should you follow your child's ideas at times and at other times see to it that he follows yours. Because it is sometimes appropriate for one of you to carry most of the ideas, as in relating a story or giving directions, there are natural opportunities for you to hear your child's ideas and others for him to listen to yours.

We find that adults and children are much more likely to stay in conversations if they expect their ideas will be heard. Therefore, we encourage you to have several brief conversations with your child every day, conversations in which you have no job to get done or lesson to teach. Simply tell yourself that the goal is to listen to his ideas and make sure he listens to some of yours on the same topic. This will take very little time, less than a minute in most cases. It will require that you make sure you each have a say on the topic.

Dad: "Hey, your bike looks broken."
Charles: "It wiggles."
Dad: "Let me see. What wiggled?"

Charles: "The wheel. It wiggles and I fell. Hurt my leg."
Dad: "Let's have a look. You got a scratch."
Charles: "Ouch, don't touch."
Dad: "It's a wiggle owie. You need a wiggly doctor."
Charles: "You're silly. Fix my bike."
Dad: "What?"
Charles: "Please."
Dad: "Look, the spokes are loose."
Charles: "What's a poke?"
Dad: "Spoke, ssspoke—these wire sticks...they make the wheel strong."
Charles: "I found another loose one."
Dad: "Let's check them all."

Notice that each person led the topic at times and at other times followed the other's topic. If the father had simply fixed the bike, Charles would have missed a valuable opportunity to learn how to have an easy conversation and also to learn how to think and talk about a new topic. Charles could practice his old ideas and get some new ones from his dad.

Substrategy
Balance your give and take.

d. Initiate and respond proportionately.

By now you know that we recommend balancing what you and your child do together, whether in play or conversation. The more you balance, the more chance your child has to learn; the more your child balances, the more he lets others into his learning world. After a child has learned that his role with adults is only to respond, not to initiate, it takes a concerted effort to change that belief. If this is the case with you and your child, make yourself wait for him to initiate a topic. When you begin, accept all of his initiations, no matter how uninteresting you may find them. It is important for your child to learn that he can start conversations and that people will stay with him in them.

Similarly, you will get in the habit of expecting your child to respond, just as you would in a ping-pong game. But resist the temptation to fill in all the silences. If you don't resist, you will find you are again having conversations with yourself.

It's Your Turn

COMMENT:

Before I learned to take turns and to realize my son Vern had to stay in conversations to learn much, I thought my job was to tell him as much as I could. Now I feel much of that was wasted time, and I remember Vern not liking it at all. I found that waiting and expecting Vern to say something and accepting the little things he said were very hard at first. Then, instead of your ping-pong idea, I kept the idea of a pendulum in mind. When I talked, the pendulum ball was with me; then when I waited it went to Vern; then it came back to me. Whenever the pendulum in my mind was stuck, I either stopped talking and let it go or I signalled for Vern to give me a turn. When I pictured and easy back-and-forth swing of the ball, I took it as a guide to our conversations.

REPLY:

That is a creative way to help yourself in the important job of balancing. We find that when parents and teachers begin to realize how a balanced give-and-take is necessary for children developing conversations, they become consistent and firm about expecting something back from children who are often willing to get much more than they give.

Rate yourself on a scale of 1 to 9, where 1 = not often or very poorly, 5 = neutral, and 9 = very frequently or quite well.

_____ 1. I keep my child talking back and forth.
_____ 2. I expect my child to stay in conversation with him.
_____ 3. I allow my child to share conversations with me.
_____ 4. I initiate and respond about equally with my child.

39. HAVE SOCIAL, FRIENDLY CONVERSATIONS WITH THE CHILD

However friendly adults may feel toward children, we rarely see that friendliness translated into frequent, social conversations that last much longer than very limited contacts. A major conclusion of widespread research on child development and our own 20 years of working with children is that a child will learn social and communicative skills to the extent he has a persistent habit of conversations across his daily routines. Children will develop ideas, social skills, and self-esteem to the extent that they have practice in balanced responsive conversations. Children with delays, in particular, may need the support and motivation only available in regular conversations.

More than any other training, your child needs to be engaged with other people largely in friendly, social conversations. "What do you mean?" you may say, "I'm friendly with my child." Please understand, we do not question the feelings of any adults toward their children, but feelings are only the first step. Frequent, friendly *conversations* are just as necessary for your child to benefit from your friendliness as to build friendships with others. If your child is to grow to appreciate life to its potential, he must see people as potential partners for conversation. Just the sight of a person he knows should signal him to communicate and stay for a little conversation. Just as your child sees a ball as a cue to throw, a book to look at and read, or a treat to eat, we want you to become a clear signal for him to have a conversation. Your easy, frequent, social conversations should help your child move away from seeing you as only a caretaker and director and more as a conversational partner.

a. Communicate for a variety of social reasons.
We see some adults who are friendly with children but who say little more than "Hi," "Bye," "You're a pretty girl," and "Good talking... walking... drawing." Your child needs more than superficial verbal pats on the back. Just watching one of our children playing house with a parent, clinician, or teacher illustrates the many reasons that people participate in conversation. The adult might say "Look at the mess in there" (here the reason is to make social contact). "You could be the mommy" (give social contact). "You look pretty today" (give attention). "I like playing house" (show general interest). "That's nice, you hug the dolly. Let

me hug you" (give support and show affection). "I think the table goes in here" (express thoughts). "That's too big for that spot" (give information). If you think of a conversation as making up a story or solving a problem, it is easy to see how one friendly comment leads to another. Be sure to share the lead with the child. Talk sometimes about what he just said; at other times, about your own images and ideas.

Many ways to show friendship.

Substrategy

b. Communicate more for enjoyable social contact than to get something done.

While there are certainly times to communicate to get things done, they cannot be frequent enough for your child to learn language and conversation. It is easy to see how adults get in the habit of instrumental communications. It's perfectly natural to direct and control a child, especially a child with delays in development. Nevertheless, if you want your child to join the social world, you must show him one at home and in school.

Be more a partner than a boss.

Whenever we first tell parents and teachers to focus on social rather than instrumental communication, we hear reactions like this: "But my child needs to learn [this or that]. He needs me to teach him." Just as often, we repeat our plea: "The more you teach in directive ways, the more passive and less social he will become." We wish there were some universal way to help adults realize that it is through friendly, incidental contacts that children will learn to be steady communicators. We consistently get more responses when we contact children with friendly, low-stress communications such as "Look at that red hair—I've got black hair" or "It's cold outside," rather than with controlling communications like "Where do you go to school?" or "Tell me how many fingers I have up" or "Can you tell me how the lawn mower works?"

When adults contact a child just for the enjoyment, the child stays longer, giving him more chances to learn and to generalize his communication skills across more situations and ideas. We want the world to define your child as a "communicator" in the same way it defines him as an eater, sleeper, and a mover. If in turn he sees the world as a friendly place to communicate, he will become a successful communicator.

Substrategy

c. Comment and wait with no stress for a particular response.

If we could recommend only one strategy to build a conversation, it would be to *comment and wait.* When you comment, you express what you think or see without making any demand for a particular answer. A comment gives the child the freedom to say anything, to choose from any of a great number of images that your comment might have created for him. Comments are also valuable because the child cannot fail. Any response that keeps the conversation going is a success.

Clearly expect "something."

When you comment, try to talk about some things the two of you both know about or share in your immediate experience. Be sure to keep matching—the more you communicate the way your child does, the more likely he will stay and communicate with you. And, eventually, he will communicate more in the ways you do.

Compare these examples of a directive and a commenting adult, looking at a picture book with a child.

Example:

Directing

Adult	**Child**
"Look at that boy. What is he doing?"	"It's gonna rain."
"Yes, but what is that boy doing? That boy there?"	"Gonna get wet."
"No, he's inside. I want to know what he's doing now."	(Closes the book.)

Example:

Commenting

Adult	**Child**
"So many things in that picture."	"Clouds, it's raining."
"The clouds are dark and big. I smell rain."	"Not raining yet."
"Everything still looks dry."	"Get inside, kids."
"I'll get their raincoats."	"No, afraid of lightning."

Commenting keeps a child longer.

Notice that, in the directive example, the conversation never developed for the child so that he could learn new ideas or have his own ideas supported. In the commenting example, the adult gave the child open-ended images, letting the conversation take the shape of the child's motivations. Notice also that the child followed the adult's ideas, even though no questions were needed to keep him involved. We find that commenting results in much longer conversations than do questions and commands; it also allows both the child and adult to create and actively build the conversation. Conversations appear to build to the extent that each partner can participate actively with his own ideas. We rarely see children pursuing conversations with partners who do not give them the freedom to develop their own ideas.

Substrategy

d. Reply to a verbal child's comments.

Once you develop a strong and warm conversational relationship with your child, your simplest responses can serve as strong rewards that keep your child communicating with you. Of the many kinds of responses you can make, replies often work the best. When you reply, you respond to your child with no stress, no questions, no testing. A reply is a response that is sensitive to your child's message. A reply tells your child that you were listening and that you are responding to what he said, but that you have no intention of controlling what he next says.

When you reply, you do need to match the child with a response that is meaningful in terms of what he just said. It may seem strange, but we strongly encourage you not to "think" much when you reply. Just watch and listen, and you will automatically know how to reply. If you stop to think you remove yourself from the moment, and your reply will not be as genuine as it may have been had it been spontaneous.

Replies give the child freedom.

Without our continued attention, many children are not likely to get into a habit of talking. Many children we know use their talk mainly to play alone. Because they do not have the habit of talking for a response, they get few responses and, as a result, they talk less to others. Avoid the habit of accepting any child talk but not responding to it. Often adults are so pleased just to hear the child talk that they fail to encourage him to stay for more with their own replies. Consider your own easy replies as the fuel that keeps your child communicating.

When you reply, try to give your child as much freedom to continue as possible. We try to reply in a way that gives a child an image or idea that he can respond to in a variety of ways. Again, there are no predetermined right answers; the goal is to get a conversational habit going, not to get the child to perform in a specific way.

Ask yourself: What can I say to keep him talking with me?

Example:

Poor replying

Child	Adult
"Look, there's an Eskimo."	"Let's look at the other book."
"I want this one, the Eskimos."	"All right, where do they live?"
"In the snow."	"No. I mean what country?"
"Cold country."	"No, the name of the country."
"Let's look at the pictures."	"Canada, that's where Eskimos live."

Example:

Effective replying

Child	Adult
"Look at the Eskimos."	"They look cold."
"Snow's cold ... but they have warm coats."	"They sure do; they look like bearskin."
"A whole bear?"	"Maybe only parts. Bears are much bigger than most people."
"His face still looks cold."	"Maybe he needs a scarf."
"He can get a bear scarf."	

In the first example, the adult was replying from her own agenda. She even ignored or negated what the child was saying. We would predict the child would not stay or return much for that adult. In the second example, the adult responded meaningfully to the child's messages, and the child reciprocated by staying and replying meaningfully to the adult's communications. The adult's replies were friendly and supportive. Although she did not direct or control, the adult took advantage of many opportunities to teach the child something new.

Substrategy

e. Balance between taking the child's point of view and your own.

It is not unusual to find that a child talks mostly about himself, to the exclusion of your concerns. Some of this ego-centered speech is quite normal and even useful for learning (Piaget, 1952). Nevertheless, if you have spent much time with a child who talks only about his concerns, you have surely concluded on occasion that "enough is enough." Certainly, we do not expect children to have conversations mainly on adult topics. Still, it is possible now and then in conversations to shift the talk to what you are doing. There are at least two reasons for gradually directing your child to see your point of view. First, not even loving parents and devoted teachers or clinicians can be expected to stay long in such one-sided conversations; they need affirmation, as does the child. Second, a parent or teacher has a major responsibility to help a child become the kind of person that others in society will stay with. And people in society want children who sometimes see things their way.

Example:

Poor balance

Child	Adult
"I want some pudding."	"What else for supper?"
"Just pudding."	"You need vegetables, too."
"Pop too."	

Example:

Close balance

Child	Adult
"I want some pudding."	"That's your favorite dessert."
"After supper?"	"After your beans and wieners."
"You like that food?"	"I hope you do too someday."

Substrategy

f. Allow the child freedom of expression.

Children are often more like us than we think. The freer we feel to express our thoughts without fear of judgment or redirection, the more likely we are to continue a conversation. By commenting and replying without pressuring your child to perform, you can let him know that you are interested in his ideas. Since children often communicate much less than they know, we need to allow them to express all the knowledge that is suppressed by adults who control conversations. Unless a child feels free of judgment and failure in an interaction, he is not likely to communicate much of what he knows. Consequently, unless we are friendly to and accepting of children with delays, they are apt to appear much less intelligent than they really are.

The freer a child is to express himself, the more intelligent he will seem and the more desirable conversation partner he will be.

When you are engaged in a conversation with a child, think of talking as if it were creative play. Enjoy watching and hearing your child create new ideas. When your child is free to talk, he will be more interesting to you and others. No longer will he be simply reflecting your ideas or answering your questions; he will be giving you the rewards that keep people in relationships. You can experience the excitement of seeing your child open up, seeing him act as though he has something to say that others want to hear. You do not want your child to be just a responder when he can be so much more.

Substrategy

g. Follow rules of social appropriateness.

When an adult and child have generalized their habit of conversation to their daily routines, they are then ready to shape those conversations to begin showing the rules society expects. We encourage you to gently redirect your child toward these rules. The basic rules for conversation include many we have discussed for building the earlier partnerships in play, communication, and language. However, we find that many of these rules do not automatically generalize when adults and children are in conversations.

Often adults must intentionally show their child the following rules: Communicate for a response; wait silently, responding to the partner's intent; be clear; be succinct; and be flexible to repair miscommunications. At the same time, show your child what not to do in conversations: Don't interrupt; don't ignore the other's message; don't ramble; don't communicate only to yourself; don't change the topic abruptly; and don't fail to clarify when you are not understood.

It's Your Turn

COMMENT:

As a teacher, I used to find questions and commands were the easiest ways to talk to students. Then I learned to be conversational. I saw that comments and replies got children to stay more and to show me more of what they had learned. It was hard to reduce questions, but I did it because it improved my teaching and the children's participation. At first, I didn't know what to say; I knew questions, but I didn't know what to comment about. Then I decided everything in the room—persons, things, words, and actions—was fair game. In a few weeks, the class was talking about everything in the room, often in humorous ways. Everyone's job was to pair up and make up a story every day about something happening in the room. Since everyone was familiar with the ideas, the stories occasionally got pretty rowdy with up to eight children contributing. I have now made commenting conversations unthreatening ways for children to learn some of the most difficult parts of the curriculum.

REPLY:

We are very hopeful when we meet creative teachers like you. Once a teacher has a strong conversational relationship with her students, she can use it to increase the cooperation of children and to help children generalize what they learn to the social relationships for which they need much of their learning.

COMMENT:

In my rush to get Nick ready for school, I taught him what I thought he needed. I saw that he dreaded these sessions, but I saw it as my duty. I found, to my despair, that while we used to have a playful time together, he now avoided me. Then it was recommended that I spend times following his point of view and trying to get nothing done in particular. What happened first, after biting my tongue for week, was that I found he knew much more than I expected, certainly more than I had taught him. By the way, he showed little of what I painfully tried to teach him. Also at first, I found he seemed not to trust me, as if he was saying "Hey, don't spoil my fun." Soon I learned what he knew and cared about, and then we started having little conversations, but I avoided any pressure for right answers. I was so surprised; in easy conversations he showed me he knew many "right" answers without my needing to question or command him. After conversations like this for almost 2 months, he really rewarded me. He started being interested in my ideas. Now I feel we are becoming partners.

REPLY:

Sometimes, like this, there is no need for a reply.

Self-Assessment: How Are You Doing?

Rate yourself on a scale of 1 to 9, where 1 = not often or very poorly, 5 = neutral, and 9 = very frequently or quite well.

_____ 1. I communicate with my child for many social reasons.
_____ 2. I communicate more for enjoyment than to get something.
_____ 3. I comment and wait for my child to respond.
_____ 4. I keep my child in conversations.
_____ 5. I take my child's point of view in conversations.
_____ 6. I support my child to talk freely.

40. DIRECT CHILD EFFECTIVELY

When we first encourage a parent or professional to reduce her questions, commands, and other directive ways of talking to a child, the adult is usually surprised. Many adults even tell us that this advice makes no sense to them. Their position can be described in these words: "I have a child whose learning is delayed, so I have to teach him. How else do you teach other than with questions and commands? Who is going to direct him if I don't?" We find this attitude deeply ingrained not just in parents but in many clinicians and teachers. Understandably this attitude is an almost-natural reaction to someone in need. It can be changed if you carefully watch its frequent effects—it quiets the child. Once many of these adults see that their child actually stays longer and communicates more without that pressure to perform, they not only begin to question and direct less but also find they work less and enjoy the time they spend with the child more.

Surprise: The less you demand the more you get.

Another reason to limit your directiveness with your child is that you may not want to get from your child what you give him. Consider the possibility that your child is likely to become the kind of person that you are to him. You need to decide which of your images you want him to mirror. Too many of the children brought to us interact with others mainly with questions, commands, and other controlling communications that pay little attention to others. These children often look and sound much like their parents and teachers. Regardless of where they learn this style, it clearly does not encourage others to build relationships with them.

When we discuss this situation with adults, they usually agree that their overriding goal is for the child to be accepted in conversational relationships in school, work, and play. We then work carefully with both parents and professionals to show them that they are not getting the kind of child they want as a result of their directiveness. Accepting this reality usually helps them begin to work toward becoming the kind of conversational partner that people want to be with. That role, then, serves as a model that we provide as a conversational style for their children to learn.

As with most ideas in this model, however, balance is the key. Adults have certain responsibilities for the child that call for them to be directive at times. Your child needs to be safe, clean, and courteous; sometimes commands are both necessary and acceptable ways to get a job done. At other times, you need to give information to your child or get information from him; at many times, questions and directions are helpful or necessary in such tasks. Thus questions and commands are important tactics you can use to regulate your child. But take great care to prevent a directive style from defining your entire relationship as a series of orders and tests.

Watch your balance: Is it more ● or more o ? ● = directive o = social

Consider for a moment how much of a person's life is taken up with directive interactions, either controlling or being controlled. Make a few circles on a paper. in one of the circles, darken the amount that you think represents the portion of your life spent in directing and controlling communications. For example, a teacher may estimate that two-thirds of her time at school is spent directing students. A mother might feel she spends a similar percentage of her day questioning, commanding, and regulating. In contrast, parents and professionals who have learned to interact with their children as conversation partners report that their circles are darkened (that is, directive) only 10 to 20%.

Using the same approach, look at a child a few years older than yours, one who has a rich social life—the kind of relationships you'd like for your child. Draw a circle for this older child. How much of it is darkened? We predict that you want your child to be a person who has mainly friendly conversations, whose directive time would be limited to meeting needs but would not be the majority of time. Now draw the circle for your child. What proportion is dark with directions, questions, and other kinds of controlling contacts? Our goal is to help you help your child have a lighter circle, that is, to become increasingly more social in contacts with people.

Substrategy

a. Question and command in a matched way, then wait.

As we have said, there are certainly times when questions and commands are appropriate and helpful, as long as they do not dominate your relationship with your child. When you do need to be directive, your questions should get answers and your commands should get cooperation. Because children often ignore questions and commands, here are some ways to make your questions and directions work.

Make sure your questions are genuine. You really want an answer.

First, we try to cut down our "rhetorical" talk, by which we mean talking at someone rather than talking specifically to get a response. We see many adults who ask questions but clearly do not expect an answer. For example, adults may say, "Why did you mess up my floor?" or "Where did you get that? I bet Davey gave it to you" or "Are you playing with those soldiers again?" In each case, the child easily learns that no response is required. He may learn to expect to be talked at and not to respond. Similarly, adults give commands but do little to enforce them. In both cases, rhetorical questions and unenforced commands, the child is learning that he is not required to talk with adults. All he has to do is ignore the adult and the adult will keep talking, relieving him of the responsibility.

Some parents are in the habit of asking questions but not waiting for a response. We frequently hear a string of talk like this: "Where's your brother? Oh, he's with dad, right? They went to get grandma." When life is full of questions that do not allow a response, a child may stop trying to answer, later not knowing what to do with a real question. Thus, one strategy you can practice is to ask only real questions, questions you genuinely want answered and will wait silently for. The importance of taking turns and the need for give-and-take in balanced turntaking apply to questions and commands as much as to conversations or play. If you ask a question, your child needs time to search for his answer. We strongly discourage many questions because they make communication more difficult for the child and because it is essential that your child not see conversation as a task to avoid. Thus, even though questions can be very valuable, keep them to a minimum and ask them so that you get an answer.

Follow through on your questions and commands.

Second, we encourage you to follow through on questions and commands. A young child or a child with delays is likely not to respond to questions mainly because of the work they involve for him. It is important that we impress on the child that we do expect a response and will gently keep him there for some kind of response (anything at first). However, when a mother says, "Stay here, don't go out, come on, stay in here, you don't want to go out, stay with mommy ..." and then allows the child to go out, her commands are effectively just another form of talking to herself. Although we rarely command a child, when we do, we communicate the message once, wait for a response, repeat it with an authoritative ("I mean it") tone if necessary, wait again, and if necessary physically fetch the child on the third try. Once a child knows you will follow through on your commands, even a soft word will begin to work.

Third, match the child carefully. A major strategy that applies at every level of the **ECO** model, *matching* means communicating at the child's level, giving him a model that he can try to do. When we do not match a child's skills and interests, we are likely to lose him. Matching also means communicating within his current experiences—the more you question him about things he know and cares about, the more likely he will stay.

If used sparingly, then, questions can help build conversations. The questions that help are ones that move the conversation along and build a topic. They are questions that keep the two of you together rather than creating dead ends, failing to shift the balance of power back and forth between the two of you. We also try to avoid questions that get into a rut of show and tell, such as "What's your name?" ("Jack") "Where do you live?" ("Mommy's house") "Who else lives there?" ("Joseph") "I bet you like Carmen, don't you?" ("Uh, uh"). Though common, these routines have the effect of allowing the child to be passive and discouraging him from participating in conversations. Avoid becoming your child's inquisitor; instead, become one of the conversation partners he needs.

Substrategy

b. Use nonverbal questions or commands.

Often when you are in touch with a child (or with an adult for that matter), you can most effectively question and command by communicating nonverbally, by raising an eyebrow, pointing clearly, shrugging your shoulders, or by many similarly clear actions that do not require a verbal exchange. While our main concern is that you develop conversational relationships with your child, we recognize that there are actually some times when conversations can get in the way of communication. If a command is needed, if a question is appropriate, if a "no" is warranted, then a simple point, a questioning face, or a head shake may do the job. A conversation at those times may only lead you away from the topic that needs immediate attention.

Directions often work best without words.

Watch all of the ways that your child controls you with nonverbal behavior; then watch yourself. One great advantage of using nonverbal questions and commands may be that they allow you to save your words for developing conversations that are positive and nondemanding. Carolyn, who is raising three boys on her own, saves her talk for friendly discussions. When she needs to regulate her children, she uses her face and hands and a mournful sound or a knock on a table very convincingly. And she finds that silence is also an extremely effective message, more effective in fact than discussing whatever it is that needs to be done. Children with language delays, even more than nondelayed learners, should not develop negative associations with adults' talking to them.

Another value of very brief or mostly nonverbal communications for questioning and commanding is that they avoid tedious, often circular, conversations between adults and children. For example, here is a typical exchange when a mother has decided the child needs to stay inside: "I wanna go out." "You still have a little cold." "But I feel better." "You can still get sick." "I won't get sick." "Oh, but you could." "I still wanna go out." "You don't want to get sick." "I don't care,

I want to play." And on and on. Although we want more and more conversations for you and your child, this is not the kind we encourage. The more this mother talked, the more she reinforced the child's pleas. After one brief explanation, such as "I don't want to take the chance of you getting sick," any further pleas can be effectively dispensed with by a firm head shake and silence (or simply by silence as a message that that conversation is over).

Sometimes we find adults delicately balanced between being an effective authority when needed and appreciating the child's need to understand a situation. We are concerned that conversations between children and their important adults do not become mainly tugs of war that adults want to flee or command stations that children will avoid. We are very apprehensive when we hear that the bulk of parents' conversations with their children consists of disputes or struggles for power. We feel deeply that, because the conversation is the primary place where a child learns to be social and communicative, it should be kept clear of distractions that reduce communication. Power disputes are not worth the loss of all the learning and attachment that conversations provide.

Substrategy

c. Use authentic questions and commands rather than routinized requests to get the child to perform.

It is easy to question and command a child out of habit without actually expecting a response or to accept rote responses that add little to a conversation. An authentic question is one you genuinely want a response to and one that truly adds to the conversation.

Although this book is concerned primarily with developing a conversation habit during the years that children move from nonverbal to verbal communication, there are similarly effective ways to further develop productive conversation with children in school age and beyond. Haim Ginott was a pioneer in his concern that parents and children have fair conversations. His work, and that of his followers, is helpful for developing stages of conversation beyond the childhood years that are the primary focus of this book (Faber & Maglish, 1980; Ginott, 1969).

Substrategy

d. Question or direct the child with no apparent stress.

Most of the delayed children we have known have had a long history of failures, whether in trying to walk, talk, be understood, or fit into rewarding opportunities for learning. Until they give up and assume a generally passive role, these children face stresses with most attempts to learn. Because social and communicative skills can only develop when the child is in a rich habit of conversations, we as adults must always try to reduce these stresses so that the child will stay in the relationships he needs.

Stress, of course, is a necessary part of learning, as exemplified in the stresses that motivate us to learn something new or to solve a problem or to maintain a conversation. Where there is incentive, the stress can be motivating. But when the child is repeatedly failing to communicate with you or when he has little opportunity to participate with you, the stress can be destructive. A child who regularly faces doing everything on another person's terms, who rarely has someone follow his lead, may conclude that the outcome is not worth the effort. One test of whether the interaction is too stressful for the child is whether or not he stays with you. If he leaves you, look at how you could alter your strategies and expectations to allow him success with you. As we have seen at every stage throughout this book, keeping the child actively participating with you remains the indispensable task and the invaluable opportunity for helping him learn to become more social and communicative.

It's Your Turn

COMMENT:

We are parents of five children aged 2 to 9. We know that conversations are important but often have no idea how to keep the children talking with us.

REPLY:

First, I commend you for still valuing conversations in a family of seven where silence might be your fondest hope. When we try to keep a child in conversations we shift among several strategies. Occasionally, we will imitate what a child says, giving him a chance to build on his own ideas. Other times we will create new images about the topic, extending it one step further. Creating images for the child can help him have more to talk about. For example, if your daughter talks about the snow and you feel stuck in the conversation, think of the snow and you will come up with images such as "I wonder where the birds are now," "I'll bet mail carriers get wet and cold," or "Snow has to be wet for snowballs." Building images helps the child move from conversations that depend on the concrete here and now to ones that build on an endless resource—his own imagination.

Another general strategy to keep conversation going is to put yourself in your child's position. Imagine you are your child, then talk about things from that point of view. Taking this perspective helps us avoid talking about things that are irrelevant to the child and lets us easily focus on the child's concerns.

COMMENT:

I am a mother with three children, ages 4, 7, and 9. I have much friendlier conversations with the 4-year-old girl that I had with the others. One thing I have done much differently with her than with the older ones was to learn when to have a conversation and when not to have one. I used to try to reason everything out with the older children and often found myself locked in conversations and giving up my responsibility to raise them. I'm here to say that once you learn when not to have conversations with children, you come to have better ones when they are appropriate.

REPLY:

That sounds like wise judgment to us.

Self-Assessment: How Are You Doing?

Rate yourself on a scale of 1 to 9, where 1 = not often or very poorly, 5 = neutral, and 9 = very frequently or quite well.

_____ 1. I consciously keep my child longer in conversations than before.
_____ 2. I use nonverbal questions as well as verbal ones.
_____ 3. I communicate with him more for enjoyable reasons than to get a job done.
_____ 4. I keep my questions and commands to only when I need information from my child.
_____ 5. When I do question or direct my child, he responds quickly.
_____ 6. I believe that low-stress conversations are necessary for my child to learn.
_____ 7. In our conversations, I allow my child considerable freedom of expression.

Sample Resources for Becoming Conversation Partners

ECOScale: Becoming Conversation Partners
ECO Tutor: Becoming Conversation Partners
ECO Link: Becoming Conversation Partners
Conversation Routine
IEP/Problem Solver
ECO Practice Plan and Record

BECOMING CONVERSATION PARTNERS

INTERACTIVE GOAL

34. Become conversation partners.
    a. Communicate for social reasons.
    b. Limit instrumental and controlling communication.
    c. Play an active rather than passive communication role.

INTERACTIVE PROBLEM

35. Poor conversations.
    a. Lack of communicative responding between the two.
    b. Directive, controlling style.
    c. Minimal topic sharing.
    d. Failure to follow each other's lead.
    e. Academic or instrumental flow.
    f. Rigid roles rather than flexible partnerships.
    g. Few reasons for communication.
    h. Lack of a developed conversational topic.

CHILD GOALS

36. Converse for a variety of reasons.
    a. Communicate verbally for a variety of reasons.
       1. Self-directed reasons.
       2. Instrumental reasons.
       3. Social reasons.
    b. Communicate in socially appropriate ways.
    c. Favor social over instrumental communications.
37. Stay in verbal conversations.
    a. Balance turns with partner.
    b. Follow discourse rules to maintain, shift, and develop topics.
    c. Converse in a comfortable style.
    d. Comment more than question or command.

ADULT STRATEGIES

38. Maintain balanced conversations.
    a. Keep a verbal child talking in a back-and-forth exchange.
    b. Communicate and show expectation for a response.
    c. Share the conversational load with a verbal child.
    d. Initiate and respond proportionately.

39. Have social, friendly conversations with the child.
    a. Communicate for a variety of social reasons.
    b. Communicate more for enjoyable social contact than to get something done.
    c. Comment and wait with no stress for a particular response.
    d. Reply to a verbal child's comments.
    e. Balance between taking the child's point of view and your own.
    f. Allow the child freedom of expression.
    g. Follow rules of social appropriateness.
40. Direct child effectively.
    a. Question or command in a matched way, then wait.
    b. Use nonverbal questions or commands.
    c. Use authentic questions and commands rather than routinized requests to get the child to perform.
    d. Question or direct the child with no apparent stress.

ECO Tutor

Interactive Goal: Becoming Conversation Partners

<table>
<tr>
<td>What Is It?</td>
<td>Conversation partners are two people who are in the habit of talking with each other as a natural part of their time together. As a conversation partner, your child will learn to be social and communicative naturally from any one willing to have conversations with him. As a conversation partner with your child, you will be in the position to help your child to communicate with no extra effort. For children with delays, conversations are not optional, inconsequential events (as they are often viewed). Rather, conversations are both the place and the process for your child to learn to be social and communicative.</td>
</tr>
<tr>
<td>What Do Conversation Partners Do?</td>
<td>Being a conversation partner may seem easy—something that comes without learning. Certainly we do not remember being taught how to have conversations. Nevertheless, conversations are learned, and children with delays need careful help here so that they become as communicative and social as they can be.</td>
</tr>
<tr>
<td>What To Look For and Strategies That Can Help</td>
<td>What do conversation partners do with a child?

— They take turns with him.
— They wait with interest for what he has to say.
— They show they expect him to talk.
— They keep him with them if the conversation stops.
— They respond sensitively to his concerns and changes in his ideas.
— They match or fine-tune their talk to his ability.
— They talk about his interests.
— They stay on his topics.
— They try to keep him on their topics.
— They communicate more for the pleasure of his company and less to get a job done.

While they do not usually try to teach, both partners often learn from conversations.

— They learn without either person controlling the other.
— They accept each other and expect him to do his part.
— They often want to return for more.</td>
</tr>
</table>

LESS LIKE THIS

Therapist: "Can you get a book to read?"
Daisy: *"Wild Things."*
Therapist: "What's Max doing with that fork? That looks dangerous. You wouldn't do that, would you?"
Daisy: "I don't know."
Therapist: "Why did his mother send him to bed? Did he get his supper?"
Daisy: "I don't know."
Therapist: "How come those trees are in his room?"
Daisy: "Monsters are coming."
Therapist: "Okay, but tell me about the trees first."
Daisy: "I want to see the monsters."

MORE LIKE THIS

Therapist: "I want to read with you."
Daisy: "I got the *"Wild Things."*
Therapist: "Max looks like the wild thing."
Daisy: "Wild Max, chasing the dog."
Therapist: "I hope the dog gets away."
Daisy: "He does. And Max goes to bed."
Therapist: "Look! Trees in his bedroom."
Daisy: "Not real trees, he's dreaming."
Therapist: "He's dreaming about monsters."
Daisy: "Monsters want to scare Max."
Therapist: "Max isn't scared."
Daisy: "No! The monsters are scared."
Therapist: "Max is a tough guy."
Daisy: "Yeah, monsters like tough guys."

Why Less?

This example shows a pattern we often see between adults and children. The adult is controlling most of the conversation, leading the topic, and directing the child with questions and commands. The child has little opportunity to express her own ideas, and clearly she has ideas of her own. The adult mismatches regularly by saying much more than the child. Notice that Daisy takes a passive role, offering little of her own ideas. The therapist is not showing the girl what next to say and she misses the opportunities to build on the girl's ideas, as when she said "monsters are coming." The therapist seems more concerned with getting certain things done than helping the child be a conversation partner. This conversation seems to be more work than enjoyment; notice that none of the therapist's questions and commands get much from Daisy. Conversations like this may strongly discourage children from staying and learning with people. And a passive child may build fewer relationships than she needs to develop her potential.

Why More?

Notice the easily balanced partnership here. Each person has the freedom and success needed to keep the child learning through conversations. Here the conversation is more play than work, yet the child shows considerably more language. Daisy is learning without any old-fashioned teaching with questions and commands. This is an example of a conversation that is *balanced, nondirective, responsive, matched*, and *enjoyable*. Daisy is learning new language she hears without any direct attempts to teach her.

Why Is It Important?

The conversation is *balanced*; each person takes her turn, then waits for the other to talk. The conversation is *matched* in two ways: the therapist talks at the child's level and talks about the child's interests.

The conversation is *responsive*; each person responds meaningfully to what the other says. The therapist supports what Daisy says and shows her how to talk more about it. The conversation is *nondirective*; no one is in control and easy comments allow the child to talk freely from her own ideas. The therapist offers the child "guided freedom" as she leads the child to talk in ways that follow her lead.

Finally, the conversation is *enjoyable*; notice the ease and playfulness that naturally helps the conversation and the learning continue. This is the kind of conversation that we predict would successfully keep the child who needs to learn to be social and communicative.

**ECO
Link**

Becoming Conversation Partners
HOW YOU CAN HELP A CHILD LEARN TO HAVE CONVERSATIONS

*TO WHAT
EXTENT DO YOU
AND YOUR
CHILD HAVE
CONVERSATIONS?*

1. Are conversations a natural and frequent part of your time with your child?
2. Do you believe conversations are important for your child's development?
3. Are your conversations with your child more like work or play?
4. Do you both actively participate in conversations or are they often one-sided?
5. In conversations do you and your child respond to and appreciate each other's ideas?
6. Do your conversations have many purposes—companionship, learning, assistance, persuasion, enjoyment, and others?

*HOW WILL YOU
KNOW IF YOUR
CHILD IS YOUR
CONVERSATION
PARTNER?*

1. He will communicate socially—to comment, reply, attend, and show affection and friendship.
2. He will actively participate, initiating, responding, and building on a topic.
3. He will communicate about your ideas as well as his own.
4. He will enjoy conversations and often prefer them to being alone.
5. He will communicate in ways that are socially appropriate to the situation.

*HOW WILL YOU
KNOW IF THERE
IS A PROBLEM
IN YOUR
CONVERSA-
TIONAL
RELATIONSHIP?*

1. You will communicate in rigid patterns such as question/answer or command/comply.
2. One person will ignore the other's ideas and insist on his own topics.
3. Your conversations sound more like school or work than fun or friendship.
4. There is little give and take; rather, mostly give or mostly take.
5. One person often takes a passive role, responding much more than initiating.
6. One person frequently dominates the conversation and rarely waits for the other.
7. You will move rapidly across topics, without developing ideas.
8. Your conversations are neither interesting nor enjoyable.
9. Communication is often inappropriate, with interruptions, speaking off topic, or otherwise disrupting the flow.

*HOW CAN YOU
BUILD A CON-
VERSATIONAL
PARTNERSHIP?*

1. Communicate *for* a response, not *at* the child.
2. Wait and expect; give the child time and signals to continue.
3. Balance the conversation; initiate and respond about as much as the child.
4. Show the child you expect "something more" rather than anything in particular.
5. Respond appreciatively to the child's actions and words.
6. Match the child's language level and ideas.
7. Be nondirective by commenting and replying more than questioning and commanding.
8. Build a habit of keeping your child for more than one turn.
9. Make conversations friendly and successful for the child.

1. Communicating mainly with questions or commands.
2. Ignoring the child's interest or regularly leading him to your topic.
3. Dominating the conversation and not waiting for the child to take part.
4. Mismatch; communicating far above the child's language or interest level.
5. Anything that serves to make the child passive or noninteractive.
6. Correcting your child's language or giving him discouraging feedback.
7. Being satisfied with brief contacts with your child that do not develop.

**Conversation
Routine**

DAILY LIVING: Eating Verbal Level Example

Make the natural events in your day into opportunities for friendly, social conversations with your child. Consider these contrasting examples. Try to avoid limited contacts such as the one on the left. Try to find something you can share with your child, as in the example on the right. Turn just another routine into a joint activity in which your child can stay and learn with you.

LESS LIKE THIS

Adult: "Everyone is at the dinner table except you, Annie."
Child: (Continues to play in the other room.)
Adult: "Don't make me come and get you." (Walks into the other room to get Annie, picks her up, walks her to the kitchen, and puts her in the chair in front of her prepared plate."
Child: "Yuck, I no like." (Pushes the plate away.)
Adult: "Oh, come on, eat a little something. Do it for mommy, okay?"
Child: "No way. I no like."
Adult: "You go to your room then. This is our dinner and I'm not spoiling it."
Child: "No, no, I want cookie."
Adult: (Picks up Annie, takes her to her room.)

Avoid These Problems:
**Directive, Controlling, Dominating;
Lack of Active Togetherness**

The child has no control in the ongoing action of dinner. Her only way to assert herself and gain attention is to make a nuisance of herself by not coming to the kitchen and not eating dinner. Mom attends reactively to the negative aspects of the situation, rather than setting up a situation to guarantee success.

MORE LIKE THIS

Adult: "Annie I need help!" (Calling to another room.)
Child: "I help!" (Comes to the kitchen.)
Adult: (Mom has everything on the table except spoons. She extends them to the child.)
Child: "I set table?" (Takes the spoons and walks to the table, and places one on each plate.)
Adult: "Everyone, come to dinner!"
Child: "Dinner, dinner." (calling too, with a note of importance.)
Adult: "I love spaghetti!" (Puts some on her plate.)
Child: "Me too, me too." (Reaches to get some herself.)
Adult: (Assists her, covering Annie's hand with her own.)
Child: "I got some!" (Dives into her food.)

Try These Strategies:
Direct Child Effectively, Match Child Behavior

Here, Mom still wants the child to eat dinner, but she knows how to get what she wants through effective communication. First, she enlists the help of the child in setting the table and calling the family, using comments rather than commands. Then, she models enjoying the food, which the child follows both behaviorally and conversationally.

VARIATIONS:
Eating a snack, taking medicine.

Early Verbal
CHILD GOAL: Converse for a Variety of Reasons
PROBLEM: Lack of Playfulness
(the adult who focuses on "right" and "wrong" or "good" and "bad")

Dad spends his spare time at home with Paul by playing "quiz" games to find out what he knows. When they go out in public together, Dad tries to make sure Paul does good things, such as eating neatly or keeping his hands off other people's things. He feels strongly that these two goals constitute his major responsibility with his child.

At Home

Dad:	"Paul, can you tell Dad your whole name?"
Paul:	"Paulie."
Dad:	"No, that's not your whole name. Say, 'Paul Thomas.' That's your whole name. Like my whole name is Bill Thomas and Mommy's whole name is Denise Thomas. What is your whole name?"
Paul:	"My whole name?" (Thinks a minute.) "Thomas."
Dad:	"No, that's not right. It's Paul Thomas. We'll work on it again Friday."
Paul:	"Friday—Paul Friday?"
Dad:	"No. I said we'll work on it Friday." (Puts his head in his hands in frustration.)

At a Restaurant

Dad:	"Let's sit up nice and tall in our seats."
Paul:	(Imitates his father's tall and straight sitting.)
Dad:	"Good boy, you look like Daddy."
Paul:	"I daddy."
Dad:	"No, you're not Daddy. You look like Daddy."
Paul:	(Opens up a pack of sugar and dumps it on the table.)
Dad:	"Paul, that's bad behavior. I don't like it."
Paul:	(Eats a little from his finger.)
Dad:	"Don't do that. No. I've told you that a million times."

ECO | Partnership Plan

The **ECO** Partnership Plan contains those elements of an Individual Family Service Plan (IFSP) or Individual Education Program (IEP) that specify **ECO** goals and objectives to enhance a child's social and communicative development. Refer to current ECOScales for present levels of development and performance and for new goals.

Child Name: **Paul**   Birth Date: **8/21**   Parents: **Denise and Bill**

Date of ECOScales: **3/14**   Examiner: _____

Present Levels of Development and Performance   Linguistic but minimally conversational; verbal level

Child Goal   Converse for a variety of reasons

Objectives   Communicate verbally to be instrumental (3/10 remarks)

Communicate verbally to be social (7/10) Favor social over instrumental

Partnership Goal   Become Conversation Partners

Objectives   Communicate for social reasons   Limit instrumental, controlling talk

Priority Problem: Poor Conversations

Subproblem   Few reasons for communication

Directive, controlling style

Adult Strategies   Have social, friendly conversations with Paul

Substrategies   Direct Paul effectively   Use authentic questions and commands

Develop verbal topics   Share choice of topic with Paul

Build a topic with new ideas and vocabulary matched to Paul's level

Practice Activities
People Only   Trading funny comments

2-3 Times a day   2-3 Minutes each

People and Things   Play catch, build blocks

1-2 Times a day   2-3 Minutes each

Daily Routines (practice one a day)   Doing dishes, bathtime

Spontaneous

ECO | Practice Plan and Record

PRACTICE PLAN   Refer to current ECOScale for goals; see other ECOScales for old goals to maintain.

Interactive Goal Become conversation partners (Tony and Teresa - teacher) in school

Objectives

Priority Problem Poor conversations

Child Goal Stay in verbal conversations

Objectives Follow discourse rules to maintain,   Balance turns with partner
shift, & develop topics

Adult Strategies Maintain balanced conversations
Keep Tony talking - "back & forth exchange"   Balance taking your/Tony's point of view

Targets to Decrease TONY: Not developing a topic   2) Minimal topic sharing

Practice Activities TERESA: 1) Limit questions & commands to authentic ones 2) Not following Tony's lead

People Only Exchange comments about daily events

How Often __1-2__ Times a day   __4-5__ Minutes each

Where

People and Things Pretend play with kitchen toys   Pushing cars & trucks

How Often __1-2__ Times a day   __4-5__ Minutes each

Where

Daily Routines
(practice one a day) Snack time   clean-up
bathroom

Spontaneous Salt and pepper your strategies across the day.   Make interactions/communications a habit.

PARTNERSHIP CALENDAR

Week	MONDAY	TUESDAY	WEDNESDAY	THURSDAY	FRIDAY	SATURDAY	SUNDAY
1	3 3	3 3	3-4 3	4 3-4	NO TIME		
2	2 2	4 3	4 4	5 5	4 3		
3							
4							
5							

How to Use the Calendar

1. Select one goal each for child and adult. Observe one planned activity a day.
2. After observing, rate child and adult (you or someone else) on the goals listed in the Practice Plan. Use a 1 to 9 scale:
   1-2 = no evidence   3-4 = little evidence   5 = some evidence   6-7 = increasing evidence   8-9 = strong evidence
3. Rate the child (c) in top half and adult (a) in bottom half of each cell. Be sure to practice across many activities. Try some of the following; check the ones you practice.
   People only: __ sounds __ actions ✓ conversations __ your choice _____
   People and things: ✓ toys __ books __ games __ your choice _____
   Daily routines: __ getting up __ dressing __ bathing ✓ meals __ TV __ car __ bedtime
                      __ shopping __ visiting __ household chores __ your choice _____

ECO | Practice Plan and Record

PARTNERSHIP DIARY

Watch your progress and help your habits grow. Quickly, comment on how interactions with your child went today. Say anything: progress, problems, ideas, changes. Mention both child and adult occasionally.

Week 1

Monday
We played in the kitchen today. I asked fewer questions than usual & Tony played with me longer than usual. Not sure it was a "conversation," though.

Tuesday
We stayed together today, while we played cars. But it still seems like we both do a lot of labeling and don't really build a topic.

Wednesday
I saw an improvement today in myself. When it seemed like the conversation was ending, I made a comment about something Tony was doing. Then he made a comment back.

Thursday
Tried what I did yesterday. This keeps Tony for another turn.

Friday
Too busy in class today – Valentine's Day party.

Saturday

Sunday

Week 2

Monday
Terrible day!! I was really feeling exhausted from the weekend and it seems like in all my interactions I used a lot of questions/commands.

Tuesday
I didn't like the way I was yesterday – Tony really stayed away. Today we were fairly balanced – said about as much as the other.

Wednesday
Great conversation at snack time. We kept exchanging silly comments about the crackers & juice – lasted 5 minutes.

Thursday
RED LETTER DAY!! Very easy, comfortable conversation while looking out the window! Very natural. I don't think I asked a single question.

Friday
Not like yesterday. When Tony didn't initiate, I had to tell myself to wait for anything. Today's conversations were slower than yesterday's, but when I waited Tony talked.

Saturday

Sunday

Extra Hints to Remember
Remember, you should both have an active conversational role. Conversations should be easy, back & forth, not stressful. Comment, then wait for Tony, and don't stress any particular response.

Part

INTERVENTION RESEARCH

9 | Research and Clinical Implications

SOCIAL PLAY

social play

TURN TAKING

turn taking

COMMUNICATION

communication

LANGUAGE

language

CONVERSATION

conversation

The clinical model presented in this book and the related intervention program (MacDonald & Gillette, 1989) are the result of a series of clinical research studies spanning 17 years. The primary purposes of the studies have been to identify some of the critical competencies involved in social and communicative development and to determine clinical approaches for building those competencies within a child's daily relationships with significant others. This chapter will address four topics: a brief history of the program, the design of the treatment program, the findings of a study of 25 parent/child pairs in quantitative and qualitative terms[1], and descriptive profiles of the children and parents before and after treatment.

BACKGROUND

Since 1971, the language and communication program at The Nisonger Center at Ohio State University has integrated graduate training, clinical service, research, and program development into a unified approach to the communication problems of children with developmental delays. During that time we were faced with a professional dilemma. On the one hand, professional fields addressing communication disorders of children (e.g., speech and language pathology, special education, and others) focused primarily on structural aspects of language such as syntax, articulation, and vocabulary. On the other hand, we were confronted with a widespread population of people with no speech or extremely limited use of the language they did have. Consequently, federally mandated education programs were linking these children with delays with clinicians and teachers who had little or no training in preverbal and preconversational development and intervention. Further, they had little experience in addressing the social contexts in which children learn language, that is, the interactive relationships between children and their parents and significant others. The traditional models for serving children with communication delays followed the one-to-one therapy model with little direct attempt to influence the interactive styles of the adults who have regular influence on the child.

The intervention model presented in this book is a direct attempt to unite parents, clinicians, and teachers in activating natural social relationships as the locus and process for social and communication development.

Several problems continually faced us as we investigated how to train professionals and serve clients with communication delays. One obvious dilemma was the high incidence of noninteractive and nonverbal children, coupled with the lack of proven clinical approaches to their communication development. Two related problems were the minimal attention paid by professional approaches to early interaction skills and the less than minimal attention paid to the role of preverbal communication in educational and social development. But perhaps more influential, little or no attention had been given to the roles of parents, teachers, and significant others in building more interactive and communicative relations with delayed children. In fact, until recently, therapy by a speech clinician in an isolated set-

[1]Yvonne Gillette coordinated much of the clinical and research activity described in this report.

ting had been the traditional approach to such disorders, disorders that clearly require a more naturalistic approach (Bronfenbrenner, 1979; Wells, 1981).

Not only had educational and clinical approaches just recently begun to address preverbal communication and interaction, the existing approaches to verbal language and conversation were also problematic because they were developed for children who already had the interactive skills and pragmatic rules for establishing the relationships needed for learning. It is now clear that large populations of children with some expressive language are limited in their social uses of language. The need for rich pragmatic uses of language for a wide range of social rates has been identified as a primary problem beyond having language *per se* (Fey, 1986; Lund & Duchan, 1983; Wells, 1981).

When language itself is pursued within educational curricula, the focus has usually been on academic concepts such as numbers and colors rather than on child-based language with high probability of communicative use. Beyond language *per se*, those conversation skills necessary to build socially acceptable relationships had not yet been systematically integrated into clinical and educational approaches. Finally, those having the most intimate contact with children—parents and teachers—regularly expected the speech clinician to solve the child's communication problems without any active participation from them. But there is now growing evidence that parents and teachers play an influential role in language development (Bronfenbrenner, 1979; Bruner, 1984; Mahoney, 1988; Marfo, 1988; Stern, 1985).

In an attempt to address these problems, we have targeted two primary goals in our programs: (1) the development of assessment and treatment tools to support professionals in their work with preverbal and minimally communicative people; and (2) the investigation of the role of parents' relationships in helping children learn to interact and communicate, so as to maximize the children's potential for integration into society.

This chapter presents findings from a series of clinical research studies. The work began with studies into the content of first language training; it explored an alternative to the academic targets in existing curricula by emphasizing child-based targets—which were then evolving from the semantic revolution in child language study (Bloom, 1973; Brown, 1973; Leonard, 1984). Our series of studies of nondelayed and delayed children revealed consistent meanings in both groups' first language (MacDonald & Horstmeier, 1978). These findings were then integrated into an assessment approach (MacDonald, 1978) and a series of teaching programs (Horstmeier & MacDonald, 1978). At that time, the work was a joint venture between the disciplines of speech pathology and special education and was conducted both in parent-based programs and in classrooms.

In the years that yielded the work mentioned above, we were mainly studying the performance of the child. Soon it became apparent that we were missing half of the developmental process and that learning communication is a reciprocal function of the interaction of two persons, child and adult (whether parent or professional). At the same time, theorists of several orientations were reaching similar conclusions and providing substantial support for studying and treating the interactive dyad, rather than the child alone, as the valid client, in cases where communication delay is the presenting problem (Bateson & Jackson, 1964; Bronfenbrenner, 1979; Bruner, 1974; Field, 1980a, 1980b; Greenspan, 1985; Skinner, 1957; Watzlawick, Beavan, & Jackson, 1967). Each of these diverse theorists argued that a person's communication is a function of the joint activities, expectations, contingencies, intentions, and motivations that are unique to the ongoing relationships. Consequently, we now view the parent or significant caregiver as our primary client, with the child's development being regarded in large part as a function of the interaction strategies employed by parents and significant others.

Both our research work and direct clinical intervention with parents and teachers directed us to study the adult's roles in relating to and helping delayed children. Consequently, a series of programs emerged. First, we followed up on the growing literature concerning adult communication with children (Cross, 1978; Mahoney & Robenalt, 1986; Moerk, 1972; Snow & Ferguson, 1978) by studying the interactive, communicative, linguistic, and pragmatic styles of parents and teachers (Almerico, 1979; Lombardino, 1978; Owens, 1979; Owens & MacDonald, 1982). We then began designing an assessment system with a parallel model for training parents to become primary communication teachers (MacDonald & Gillette, 1984, 1985a, 1986).

The remainder of this chapter presents the clinical treatment design and data analyses utilized in studying the **ECO** model as well as the research finding to date. As the assessment system and model is composed of four scales (see table 9.1), the research findings are related to them: the Child Goals Scale, the Adult Strategy Scale, the Interaction Scale, and the Interactive Problems Scale. Implications of these findings will be discussed to some extent in the body of this chapter; however, you will find in-depth discussions of the **ECO** behaviors throughout this book.

CLINICAL TREATMENT DESIGN

Treatment Program
The **ECO** model was designed to enhance adult-child interactions in ways that strengthen the child's social and communicative skills. The primary approach to relationship building is training parents to understand and personally integrate a series of strategies into direct and spontaneous contacts with their children. Speech-language pathologists taught each parent about the reasons for targeting preverbal skills in the child and including the parent as a primary teacher. The professionals also worked with parents to identify priority problems in their interactions with their children and then provided a rationale for why these problems might interfere with the child's interaction and communication development. In addition to establishing strategies to guide the adults' interactions with children, the professional and parent together determined specific goals that the parent–child pair would work toward. It was reasoned that both education and clinical practice were necessary to help parents adapt their interactive behavior to their children's emerging skills.

The Adult Strategies
The program emphasized developing a finely tuned interactive style (Bruner, 1984) that focused on five primary social principles: balance, match, responsiveness, nondirectiveness, and emotional attachment (see chapter 2 describing the prin-

ciples). Parents learned to *balance* their interactions by allowing the child time to participate and by establishing a style of give and take in which neither person dominated the interaction and both shared the exchange in taking turns and maintaining extended contacts. This principle of balanced turntaking was taught regardless of the child's level of communication. Turntaking was viewed as a pervasive style that facilitates interactions from primitive contacts to full conversations.

As the second principle, *matching*, was taught, parents learned to act and communicate in ways their child could do. Matching allowed parents to provide models that the child was likely to master physically, communicatively, and cognitively.

Table 9.1
Item Number and Description of ECOScale Items Rated in Study of Effectiveness of **ECO** *Treatment*

CHILD GOALS

1. (14)* Use actions in functional and meaningful ways
2. (13) Show a turntaking play style
3. (22) Intentionally communicate with others
4. (23) Communicate nonverbally
5. (24) Begin to communicate verbally
6. (25) Make self understood
7. (30) Use varied vocabulary
8. (31) Follow grammatical rules
9. (36) Converse for a variety of reasons
10. (37) Stay in verbal conversations

ADULT STRATEGIES

1. (15) Maintain and balance turntaking
2. (17) Wait, signal, and expect
3. (16) Match the child's behavior
4. (18) Imitate and animate
5. (26) Match child communication progressively
6. (27) Respond to the child
7. (32) Verbally match child experiences and communications
8. (33) Develop verbal topics
9. (38) Maintain balanced conversations
10. (39) Have social, friendly conversations with the child
11. (40) Direct child effectively

INTERACTIVE GOALS

1. (1) Becoming play partners
2. (10) Becoming turntaking partners
3. (19) Becoming communicating partners
4. (28) Becoming language partners
5. (34) Becoming conversation partners

PROBLEMS

1. (3) Directive, controlling style (adult)
2. (21) Mismatch (adult)
3. (12) Low interactive participation (child)
4. (20) Low communicative participation (child)
5. (29) Low verbal and pragmatic skills (child)
6. (11) Lack of active togetherness (interactive)
7. (2) Lack of playfulness (interactive)
8. (35) Poor conversations (interactive)

* *Final ECOScale item number.*

Matching relates to the findings that children are often more motivated to learn and pursue learning if the tasks are ones they can succeed at and feel competent about (Bruner, 1983; Girolometto, 1986; Hunt, 1961; MacDonald & Gillette, 1988; Mahoney, 1989; Vygotsky, 1962).

The third principle, *responsiveness*, relates to the degree to which adults sensitively respond to the child's social contacts, his preverbal actions and messages, and his linguistic messages (Cross, 1984, 1985; Mahoney, 1988; Snow, 1984).

The fourth principle, *nondirectiveness*, is based on the observation that children appear to learn most efficiently and become more interactive when they have freedom to initiate and respond from their own experiences and motivations (Goldberg, 1977; Mahoney, 1988). In the program, parents learn to reduce their directions and controls of the children by limiting questions, commands, and other adult-directed communications.

The final principle is *emotional attachment*. In order to help parents and others become natural reinforcers to children and motivate the children to become social, we taught parents to make interactions mutually enjoyable, that is, sources of competence rather than sources of unreasonable challenges.

Clinical Procedures

Prior to the treatment program, participants were videotaped three times over 2 months. This was during the control phase. The treatment program ran for 6 months with biweekly sessions of 1½ hours followed by three monthly posttreatment sessions. Each session was videotaped, and the videotaping was standardized to include a sample of people play (no toys), single-toy play, and multiple-toy play. Each session had four training components that served as guidelines for conducting the programs. An outline of a sample treatment session follows.

Professional Treatment Session Components

Each professional treatment session consisted of four components: assessment of parent and child, education and negotiation for a treatment plan, model feedback training, and home program training.

1. *Assessing parent and child* Each session began with a two-step assessment of the child and parent in terms of the previous session's treatment targets.

Step One:
Update

The parent provided a qualitative picture of interactions with the child in the home. The discussion enabled the professional to determine the parent's level of understanding of and attitudes toward the program goals. Parent and professional reviewed the home treatment records. They then discussed frequency and quality of home treatment and the appropriateness of the current child targets, adult strategies, and the play context prescribed.

Step Two:
Observation

During video recording, the professional directly observed the pair carrying out interactions on three activities: play without toys, play with one toy, and play with five toys available for interaction. This observation aided the professional in assessing the parent's use of training strategies and the status of the child's social and communicative goals.

2. *Education and negotiation for a treatment plan* Before deciding on a treatment plan, the professional educated parents to the rationale for the targets and

strategies selected. They discussed developmental information and the role of the parent's interaction style, in order to help the parent integrate the goals into her perceptions and roles with the child rather than use them only as discrete techniques. With this information the parents were in the position to negotiate the plan actively with the professional.

The professional and parent reviewed the assessment findings and negotiated a home treatment plan designed to reduce problems and achieve child goals. This prescription included selection of a priority problem, a child goal, and strategies for the parent. Conversation routines (the contexts for treatment) were also prescribed. Figure 9.1 shows an example of a treatment prescription for the priority problem of parent dominance. This problem occurs when the adult does and says more than the child, so that the child has little opportunity to participate or to practice his competencies.

Figure 9.1
Sample home treatment prescription

Priority problem: Parent dominance

Child goal: Frequent participation in action turntaking sequences 2–3 turns in length

Adult strategies:
1. Imitate the child.
2. Wait and signal for child's turn.
3. Communicate with gestures, sounds, single words.

Practice activities:

Direct:
1. People only play: exchange movement and sounds
2. People and things play: Pegboard

Daily routines:
1. Mealtime
2. Car

See *ECO Resources* (Gillette & MacDonald, 1989) for samples of conversation routines, IEPs and **ECO** Item Tutors used to instruct parents regarding each target and strategy.

3. *Model-Feedback Training* The professional and the parent then engaged in a series of demonstrations of the conversation routines to be carried out at home. The professional followed an agenda that involved practicing the direct training routines to be used in the home treatment and less structured activities meant to stimulate spontaneous and generalized learning in each activity. The professional demonstrated the targets or strategies with the child and focused on the strengths and limitations observed in the parent. The parent immediately repeated the activity with the child. After the parent practiced, the professional commented on her performance or provided additional models before proceeding to the next activity. This sequence allowed immediate refinement of the strategies as the practice moved from one activity to the next. This method provided the parent with demonstrations as well as opportunities to practice. Consequently, it did not depend on the parent understanding the professional's language. Depending on the

relative needs for education and practice, model-feedback training often accounted for the bulk of the training session.

4. *Planning Home Treatment* Home treatment was designed to establish new interactive habits between the parent and child. Each session ended with the professional and parent reviewing the prescription and negotiating any changes determined to be needed after the model-feedback training. The purpose of home training was not to place the parent into the role of teacher but to develop an interactive partnership between parent and child. The goal of this partnership was to provide the social context the child needed for learning to communicate.

Two types of interaction training were programmed: direct and spontaneous. Direct training involved brief (1- to 5-minute) joint play activities in which the parent practiced her strategies and built predictable social routines in which the child could develop his interactions first into communications, then into language and conversation. Spontaneous training involved contacting the child at least 10 times each day and engaging him in brief interactions appropriate to the moment. This was a critical part of home training because communicative development depends, in large part, on the habit of interacting during the natural course of the day. A general goal for spontaneous training was that the adult and child stay in increasingly longer interactions during incidental contacts.

In direct training sessions, the parent learned how spontaneous contacts provided the opportunity to incorporate those skills into making extended interaction a habit for the dyad. The parent was expected to chart ratings for targets, problems, and strategies and direct training activities. Spontaneous contacts were recorded once or twice per day on a special calendar provided for that purpose.

EXPERIMENTAL RATINGS AND INTERRATER RELIABILITY

In preparation for the study of parent-child interactions before and after **ECO** intervention, a study was made of the extent to which different raters agree on their ratings of *ECOScale* items. The reliability study consisted of three different phases: an initial training phase, a phase in which the trained raters were checked by a program developer in preparation for the experimental study, and a phase in which a program developer checked the trained raters' judgments of experimental data. All three phases used a method developed by Rosenberg and Robinson (1985) for calculating agreement. In this method, each point of discrepancy on the 9-point *ECOScales* is converted to 11% discrepancy. Thus, if one rater rated an item as 6 and another rater rated the item as 5, the level of agreement between the two is said to be 89% (100% minus 11%). To ensure an average discrepancy no larger than plus or minus 1 scale point, the investigators established 89% as the criterion at or above which they considered the rater to be reliable.

Initial Training to Criterion

To train to a criterion for interrater agreement established by the program developers, each rater rated at least 15 hours of videotaped interaction samples on one of the four *ECOScale* partnership scales (child goals, adult strategies, interactive goals, or problems). The ratings were compared with ratings made by a program developer. A rater was trained to criterion by observing an interaction sample, rating the sample on all of the items on one of the four partnership scales, observing the tape again, and revising scores as needed based on the second observation. Then the rater compared scores with a rating made by a trained rater. The two raters then discussed discrepancies based upon their clinical experience as well as the current relevant literature. The discussion continued until the two raters agreed upon a rating. Training continued until raters achieved a minimum of 89% agreement across a minimum of 10 training tapes.

Preexperimental Reliability

To compute interrater agreement on the *ECOScales* in preparation for the experimental study of **ECO** program treatment effects, raters also rated nine 3-minute videotaped samples of adult–child play. These samples were collected to represent the range of handicapped children commonly assessed with the *ECOScales* and to reflect a range of levels of effectiveness with the adult strategies. Each rater independently viewed each sample twice, rated the tape on one of the *ECOScales*, and viewed the sample again to allow revision of the original rating. This tape allowed a rater to demonstrate reliability on samples illustrating low, middle, and high values of the scale. The raters were considered trained when they independently achieved 89% agreement with the criterion ratings for the samples on the videotape. Tables 9.2 through 9.5 present the preexperimental percentage agreements for the raters by the criterion rater (one of the program developers) and two different raters.

Table 9.2 Percentage Agreement between a Criterion Rater and Two Raters on the Adult Strategies Items of the ECOScales in Preparation for an Experimental Study

Items	Rater 1	Rater 2
1. Maintain and balance turntaking	90.2	91.4
2. Wait, signal, and expect	90.2	89.0
3. Match child behavior	89.0	89.0
4. Imitate and animate	86.6	90.2
5. Match child progressively	93.9	86.6
6. Respond to the child	87.8	86.6
7. Verbally match child	95.1	86.6
8. Develop verbal topics	95.1	82.9
9. Maintain balanced conversations	86.6	80.4
10. Have social conversations	89.0	82.9
11. Direct child effectively	95.1	91.4
Average Reliability	90.7	87.0

$N = 9$

Table 9.3 Percentage Agreement between a Criterion Rater and Two Raters on the Child Goals Items of the ECOScales in Preparation for an Experimental Study

Items	Rater 1	Rater 2
1. Use actions functionally, meaningfully	93.9	93.9
2. Show a turntaking play style	91.8	86.3
3. Intentionally communicate	87.8	87.8
4. Communicate nonverbally	90.2	89.0
5. Communicate verbally	92.7	89.0
6. Make self understood	86.6	92.7
7. Use varied vocabulary	96.3	90.2
8. Follow grammatical rules	85.1	92.7
9. Converse for a variety of reasons	91.4	93.4
10. Stay in verbal conversations	93.9	92.7
Average Reliability	90.9	90.8

$N = 9$

Items	Rater 1	Rater 2
1. Becoming play partners	90.2	87.7
2. Becoming turntaking partners	94.3	84.1
3. Becoming communicating partners	87.7	86.5
4. Becoming language partners	87.7	82.8
5. Becoming conversational partners	93.8	92.6
Average Reliability	90.8	86.7
$N = 9$		

Items	Rater 1	Rater 2
ADULT		
1. Directive, controlling style	90.2	84.1
2. Mismatch	89.0	82.8
CHILD		
3. Low interactive participation	81.6	74.8
4. Low communicative participation	84.1	75.5
5. Low verbal and pragmatic skills	81.6	76.6
INTERACTIVE		
6. Lack of active togetherness	90.2	84.1
7. Lack of playfulness	89.0	85.3
8. Poor conversations	84.1	78.0
Average Reliability	86.2	80.6
$N = 9$		

Experimental Reliability

To maintain an acceptable level of interrater reliability throughout the experimental study of **ECO** treatment effects, one of the program developers rated more than 25% of the 115 four-minute videos and compared ratings with the ratings made by the judges. The same method of viewing and rating described for the preexperimental phase was used for the experimental phase. That is, two judges rated the experimental tapes, which involved dyads not rated in the preexperimental tapes. Tables 9.6 through 9.9 present the percentage of agreement between the ratings of the experimental samples by the program developer and each of the two raters participating.

To control for possible rater bias resulting from expectations of progress over time, the experimental procedure included randomizing samples of the videotaped interactions prior to rating. Each sample ran 4 minutes and consisted of the second through fifth minutes from a 5-minute interaction. A rater observed the sample, rated the sample on the scale items, observed the sample again, and revised scores as needed. The two raters measured reliability by rating 25% of the experimental tapes and computing percentage of agreement between their ratings. The results of the study are described in the validity section of this chapter.

Items	Rater 1	Rater 2
1. Maintain and balance turntaking	89.1	87.2
2. Wait, signal, and expect	90.4	88.2
3. Match child behavior	86.3	89.8
4. Imitate and animate	84.9	88.2
5. Match child progressively	93.8	89.0
6. Respond to the child	87.6	89.0
7. Verbally match child	89.0	86.5
8. Develop verbal topics	89.0	89.0
9. Maintain balanced conversations	88.3	92.4
10. Have social conversations	88.3	85.6
11. Direct child effectively	89.0	88.2
Average Reliability	88.7	88.5

$N = 29$

Items	Rater 1	Rater 2
1. Use actions functionally, meaningfully	95.6	90.7
2. Show a turntaking play style	86.8	90.1
3. Intentionally communicate	91.2	92.9
4. Communicate nonverbally	90.1	89.0
5. Communicate verbally	90.1	96.7
6. Make self understood	94.5	95.6
7. Use varied vocabulary	91.2	97.3
8. Follow grammatical rules	95.6	89.0
9. Converse for a variety of reasons	97.8	96.7
10. Stay in verbal conversations	97.8	96.2
Average Reliability	93.1	93.4

$N = 30$

Items	Rater 1	Rater 2
1. Becoming play partners	91.4	92.2
2. Becoming turntaking partners	92.1	85.0
3. Becoming communicating partners	84.7	97.4
4. Becoming language partners	89.6	94.1
5. Becoming conversational partners	93.2	96.7
Average Reliability	90.2	93.1

$N = 35$

Table 9.9
Percentage
Agreement
between a
Criterion Rater
and Two Raters
on the Problems
Items of the
ECOScales in an
Experimental
Study of ECO
Treatment Effects

Items	Rater 1	Rater 2
ADULT		
1. Directive, controlling style	87.7	93.2
2. Mismatch	89.0	91.7
CHILD		
3. Low interactive participation	86.9	87.2
4. Low communicative participation	91.3	91.1
5. Low verbal and pragmatic skills	90.8	96.1
INTERACTIVE		
6. Lack of active togetherness	90.2	89.6
7. Lack of playfulness	90.6	88.3
8. Poor conversations	91.5	92.0
Average Reliability	89.8	91.2

$N = 35$

CLINICAL JUDGMENTS OF PARENT-CHILD INTERACTIONS BEFORE AND AFTER ECO INTERVENTION

The effectiveness of the **ECO** model for developing child goals and adult strategies together was studied by using the *ECOScales* to rate videotaped interaction samples of parent-child pairs over a period of several months. A total of 25 dyads were involved in the study. The children ranged in age from 23 to 64 months at the time of the first sample, with a median age of 38 months. Twelve of the 25 children were diagnosed as having Down syndrome, 4 others were diagnosed as autistic, 4 others as severely retarded. Of the remainder, 4 were language delayed with no diagnosis of retardation, and 1 was deaf with spina bifida. Based on assessments with the Receptive-Expressive Language Scale (REEL) (Bzoch-League, 1970) and the Adaptive Behavior Scales for Infants (ABSI) (Leland, Shoaee, McElwain, & Christie, 1980), all children displayed a delay of at least one year in communication and at least one other area of development.

The adults in all cases were parents, and they represented a relatively broad spectrum of socioeconomic levels and backgrounds. In all but one case, the mother was the participant in the program. Of these 25 mothers, 18 were primarily homemakers or homemakers who also did some work outside the home (one a librarian and one a nurse). The remaining mothers included an office worker, a computer specialist, a business executive, two nurses, a mail clerk, a bank teller, and a teacher's aide. The only father in this group was a physician.

The design of the study called for rating five samples of parent–child interaction videotaped on five separate occasions over a period of 8 months. The occasions of the videotaping corresponded to five key points in the program of **ECO** assessment and treatment:

1. One month before treatment began;
2. The day treatment started but before any recommendations were made;
3. Three months after the beginning of the program;
4. The end of the program, 6 months after it had begun;
5. One month after the program ended.

On each occasion, a total of five play sessions were videotaped, each with a different toy. The rated samples were all drawn from the second of the five play sessions and consisted of the second through the fifth minutes. The first session was eliminated to allow the dyad time to adapt to the setting.

Each of the selected videotaped samples was rated on 34 of the final 40 *ECOScale* items (6 more items were added after the study was underway). The same rater rated all samples for a particular *ECOScale* item, though different raters were assigned to different groups of *ECOScale* items. Thus, several different raters were used in the study but only one rater rated any given item. All raters used the 9-point scale consistently used with the *ECOScales* (MacDonald & Gillette, 1989); see table 9.10 for a description of the scale values.

Table 9.10
Scale Values and Definitions Used to Rate Subject Pairs

Scale Values for Child Goals, Adult Strategies, and Interaction Goals: 1–2 = low; 3–4 = low–mid; 5 = mid; 6–7 = high–mid; 8–9 = high; "N" = Does not apply

1–2 LOW:	Quality of the skill is poor; there is no evidence of a habit beginning. The quantity and duration of the examples are negligible or inappropriate.
3–4 LOW-MID:	Quality of the skill is weak but there is a little evidence of a habit beginning. There are few examples or they are of fleeting duration. Quantity and duration of the examples are seldom appropriate.
5 MID:	Quality of the skill is fair and there is evidence of a habit emerging. There are occasional examples or they are of brief duration. Quantity and duration of the examples are approaching an appropriate level.
6-7 HIGH-MID:	Quality of the skill is good and appears to be a stable habit. There are many examples or the duration is adequate. Quantity and duration of the examples are almost appropriate.
8-9 HIGH:	Quality of the skill is outstanding and involves creative use. Quantity and duration of the examples are appropriate.
"N"	Use "N" when you feel the descriptor does not apply to the dyad you have viewed.

Scale Values for Problems: 1-2 = low; 3-4 = low-mid; 5 = mid; 6-7 = high-mid; 8-9 = high; "N" = does not apply

1-2 LOW:	The problem is major and the quantity or duration of the examples indicates that the problem is a habit.
3-4 LOW-MID:	The problem is serious and the quantity or duration of the examples indicates that the problem is almost habitual.
5 MID:	The problem is moderate and the quantity or duration of the examples indicates that it is becoming a habit.
6-7 HIGH-MID:	The problem is mild and the quantity or duration of the examples indicates that it is a weak habit.
8-9 HIGH:	The problem is almost nonexistent as indicated by the quantity and duration of the examples.
"N"	Use "N" when you feel the descriptor does not apply to the dyad you have viewed.

Before rating the samples in this study, each rater was trained on separate 3-minute videotaped samples of other dyads, with a criterion of 88% agreement between the rater and one of the program developers, who acted as the criterion rater. To control for effects related to expectations about the benefits of treatment, the order of presentation of the five samples for each dyad was randomized. Thus, for any given observation, the rater did not know if he or she was observing the first, second, third, fourth, or fifth of the five.

As noted above, all five samples were rated on a total of 34 of the final 40 *ECOScale* items. As Table 9.11 illustrates, these 34 items represented 10 child goals, 11 adult strategies, 8 interactive problems, and 5 major interactive goals (Social Play, Turn-taking, Preverbal and Nonverbal Communication, Language, and Conversation) that represent the five sets of **ECO** competencies. All of these are discussed in detail in chapters 4 through 8 of this book. The component behaviors for each competency are discussed there and listed in the *ECOScales*, raters used the components to determine their ratings.

CHILD GOALS

1. (14) Use actions in functional and meaningful ways
2. (13) Show a turntaking play style
3. (22) Intentionally communicate with others
4. (23) Communicate nonverbally
5. (24) Begin to communicate verbally
6. (25) Make self understood
7. (30) Use varied vocabulary
8. (31) Follow grammatical rules
9. (36) Converse for a variety of reasons
10. (37) Stay in verbal conversations

ADULT STRATEGIES

1. (15) Maintain and balance turntaking
2. (17) Wait, signal, and expect
3. (16) Match the child's behavior
4. (18) Imitate and animate
5. (26) Match child communication progressively
6. (27) Respond to the child
7. (32) Verbally match child experiences and communications
8. (33) Develop verbal topics
9. (38) Maintain balanced conversations
10. (39) Have social, friendly conversations with the child
11. (40) Direct child effectively

INTERACTIVE GOALS

1. (1) Becoming play partners
2. (10) Becoming turntaking partners
3. (19) Becoming communicating partners
4. (28) Becoming language partners
5. (34) Becoming conversation partners

PROBLEMS (primary focus)

1. (3) Directive, controlling style (adult)
2. (21) Mismatch (adult)
3. (12) Low interactive participation (child)
4. (20) Low communicative participation (child)
5. (29) Low verbal and pragmatic skills (child)
6. (11) Lack of active togetherness (interactive)
7. (2) Lack of playfulness (interactive)
8. (35) Poor conversations (interactive)

Tables 9.12, 9.13, and 9.14 present information that seems especially important to an analysis of the differences in ratings related to **ECO** treatment. Table 9.12 presents data taken at Occasions 1 and 2, the first and second samples, both taken before treatment began. Table 9.13 data were taken at Occasions 2 and 4, the second and fourth samples, taken immediately before treatment began and immediately after it concluded 6 months later. Table 9.14 data were taken at Occasions 1 and 5, the first and fifth samples, taken before treatment and 1 month after treatment ended.

Table 9.12 presents, among other data, the mean scores from Occasions 1 and 2 (the control phase) for each *ECOScale* item rated, the difference between the means for each set, and the results of a *t* test for related samples to determine if the differences were significantly different from zero. As the data in table 9.11 show, differences for Occasions 1-2 (mean of Occasion 2 minus mean of Occasion 1) were generally not significant. Thus, neither the children nor the parents changed significantly across the two pretreatment video samples on any of the 34 measures related to the treatment program. In contrast, differences for Occasions 2-4, reported in table 9.13, were significant for all items except one, most beyond the .001 level. Differences for occasions 4–5, reported in table 9.14, were generally not significant for any items except one (only two adult strategies showed significant differences, and those both reflected lower ratings for Occasion 5 than for Occasion 4). In other words, as groups, the children and parents changed their social and communicative behaviors positively during the time of the treatment program and remained relatively stable during the first month following the conclusion of the 6-month treatment program.

Although the ratings of all the adult strategies diminished at least minimally during the month after treatment ended, the ratings of Occasion 5 show that more child goals were rated higher than were rated lower. Viewed together, these somewhat conflicting patterns may actually be more encouraging than not. At least they seem to suggest that once children become more communicative they do not necessarily regress, even when their parents are unable to remain completely consistent in applying their newly learned adult strategies. Of course, these data imply a need for continued involvement by the professional, not only to monitor the results of treatment but also to continue to provide, support guidance, and feedback to parents.

Tables 9.15 through 9.17 report data on summaries of the ratings for items for each pair of occasions compared in tables 9.12 through 9.14. Since the *ECOScales* item ratings can be summed to produce a set of **ECO** Competencies scales or a set of **ECO** Interaction scales, both are reported in tables 9.15 through 9.17. To provide a picture of these scales, figures 9.2 through 9.7 illustrate the changes in ratings for the Interaction scales and Competencies scales for all three of the occasions compared. Finally, to illustrate the change in specific items across the treatment period, figures 9.8 through 9.11 show the changes in individual *ECOScales* items reported in table 9.12. The items are organized in the figure as they are in the table: by Child Goals (figure 9.8), Adult Strategies (9.9), Interactive Goals (9.10), and Problems (9.11).

Table 9.12
Ratings on
ECOScale Items
Observed at
Occasions 1 and
2 (Before ECO
Treatment) with t
tests and Effect
Sizes (largest
n = 25 dyads)

	Occasion 1		Occasion 2		Difference		(Occasion 2 Minus 1)		Effect
Child Goals	M	SD	M	SD	M	SD	t	p ‹	Size
1. (14) Use actions function- ally, meaningfully	3.88	1.05	4.12	1.27	0.24	0.93	1.30	0.21 NS	0.21
2. (13) Show a turntaking play style	2.92	1.32	3.08	1.41	0.16	1.18	0.68	0.50 NS	0.12
3. (22) Intentionally communi- cate with others	3.60	1.19	3.76	1.20	0.16	0.94	0.85	0.40 NS	0.13
4. (23) Communicate nonverbally	2.52	0.71	2.40	1.00	−0.12	0.93	−0.65	0.52 NS	−0.14
5. (24) Communicate verbally	2.10	1.30	2.33	1.39	0.24	0.89	1.23	0.23 NS	0.18
6. (25) Make self understood	2.52	1.03	2.67	1.02	0.14	0.79	0.83	0.42 NS	0.14
7. (30) Use varied vocabulary	1.76	1.09	1.90	1.04	0.14	0.91	0.72	0.48 NS	0.13
8. (31) Follow grammatical rules	1.33	0.73	1.29	0.56	−0.05	0.67	−0.33	0.75 NS	−0.07
9. (36) Converse for a variety of reasons	1.81	1.25	1.71	0.96	−0.10	0.62	−0.70	0.49 NS	−0.09
10. (37) Stay in verbal conversations	1.38	1.07	1.43	0.81	0.05	0.50	0.44	0.67 NS	0.05
Adult Strategies									
1. (15) Maintain and balance turntaking	3.21	1.38	3.04	1.12	−0.17	1.31	−0.62	0.54 NS	−0.13
2. (17) Wait, signal, and expect	3.08	1.41	2.92	1.28	−0.17	1.09	−0.75	0.46 NS	−0.13
3. (16) Match child behavior	3.08	1.59	3.04	1.23	−0.04	1.30	−0.16	0.88 NS	−0.03
4. (18) Imitate and animate	3.46	1.44	3.17	1.24	−0.29	1.43	−1.00	0.33 NS	−0.22
5. (26) Match child communi- cation progressively	2.83	1.49	2.63	1.24	−0.21	1.25	−0.82	0.42 NS	−0.15
6. (27) Respond to child	3.83	1.40	3.42	1.35	−0.42	1.64	−1.24	0.23 NS	−0.30
7. (32) Verbally match child communications	2.96	1.16	2.75	1.39	−0.21	1.32	−0.77	0.45 NS	−0.16
8. (33) Develop verbal topics	2.83	1.37	2.42	1.25	−0.42	1.50	−1.36	0.19 NS	−0.32
9. (38) Maintain balanced conversation	2.75	1.33	2.67	1.40	−0.08	1.41	−0.29	0.78 NS	−0.06
10. (39) Have social, friendly conversations	3.04	1.49	2.83	1.34	−0.21	1.44	−0.71	0.49 NS	−0.15
11. (40) Direct the child effectively	3.92	1.91	3.67	1.79	−0.25	1.89	−0.65	0.52 NS	−0.14
Interactive Goals									
1. (1) Becoming play partners	3.80	0.96	3.72	1.06	−0.08	1.22	−0.33	0.75 NS	−0.08
2. (10) Becoming turntaking partners	3.08	0.86	3.08	1.04	0.00	1.15	0.00	1.00 NS	0.00
3. (19) Becoming com- municating partners	2.56	0.96	2.56	0.87	0.00	0.91	0.00	1.00 NS	0.00
4. (28) Becoming language partners	1.72	0.94	1.84	0.80	0.12	0.83	0.72	0.48 NS	0.14
5. (34) Becoming conversation partners	1.40	0.76	1.44	0.58	0.04	0.68	0.30	0.77 NS	0.06
Interactive Problems (primary focus)									
1. (3) Directive, controlling style (adult)	4.44	1.71	4.24	1.48	−0.20	2.04	−0.49	0.63 NS	−0.13
2. (21) Mismatch (adult)	3.84	1.31	4.08	1.29	0.24	1.61	0.74	0.46 NS	0.18
3. (12) Low interactive par- ticipation (child)	4.48	1.45	4.20	1.44	−0.28	1.46	−0.96	0.35 NS	−0.19
4. (20) Low communicative participation (child)	3.72	1.59	3.68	1.52	−0.04	1.43	−0.14	0.89 NS	−0.03
5. (29) Low verbal, pragmatic skills (child)	1.68	0.90	1.92	0.86	0.24	1.05	1.14	0.27 NS	0.27
6. (11) Lack of active togetherness (child/adult)	3.60	1.35	3.68	1.14	0.08	1.50	0.27	0.79 NS	0.06
7. (2) Lack of playfulness (child/adult)	4.92	1.55	4.64	1.55	−0.28	1.84	−0.76	0.45 NS	−0.18
8. (35) Poor conversations (child/adult)	1.56	0.71	1.88	1.20	0.32	1.38	1.16	0.26 NS	0.32

Table 9.13
Ratings on ECOScale Items Observed at Occasions 2 and 4 (Before and After ECO Treatment) with t tests and Effect Sizes (largest n = 25 dyads)

	Occasion 2		Occasion 4		Difference		(Occasion 4 Minus 2)		Effect
	M	SD	M	SD	M	SD	t	p <	Size
Child Goals									
1. (14) Use actions functionally, meaningfully	4.12	1.27	4.84	1.03	0.72	1.10	3.27	0.01	0.62
2. (13) Show a turntaking play style	3.08	1.41	5.04	1.54	1.96	1.57	6.25	0.001	1.33
3. (22) Intentionally communicate with others	3.76	1.20	5.28	1.57	1.52	1.26	6.02	0.001	1.09
4. (23) Communicate nonverbally	2.40	1.00	3.32	1.03	0.92	0.86	5.34	0.001	0.91
5. (24) Communicate verbally	2.32	1.36	3.41	2.02	1.09	1.23	4.16	0.001	0.63
6. (25) Make self understood	2.64	1.00	3.45	1.34	0.82	1.05	3.65	0.01	0.69
7. (30) Use varied vocabulary	1.86	1.04	2.73	1.88	0.86	1.32	3.07	0.01	0.57
8. (31) Follow grammatical rules	1.27	0.55	1.82	1.01	0.55	0.80	3.20	0.01	0.67
9. (36) Converse for a variety of reasons	1.68	0.95	3.00	1.88	1.32	1.49	4.14	0.01	0.89
10. (37) Stay in verbal conversations	1.41	0.80	2.50	2.11	1.09	1.93	2.66	0.05	0.68
Adult Strategies									
1. (15) Maintain and balance turntaking	3.04	1.12	6.46	1.47	3.42	1.67	10.05	0.001	2.61
2. (17) Wait, signal, and expect	2.92	1.28	6.38	1.66	3.46	1.84	9.20	0.001	2.33
3. (16) Match child behavior	3.04	1.23	6.42	1.50	3.38	2.00	8.28	0.001	2.46
4. (17) Imitate and animate	3.17	1.24	6.54	1.77	3.38	1.47	11.26	0.001	2.21
5. (26) Match child communication progressively	2.63	1.24	6.25	1.59	3.63	2.04	8.71	0.001	2.53
6. (27) Respond to child	3.42	1.35	6.42	1.69·	3.00	1.96	7.51	0.001	1.96
7. (32) Verbally match child communications	2.75	1.39	5.79	1.67	3.04	2.05	7.26	0.001	1.98
8. (33) Develop verbal topics	2.42	1.25	5.67	1.58	3.25	2.03	7.85	0.001	2.28
9. (38) Maintain balanced conversation	2.67	1.40	6.21	1.50	3.54	1.89	9.19	0.001	2.44
10. (39) Have social, friendly conversations	2.83	1.34	6.58	1.47	3.75	1.65	11.14	0.001	2.66
11. (40) Direct the child effectively	3.67	1.79	7.58	1.14	3.92	2.28	8.41	0.001	2.62
Interactive Goals									
1. (1) Becoming play partners	3.72	1.06	6.08	1.35	2.36	1.38	8.55	0.001	1.94
2. (10) Becoming turntaking partners	3.08	1.04	5.00	1.55	1.92	1.53	6.29	0.001	1.45
3. (19) Becoming communicating partners	2.56	0.87	4.12	1.74	1.56	1.66	4.70	0.001	1.13
4. (28) Becoming language partners	1.84	0.80	2.80	1.76	0.96	1.62	2.96	0.01	0.70
5. (34) Becoming conversation partners	1.44	0.58	2.16	1.40	0.72	1.37	2.63	0.05	0.67
Interactive Problems (primary focus)									
1. (3) Directive, controlling style (adult)	4.24	1.48	6.88	1.24	2.64	1.91	6.90	0.001	1.94
2. (21) Mismatch (adult)	4.08	1.29	6.60	1.15	2.52	1.66	7.58	0.001	2.06
3. (12) Low interactive participation (child)	4.20	1.44	5.76	1.56	1.56	1.85	4.22	0.001	1.04
4. (20) Low communicative participation (child)	3.68	1.52	4.96	1.99	1.28	1.77	3.62	0.01	0.72
5. (29) Low verbal, pragmatic skills (child)	1.92	0.86	2.84	1.93	0.92	1.73	2.66	0.05	0.62
6. (11) Lack of active togetherness (child/adult)	3.68	1.14	6.00	1.53	2.32	1.65	7.02	0.001	1.72
7. (2) Lack of playfulness (child/adult)	4.64	1.55	6.68	1.80	2.04	2.07	4.92	0.001	1.22
8. (35) Poor conversations (child/adult)	1.71	0.86	2.25	1.54	0.54	1.59	1.67	0.11 ns	0.43

Table 9.14
Ratings on
ECOScale
Items Observed
at Occasions 4
and 5 (After
ECO Treatment)
with t tests and
Effect Sizes
(largest
n = 25 dyads)

| | Occasion 4 | | Occasion 5 | | Difference | | (Occasion 5 Minus 4) | | Effect |
	M	SD	M	SD	M	SD	t	p ⟨	Size
Child Goals									
1. (14) Use actions functionally, meaningfully	4.86	1.06	5.19	1.33	0.33	1.02	1.50	0.15ns	0.28
2. (13) Show a turntaking play style	4.95	1.50	5.05	1.32	0.10	1.34	0.33	0.75ns	0.07
3. (22) Intentionally communicate with others	5.14	1.53	5.19	1.36	0.05	1.36	0.16	0.87ns	0.03
4. (23) Communicate nonverbally	3.24	0.94	3.52	1.21	0.29	1.23	1.06	0.30ns	0.26
5. (24) Communicate verbally	3.16	1.98	3.11	1.66	−0.05	1.43	−0.16	0.87ns	−0.03
6. (25) Make self understood	3.37	1.38	3.26	0.93	−0.11	1.15	−0.40	0.69ns	−0.09
7. (30) Use varied vocabulary	2.63	1.89	2.42	1.35	−0.21	1.08	−0.85	0.41ns	−0.13
8. (31) Follow grammatical rules	1.74	0.99	1.89	1.37	0.16	0.96	0.72	0.48ns	0.13
9. (36) Converse for a variety of reasons	2.63	1.71	2.79	1.44	0.16	1.17	0.59	0.56ns	0.10
10. (37) Stay in verbal conversations	2.16	1.89	2.05	1.68	−0.11	0.94	−0.49	0.63ns	−0.06
Adult Strategies									
1. (15) Maintain and balance turntaking	6.53	1.17	6.11	1.24	−0.42	1.57	−1.17	0.26ns	−0.35
2. (17) Wait, signal, and expect	6.37	1.34	5.95	1.39	−0.42	1.77	−1.03	0.31ns	−0.31
3. (16) Match child behavior	6.42	1.22	5.95	1.27	−0.47	1.47	−1.41	0.18ns	−0.38
4. (18) Imitate and animate	6.53	1.50	5.68	1.53	−0.84	1.71	−2.15	0.05	−0.56
5. (26) Match child communication progressively	6.32	1.25	5.74	1.41	−0.58	1.68	−1.50	0.15ns	−0.43
6. (27) Respond to child	6.58	1.54	6.00	1.53	−0.58	1.77	−1.42	0.17ns	−0.38
7. (32) Verbally match child communications	6.00	1.63	5.68	1.49	−0.32	1.53	−0.90	0.38ns	−0.20
8. (33) Develop verbal topics	5.68	1.38	5.37	1.30	−0.32	1.67	−0.83	0.42ns	−0.24
9. (38) Maintain balanced conversation	6.21	1.23	5.84	1.30	−0.37	1.16	−1.38	0.18ns	−0.29
10. (39) Have social, friendly conversations	6.63	1.26	6.11	1.10	−0.53	1.12	−2.04	0.06ns	−0.45
11. (40) Direct the child effectively	7.37	1.16	6.63	1.26	−0.74	1.52	−2.11	0.05	−0.61
Interactive Goals									
1. (1) Becoming play partners	5.89	1.37	5.79	1.27	−0.11	1.49	−0.31	0.76ns	−0.08
2. (10) Becoming turntaking partners	4.74	1.37	5.05	1.51	0.32	1.16	1.19	0.25ns	0.22
3. (19) Becoming communicating partners	3.74	1.56	4.00	1.45	0.26	1.41	0.81	0.43ns	0.17
4. (28) Becoming language partners	2.32	1.45	2.47	1.47	0.16	1.12	0.62	0.55ns	0.11
5. (34) Becoming conversation partners	1.79	1.03	1.89	1.37	0.11	0.94	0.49	0.63ns	0.09
Interactive Problems (primary focus)									
1. (3) Directive, controlling style (adult)	6.68	1.34	6.42	1.12	−0.26	1.56	−0.74	0.47ns	−0.21
2. (21) Mismatch (adult)	6.47	1.17	6.32	1.06	−0.16	1.30	−0.53	0.60ns	−0.14
3. (12) Low interactive participation (child)	5.53	1.43	5.47	1.43	−0.05	1.47	−0.16	0.88ns	−0.04
4. (20) Low communicative participation (child)	4.74	2.00	4.79	1.93	0.05	1.93	0.12	0.91ns	0.03
5. (29) Low verbal, pragmatic skills (child)	2.42	1.35	2.37	1.50	−0.05	1.13	−0.20	0.84ns	−0.04
6. (11) Lack of active togetherness (child/adult)	5.68	1.29	5.63	1.42	−0.05	1.47	−0.16	0.88ns	−0.04
7. (2) Lack of playfulness (child/adult)	6.53	1.84	6.32	1.57	−0.21	1.55	−0.59	0.56ns	−0.12
8. (35) Poor conversations (child/adult)	1.94	1.06	2.06	1.35	0.11	0.90	0.52	0.61ns	0.09

Table 9.15
Ratings on ECO
Competencies
and Interaction
Scales Observed
at Occasions 1
and 2 (Before
ECO Treatment)
with t tests and
Effect Sizes
(largest
n = 25 dyads)

	Pretreatment		Posttreatment		Difference		(Post Minus Pre)		Effect
	M	SD	M	SD	M	SD	t	p <	Size
Child Goals	23.86	9.14	24.62	8.19	0.76	4.67	0.75	0.46 NS	0.09
Adult Strategies	35.00	14.16	32.54	12.62	−2.46	12.35	−0.98	0.34 NS	−0.18
Interactive Goals	12.56	3.62	12.64	3.63	0.08	3.34	0.12	0.91 NS	0.02
Interactive Problems	28.24	7.80	28.32	7.13	0.08	7.74	0.05	0.96 NS	0.01
Play Items	13.16	3.65	12.60	3.38	−0.56	4.21	−0.66	0.51 NS	−0.16
Turntaking Items	30.67	9.23	30.29	8.27	−0.38	7.72	−0.24	0.81 NS	−0.04
Communication Items	28.14	8.14	28.00	7.46	−0.14	5.64	−0.12	0.91 NS	−0.02
Language Items	12.57	4.32	12.43	4.33	−0.14	4.07	−0.16	0.87 NS	−0.03
Conversation Items	16.14	6.02	16.33	4.90	0.19	4.39	0.20	0.84 NS	0.03

Table 9.16
Ratings on ECO
Competencies
and Interaction
Scales Observed
at Occasions 2
and 4 (Before
and After ECO
Treatment) with t
tests and Effect
Sizes (largest
n = 25 dyads)

	Pretreatment		Posttreatment		Difference		(Post Minus Pre)		Effect
	M	SD	M	SD	M	SD	t	p <	Size
Child Goals	24.45	8.03	35.64	13.07	11.18	9.33	5.62	0.001	1.03
Adult Strategies	32.54	12.62	70.29	15.17	37.75	18.38	10.06	0.001	2.71
Interactive Goals	12.64	3.63	20.16	7.18	7.52	6.42	5.85	0.001	1.32
Interactive Problems	28.21	7.26	41.33	8.07	13.13	8.62	7.46	0.001	1.71
Play Items	12.60	3.38	19.64	3.56	7.04	4.14	8.51	0.001	2.03
Turntaking Items	30.29	8.27	52.46	11.36	22.17	10.96	9.91	0.001	2.23
Communication Items	28.00	7.46	43.76	10.98	15.76	9.29	7.77	0.001	1.68
Language Items	12.43	4.33	22.14	8.13	9.71	7.38	6.03	0.001	1.49
Conversation Items	16.35	5.03	30.25	7.62	13.90	8.49	7.32	0.001	2.15

Table 9.17
Ratings on ECO
Competencies
and Interaction
Scales Observed
at Occasions 4
and 5 (After ECO
Treatment) with t
tests and Effect
Sizes (largest
n = 25 dyads)

	Pretreatment		Posttreatment		Difference		(Post Minus Pre)		Effect
	M	SD	M	SD	M	SD	t	p <	Size
Child Goals	34.11	12.34	34.89	10.53	0.79	8.82	0.39	0.70	0.07
Adult Strategies	70.63	12.59	65.05	13.02	−5.58	15.00	−1.62	0.12	−0.44
Interactive Goals	18.47	5.98	19.21	6.36	0.74	4.64	0.69	0.50	0.12
Interactive Problems	40.56	7.41	39.72	8.41	−0.83	7.41	−0.48	0.64	−0.11
Play Items	19.11	3.68	18.53	3.29	−0.58	3.66	−0.69	0.50	−0.17
Turntaking Items	51.61	9.10	50.28	9.49	−1.33	9.51	−0.59	0.56	−0.14
Communication Items	43.19	8.66	43.94	7.29	0.75	9.06	0.33	0.75	0.09
Language Items	21.19	5.80	21.19	6.75	0.00	5.54	0.00	1.00	0.00
Conversation Items	29.33	6.22	28.80	5.45	−0.53	6.19	−0.33	0.74	0.09

The pattern of changes in *ECOScale* items across the five competencies scales (Play, Turntaking, Communication, Language, and Conversation) and the four interaction scales (Child Goals, Adult Strategies, Interactive Goals, and Problems) are noteworthy. Because the Interaction scales and the Competencies scales are simply different classifications of the same *ECOScales* items, these figures reflect patterns of increase for the Competencies scales that are highly similar to those found for the Interaction scales. Much of the positive change across all the competencies can be explained by the large increases in the ratings of the Adult Strategies items in each competencies scale. Although *t*-test results reported in table 9.13 reveal significant differences for both child and adult performances from pretreatment to posttreatment, figures 9.8 and 9.9 illustrate that parents were judged as making greater changes than the children. Indeed, on average the raters' post-treatment ratings of the adult strategies were more than double their pretreatment ratings. Nevertheless, the ratings on the Child Goals items were all positive. And although changes in Child Goals were highest on Turntaking and Communication items, there were increases in the Child Goals items in the Language and Conversation competencies.

Although results of t tests and their associated significance levels are helpful to researchers, they communicate little to average parents or teachers. Furthermore, the fact that a given difference between two means is statistically significant tells no one, not even the researcher, about the prevalence of such differences in everyday life. Thus, the presence of a statistically significant difference does not necessarily guarantee that the difference is meaningful in any practical way. (On the other hand, differences obtained in small-sample studies often lack statistical significance due to sample size and would be both meaningful and significant if obtained for a larger sample. This was not the case in this study, in spite of the relatively small number of pairs rated. In fact, nearly all of the differences between pretreatment and posttreatment were statistically significant.)

As figure 9.2 shows, the raters judged that the child goals, adult strategies, interactive goals, and problems changed minimally before the treatment began. The general lack of change in ratings from Occasion 1 to Occasion 2 suggests how stable parent–child interactions can be when the child has a history of communication delay (the reason all the pairs were referred to the **ECO** project). Figure 9.3 illustrates the changes in ratings from pretreatment (Occasion 2) to posttreatment (Occasion 4), showing that judges evaluated the adults and children higher on all scales. Figure 9.4 shows that the raters judged the child goals, adult strategies, interactive goals, and problems to remain relatively stable after the treatment began. Figures 9.5 through 9.7 illustrate the same changes when the items are organized as Competencies scales (Play, Turntaking, Communication, Language, and Conversation).

Figure 9.2
Change in Ratings on ECO Interaction Scales Before Treatment (Occasions 1 and 2)

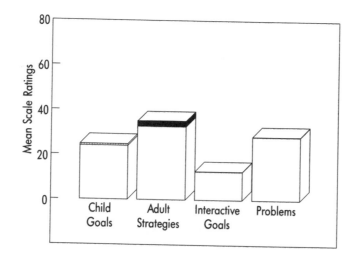
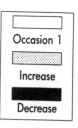

Figure 9.3
*Change in
Ratings on ECO
Interaction
Scales During
Treatment
(Occasions 2
and 4)*

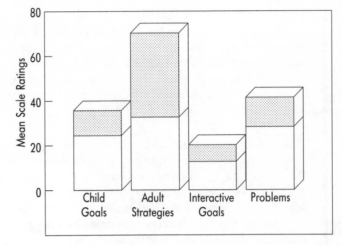

Figure 9.4
*Change in
Ratings on ECO
Interaction
Scales After
Treatment
(Occasions 4
and 5)*

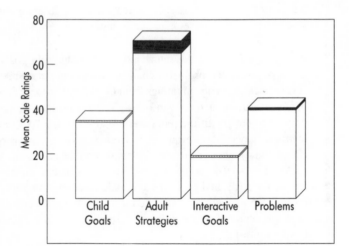

Figure 9.5
*Change in
Ratings on ECO
Competencies
Scales Before
Treatment
(Occasions 1
and 2)*

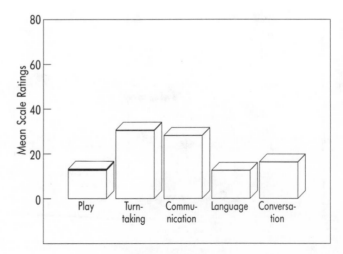
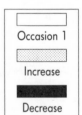

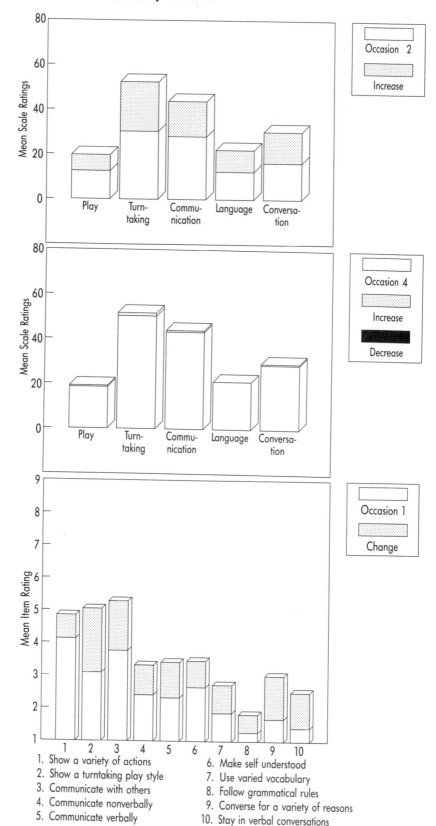

Figure 9.6
Change in Ratings on ECO Competencies Scales During Treatment (Occasions 2 and 4)

Figure 9.7
Change in Ratings on ECO Competencies Scales After Treatment (Occasions 4 and 5)

Figure 9.8
Change in Ratings on ECO Child Goals Items During Treatment (Occasions 2 and 4)

1. Show a variety of actions
2. Show a turntaking play style
3. Communicate with others
4. Communicate nonverbally
5. Communicate verbally
6. Make self understood
7. Use varied vocabulary
8. Follow grammatical rules
9. Converse for a variety of reasons
10. Stay in verbal conversations

Figure 9.9
Change in Ratings on ECO Adult Strategies Items During Treatment (Occasions 2 and 4)

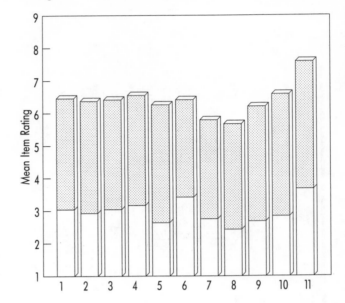

1. Maintain and balance turntaking
2. Wait, signal, and expect
3. Match child behavior
4. Imitate and animate
5. Match child behavior progressively
6. Respond to child

7. Verbal match of child communications
8. Develop verbal topics
9. Maintain balanced conversation
10. Have social, friendly conversation
11. Direct the child effectively

Figure 9.10
Change in Ratings on ECO Interaction Goals During Treatment (Occasions 2 and 4)

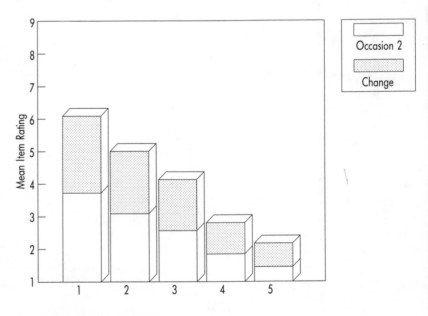

1. Becoming play partners
2. Becoming turntaking partners
3. Becoming communication partners
4. Becoming language partners
5. Becoming conversation partners

Figure 9.11
Change in
Ratings on ECO
Problems Items
During Treatment
(Occasions 2
and 4)

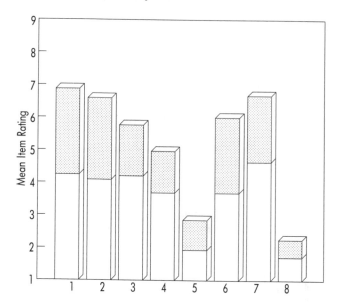

1. Directive, controlling style
2. Mismatch
3. Low interactive participation
4. Low communicative participation

5. Low verbal participation
6. Lack of active togetherness
7. Lack of playfulness
8. Poor conversations

To help in interpreting the differences in *ECOScale* ratings reported in tables 9.12 to 9.17, each difference is also expressed as an *effect size*, which represents the difference between the two ratings for an item or scale divided by the common variance for the two ratings. (For example, in table 9.12, the effect size for "Show a variety of actions" was computed by subtracting the Occasion 1 rating for the item from the Occasion 2 rating for the item and dividing the result by the square root of the average of the squared standard deviations for the two occasions.) An advantage of the effect size is that there are conventional guidelines established for judging the meaningfulness of effect sizes.

Cohen (1988) has suggested a three-level classification of magnitudes of effect sizes—small, medium, and large, corresponding to effect sizes of .2, .5, and .8, respectively—which he explains by way of examples.

> In new areas of research inquiry, effect sizes are likely to be small (when they are not zero!). This is because the phenomena under study are typically not under good experimental or measurement control or both. . . . A medium effect size is conceived as one large enough to be visible to the naked eye. That is, in the course of normal experience, one would become aware of an average difference in IQ between clerical and semi-skilled workers or between members of professional and managerial occupational groups (Super, 1949, p. 98). . . . When our two populations are so separated as to make [the effect size] = .8 . . . the highest 65.5% of the B population exceeds the lowest 65.5% of the A population. . . . Such a separation, for example, is represented by the mean IQ difference estimated by the difference estimated between holders of the Ph.D. degree and typical college freshmen, or between college graduates and persons with only a 50–50 chance of passing in an academic high school curriculum (Cronbach, 1960, p. 174). These seem like grossly perceptible and therefore large differences, as does the mean difference in height between 13- and 18-year-old girls, which is of the same size. (pp. 25-27)

Table 9.18 uses Cohen's classification for the *ECOScale* data reported in Tables 9.12, 9.13, and 9.14 (and adds another category of "very large" for effect sizes of 1.2 or larger). Even a casual inspection of table 9.18 shows that the magnitudes of the changes in child–adult interaction vary markedly with the introduction of **ECO** treatment. Of equal interest, however, is the pattern of changes in *ECOScale* items across the competencies and the types of items (child goal, adult strategy, interactive goal, and interactive problems).

First of all, the comparison of Occasions 1 and 2 (table 9.12) suggests how stable parent-child interactions can be when the child has a history of communication delay (the reason all the dyads were referred to the **ECO** project). Only a very few (5 of 34) of the effect sizes for occasions prior to treatment showed any meaningful change (and in fact, none were statistically significant, either). In contrast, virtually all of the effect sizes (66 of 68) for the two analyses involving pre-post treatment comparisons (tables 9.13 and 9.14) were medium, large, or very large (in fact, only two were not statistically significant at the .05 level). Figures 9.4, 9.5, 9.6, and 9.7 illustrate the changes that are reported as effect sizes in tables 9.12 through 9.14.

The effect sizes of the items and the Competencies and Interaction scales made up of these items may provide some valuable clues to the reasons that **ECO** principles can foster change in parent–child interactions. Note that the largest effect sizes among individual *ECOScale* items were consistently those for adult strategies (without exception, every change in adult strategy after **ECO** treatment resulted in an effect size classified as "very large"). This might have been predictable, given highly motivated parents who were willing to come to an unfamiliar facility and an unknown program in an effort to help their delayed children become more communicative. What might have been less predictable, however, is that the parents would be willing to change their own interactive style with their children as a way of stimulating their children to change. Consider that many of the parents had to learn new, even foreign skills that seemed at first to counter to their own personal style and to their expectations for how best to teach their children.

Equally encouraging is the fact that all of the effect sizes for the child goals were classified as medium, large, or very large. The early treatment emphasis on social play and turntaking is also reflected in the "very large" effect sizes for the interactive goals of "becoming play partners" (1) and "becoming turntaking partners" (10). Likewise, the largest effect size observed for child goals was "showing a turntaking play style" (13). Child goals of "intentionally communicating with others" (22), "communicating nonverbally" (23), and "conversing for a variety of reasons" (36) also resulted in "large" effect sizes. Contrast these with those child goals with only medium effect sizes, "beginning to communicate verbally" (24), "using varied vocabulary" (30), "following grammatical rules" (31), and "stay in verbal conversations" (37). Given the group of children in the study, many with moderate to severe delays, one would expect less growth on these later, more verbally oriented goals than one would on goals which could be accomplished more readily by nonverbal means. On the other hand, this group of children with their parents still made pre-post gains (Occasions 1 to 5) in the major interactive goals of language and conversation that were classfied as "medium."

	Before Treatment to Beginning of Treatment (Occasions 1 to 2)	Beginning of Treatment to End of Treatment (Occasions 2 to 4)	End of Treatment to Month after Treatment (Occasions 4 to 5)
Child Goals			
1. (14) Use actions functionally, meaningfully	Small	Medium	Small
2. (13) Show a turntaking play style	No Effect	Very Large	No Effect
3. (22) Intentionally communicate	No Effect	Large	No Effect
4. (23) Communicate nonverbally	No Effect	Large	Small
5. (24) Begin to communicate verbally	No Effect	Medium	No Effect
6. (25) Make self understood	No Effect	Medium	No Effect
7. (30) Use varied vocabulary	No Effect	Medium	No Effect
8. (31) Follow grammatical rules	No Effect	Medium	No Effect
9. (36) Converse for a variety of reasons	No Effect	Large	No Effect
10. (37) Stay in verbal conversations	No Effect	Medium	No Effect
Adult Strategies			
1. (15) Maintain and balance turntaking	No Effect	Very Large	Small
2. (17) Wait, signal, and expect	No Effect	Very Large	Small
3. (16) Match child behavior	No Effect	Very Large	Small
4. (18) Imitate and animate	Small	Very Large	Medium
5. (26) Match child communication progressively	No Effect	Very Large	Small
6. (27) Respond to child	Small	Very Large	Small
7. (32) Verbally match child communications	No Effect	Very Large	Small
8. (33) Develop verbal topics	Small	Very Large	Small
9. (38) Maintain balanced conversations	No Effect	Very Large	Small
10. (39) Have social, friendly conversation	No Effect	Very Large	Small
11. (40) Direct the child effectively	No Effect	Very Large	Medium
Interactive Goals			
1. (1) Becoming play partners	No Effect	Very Large	No Effect
2. (10) Becoming turntaking partners	No Effect	Very Large	Small
3. (19) Becoming communicating partners	No Effect	Large	No Effect
4. (28) Becoming language partners	No Effect	Medium	No Effect
5. (34) Becoming conversation partners	No Effect	Medium	No Effect
Interactive Problems (primary focus)			
1. (3) Directive, controlling style (adult)	No Effect	Very Large	Small
2. (21) Mismatch (adult)	No Effect	Very Large	No Effect
3. (12) Low interactive participation (child)	No Effect	Large	No Effect
4. (20) Low communicative participation (child)	No Effect	Medium	No Effect
5. (29) Low verbal, pragmatic skills (child)	Small	Medium	No Effect
6. (11) Lack of active togetherness (child/adult)	No Effect	Very Large	No Effect
7. (2) Lack of playfulness (child/adult)	No Effect	Very Large	No Effect
8. (35) Poor conversations (child/adult)	Small	Small	No Effect

Table 9.18
Magnitudes of Effect Sizes of ECOScale Items Observed at Selected Intervals Before and After ECO Treatment

In short, the magnitude of these changes, the consistent and interpretable patterns of the effect sizes that reflect them, and the stability of the changes one month after treatment ended all seem highly encouraging for improving the communicative ability of children with moderate to severe delays. These data also appear to support the **ECO** principles that focus on social interaction and active parental participation as keys to a child's language learning. These data help to illustrate the recurring theme in **ECO** that, *when adults change the ways in which they interact with delayed children, the children change the ways in which they interact with the adults.* This principle of reciprocity is the core message of this book, a central principle that parents of children with communication delays practice in order to help their children to learn and grow.

SOCIAL VALIDITY OF THE FINDINGS: JUDGMENTS OF UNINVOLVED PEOPLE

Two recurring themes in this book are that children who are more communicative are more socially engaging to the adults around them and that adults are more likely to interact with children they find socially engaging. Therefore, an important question in evaluating the outcomes of **ECO** treatment is whether the child becomes more socially engaging to others as a result of the newly gained competencies for interaction and the dyad is viewed as a positive partnership.

A general goal of the **ECO** model is to help adults and children have more interactive and communicative relationships. The study described above illustrates one measure of progress, the reliable assessment by professionals using the *ECOScales*. However, beyond professional judgments we are interested in the extent to which uninvolved members of society agree with the professional findings. Consequently, a study was conducted to address the following questions: Does a sample of individuals not involved in the **ECO** program see differences between interactions before and after treatment? Do they see improvements in the goals selected for the children and adults in the program?

To study these questions, videotaped samples of parent–child interactions before and after **ECO** intervention were collected for a total of six children. These six children represented three levels of delayed development—severe, moderate, and mild—and varied diagnostic categories including Down syndrome, behavior disordered, autistic, autistic-like, and severely retarded. The pretreatment video samples were selected from a 2-month control phase during which the **ECO** staff recorded play sessions and administered the Adaptive Behavior Scale for Infants (ABSI) (Leland et al., 1980). The posttreatment video came from the sample taped 6 months later, after an average of 10 biweekly treatment sessions and daily home programming. For this video sample, the clinicians instructed the parents to "play with your child as you usually do at home."

The video samples were shown to 18 raters whose familiarity with the **ECO** program varied. Three of the raters were mothers of handicapped children, 3 were speech/language pathologists, 6 were graduate students, 1 was a nurse, and 5 were adults not involved with handicapped children or special education. None of the raters had been directly involved in the program that yielded the tapes. A total of 12 one-minute video samples were rated in two ways.

First, each rater evaluated the degree of perceived dissimilarity between various pairs of video samples (ranging from as few as 22 pairs to as many as 66—the total number of possible pair comparisons). A 5-second pause was inserted between the compared samples, and a 10-second pause was inserted between each of these pairs so that a judgment could be made and recorded. The raters used a 9-point scale to rate the degree of dissimilarity between the samples in a pair, with 1 indicating the greatest similarity and 9 the least. A multidimensional scaling analysis (Gillette & MacDonald, 1988) of these dissimilarity ratings indicated that the raters saw consistent differences between pre and post samples but saw no systematic differences related to the children's levels of adaptive functioning as measured by the ABSI.

Second, the raters then rated the samples on a series of attributes related to the goals of treatment. The attribute scale categorized the goals of the program in terms of the parent–child interaction, the child, and the parent. These attributes are listed in table 9.19, as is an overall rating computed by summing the ratings on the 10 attributes. The attributes were also rated using a 9-point scale, with 1 for a judgment that the attribute was a poor description of the interaction and a 9 for a judgment that the attribute was an excellent description. An analysis of these ratings for all six subjects is summarized in table 9.20 and includes results of t tests of the differences between pre and post means and effect sizes (computed as described earlier in this chapter). Table 9.21 reports the data for the two dyads that included children with severe delays; table 9.22, the data for the two dyads including children with moderate delays; and table 9.23, the data for the two dyads including children with mild delays.

Table 9.19
Social Attributes of Parent-Child Interaction Rated Before and After ECO Treatment by 18 Raters

1.	Playful	The interaction is playful.
2.	Each Other	The parent and child are communicating with each other.
3.	Interesting	The activity is interesting.
4.	Understandable	The child sends understandable messages (gesture, word, sound).
5.	Matching	The parent communicates in ways that are similar to the child's.
6.	Social	The child's behavior is socially acceptable.
7.	Parent Plays	The parent plays as well as talks.
8.	Partnership	The interaction is a partnership.
9.	Responsive	The parent responds to the child.
10.	Conversation	The conversation is interesting.
11.	Overall Rating	Sum of the 10 ratings.

Table 9.20
Ratings of Social Attributes of Parent-Child Interaction Before and After ECO Treatment with t tests and Effect Sizes: Severe, Moderate, and Mild Developmental Delays (largest n = 18 raters × 6 dyads)

	Pretreatment		Posttreatment		Difference		(Post Minus Pre)		Effect
	M	SD	M	SD	M	SD	t	p ⟨	Size
1. Playful	3.60	2.21	6.24	1.93	2.64	2.76	9.92	0.001	1.27
2. Each Other	3.46	2.29	6.71	2.01	3.25	2.69	12.50	0.001	1.51
3. Interesting	3.48	2.19	6.06	2.15	2.57	2.37	10.25	0.001	1.19
4. Understandable	3.73	2.25	6.08	2.29	2.36	2.47	9.85	0.001	1.04
5. Matching	3.24	2.33	6.86	1.85	3.62	2.86	13.09	0.001	1.72
6. Social	5.26	2.52	6.64	2.29	1.38	2.39	5.98	0.001	0.57
7. Parent Plays	3.92	2.43	7.14	1.86	3.22	2.80	11.91	0.001	1.49
8. Partnership	3.04	2.27	6.73	2.16	3.69	2.72	14.05	0.001	1.67
9. Responsive	4.08	2.57	7.50	1.58	3.41	2.75	12.81	0.001	1.60
10. Conversation	2.67	2.11	5.34	2.69	2.66	2.83	8.88	0.001	1.10
11. Overall Rating	6.21	4.02	11.56	4.03	5.35	5.03	10.03	0.001	1.33

Table 9.21

Ratings of Social Attributes of Parent-Child Interaction Before and After ECO Treatment with t tests and Effect Sizes: Severe Developmental Delays (largest n = 18 raters x 2 dyads)

	Pretreatment M	SD	Posttreatment M	SD	Difference M	SD	(Post Minus Pre) t	p <	Effect Size
1. Playful	2.89	1.91	5.06	1.93	2.17	2.29	5.69	0.001	1.13
2. Each Other	2.08	1.66	4.94	1.96	2.86	2.40	7.14	0.001	1.58
3. Interesting	2.53	1.74	4.90	2.11	2.37	2.40	5.40	0.001	1.23
4. Understandable	2.39	1.69	4.08	1.98	1.69	2.41	4.21	0.001	0.92
5. Matching	2.42	1.78	5.86	2.26	3.44	3.03	6.83	0.001	1.70
6. Social	3.31	2.38	4.39	2.11	1.08	3.20	2.03	0.05	0.48
7. Parent Plays	3.86	2.26	6.44	1.96	2.58	2.50	6.20	0.001	1.22
8. Partnership	2.06	1.80	5.17	2.48	3.11	2.64	7.08	0.001	1.44
9. Responsive	3.67	2.37	6.39	1.93	2.72	2.58	6.33	0.001	1.26
10. Conversation	1.47	0.82	3.33	2.31	1.87	2.27	4.50	0.001	1.08
11. Overall Rating	4.43	2.51	8.47	3.60	4.03	3.98	5.55	0.001	1.30

Table 9.22

Ratings of Social Attributes of Parent-Child Interaction Before and After ECO Treatment with t tests and Effect Sizes: Moderate Developmental Delays (largest n= 18 raters x 2 dyads)

	Pretreatment M	SD	Posttreatment M	SD	Difference M	SD	(Post Minus Pre) t	p <	Effect Size
1. Playful	5.26	2.02	6.11	1.79	0.86	2.46	2.06	0.05	0.45
2. Each Other	5.49	1.98	7.17	1.54	1.69	2.45	4.08	0.001	0.95
3. Interesting	4.79	2.23	6.14	2.07	1.34	1.99	3.64	0.01	0.63
4. Understandable	4.94	2.11	6.40	2.02	1.46	2.13	4.04	0.001	0.71
5. Matching	4.83	2.44	7.23	1.63	2.40	2.89	4.91	0.001	1.16
6. Social	6.37	2.03	7.29	1.62	0.91	1.63	3.31	0.01	0.50
7. Parent Plays	5.00	2.28	6.77	2.02	1.77	2.31	4.53	0.001	0.82
8. Partnership	4.80	2.21	7.20	1.61	2.40	2.45	5.79	0.001	1.24
9. Responsive	5.94	2.22	8.14	1.03	2.20	2.47	5.27	0.001	1.27
10. Conversation	4.52	2.31	5.72	2.34	1.21	2.41	2.70	0.05	0.52
11. Overall Rating	9.72	4.08	11.83	3.40	2.10	3.91	2.89	0.01	0.56

Table 9.23

Ratings of Social Attributes of Parent-Child Interaction Before and After ECO Treatment with t tests and Effect Sizes: Mild Developmental Delays (largest n = 18 raters x 2 dyads)

	Pretreatment M	SD	Posttreatment M	SD	Difference M	SD	(Post Minus Pre) t	p <	Effect Size
1. Playful	2.69	1.77	7.56	1.11	4.86	1.85	15.73	0.001	3.29
2. Each Other	2.86	1.71	8.03	0.97	5.17	1.99	15.56	0.001	3.72
3. Interesting	3.17	2.00	7.13	1.70	3.97	1.97	11.01	0.001	2.14
4. Understandable	3.89	2.19	7.78	0.93	3.89	2.15	10.86	0.001	2.31
5. Matching	2.53	1.95	7.50	1.06	4.97	2.01	14.87	0.001	3.17
6. Social	6.14	1.91	8.28	0.70	2.14	1.90	6.76	0.001	1.48
7. Parent Plays	2.92	2.36	8.19	0.95	5.28	2.33	13.62	0.001	2.93
8. Partnership	2.31	1.72	7.83	1.23	5.53	2.02	16.41	0.001	3.70
9. Responsive	2.69	1.98	7.97	0.94	5.28	2.20	14.40	0.001	3.40
10. Conversation	2.10	1.58	6.97	2.06	4.87	2.39	11.16	0.001	2.65
11. Overall Rating	4.60	2.88	14.40	2.61	9.80	3.66	14.66	0.001	3.56

As with the data reported in tables 9.12 through 9.14, the results of these analyses reflect acutely perceptible differences between the quality of parent–child interactions before and after **ECO** treatment. All but one of the effect sizes for the group of six dyads are "very large" as classified by the categories used above, and that one attribute—"The child's behavior is socially acceptable"—yielded an effect size classified as "medium." It is also interesting to note that, despite relatively small numbers of ratings (no more than 36 per attribute in tables 9.21 through 9.22), the *t* tests of differences between pretreatment and posttreatment means were significant beyond the .05 level for all attributes, and most were significant beyond the .001 level.

It is also interesting to note the variability exhibited by these six dyads. Examining the results by level of developmental delay, as reported in tables 9.21, 9.22, and 9.23, suggests that children with mild delays may make very pronounced changes in as short a time as the six months between the samples rated in this study. Perhaps surprisingly, the dyads in which the child's developmental delays were severe exhibited larger effect sizes than the dyads in which the child's delays were moderate. Although the number of ratings for each of these groups is relatively large for a clinically based study ($n = 36$ ratings for each attribute reported in tables 9.21 through 9.23), the fact that only two children at each level of delay were rated prohibits any reasonable inferences regarding the increase in communicative ability or social acceptability as a function of the level of developmental delay.

On the other hand, consider the smallest of the effect sizes reported in these tables. Social acceptability, as indicated by the attribute, "The child's behavior is socially acceptable," showed the smallest amount of change. The next smallest change was shown for the attribute "The child sends understandable messages." And the third smallest change was shown for the attribute "The conversation is interesting." **ECO** treatment appears to increase a child's communicative ability more perceptibly than the child's intelligibility. Furthermore, the child is still likely to be perceived as less socially acceptable than a nondelayed child might be. Yet even in these conclusions are the **ECO** principles evident: a child with communication delays generally must increase his interactive skills, including turntaking and preverbal or nonverbal communication skills, before he or she can become verbal, verbally intelligible, or highly conversational. The steps to be taken are often small, and the parent must respond with small, progressively matched steps that show the child only a little more, just as much as the child can reach for and succeed at.

Nevertheless, parents and clinicians can find encouragement by noting that raters did perceive improvement for children with all these levels of delay. Only 3 of the 30 attribute effect sizes in tables 9.21 through 9.23 were low enough to be rated "small" by Cohen's (1988) classification. All others were at least "medium," which in Cohen's words "is conceived as one large enough to be visible to the naked eye." Moreover, 23 of the 30 attribute ratings reported in these three tables yielded effect sizes classified as "large" by Cohen's classification, sizes that, in his words, seem to be "grossly perceptible." Such changes are critical for children who must first become interactive if they are ever to become conversational enough to learn from the natural teachers—parents, teachers, other adults, other children—whom every child encounters in daily living. To conclude, uninvolved judges were in close agreement with the experimental analyses of the program in that they consistently discriminated between pre- and posttreatment interactions and they saw positive changes in attributes of both child and adult interaction that were addressed by the **ECO** program.

DISCUSSION

The study of these 25 parent–child pairs provides initial analyses of preconversational children in terms of their patterns of interaction and their parents' patterns of interactions with them. The study addresses three general questions. First, what interactive and communicative patterns does the **ECO** model reveal in preschool children and their parents? We will refer to the data addressing this question as the "pretreatment" findings; that is, the dyad's performance before any direct interaction training. Second, how do the children and parents change their interactive and communicative style through a 6-month treatment program based on interaction? We will refer to data that address this question as "posttreatment" findings. Third, how do independent observers view the parents and children before and after the interactive treatment? We will refer to the data addressing this question as the "social validity" findings, in that they speak to the degree to which uninvolved observers see pre- and postperformances as reliably different and the extent to which they observe changes in the directions addressed by the programs.

What were the patterns of interaction of the parents and children?

This study describes a sample of preschoolers and their parents as videotaped during play with toys in a clinic setting. The children in the study included children who were primarily noninteractive, interactive but not regularly communicative, nonverbally communicative but not linguistic, and minimally linguistic but not conversational. Consequently, the patterns described here are general guidelines to the interaction styles of the children and their parents.

We will describe the interactive profiles, before and after treatment, for the children and parents for each of the five developmental areas addressed in the model: social play, turntaking interaction, preverbal communication, language, and conversation. Recall that the judges used a 1 to 9 rating scale, in which scores of 1 or 2 (low) indicated poor or negligible performance with no evidence of a habit emerging. A score of 3 or 4 (low–mid) indicated a weak skill with only fleeting evidence. A score of 5 (mid) indicated some evidence of a habit emerging, with occasional examples of brief duration. A score of 6 or 7 (high-mid) suggested the quality of the skill was good with evidence of a habit emerging: quantity and duration of examples were often appropriate. A score of 8 or 9 was reserved for outstanding and creative use of the skill; the skill appeared to be an assertive habit finely tuned to the partner.

SOCIAL PLAY

How much real interaction was seen when the parents and children played together?

In social play, both child and adult play in truly joint shared activities, balancing their participation, being sensitive to the other's intentions, and interacting more for the internal motivation of being together than directing and controlling each other toward a goal. It is through social play that the parent and child are expected to learn the reinforcing value of contact with people and the basic rules for engaging and maintaining contact with others.

Pretreatment

Child Profile

The children performed in the low-mid range of staying in play with their parents. They often played alone, rarely initiating or maintaining contact with the adult. While some children occasionally initiated contact or responded to a parent's contact, rarely did they both initiate and respond. The children also rarely stayed in the same activity as the parent, especially voluntarily. While they occasionally played functionally and symbolically alone, they did less meaningful and more responsive play with their parents. To summarize, while some children showed some active interest in playing with their parents, the strong trend was to play alone and not to join into interactions with their parents.

Parent Profile

The parents were judged as performing in the low end of the low-mid range of rating. One finding across parents was that they did not keep childlike play going; they seemed to maintain an adult style throughout the play. Consequently, the parents usually did not match their child by acting and communicating in ways the child could perform. A frequent pattern was for the parent to talk, often in unbroken streams, as the child played; consequently there was little joint activity that would offer the shared meanings the child needed if he were to develop language. Using an adult style, the parents often communicated about academic and adult concepts that neither fit the child's experiences and interests nor provided readily communicable language. The parents regularly controlled the interaction with directions or physical assistance, often missing the child's cues that could show his motivations. To summarize, while the parents occasionally appeared to enjoy their children, they did not appear to see themselves as a play partner but rather as a regulator.

Posttreatment

Child Profile

After treatment the children played more actively with their parents, rather than in the solo or parallel patterns we saw before the program. In general they stayed in joint activities with their parents, with their behavior showing considerably more influence of their parents than before. Not only did they stay, they were no longer primarily passive and responsive. The majority of children showed a beginning habit of initiating contact and assertively keeping the parent in the interaction. Most of the children showed a greater range of play behaviors, which means they had more behaviors that could become communications. Not only was the children's play more interactive, it often appeared to be more meaningful and symbolic. Thus, most of these children appeared to take a more social role in play after treatment.

Parent Profile

The parents of the children changed considerably more in their social play skills than did the children. As a general rule, the parents became more childlike and playful, thus appearing more accessible to their children. The parents actively kept their children's play going rather than allowing solo play as they had before. Their general childlike style also involved matching the children's actions and communications, thus modeling behaviors the children could likely perform. Another way the parents matched the children was to communicate more about the child's activities than the adults' agenda, as had often occurred before programming. These parents often allowed the children to control the play more; they acted less as regulators or caretakers than as play partners.

TURNTAKING

Turntaking refers to the habit of reciprocal interactions in which the child and adult interact in a balanced, give-and-take style. They share turns meaningfully, with both child and adult initiating and responding nearly equally. Each has similar control and direction of the exchange. The key to turntaking interactions is that they become the natural and increasingly extended way of being with people.

Pretreatment

Child Profile

While the children often responded to a parent's contacts, they rarely initiated to the parent. When the children did interact, it was usually for brief exchanges, one to two turns. None of the children seemed to be in the habit of initiating and maintaining interactions. Those habits are widely reported in infants and are critical to developing social and communicative skills. While some children tended to dominate turns, most of them played a passive role when their parents dominated. A striking finding was the high frequency of parallel play; often the children showed little parent-directed behavior when they were obstensibly playing together. They did not interact back and forth; rather, the children acted as if they did not know that being with someone meant they were to interact.

Parent Profile

The parents rarely took turns with their children beyond initiating or responding and then ending the interaction on a topic. Occasionally they allowed the children to dominate turns, acting or communicating several times before the parent would. More commonly the parents dominated turns, doing or saying a number of things consecutively without waiting or signaling for the child to participate. A strikingly common finding was that parents did not wait for their child with delays to interact; they appeared to create an atmosphere of not expecting the child to participate. In subsequent interviews, parents often reported that they either had few expectations or that they did not know what expectations were appropriate.

When parents did attempt to interact, they regularly mismatched the child, thus giving the child a behavior model he was unlikely to follow. In these interactions, the parents, while occasionally responding to verbal turns, were remarkably consistent in not responding to the children's actions and nonverbal interactions. With these primarily preverbal children, parents did not interacted at the appropriate developmental levels so that the children would become social and communicative.

Posttreatment

Child Profile

A majority of the children now began to show more of a give and take style of interaction than the generally passive or solo style they showed before programming. While they responded more regularly to their parents' contacts, a more striking finding was that the children now began to initiate contacts and were generally more socially assertive.

As the children learned to take turns they appeared to be more active participants with their parents. In many cases they became not only interactive but reciprocal, exchanging turns in ways that appeared to take their parents' perspective. Several of the children began to spontaneously show the rules of turntaking, such as waiting for their partners' turns, signaling when a turn is delayed, and even physically prompting their parents' turns. Many of the children appeared more strongly motivated to interact, as evidenced by actively maintaining their parents in interaction. In summary, the children showed a greater awareness that people are there to socialize with. This attitude was in contrast with their isolation before treatment. In addition, the children's turns often reflected the parents' behavior, suggesting an increasing sensitivity to the adults' behavior. No longer were most of the children engaged in extended solo or parallel situations. Finally, the children showed a greater balanced exchange in interaction, with fewer episodes of being primarily passive or dominant than earlier.

Parent Profile

Perhaps the major change in the parents was that *they did less after treatment.* They regularly waited silently and allowed their children enough time to process the parents' turns and act on their own. The parents often showed visible expectations and, after waiting, signaled the child to act. Given the generally reduced speed of response of children with delays, this habit of waiting appeared to change the nature of the relationships considerably. As the parents began to assume a give-and-take style, a balance developed; they acted and communicated less and allowed the children to do more. As the parents did less, they often matched their children, doing things closer to their children's abilities. Several appeared to learn to imitate and act with more animation, to which the children often responded readily. In summary, by doing less and by sharing turns with their children, the parents often established an interactive balance that allowed the children to socialize and communicate.

NONVERBAL COMMUNICATION

What kinds of nonverbal messages did the parents and children exchange?

The competency of nonverbal communication involves a finely tuned relationship between parent and child. The child sends messages with any sound or movements, and the parents carefully match the child's attempts so as to support them and show him a feasible next way to communicate. Nonverbal communication is a valuable habit that precedes and facilitates language development; it is seen as an indispensible tool for helping the child build social relations for both cognitive and communicative development.

Pretreatment

Child Profile

The average ratings for nonverbal communication and being understood were in the low range of the scale. The general rating of "communicates with others" was somewhat higher, in the low-mid range. In general the children only rarely communicated intentionally in the play sessions. While most of the children used potentially communicative sounds and movements, they appeared to do so more to accompany their play than to exchange messages with their parents. When they did communicate, their exchanges were usually too brief to expect the child to learn communication from his parent. Further evidence that few communicative habits had developed lies in the minimal degree to which the children altered their communication in response to their parent's communications.

Parent Profile

The parents did not use the preverbal ways to communicate that characterized their child's communications. In a general way, many parents did not seem to regard the child's preverbal attempts as valid communications. Evidence for this lies in two pervasive findings. The first finding was that the parents generally mismatched the children using communications far beyond the children's performance level. Thus the parents did not usually provide models for communications the child could imitate or ever adapt to his own level.

The second broad finding was that the parents generally failed to respond to the children's actions, sounds, and body language that are the beginnings of language. Thus, they did not give their children a strong base of support for their emerging communications. In summary, parents appeared to provide neither the kinds of models the children were ready to perform nor the kinds of support that would motivate and reinforce the child's new attempts to communicate. Interviews with parents revealed that they had not known that early sounds and gestures are important for language or that their own communication influenced the children's rate or style of communication.

Posttreatment

Child Profile

After treatment, the majority of the children communicated more frequently and with a greater range of movements, sounds, and words than before. No longer were their communications primarily responsive; they communicated to initiate contacts and to keep them going.

The children's communications now seemed a more integral part of their play and less a response to directives. The children shifted from nonverbal communications to verbal ones. Many children became communicative whereas before treatment they had sent messages very infrequently. An interesting finding was that several children who now directed their communication to their parents had often been self-directed before treatment. The children who were verbal were judged as more intelligible after treatment than before. While the majority of the children were primarily nonverbal, they did show marked increases in their range of sounds and gestures. Furthermore, their communications were more effective. Thus, the children appeared to be developing their nonverbal communication in several ways, and their parents appeared to be pacing themselves to the children. A primary change across treatment appears to be that the children view themselves as communicators—not only as responders or occasional initiators, but as people who see communication as a socially required and motivating action to take with people.

Parent Profile

It is here where many parents made their strongest gains. During the program, they moved from communicating as adults, far above the children's capabilities, to communicating in ways matched to the children, within their abilities. As the parents communicated more like their children, they also became more responsive to the children's emerging communications. No longer did they ignore the actions and sounds that could become communications. Rather they matched these emerging communications, thus often immediately providing instructive feedback to the child.

By matched responding, they appeared to fine-tune their communication in ways that their child could master both physically and cognitively. The physical and communicative similarity between the parents and children was visible after the program. The parents' development of a turntaking style appeared to provide a rhythm for the interactions that help to maintain and extend the number of turns exchanged. This turntaking style allowed for a repetitive feedback system in which the parent could immediately respond to the child in a matched way that would give the child a model for how to communicate next. The parents revealed a sensitivity to a wide range of behaviors that was not observed before treatment. Not only did they show the children some next steps to communicating with matched responding, this style also appeared to reinforce and support the child in using any behaviors available to communicate.

LANGUAGE

Language develops as the child transfers his experiences, interests, and preverbal communications into words and other symbols. Parents can promote a child's language by using language that is cognitively matched to the child's thinking and ability level and that is frequently communicatively useful to the child. Language appears to develop more efficiently within natural contacts dealing with child-world notions than within teaching lessons that focus on academic and adult-driven notions.

Pretreatment

About half of the children communicated regularly with words, usually one to three words at a time. When they talked, the children usually responded rather than initiated. Their speech was of three types: first, they talked about their immediate experiences, often people, objects, locations, and actions; second, they responded to their parents' questions and commands; third, they used a few words stereotypically for many messages, such as "dat," "bye," and "more." From the play contexts, we felt that the children regularly communicated less in words than they knew. Often their gestures and sounds were communicatively effective with their parents, even when the children occasionally showed they could use words for the same messages. In other words, the children seemed to use the language they had very infrequently; while they "could" talk, they did not appear to view themselves as habitual speakers.

Parents were rated "low" on their skill in matching their language to the children's experiences and communications and their skill in building topics, indicating minimal evidence. The parents' language often followed an adult agenda more than being responsive to the child's apparent motivations. While the parents often used more language than the children could produce, they did not seem to frequently respond to the children in ways that would give them words for their sounds, gestures and unintelligible words. The parents used language that would be unlikely to be used in communications by the children. Consequently, as interviews corroborated, the parents appeared unaware of the role their language could have on their child's development.

Posttreatment

During the 6-month program, the children's use of verbal vocabulary increased from low to mid-low. These gains occurred in about half of the children. Thus, while the other half were still learning to become interactive or nonverbally communicative, the children who did talk, talked more and about a greater variety of meanings. They used language for those early child meanings found in normally developing children. That is, they talked about people, actions, objects, and feelings more than they did about academic concepts or adult words. While many children appeared to begin to use words imitatively, they also initiated their language. It was noted that when the parents waited silently for the child to talk, the child often used his own words rather than those of his parents. A major change for many children was that they now appeared to know what to do with words and to define words as an integral part of interactions. Before the program, the children appeared to use words mainly to respond or to get needs met, and not as a natural way of being with people.

The parents generally changed their language by more closely matching the children's experiences, intentions, and communication level. That is, rather than talking at adult levels and about their own ideas, the parents moved more into the children's world by talking in ways the children could talk. The parents' language began to lead the children from their words to creating sentences by following the children's meanings and combining them. Much more than before treatment, the parents sensitively responded to the children in ways that showed them the next step in talking. Another change in the parents was an increase in keeping the children on a topic beyond one or two turns. Before the program, parents usually allowed the children to communicate once and then leave the interaction; after the program, many parents made visible and often successful efforts at keeping the children talking about the topic, thus exposing them to greater natural language and cognitive development.

CONVERSATION

What are the reasons the parents and children talk and what kind of conversations do they have?

The competency of conversation involves the range of social, instrumental, and self-directed reasons the parents and children communicate. Conversation skills also involve having verbal exchanges both spontaneously and for specific purposes. The rules of balance, responsiveness, match, and nondirectiveness help to keep children voluntarily building relationships through conversation.

Pretreatment

Child Profile

The children appeared to enter into verbal exchanges of more than one turn to communicate for two major reasons. The first was to make demands or otherwise control the parent; the second, to respond passively to the parent's commands and questions. Some children also talked or made sounds for noncommunicative reasons such as accompanying their own actions. Few social conversations—ones for the social exchange itself—were observed. The children did not yet seem to have the habit of commenting, replying, and otherwise having a conversation with no external job to get done. One nearly consistent finding was that the children rarely stayed in a conversation longer than two or three turns. Thus, whatever learning through conversation was possible, these children avoided much of it.

Parent Profile

In a few words, the parents' initial conversations may be described as directive and dead-end. They failed to maintain exchanges beyond brief contacts. The parents did little to encourage the children to stay in conversations; when children left a conversation, parents nearly always allowed them to go. Extended talking on a topic did not seem to be a value held by the parents. One potential reason for the brief conversations was that the parents primarily questioned, commanded, and otherwise directed the conversation from their own perspectives rather than guiding the conversations socially from the child's perspective. The parents' communications often appeared rhetorical; that is, they often talked *at* the child with little apparent expectation or time allowed for a response. The parents rarely pursued the child for a response if the child ignored a communication. Parents reported little awareness of the value of conversations for the child's social and communicative learning.

Posttreatment

Child Profile

While the children's major changes were in their interactive and communicative skills, not in verbal conversations, they did begin to communicate for more social and fewer instrumental reasons. Thus, even the children with emerging language were beginning to use language for those social reasons that would eventually be used to build conversation skills. Now that most of the children had learned to stay in social interactions, they communicated less often to themselves and more often to others. They visibly looked for a response. Many of the children, even those still predominately preverbal, performed as conversationalists; that is, they exchanged balanced turns, began to take the other's perspective, and reciprocated with their partner. In general, they acted more as communicative partners than as loners. For many dyads, language now appeared to play a strong functional role in uniting the children with their parents, in contrast to the either instrumental or ineffective role language had played before the program.

Parent Profile

After the program the parents were much more social than controlling and maintained more balanced conversations with the children. These changes were some of the strongest in the program. Parents used many fewer questions and demands and more nondirective comments and replies. Their communications were also more effective, that is, their children responded to them more. They appeared to actively keep the children in increasingly longer conversations. In being more social and conversational, the parents offered the children more options for what to do in the conversations. Most parents now appeared to define their relationship with their child as a balanced one that was facilitated by conversation. They used conversation as the primary tool for being together. Thus, the parents appeared to engage in conversation less often to accomplish something and more often as a natural way of being with their child.

SUMMARY

This series of studies illustrates a program for assisting parents and children in developing a closer social and communicative learning relationship. The **ECO** model provides direction for beginning and strengthening these relationships. A core assumption of the model is that children need intimate, balanced relationships if they are to learn to be social and communicative. Although the **ECO** program is only a beginning, with more issues raised than resolved, these findings at least suggest an optimistic beginning.

10 | *Directions for the Future*

SOCIAL
social

PLAY
play

TURN TAKING
turn taking

COMMUNICATION
communication

LANGUAGE
language

CONVERSATION
conversation

The partnership model for social and communication development presented here encourages a number of changes in the educational and domestic management of preconversational children. The education of young children with delays is becoming increasingly supported by law, and research and model programs are demonstrating a greater potential for these children. With these advances, it is particularly timely that we consider what educational and clinical approaches are appropriate for these children who have little history of systematic education. A related fact is that relatively few training programs have been available to teachers, clinicians, or parents to acquire competencies need for fostering social and communicative development. In fact, U.S. laws mandating education for handicapped children have predated the systematic training required to respond to those mandates. It is now time to propose educational and clinical models that prepare both children and their responsible adults to meet not only the letter and spirit of the new laws but the genuine needs of the children.

CHALLENGES AND DILEMMAS

1. Developmental needs, legal mandates, and ethical considerations argue forcibly for systematic attention to the social development of preconversational children.
2. Parents and other caregivers are inevitably influencing their children's social and communicative development, yet they have virtually no access to education for that task.
3. Few professionals have access to developmental and practical training in early parent-child relationships, including training in productive adult interaction styles for communication development.
4. Professional and educational approaches to communication development have focused predominantly on structural aspects of language for children who have conversational competencies needed to develop advanced speech and language for communication.
5. Professionals are legally mandated to serve a population whose developmental competencies they have not been trained to serve.
6. Parents have legal access to direct involvement in individual education plans, yet they rarely have access to education that would make them competent for that involvement.

COMMITMENT TO A SOCIAL DEVELOPMENT CURRICULUM

Rather than assume that homes will inevitably provide adequate social development for children to learn in school and in daily routines, we must ensure that children have the social and communicative skills they need for spontaneous learning and generalization of adult-directed learning. This commitment to social development will ensure that systems do not invest in educational and clinical goals that cannot be met without first helping the children develop a stable social and communicative base. Once social interaction skills are seen as prerequisite goals for speech, language, and didactic learning, they will assume a real priority in clinical, educational, and parental intervention.

With social and communicative competencies as the primary goals for children with delays, professionals and parents will need to reassess their view of the learning process. No longer can a didactic approach alone suffice—one in which the child follows the adult's agenda and plays only a passive role in learning. The methods of partnership illustrated in this book must become a part of the curriculum of schools, clinics, and personal relationships.

The teaching models developed for children with intact social habits are inadequate for children who have yet to develop the social relations that make people accessible and that facilitate their learning from others spontaneously. Parents and professionals need to discover that learning is inevitable in their interactions with children and that the choice of interaction styles profoundly influences how and what the child learns with them. Consequently, one direction for future approaches with children is for adults to assume balanced, reciprocal partnerships with them. In those partnerships, the adults both respond to and match the child's cognition, communication, and motivation, rather than assuming that the child "learns only from events where the adults intended to teach."

INCREASINGLY PROMINENT ROLE OF PARENTS

After 17 years of working directly with parents and their children with delays, one conclusion cannot be ignored: educating parents and involving them in the clinical effort are as essential to the children's social and communicative development as attention to the children themselves. The role of the parents is so central that it is reasonable to ask this: Might we not get more efficient use of our effort and expenditures if we shifted a greater proportion of them to the parents?

What roles can parents play in their child's social and communicative development? Given their inevitable influence, parents' first role needs to be that of student. Not only are parents rarely trained, except naturalistically, in parenting skills, they appear to know little about the stages of their child's early development and to appreciate even less the importance of their own role in the child's becoming social and communicative.

Concurrent with education programs, parents need to build productive learning relationships with their children. They need to learn to fine-tune themselves to their children, thereby building emotional attachments that foster spontaneous learning. Contrary to many parents' and teachers' expectations, becoming teachers in the didactic style is not the appropriate first goal for parents of preconversational children. When parents become teachers, concerned with skills and answers, they risk interrupting the reciprocal, give-and-take relations within which they and the child share the balance of power. It is the give-and-take that leads to successes that motivate a child to stay interactive.

In order to establish effective parent education and clinical training, the work must not be piggy-backed onto the duties of already overloaded teachers and clinicians. One option is to redefine the role of teachers, clinicians, and other professionals from that of didactic teacher to child-oriented, contingently interactive partner. Experiences with professionals indicate that some adults can adjust to this profound turnaround in attitude and behavioral style and that others may not. Because of the magnitude of the changes required, we might ask if children with developmental delays would benefit from a new profession of early development specialist, whose competencies would lie in early developmental processes of both parent and child. This new professional could educate parents to understand, observe, and participate productively in early social and communicative processes. As long as preconversational children and their parents seek out professionals trained only in didactic and academic competencies useful mainly to children with stable conversation habits, it is difficult to see how a genuine curriculum of social interaction competencies will develop or become widespread.

Professionals need to learn that social and communicative competencies are not extraneous goals or goals to address after academic skills have been taught. There is an undeniable need for a population of professionals and parents who see social and communicative development as their most vital goal, in the same way that a third grade teacher sees literacy as a major responsibility to her children.

INTERACTIVE CLASSROOMS

Many children learn, far too easily, to assume a passive, responsive role in academically oriented classrooms. If we accept that the preconversational child's major task is to learn to be social, then classrooms must become socially supportive environments so that children may avoid the passive roles and learned helplessness that results.

An interactive classroom is an environment with the foremost goal of stimulating extended interaction within developmentally matched but challenging activities. Thus, a primary goal in the child's education plan in such a classroom would be to stay for increasingly longer turns in play, spontaneous contacts, and learning tasks. While the interactions would be playful, they would also be contingent, that is, as carefully cued and reinforced as any indispensible learning goal. Before we can construct developmentally interactive classrooms, however, professionals must be educated into the facilitative roles they can play in becoming learning partners in play, turntaking, preverbal communication, language, and conversation.

SUMMARY

This book has introduced a new model for social and communicative development of developmentally delayed children. Its focus is the preconversational child who has yet to develop a stable or generalized habit of spontaneous conversation. The model is forged from two perspectives, the literature on the development of parent-child interaction in the first few years after birth and a series of clinical research projects that have investigated parent-child interaction within intervention programs. The unifying concept of the **ECO** model is partnership, defined as generalized habit of balanced, reciprocal interactions maintained by a sensitively matched and responsive adult who is frequently child-directed and who fosters emotional attachment. The model is ecological in the sense that it addresses development as a two-person process, one that considers the adult-child dyad as the primary unit to be studied rather than the child as the only "client." The model encourages curriculum that focuses on perpetually building partnerships in five competency areas not traditionally included in programming for parents or classrooms.

References

Ainsworth, M.D. (1972). Individual differences in the development of attachment behaviors. *Merrill Palmer Quarterly, 18,* 2.

Almerico, T. (1979). *The maternal pragmatic environment of replies and declarations in non-delayed and delayed children.* Unpublished masters thesis, The Ohio State University.

Austin, J. (1962). *How to do things with words.* London, England: Oxford University Press.

Bandura, A. (1977). *Modeling social learning theory.* Englewood Cliffs, NJ: Prentice-Hall.

Barnes, S., Gutfreund, M., Sattersly, D., & Wells, G. (1983). Characteristics of adult speech which predict children's language development. *Journal of Child Language, 10,* 65-84.

Bates, E. (1976). *Language and context: The acquisition of pragmatics.* New York: Academic Press.

Bateson, G., & Jackson, D. (1964). Some varieties of pathogenic organizations. In D. McK. Rioch (Ed.), *Disorders of Communication, 42,* 270-283.

Bateson, G., Jackson, D., Haley, J., & Weakland, J. (1956). Toward a theory of schizophrenia. *Behavioral Science, 1,* 251-264.

Bell, R.Q. (1968). A reinterpretation of the direction of effects in studies of socialization. *Psychological Review, 75,* 81-95.

Bell, R.Q. (1971). Stimulus control of parent or caregiver by offspring. *Developmental Psychology, 1,* 63-72.

Bell, R.Q. (1979). Parent, child, and reciprocal influences. *American Psychologist, 34,* 821-826.

Bell, R.Q., & Harper, L.V. (1977). *Child effects on adults.* Hillsdale, NJ: Lawrence Erlbaum.

Berger, J., & Cunningham, C.C. (1983). Development of early vocal behaviors and interactions in Down's syndrome and nonhandicapped infant-mother pairs. *Developmental Psychology, 19,* 322-331.

Blacher, T. (1984). Sequential stages of parental adjustment to the birth of a child with handicaps: Fact or artifact 7. *Mental Retardation, 22,* 55-68.

Bloom, L. (1973). *One word at a time. The use of single word utterances before syntax.* The Hague, Netherlands: Mouton.

Bloom, L., & Lahey, M. (1978). *Language development and language disorders.* New York: John Wiley.

Brazelton, T.B. (1973). *Neonatal Behavioral Assessment Scale.* Philadelphia: Lippincott.

Brazelton, T.B., Koslowski, B., & Main, M. (1974). The origins of reciprocity: The early mother-infant interaction. In M. Lewis & L.A. Rosenblum (Eds.), *The effect of the infant on its caretaker.* New York: John Wiley.

Bromwich, R.M. (1981). *Working with parents and infants: An interactional approach.* Baltimore: University Park Press.

Bronfenbrenner, U. (1979). *The ecology of human development.* Cambridge: Harvard University Press.

Bronfenbrenner, U. (1986). Ecology of the family as a context for human development: Research perspectives. *Developmental Psychology, 22,* 723-742.

Brown, R. (1973). *A first language: The early stages.* Cambridge: Harvard University Press.

Bruner, J. (1974). From communication to language: A psychological perspective. *Cognition, 3,* 255-277.

Bruner, J. (1975). The ontogenesis of speech acts. *Journal of Child Language, 2,* 1-19.

Bruner, J. (1977a). Early social interaction and language acquisition. In H.R. Schaffer (Ed.), *Studies in mother-infant interaction.* New York: Academic Press.

Bruner, J. (1977b, May). *The role of dialogue in language acquisition.* Paper presented at conference on the child's conception of language, Max Planck Society in Linguistics.

Bruner, J. (1978a, March). *Acquiring the use of language.* Parts of this paper were presented at the Berlyne Memorial Lecture at the University of Toronto, Toronto, Canada.

Bruner, J. (1978b). Human growth and development. In J. Bruner & A. Garton (Eds.), *Wolfson College Lectures, 1976.* Oxford, England: Clarendon Press.

Bruner, J. (1978c). Learning the mother tongue. *Human Nature, 1,* 42-48.

Bruner, J. (1983). *Child talk.* New York: W.W. Norton.

Bruner, J., Roy, C., & Ratner, N. (1980). The beginnings of request. In K.E. Nelson (Ed.), *Children's language* (Vol. 3). New York: Gardner Press.

Buckhalt, J.A., Rutherford, R.B., & Goldberg, K.E. (1978). Verbal and nonverbal interaction of mothers with their Down syndrome and nonretarded infants. *American Journal of Mental Deficiency, 82,* 337-343.

Bullowa, M. (Ed.). (1979). *Before speech: The beginnings of interpersonal communication.* Cambridge, England: Cambridge University Press.

Bzoch, K.R., & League, R. (1970). *The receptive-expressive emergent language scale for the measurement of language skills in infancy.* Gainesville, FL: The Tree of Life Press.

Chapman, R. (1978). Comprehension strategies in children. In J. Kavanaugh & W. Strange (Eds.), *Speech and language in the laboratory, school and clinic.* Cambridge: MIT Press.

Cheseldine, S., & McConkey, R. (1979). Parental speech to young Down's syndrome children: An intervention study. *American Journal of Mental Deficiency, 83,* 612-620.

Clark, H., & Clark, E. (1977). *Psychology and language.* New York: Harcourt Brace Jovanovich.

Clezy, G. (1984). Interactive analysis. In D. Miller (Ed.), *Remediating children's language.* San Diego: College-Hill Press.

Cohen, J. (1988). *Statistical power analysis for the behavioral sciences* (2nd ed.). Hillsdale, NJ: Lawrence Erlbaum.

Cole, M., et al. (1978). *L.S. Vytgotsky: Mind in society.* Cambridge: Harvard University Press.

Conant, S., Budoff, M., Hecht, B., & Morse, R. (1984). Language intervention: A pragmatic approach. *Journal of Autism and Developmental Disorders, 14,* 301-317.

Conti-Ramsden, G., & Friel-Patti, S. (1983). Mother's discourse adjustments to language-impaired and non-language-impaired children. *Journal of Speech and Hearing Disorders, 48,* 360-367.

Conti-Ramsden, G., & Friel-Patti, S. (1984). Mother-child dialogues: A comparison of normal and language impaired children. *Journal of Communication Disorders, 17*(1), 19-35.

Crnic, K., Greenberg, M.T., Robinson, N.M., & Ragozin, A.S. (1984). Maternal stress and social support: Effects on the mother-infant relationship from birth to eighteen months. *American Journal of Orthopsychiatry, 54,* 224-235.

Crnic, K., Greenberg, A., & Slough, N. (1986). Early stress and social support influences on mothers' and high-risk infants' functioning in late infancy. *Infant Mental Health Journal, 7,* 19-48.

Cross, T.G. (1978). Mother's speech and its association with rate of linguistic development in young children. In N. Waterson & C.E. Snow (Eds.), *The development of communication.* New York: John Wiley.

Cross, T.G. (1985). Habilitating the language-impaired child: Ideas from studies of parent-child interaction. *Topics in Language Disorders, 4,* 1-14.

Cunningham, C. E., Reuler, E., Blackwell, J., & Deck, J. (1981). Behavioral and linguistic developments in the interactions of normal and handicapped children with their mothers. *Child Development, 52,* 62-70.

Dale, P.S. (1980). Is early pragmatic development measurable? *Journal of Child Language, 7,* 1-12.

Davis, A.J., & Hathaway, B.K. (1982). Reciprocity in parent-child verbal interaction. *The Journal of Genetic Psychology, 140,* 169-183.

Deci, E. (1975). *Intrinsic motivation.* New York: Plenum Press.

deVilliers, J., & deVilliers, P. (1978). *Language acquisition.* Cambridge: Harvard University Press.

Dobe, L. (1989). A study of unteraction styles and patterns of mothers of preverbal children. Unpublished master's thesis. The Ohio State University.

Dore, J. (1975). Holophrases speech acts and language universals. *Journal of Child Language, 2,* 21-40.

Dunst, C. (1978). A cognitive-social approach for assessment of early nonverbal communicative behavior. *Journal of Child Communicative Disorders, 2*(2).

Dunst, C.J. (1985). Communicative competence and deficits: Effects on early social interactions. In E. McDonald & D. Gallagher (Eds.), *Facilitating social-emotional development in the young multiply handicapped child.* Philadelphia: HMS Press.

Erheart, B. (1982). Mother-child interactions with nonretarded and mentally retarded preschoolers. *American Journal of Mental Deficiency, 87,* 20-25.

Eisenberg, J. (1985). *Conversational development between parents and handicapped children: An intervention study.* Unpublished masters thesis, The Ohio State University.

Elkind, D. (1987). *Miseducation: Preschoolers at risk.* New York: Knopf.

Ellis, R., & Wells, G. (1980). Enabling factors in adult-child disorders. *First Language, 1,* 46-82.

Erickson, E. (1963). *Childhood and society.* New York: Norton.

Ervin-Tripp, S. (1978). Wait for me, roller skate. In C. Mitchell-Kernan & S. Ervin-Tripp (Eds.), *Child discourse.* New York: Academic Press.

Faber, N., & Maglich, R. (1980). *How to talk so kids will listen and listen so kids will talk.* New York: Avon.

Fey, M. (1986). *Language intervention—Young children.* Boston: College-Hill Press.

Field, T. (1978). The three R's of infant-adult interactions: Rhythms, repertoires, and responsivity. *Journal of Pediatric Psychology, 3,* 131-136.

Field, T. (1980a) *High-risk infants & children: Adult and peer interactions.* New York: Academic Press.

Field, T. (1980b). Interactions of high-risk infants: Qualitative and quantative differences. In S.B. Sawin, R.C. Hawkins, L.O. Walker, & J.H. Penticuff (Eds.), *Exceptional infant. Vol. 4: Psychosocial risks in infant-environment transactions.* New York: Brunner/Mazel.

Forehand, R., & McMahon, R. (1981). *Helping the noncompliant child: A clinician's guide to parent training.* New York: Guilford Press.

Foster, S. (1985). The development of discourse topic skills by infants and young children. *Topics in Language Disorders, 5,* 31-45.

Fraiberg, S. (1977). *Insights from the blind.* New York: Basic Books.

Freedle, R., & Lewis, M. (1977). Prelinguistic conversations. In M. Lewis & L. Rosenblum (Eds.), *Interaction, conversation, and the development of language.* New York: John Wiley.

French, P., & MacLure, M. (1981). *Adult-child conversation.* New York: St. Martin's Press.

Furrow, D., Nelson, K., & Benedict, H. (1979). Mother's speech to children and syntactic development: Some simple relationships. *Journal of Child Language, 6,* 423-444.

Gerensen, J. (1982). *Parent-child communication: An evaluation of continuing education for parents of handicapped children.* Unpublished masters thesis, The Ohio State University.

Gillette, Y., & MacDonald, J. (1988). *Evaluating parent-child communication treatment through perceptions of judges.* Unpublished manuscript.

Ginott, H. *Between parent and child.* New York: Avon.

Girolometto, L. (1986). *Developing dialogue skills of mothers and their developmentally delayed children: An intervention study.* Unpublished doctoral dissertation, University of Toronto.

Girolometto, L. (1988). Developing dialogue skills: The effects of a conversational model of language intervention. In K. Marfo (Ed.), *Parent-child interaction and developmental disabilities: Theory, research, and intervention.* New York: Praeger.

Girolometto, L., Greenberg, J., & Manolson, A. (1986). Developing dialogue skills: The Hanen early language parent program. *Seminars in Speech and Language, 7,* 367-382.

Gleitman, L.R., Newport, E.L., & Gleitman, H. (1984). The current status of the motherese hypothesis. *Journal of Child Language, 11,* 43-79.

Goldberg, S. (1977). Social competence in infancy: A model of parent-infant interaction. *Merrill-Palmer Quarterly, 23,* 263-277.

Graef, J., & Spence, I. (1976, April). *Using prior distance information in multidimensional scaling.* A paper presented at the Annual Meeting of the Psychometric Society. Murray Hill, NJ.

Greenberg, M.T., Calderon, R., & Kusche, C. (1984). Early intervention using simultaneous communication with deaf infants: The effect on communication development. *Child Development, 55,* 607-616.

Greenfield, P., & Smith, J. (1976a). *Communication and the beginnings of language: The development of semantic structure in one-word speech and beyond.* New York: Academic Press.

Greenfield, P., & Smith, J. (1976b). *The structure of communication in early language development.* New York: Academic Press.

Greenspan, S. (1985). *First feelings: Milestones in the emotional development of your baby and child.* New York: Viking Penguin.

Grice, H.P. (1975). Logic and conversation. In Y. Cole (Ed.), *Syntax and semantics.* London, England: Academic Press.

Halliday, M. (1975). *Learning how to mean: Explorations in the development of language.* London, England: Edward Arnold.

Harris, M., Jones, D., & Grant, J. (1983). The nonverbal context of mother's speech to infants. *First Language, 4,* 21-30.

Harris, S.L. (1975). Teaching language to nonverbal children with emphasis on problems of generalization. *Psychology Bulletin, 82,* 525-588.

Hart, B., & Risley, T. (1977). In vivo language intervention: Unanticipated general effects. *Journal of Applied Behavior Analysis, 3,* 407-432.

Haslett, B. (1983). Communicative functions and strategies in children's conversations. *Human Communication Research, 9,* 114-129.

Holland, A. (Ed.). (1984). *Language disorders in children: Recent advances.* San Diego: College-Hill Press.

Holtom, J. (1987). *Parent interaction strategies with handicapped children: Evaluation of a new assessment scale through measurement over intervention.* Unpublished master's thesis, The Ohio State University.

Hornby, G., & Jensen-Proctor, G. (1984). Parental speech to language delayed children: A home intervention study. *British Journal of Disorders of Communication, 19,* 97-103.

Horstmeier, D., & MacDonald, J. (1978). *Ready, set, go. Talk to me.* Columbus, OH: Charles E. Merrill.

Howlin, D. (1984). Parents as therapists. In D. Miller (Ed.), *Remediating children's language.* San Diego: College-Hill Press.

Hubbell, R. (1981). *Children's language disorders.* Englewood Cliffs, NJ: Prentice-Hall.

Hunt, D. (1961). *Intelligence and experience.* New York: Ronald Press.

Hunt, J. (1965). Intrinsic motivation and its role in psychological development. In D. Levine (Ed.), *Nebraska symposium on motivation.* Lincoln: University of Nebraska.

Jones, O.H.M. (1977). Mother-child communication with prelinguistic Down syndrome and normal infants. In H.R. Schaffer (Ed.), *Studies in mother-infant interaction.* New York: Academic Press.

Jones, O.H.M. (1980). Prelinguistic communication skills in Down's syndrome and normal infants. In T.M. Field, S. Goldberg, D. Stern, & A.M. Sostek (Eds.), *High-risk infants and children: Adult and peer interactions.* New York: Academic Press.

Kaye, K. (1976). Infants' effects on their mothers' teaching strategies. In J. C. Glidewell (Ed.), *The social context of learning and development.* New York: Gardner Press.

Kaye, K. (1977). Toward the origin of dialogue. In H.R. Schaeffer (Ed.), *Mother-infant interaction.* New York: Academic Press.

Kaye, K. (1979). Thickening thin data: The maternal role in developing communication and language. In M. Bullowa (Ed.), *Before speech: The beginnings of interpersonal communication.* Cambridge, England: Cambridge Press.

Kaye, K. (1980a). The infant as projective stimulus. *American Journal of Orthopsychiatry, 50,* 732-736.

Kaye, K. (1980b). Why we don't talk baby talk to babies. *Journal of Child Language, 7,* 489-507.

Kaye, K., & Charney, R. (1980). How mothers maintain "dialogue" with two-year-olds. In D. Olsen (Ed.), *The social foundations of language and thought: Essays in honor of Jerome S. Bruner.* New York: W.W. Norton.

Kaye, K., & Charney, R. (1981). Conversational asymmetry between mothers and children. *Journal of Child Language, 8,* 35-49.

Kogan, K.L., Wimberger, H.C., & Bobbitt, R.A. (1969). Analysis of mother-child interaction in young mental retardates. *Child Development, 40,* 799-812.

Kretschmer, R., & Kretschmer, L. (1978). *Language development and interaction with the hearing impaired.* Baltimore: University Park Press.

Kruskal, J.B., & Wish, M. (1978). *Multidimensional scaling.* Beverly Hills: Sage Publications.

Kysela, G., McDonald, L., Reddon, T., & Goebiel-Dwyer, F. (1988). Stress and supports to families with a handicapped child. In K. Marfo (Ed.), *Parent-child interaction and developmental disabilities.* New York: Praeger.

Leland, H., Shoaee, M., McElwain, D., & Christie, R. (1980). *Adaptive Behavior Scale for Infants and Early Childhood (ABSI).* Columbus: The Ohio State University.

Leifer, J.S., & Lewis, M. (1983). Maternal speech to normal and handicapped children: A look at question-asking behavior. *Infant Behavior and Development, 6,* 175-187.

Leonard, L. (1984). Normal language acquisition: Some recent findings and clinical implications. In A. Holland (Ed.), *Language disorders in children.* San Diego: College-Hill Press.

Leonard, L., Bolders, J., & Miller, J. (1976). An examination of the semantic relations reflected in the language usage of normal and language disordered children. *Journal of Speech and Hearing Research, 19,* 371-392.

Lewis, M. (1972). State as an infant-environment interaction: An analysis of mother-infant behavior as a function of sex. *Merrill-Palmer Quarterly, 11,* 95-121.

Lewis, M., & Goldberg, S. (1969). Preceptual-cognitive development in infancy. An expectancy model of mother-infant interaction, *Merrill Palmer Quarterly, 15,* 81-100.

Lewis, M., & Rosenblum, L. (1974). *Effects of the infant on its caregiver.* New York: John Wiley.

Lewis, M., & Rosenblum, L. (1977a). Interaction, conversation, and the children's language learning. *Topics in Language Disorders, 4,* 15-23.

Lewis, M., & Rosenblum, L. (Eds.). (1977b). *Interaction, conversation, and the development of language.* New York: John Wiley.

Lieven, E. (1978). Turntaking & pragmatics: Two issues in early child language. In R. Campbell & P. Smith (Eds.), *Recent advances in psychology of language.* New York: Plenum Press.

Lieven, E. (1984). Interaction style and children's language learning. *Topics in Language Disorders, 4,* 15-23.

Lombardino, L. (1978). *Maternal speech acts on non-delayed and Down's syndrome children: A taxonomy and distribution.* Unpublished doctoral dissertation, The Ohio State University.

Lombardino, L., & Mangan, N. (1983). Parents as language trainers: Language programming with developmentally-delayed children. *Exceptional Children, 49,* 358-360.

Lucas, E. (1980). *Semantic and pragmatic disorders: Assessment and retardation.* Rockville, MD: Aspen Systems Corp.

Lund, N., & Duchan, J. (1983). *Assessing children's language in naturalistic contexts.* Englewood Cliffs, NJ: Prentice-Hall.

MacDonald, J. (1978). *Environmental Language Inventory.* Columbus, OH: Charles E. Merrill.

MacDonald, J. (1982a). Communication strategies for language intervention. In D. McClowry, A. Guilford, & S. Richardson (Eds.), *Infant communication: Development, assessment and intervention.* New York: Grune & Stratton.

MacDonald, J. (1982b). Language through conversation: A communication model for language intervention. In S. Warren & J. Roger-Warren (Eds.), *Productive language teaching.* Baltimore: University Park Press.

MacDonald, J. (1983). A conversational approach to language delayed children: Problem solving for nurses. In S. Shanks (Ed.), *Nursing and management of communication disorders.* San Diego: College-Hill Press.

MacDonald, J. (1984). Teaching communication to your child. In S. Warren & A. Rogers-Warren (Eds.), *Teaching functional language.* Baltimore: University Park Press.

MacDonald, J., & Blott, J. (1974). Environmental language intervention: A rationale for diagnostic and training strategy through rules, context, and generalization. *Journal of Speech and Hearing Disorders, 39,* 244-256.

MacDonald, J., & Gillette, Y. (1984). Conversational engineering. In J. McLean & L. Snyder-McLean (Eds.), *Educational seminars in speech and language, 5*(3), 171-183.

MacDonald, J., & Gillette, Y. (1985a). *Social play: A program for developing a social play habit necessary for communication development.* Columbus: Ohio State University Research Foundation.

MacDonald, J., & Gillette, Y. (1985b). Turntaking. *Exceptional Parent, 15,* 49-54.

MacDonald, J., & Gillette, Y. (1986). Communicating with persons with severe handicaps: Roles of parents and professionals. *Journal for the Association of the Severely Handicapped, 11,* 255-265.

MacDonald, J., & Gillette, Y. (1987). *Adult/child interaction and conversation: Assessing the communication development process.* Paper presented at the annual meeting of the Society for Research in Child Development.

MacDonald, J., & Gillette, Y. (1988). Communicating partners: A conversational model for building parent-child relationships with handicapped children. In K. Marfo (Ed.), *Parent-child interaction and developmental disabilities.* New York: Praeger.

MacDonald, J., & Gillette, Y. (1989). *ECOScales manual.* San Antonio, TX: Special Press.

MacDonald, J., & Horstmeier, D. (1978). *Environmental Language Intervention Program.* Columbus, OH: Charles E. Merrill.

Mahoney, G. (1975). An ethological approach to delayed language acquisition. *American Journal of Mental Deficiency, 80,* 139-148.

Mahoney, G. (1988). Enhancing the developmental competence of handicapped infants. In K. Marfo (Ed.), *Parent-child interaction and developmental disabilities.* New York: Praeger.

Mahoney, G., Finger, I., & Powell, A. (1985). The relationship between maternal behavioral style to the development of organically impaired mentally retarded infants. *American Journal of Mental Deficiency, 90,* 296-302.

Mahoney, G.J., Glover, A., & Finger, I. (1981). Relationship between language and sensorimotor development of Down syndrome and nonhandicapped children. *American Journal of Mental Deficiency, 86,* 21-27.

Mahoney, G., Powell, A., Finnegan, C., Fors, S., & Wood, S. (1986). The transactional intervention program, theory, procedures, and evaluation. In D. Gentry & J. Olson (Series Eds.), *The family support network series: Individualizing family services* (Monograph 4) (pp. 8-21). Moscow: Warren Center on Human Development, University of Idaho.

Mahoney, G., & Powell, A. (1988). Modifying parent-child interaction: Enhancing the development of handicapped children. *Journal of Special Education, 22,* 82-90.

Mahoney, G., & Robenalt, K. (1986). Mother-child turntaking with Down syndrome and normal children. *Journal for the Division of Early Childhood, 10,* 172-180.

Marfo, K. (Ed.). (1988). *Parent-child interaction and developmental disabilities: Theory, research, and intervention.* New York: Praeger.

Martlew, M. (1980). Mother's control strategies in dyadic mother-child conversations. *Journal of Psycholinguistic Research, 9*(4), 327-347.

Mayo, C. (1979). On the acquisition of nonverbal communication: A review. *Merrill-Palmer Quarterly, 24*(4).

McConkey, R. (1988). Educating all parents: An approach based on video. In K. Marfo (Ed.), *Parent-child interaction and developmental disabilities.* New York: Praeger.

McConkey, R., & Jeffree, D. (1977). *Let me speak.* London, England: Taplinger.

McConkey, R., & O'Connor, M. (1982). A new approach to parental involvement in language intervention programs. *Child Care, Health & Development, 8,* 163-176.

McDonald, L., & Pien, D. (1982). Mother conversational behavior as a function of interactional intent. *Journal of Child Language, 9,* 337-358.

McLean, J., & Snyder-McLean, L. (1978). *Transactional approach to early language training.* Columbus, OH: Charles E. Merrill.

McLean, J., & Snyder-McLean, L. (1984). Recent developments in pragmatics: Remedial implications. In D. Miller (Ed.), *Remediating children in language.* San Diego: College-Hill Press.

McLowrey, D. (1981). *The maternal teaching styles to normally developing and developmentally delayed children.* Unpublished doctoral dissertation, The Ohio State University.

Mirenda, P., & Donnellan, A. (1986). Effects of adult interaction style on conversational behavior in students with severe communication problems. *Language, Speech, and Hearing Services in Schools, 7,* 126-141.

Moerk, E. (1972). Principles of dyadic interaction in language learning. *Merrill-Palmer Quarterly, 18,* 229-257.

Moerk, E. (1976). Process of language teaching and training in the interactions of mother-child dyads. *Child Development, 47,* 1064-1078.

Moore, M., & Meltzoff, A. (1978). Object permanence, imitation, and language development in infancy: Toward a neo-Piagetian perspective in communicative and cognitive development. In F. Minifie & L. Lloyd (Eds.), *Communicative and cognitive abilities in children.* Baltimore: University Park Press.

Murphy, J. (1983). *Parent-child conversation: Assessment and treatment with prelinguistic handicapped children.* Unpublished masters thesis, The Ohio State University.

Nelson, K. (1974). Concept word and sentence. *Psychological Review, 81*(4), 267-285.

Nelson, K. (1978). Early speech in its communicative context. In F. Minifie & L. Lloyd (Eds.), *Communicative and cognitive abilities in children.* Baltimore: University Park Press.

Nelson, K. (1980). *Children's language* (Vol. 3). New York: Gardner Press.

Newson, J. (1977). An intersubjective approach to the systematic description of mother-infant interaction. In H. Schaeffer (Ed.), *Studies in mother-infant interaction.* London, England: Academic Press.

Newson, J. (1979a). Towards a theory of infant understanding. *Bulletin of the British Psychological Society, 27,* 251-257.

Newson, J. (1979b). The growth of shared understanding between infant and caregiver. In M. Bullowa (Ed.), *Before speech: Interpersonal communications.* London, England: Cambridge University Press.

Newson, J., & Newson, E. (1963). *Infant care in an urban community.* London, England: Allen & Unwin.

Olson, D. (Ed.). (1980). *Social foundation of language and thought.* New York: W.W. Norton.

Owens, R. (1979). *Pragmatic functions in the speech of preschool-aged Downs and nondelayed children.* Unpublished doctoral dissertation, The Ohio State University.

Owens, R., & MacDonald, J. (1982). Communicative uses of early speech of nondelayed and Down's syndrome children. *American Journal of Mental Deficiency, 86,* 503-511.

Peck, C.A. (In press). Assessment of social communicative competence. *Seminars in Speech and Language.*

Peterson, G., & Sherrod, K. (1982). Relationship of maternal language to language development and language delay of children. *American Journal of Mental Deficiency, 86,* 391-398.

Piaget, J. (1952). *The origins of intelligence in children.* New York: W.W. Norton.

Piaget, J. (1954). *The construction of reality in the child.* New York: Basic Books.

Piaget, J. (1963). *The language and thought of the child.* New York: World Publishing.

Prizant, B. (1983). Language acquisition and communicative behavior in autism: Toward an understanding of the "whole." *Journal of Speech and Hearing Disorders, 48,* 286-296.

Resler, C. (1973). *Semantic rules in the language of 2, 3, & 4-year-olds.* Unpublished doctoral dissertation, The Ohio State University.

Rice, M., & Schiefelbusch, R. (Eds.). (1989). *The teachability of language.* Baltimore: Paul H. Brookes.

Richards, M.M.P. (Ed.). (1974). *The integration of a child in a social world.* Cambridge, England: Cambridge University Press.

Rosenberg, S., & Robinson, C. (1985). Enhancement of mother's interactional skills in an infant education program. *Education and Training of the Mentally Retarded,* 163-169.

Russo, J.B., & Owens, R.E.(1982). The development of an objective observational tool for parent-child interaction. *Journal of Speech and Hearing Disorders, 47,* 165-173.

Schaeffer, H.R. (Ed.). (1977). *Studies in mother-infant interaction.* New York: Academic Press.

Schiefelbusch, R., & Bricker, D. (1981). *Early language: Acquisition and intervention.* Baltimore: University Park Press.

Schiefelbusch, R., & Lloyd, L. (1974). *Language perspectives—Acquisition, retardation, and intervention.* Baltimore: University Park Press.

Schwartz, R., & Camarata, S. (1985). Examining relationships between input and language development: Some statistical issues. *Journal of Child Language, 12*, 199-207.

Schwethelm, B., & Mahoney, G. (1986). Task persistence among organically impaired mentally retarded children. *American Journal of Mental Deficiency, 90*, 432-430.

Searle, J.R. (1969). *Speech acts: An essay in the philosophy of language.* New York: Cambridge University Press.

Seibert, J., & Hogan, A. (1982). A model for assessing social and object skills and planning intervention. In D. McCloury (Ed.), *Infant communication.* New York: Grune & Stratton.

Semmel, L., & Dolley, D. (1971). Comprehension and imitation of sentences by Down's syndrome children as a function of transformational complexity. *American Journal of Mental Deficiency, 75*, 739-745.

Siegel-Causey, E., Ernst, B., & Guess, D. (1987). Elements of nonsymbolic communication and early interactional processes. In M. Bullis (Ed.), *Communication development in young children with deaf blindness: Literature review III.* Eugene, OR: Communication Skill Center for Young Children with Deaf-Blindness.

Skinner, B.F. (1953). *Science and human behavior.* New York: Macmillan.

Skinner, B.F. (1957). *Verbal behavior.* New York: Appleton-Century-Crofts.

Slobin, D. (1983). Cognitive prerequisites for the development of grammar. In C. Ferguson & D. Slobin (Eds.), *Studies of child language development.* New York: Holt, Rinehart & Winston.

Snow, C. (1972). Mother's speech to children learning language. *Child Development, 43*, 549-565.

Snow, C. (1984). Parent-child in teaching and the development of communicative ability. In R. Schiefelbusch & J. Pickar (Eds.), *The acquisition of communicative competence.* Baltimore: University Park Press.

Snow, C., & Ferguson, C. (1978). *Talking to children.* London, England: Cambridge University Press.

Snow, C., Midkiff-Borunda, S., Small, A., & Proctor, A. (1984). Therapy as social interaction: Analyzing the contexts for language remediation. *Topics in Language Disorders, 4*, 72-85.

Snyder, L.S. (1978). Communicative and cognitive abilities and disabilities in the sensorimotor period. *Merrill-Palmer Quarterly, 24*(3), 161-180.

Solnit, A., & Stark, M. (1961). Mourning and the birth of a defective child. *The Psychoanalytic Study of the Child, 16*, 523-537.

Stern, D. (1974). Mother and infant at play: The dyadic interaction involving facial, vocal, and gaze behaviors. In M. Lewis & L.A. Rosenblum (Eds.), *The effect of the infant on its caregiver.* New York: John Wiley.

Stern, D. (1977). *The first relationship: Mother and infant.* Cambridge: Harvard University.

Stern, D. (1985). *The interpersonal world of the infant: A view from psychoanalysis and developmental psychology.* New York: Basic Books.

Stern, D., & Gibbon, J. (1977). Temporal expectancies of social behaviors in mother-infant play. In E. Thorman (Ed.), *The origins of the infant's responsiveness.* New York: Lawrence Erlbaum.

Sugarman, S. (1973). *Communicative development in the prelanguage child.* Unpublished masters thesis, Hampshire College.

Sugarman, S. (1984). The development of preverbal communications: It's contribution and limits in promoting the development of language. In R. Schiefelbusch & J. Pickar (Eds.), *The acquisition of communicative compentencies.* Baltimore: University Park Press.

Sugarman-Bell, S. (1978). Some organizational aspects of pre-verbal communication. In I. Markova (Ed.), *The social context of language.* New York: John Wiley.

Sylvester-Bradley, B., & Trevarthen, C. (1978). Baby talk as an adaptation to the infant's communication. In N. Waterson & C.E. Snow (Eds.), *The development of communication.* New York: John Wiley.

Tiegerman, E., & Siperstein, M. (1984). Individual patterns of interaction in the mother-child dyad: Implications for parent intervention. *Topics in Language Disorders, 4*, 50-61.

Trevarthen, C. (1977). Descriptive analysis of infant communication behavior. In H.R. Schaeffer (Ed.), *Studies in mother-infant interaction.* London: Academic Press.

Trevarthen, L.B. (1979). Communication & cooperation in early infancy; a description of primary intersubjectivity. In M. Bullowa (Ed.), *Before speech: The beginnings of communication*. Cambridge, England: Cambridge University Press.

Tronick, E. (Ed.). (1982). *Social interchange in infancy: Affect, cognition and communication*. Baltimore: University Park Press.

Tronick, E., Als, H., & Brazelton, T.B. (1977). The infant's capacity to regulate maturality in face-to-face intervention. *Journal of Communication, 27*, 74-80.

Van Ek, J. (1977). *The threshold level for modern language learning in schools*. The Hague, Netherlands: Longman Group Ltd.

Vygotsky, L.S. (1962). *Thought and language*. Cambridge: MIT Press.

Vygotsky, L.S. (1978) *Mind in society*. Cambridge: Harvard University Press.

Warren, S., & Rogers-Warren, A. (1984). *Teaching functional language*. Baltimore: University Park Press.

Waterson, N., & Snow, C.E. (Eds.). (1978). *The development of communication*. New York: John Wiley.

Watzlawick, P., Beavin, J., & Jackson, D. (1967). *Pragmatics of human communication*. New York: W.W. Norton.

Watzlawick, P., Weakland, J.H., & Fish, R. (1974). *Change: Principles of problem formation and problem resolution*. New York: W.W. Norton.

Wells, G. (1981). *Learning through interaction*. Cambridge, England: Cambridge University Press.

White, B.L. (1975). *The first three years of life*. New York: Prentice-Hall.

White, R., & White, S. (1984). The deaf imperative: Characteristics of maternal input to hearing impaired children. *Topics in Language Disorders, 4*, 38-49.

Winnicott, D.W. (1965). *The maturational process & the facilitating environment*. London, England: Hogarth.

Young, F.W., Takane, Y., & Lewyckyj, R. (1978). ALSCAL: A nonmetric multidimensional scaling program with several differences options. *Behavioral Research Methods and Instrumentation, 10*, 451-453.

Young, J. (1988). *Developing social conversation skills: An* intervention study of preverbal handicapped children with their parents. Unpublished masters thesis, The Ohio State University.

Other ECO Program Components

Read about these ECO program components on pages 15 and 16 of this book.

ECO: A Partnership Program (kit)   90-009-N $149.00
(all components except videos and video manuals)

Ecological Programs for Communicating Partnerships   90-011-N $29.95
(224 pp.; spiral)

ECO Resources   90-012-N $49.95
(370 pp.; ring binder)

ECOScales Manual   90-013-N $19.95
(144 pp.; spiral)

ECOScales   89-012-N $15.95
(6 pp.; package of 24)

ECO Practice Plan and Record   89-013-N $14.95
(4 pp.; package of 24)

½-inch VHS Videotapes
Introduction to the ECO Program: Principles & Demonstrations   90-014-N $49.00

Manual for "An Introduction to the ECO Program"   90-024-N $7.00
(16 pp.; softbound)

Introduction to ECO/Turntaking   90-015-N $49.00

Social Play/Communication   90-016-N $49.00

Language and Conversation/Questions and Examples   90-017-N $49.00

Communicating Partners: Training Guide for Videotapes   90-020-N $14.95
(56 pp.; softbound)

ECO Video Package   90-019-N $189.00
(4 videotapes, 2 manuals)

For more information, call **1-800-888-4506** or write:
     Special Press, Inc.
     Suite 3205
     11230 West Avenue
     San Antonio, TX 78213-4925